# *Reading 1 Peter After Supersessionism*

## Series Preface

The **New Testament After Supersessionism** (NTAS) is a series that presents post-supersessionist interpretations of the New Testament. By post-supersessionism, we mean "a family of theological perspectives that *affirms God's irrevocable covenant with the Jewish people as a central and coherent part of ecclesial teaching*. It rejects understandings of the new covenant that entail the abrogation or obsolescence of God's covenant with the Jewish people, of the Torah as a demarcator of Jewish communal identity, or of the Jewish people themselves" (spostst.org). Although the field of New Testament studies has made significant strides in this direction in recent years, the volumes in this series, written by Jewish and gentile believers in Jesus, seek to advance the conversation by offering post-supersessionist readings of the New Testament that address the question of ongoing Jewish particularity, and the relationship of interdependence and mutual blessing between Jew and gentile in Messiah.

SERIES EDITORS

J. Brian Tucker
  *Moody Theological Seminary, Plymouth, MI*

David Rudolph
  *The King's University, Southlake, TX*

Justin Hardin
  *Palm Beach Atlantic University, West Palm Beach, FL*

PROJECTED VOLUMES

*New Testament After Supersessionism, Introductory Volume*
  —Justin K. Hardin, David J. Rudolph, and J. Brian Tucker

*Reading Matthew After Supersessionism*
  —Nicholas J. Schaser

*Reading Mark After Supersessionism*
  —tbc

*Reading Luke-Acts After Supersessionism*
  —Jason F. Moraff

*Reading John After Supersessionism*
  —tbc

*Reading Romans After Supersessionism*
  —J. Brian Tucker

*Reading 1 Corinthians After Supersessionism*
  —Kar Yong Lim

*Reading 2 Corinthians After Supersessionism*
  —Ryan Heinsch

*Reading Galatians After Supersessionism*
  —Justin K. Hardin

*Reading Philippians After Supersessionism*
  —Christopher Zoccali

*Reading Ephesians and Colossians After Supersessionism*
  —Lionel Windsor

*Reading Hebrews After Supersessionism*
  —David M. Moffitt

*Reading James After Supersessionism*
  —Justin Winzenburg

*Reading* 1 Peter *After Supersessionism*
  —Kelly D. Liebengood

*Reading Revelation After Supersessionism*
  —Ralph Korner

*New Testament After Supersessionism, Supplementary Volume*
  —edited by Justin K. Hardin, David J. Rudolph, and J. Brian Tucker

"In this rich and engaging book, the product of many years of research and reflection, Kelly Liebengood argues that 1 Peter can and should be read in a non-supersessionist way, despite centuries of interpretation to the contrary. Combining detailed exegesis and scholarly engagement with a critical awareness of what is at stake theologically, Liebengood argues that the author of 1 Peter does not depict a new people—the church—replacing Israel as God's people, but rather invites gentiles to appropriate 'Israelhood,' extending the people of the God of Israel to include gentiles as gentiles. Anyone interested in this fascinating letter, and the wider issues at stake, should grapple with this valuable study."

—DAVID G. HORRELL, professor of New Testament studies, University of Exeter

"In *Reading 1 Peter After Supersessionism*, Liebengood provides the most complete and thorough post-supersessionist reading of 1 Peter to date. Moving beyond the recognition that this letter is silent on the status of Jews in God's new salvific plan in Christ, Liebengood demonstrates that instead of replacing Israel with the church, this letter emplaces its gentile recipients in an Israelhood composed of both Jew and gentile. This book makes a significant contribution to the conversation of how to read 1 Peter in new ways that foster Jewish-Christian relations."

—TROY W. MARTIN, department of religious studies, Saint Xavier University

"Liebengood skillfully and sensitively navigates the intricacies of 1 Peter on his way to problematizing the traditional supersessionist interpretation of the letter. Interacting with the latest developments in the field and introducing creative solutions to questions that have long puzzled interpreters, he offers an informed and informative reading of the epistle, one that includes an innovative perspective on the 'Israelhood' that 1 Peter calls the gentiles to embrace. Petrine scholarship will long be indebted to this trailblazing work."

—TRAVIS B. WILLIAMS, professor of religion, Tusculum University

"Kelly Liebengood gives us a comprehensive, compelling, and at times even gripping scholarly argument against supersessionist readings of 1 Peter. The addressees of the letter are gentile believers in Jesus the Davidic shepherd, who need reassurance amidst suffering that they are indeed the people of the God of Israel, that in Messiah they share a form of

'Israelhood' without replacing Israel. This book commands the attention of all future interpreters of 1 Peter."

—Douglas Harink, emeritus professor of theology,
The King's University, Edmonton

"What does a New Testament letter that nowhere explicitly mentions Israel or the Jewish people offer for a post-supersessionist reading? First Peter is that letter, and Kelly Liebengood promotes a way of reading it that avoids marginalizing Jewish identity and interests. He suggests that 1 Peter participates in a Jewish restoration theology rather than a replacement theology. This is an important topic to grapple with, and I highly recommend this thoughtful book."

—Jeannine K. Brown, The David Price Professor of Biblical and
Theological Foundations, Bethel Seminary, St. Paul, Minnesota

"Liebengood will not allow contemporary readers of 1 Peter to erase Jewish people from the letter. He asserts that supersessionist readings of 1 Peter are problematic exegetically and not just ethically or ideologically. With careful analysis of 1 Peter, particularly regarding the communal imagery and eschatological outlook of the letter, and engaging studies focused on ethnic reasoning in the letter, Liebengood provides an intriguing case for absolving 1 Peter of supersessionism. *Reading 1 Peter After Supersessionism* is necessary for our study of 1 Peter. Liebengood helps us remember there is a diverse Jewish community in the background of the letter and invites us to consider how that community influences the gentile followers of a Jewish messiah."

—Dennis R. Edwards, seminary dean,
North Park Theological Seminary

"Kelly Liebengood is an expert on 1 Peter, and his book, *Reading 1 Peter After Supersessionism*, is a theological and exegetical *tour de force*, addressing systematically the issues involved with a supersessionist reading of this letter. Anyone interested in 1 Peter should read this book!"

—W. Edward Glenny, professor of New Testament studies and
Greek, University of Northwestern, St. Paul, Minnesota

# Reading 1 Peter After Supersessionism

JEWISH APOSTOLIC AFFIRMATION
OF GENTILE ISRAELHOOD

Kelly D. Liebengood

CASCADE *Books* · Eugene, Oregon

READING 1 PETER AFTER SUPERSESSIONISM
Jewish Apostolic Affirmation of Gentile Israelhood

New Testament After Supersessionism

Copyright © 2025 Kelly D. Liebengood. All rights reserved. Except for brief quotations in critical publications or reviews, no part of this book may be reproduced in any manner without prior written permission from the publisher. Write: Permissions, Wipf and Stock Publishers, 199 W. 8th Ave., Suite 3, Eugene, OR 97401.

Cascade Books
An Imprint of Wipf and Stock Publishers
199 W. 8th Ave., Suite 3
Eugene, OR 97401

www.wipfandstock.com

PAPERBACK ISBN: 978-1-4982-0769-0
HARDCOVER ISBN: 978-1-4982-0771-3
EBOOK ISBN: 978-1-4982-0770-6

*Cataloguing-in-Publication data:*

Names: Liebengood, Kelly D. [author]

Title: Reading 1 Peter after supersessionism : Jewish apostolic affirmation of gentile Israelhood / by Kelly D. Liebengood.

Description: Eugene, OR: Cascade Books, 2025 | Series: New Testament After Supersessionism | Includes bibliographical references and index.

Identifiers: ISBN 978-1-4982-0769-0 (paperback) | ISBN 978-1-4982-0771-3 (hardcover) | ISBN 978-1-4982-0770-6 (ebook)

Subjects: LCSH: Bible.—Peter, 1st—Criticism, interpretation, etc. | Jews in the New Testament. | Gentiles in the New Testament. | Jews—Election, Doctrine of.

Classification: BS2795.52 L54 2025 (print) | BS2795.52 (ebook)

I wish to thank *Religions* for granting permission to reprint (with some revisions) what was first published in "The Problem (s) of Reading 1 Peter after Supersessionism." *Religions* 14.2 (2023) 206.

To Campbell, for your sacrifice and courage. Thank you.

*Table of Contents*

*Acknowledgments* | *xiii*
*List of Abbreviations* | *xv*

Introduction: Aims and Assumptions | 1

1. The Problem(s) of Reading 1 Peter After Supersessionism | 11
2. The Problem of Identifying the Ethnic Identity of the Addressees of 1 Peter, Part 1: Reconsidering Foundational Assumptions of the Consensus | 31
3. The Problem of Identifying the Ethnic Identity of the Addressees of 1 Peter, Part 2: Situating the "Elect Sojourners" | 50
4. The Problem of Empire: Exploring the Jewish Restoration Ideology of 1 Peter | 87
5. The Problem of Temple and Priesthood in 1 Peter | 125
6. The Problem of "Race, Nation, and People" in 1 Peter 2:9–10 | 170

Conclusion: Summary and Implications | 214

*Bibliography* | 223
*Author Index* | 233
*Scripture Index* | 239

## *Acknowledgments*

WHEN BRIAN TUCKER, ONE of the editors of the New Testament After Supersessionism series, invited me to write this volume on 1 Peter, I had no idea what I was getting myself into. This has been the most difficult writing project I have undertaken, stretching me to better understand not only the text of 1 Peter, but also the Hebrew Bible, early church history, as well as Christian theology in relation to Jewish self-understanding. Not everything I had to learn in order to complete this project is reflected on the pages that follow. But this is one of the reasons it has taken me over ten years to complete.

Several significant life events also impacted my capacity to engage with this project. At the beginning of the writing stage, I was debilitated for nine months by Leptospirosis, a rare tropical disease that had me hospitalized for nineteen days and has left me with enduring challenges. Just as I was getting my research and writing feet underneath me again, I was appointed to be dean of the School of Theology and Vocation at LeTourneau University. Learning the new job occupied most of my mental capacity for a year, and as I finally got the hang of things, my father died unexpectedly. Then came the challenges of pastoring a church through the pandemic and race tensions. In the midst of that perplexing and taxing season, my mother died of a three-year battle with cancer. It was at that time that I strongly considered abandoning the project (and scholarship) forever.

But before writing an email to terminate my contract with Cascade, I went on a clarifying walk with my wife. The result was an imagination for a way forward. So, in the fall of the 2023 academic year, LeTourneau University granted me a research leave that proved to be the momentum I needed to complete the volume. I want to express my gratitude to many who made this possible: to my wife, Marietta, who gave me hope to finish the race; to Provost Ben Caldwell and President Steven Mason for their support and for permitting a research leave for an administrator; to Viktor Roudkovski, who took over many of my dean duties while I was gone; to my LeTourneau School of Theology colleagues for their variegated and insightful feedback along the way, and their steadfast encouragement; to Tyndale House for access to their lodging and wonderful library; to Carlos Gil, María José Schultz, and the faculty at the University of Deusto for their warm hospitality, engaging conversations, and access to an office and library; to my son, Campbell, who, among many things, sacrificed his first year of high school football so I could finish the book; and to the elders of One Hope Presbyterian, who had to pick up my slack while I was gone. I also want to thank David Horrell for introducing me to Carlos Gil and pointing me to the University of Deusto. Professor Horrell is also the one to blame for putting the research question of this book on my mind in the first place! There are many others who helped me along the way, some of whom will be acknowledged at varying points in the pages that follow. But I wish to conclude by giving thanks to Brian Tucker, David Rudolph, and Justin Harding for their helpful feedback on an earlier draft, and for their vision for the New Testament After Supersessionism series.

# List of Abbreviations

| | |
|---|---|
| BDAG | Walter Bauer, Frederick W. Danker, W. F. Arndt, and F. W. Gingrich, *Greek-English Lexicon of the New Testament and Other Early Christian Literature*. 3rd ed. Chicago: University of Chicago Press, 2000. |
| BZNW | Beihefte zur Zeitschrift für die neutestamentliche Wissenschaft |
| EKKNT | Evangelisch-Katholischer Kommentar zum Neuen Testament |
| JSOT | Journal for the Study of the Old Testament |
| LNTS | Library of New Testament Studies |
| NICNT | New International Commentary on the New Testament |
| SBLDS | Society of Biblical Literature Dissertation Series |
| Tacitus, *Ann.* | The Annals of Tacitus |
| WUNT | Wissenschaftliche Untersuchungen zum Neuen Testament |

# Introduction
## Aims and Assumptions

*Supersessionism teaches that the ekklēsia replaces the Jewish people as the elect community in covenant with God, in whom the divine presence resides and through whom the divine purpose is realized in the world. According to this traditional Christian view, the church is the new and spiritual Israel, fulfilling the role formerly occupied by "carnal" Israel. In the decades since the Holocaust, many Christians have repudiated this teaching. However, it would appear that few have learned to read the New Testament in a non-supersessionist manner.*[1]

## The Primary Aims of This Study

SUPERSESSIONISM, ALSO REFERRED TO as replacement theology or fulfillment theology, is the belief that Christians replace Israel as the elect community in covenant with God. It is in this new community, sometimes referred to as the church, that now "the divine presence resides and through whom the divine purpose is realized in the world. According to this traditional Christian view, the church is the new and spiritual Israel, fulfilling the role formerly occupied by 'carnal' Israel."[1]

---

1. Kinzer, *Post-Missionary Messianic Judaism*, 12. Donaldson defines supersessionism as "denoting traditional Christian claims that the church has replaced Israel in the divine purposes and has inherited all that was positive in Israel's tradition" (Donaldson, "Supersessionism and Early Christian Self-Definition," 2). Soulen notes the negative connotation of the word: "Since the early 1970s, the term supersessionism has gained steadily in currency among anglophone scholars as a quasi-technical term that identifies what they regard as an inadequate or problematic account of the church's relationship to the Jewish people, according to which the church has taken the place of the Jewish people as the people of God, and God's former covenant with the Jews is now discarded or discontinued" (Soulen, "Supersessionism").

The terms *supersessionism*, *replacement*, and *fulfillment* suggest that this new elect community now has a superior status before God, and that through a process of replacement God has completed or fulfilled a plan or promise which this new entity now benefits from. Thus, at its core, supersessionism assumes that the promises that God made to the covenant community in the Old Testament (or Hebrew Bible) no longer apply directly to Israel but instead find their "spiritual" and universalized application in another group, namely Christians, or the church, which is not Israel in the flesh. Supersessionism assumes (often implicitly, but in some cases historically in quite explicit manners) that to belong to the church, one must renounce being Jewish.[2] Christianity, in other words, is the successor, fulfiller, or replacement of Judaism. In this respect, "Jewish Christian" is an oxymoron because those two entities are incompatible. There is, in other words, a firm discontinuity between Israel and this new body (i.e., the church) that has been established, even if the titles, descriptors, privileges, and prerogatives of Israel have been retained to make such a distinction.

However, supersessionism is more than merely a belief or doctrine regarding the relationship between Israel and the church; instead, it is a claim that carries with it a *reading strategy* with assumptions that are often unexamined. Readers who have inherited a supersessionist strategy of interpretation often presume (sometimes unknowingly) that what they find in the New Testament are a variety of examples of Christians repudiating the practices of Judaism and thus abolishing Israel as the people of God. As a result, when New Testament authors refer to followers of Jesus with terms and imagery that are unique to Israel's heritage (e.g., "holy," "elect," "house of God," "holy nation," or "royal priesthood"), it is often assumed to be polemical and meant to suggest a replacement and/or repudiation of the original references. Additionally, conflicts in the Gospels between Jesus and the Pharisees, or Jesus and the scribes, or the debates Jesus had about purity laws, sabbath practices, and the temple are often uncritically assumed to entail Jesus denouncing Judaism *in toto*. In relation to Paul, it is presumed that he converted *from* Judaism *to* Christianity, repented from and renounced self-justifying Jewish practices, and promoted a law-free gospel to everyone, including Jews, because the Jewish system of worshipping God was (from the start) inadequate and incapable of dealing with the fundamental problem of sin.

---

2. See Rudolph, "Messianic Judaism in Antiquity," 25.

These are but a few glimpses of how supersessionism affects what is seen in the New Testament.

First Peter appears to emphatically support the doctrine of supersessionism and its inherited reading strategy. That is, the author seems to claim that Christians (1 Pet 4:16), by virtue of Christ's atoning sacrificial death (1 Pet 1:19; 2:24–25; 3:18; 1:2) and the sanctifying work of the Holy Spirit (1 Pet 1:2–3, 12) are now the new locus of divine presence (1 Pet 4:14). In short, they have become the new temple and the new priesthood, who offer true and legitimate sacrifices to God (1 Pet 2:5)—because they are now the new people of God, the new Israel (1 Pet 2:9–10). Commenting on the climactic passage of 1 Pet 2:9–10, Karen Jobes concludes, "Peter here makes the radical claim that those who believe in Jesus Christ—whether Jew, Gentile, Greek, Roman, Cappadocian, Bithynian, or whatever—though from many nationalities and ethnicities, constitute a new people."[3]

One aim of this book is to show that there are a number of problems that arise when we read 1 Peter in this manner. But problematizing the way 1 Peter is traditionally interpreted is challenging because for many (if not most), supersessionism itself is not regarded as a problem. This is because since the mid-second century almost every Christian tradition has tended to read the Bible with a supersessionist posture towards Israel in the flesh. But remarkably, in spite of this long-standing posture and practice, as Adam Gregerman (professor of Jewish studies) has noted, in terms of Jewish-Christian relations, we live in an exceptional time.[4] In the wake of the Holocaust, several Christian theologians from a variety of Christian traditions have become concerned with the linkage between supersessionism and antisemitism and thus have sought other ways to imagine and interpret the relationship between Israel and the church. As a result, in the past fifty years, Christian traditions that promoted replacement theology are now renouncing or repudiating their supersessionist teachings. The Roman Catholic Church, for example, in its *Nostra Aetate* (1965), affirms that God's covenant with the Jewish people has not been superseded but is forever valid.[5] The Presbyterian Church USA (1987) affirms that the church has been engrafted into the people of God established by the Abrahamic covenant, explicitly noting that Christians have

---

3. Jobes, *1 Peter* [2nd ed.], 159.
4. Gregerman, "Challenges of Post-Supersessionism."
5. Paul VI, "Nostra Aetate."

not replaced Jews.⁶ This kind of Christian rejection of supersessionism has no parallel in history. But to renounce supersessionism is one thing; it is entirely another to (re)learn how to read the New Testament in a non-supersessionist manner.

Of late, supersessionism has been rejected on moral or ethical grounds generated from within a variety of prevailing ideologies. What is noteworthy is that often such denunciations of supersessionism also include claims that the New Testament itself is to blame. Amy-Jill Levine, for example, in her provocative essay "Supersessionism: Admit and Address Rather Than Debate or Deny," claims that careful readings of New Testament texts (e.g., "historical-critical exegesis") will not lead to the denial of supersessionism.⁷ Instead, she argues that a rejection of supersessionism must be done on hermeneutical and ethical grounds. In other words, she argues that New Testament texts are themselves culpable, and that it is not just a "reception" problem that started in the second century: "It will be theologians, concerned that God not be seen as unfaithful to ancient promises, rather than exegetes who will need to make the case against supersessionism."⁸ What is more, she argues, all religious truth claims are in a sense supersessionist, improving or building upon anterior or rival traditions. For example, rabbinic Judaism replaced priestly Judaism: "Christians do it, Jews do it, we all do it. However, we can determine ways of doing it that are less harmful and perhaps even helpful."⁹ Thus, instead of trying to deny that, for example, the New Testament promotes supersessionism, Levine suggests that "it might be better for Jewish-Christian relations were each group to admit that their texts are in many places supersessionist rather than engage in exegetical gymnastics to have the texts say otherwise. Theology and ethics, rather than historical-critical exegesis, is the best way of addressing supersessionist teachings."¹⁰ Postcolonial critic Betsy Bauman-Martin targets 1 Peter in particular, insisting that scholarship has downplayed the blatant appropriation of Jewish identity and heritage by minimizing it as a mere

---

6. PC(USA), "Theological Understanding." For other Christian traditions and councils that have rejected supersessionism, see the opening section of the PC(USA) document referenced here.

7. Levine, "Supersessionism."

8. Levine, "Supersessionism," 2–4.

9. Levine, "Supersessionism," 4.

10. Levine, "Supersessionism," 6.

rhetorical strategy.¹¹ She argues that what is not readily acknowledged in 1 Peter scholarship is that this kind of appropriation is itself a kind of imperialism that degrades the integrity and identity of the culture that is being misrepresented and defined out of existence.¹²

The chief aim of this book is to show that a supersessionist reading of 1 Peter is problematic not just on ideological or ethical grounds, but more foundationally on *exegetical* grounds. That is, *pace* Levine and Bauman-Martin, in what follows, I will show how the text of 1 Peter presses its readers to not only resist a supersessionist hermeneutical posture towards Israel in the flesh but also to make sense of who God is and what God is up to in the world in a distinctively Israel-centric manner that has not always been appreciated. Given the expansive scope of the subject of supersessionism, and the fact that we stand some 1,800 years downstream a very strong current of supersessionist reading strategies of New Testament texts, I seek to offer a small contribution to a much larger ongoing conversation. In the chapters ahead, on the one hand I "play defense" by demonstrating the ways in which certain passages in 1 Peter need not and should not be read with a supersessionist posture towards Israel in the flesh. But on the other hand, I "play offense" by drawing attention to 1 Peter's indebtedness to, for example, Jewish restoration eschatology (see chapter 4) and the logic of covenant and sacrifice (see chapter 5). Attentiveness to the manner in which *Jewish* ethnic reasoning (see chapter 6) is employed in the letter for the purpose of identity formation opens fresh lines of interpretation and new ways to understand "Christian" identity as rooted in God's ongoing commitment to Israel.¹³ In the end, I hope to offer an exegetically faithful example of how to read 1 Peter in a non-supersessionist manner.

Unfortunately, given the fact that the author of 1 Peter addresses a very specific situation (see especially chapter 3 on the rhetorical exigence of the letter) and that we have limited data to work with (only one letter), not every pressing question we might have about the author's

---

11. Bauman-Martin, "Speaking Jewish," 163.

12. Bauman-Martin, "Speaking Jewish," 173–77.

13. As will be noted, I do not use social identity theory to discern the identity-formation strategy of 1 Peter. Instead, I assume that the theological perspective developed in 1 Peter invites the ideal readers to embrace a new corporate identity that offers purpose, belonging, and a concomitant new way of life that is derived from being included in the God of Israel's ongoing covenantal fidelity to Israel. For an example of the kind of theoretical approach I undertake in this book to discern identity formation in the letter, see Ok, *Constructing Ethnic Identity*, 2–10.

understanding of the relationship between Israel in the flesh and what we now call the church will be answered in ways that satisfy our curiosities. And in some cases, as we will see, the author's identity-formation strategy will raise new questions that may require us to go elsewhere for answers. But the contention of this study, as will be developed beginning in the next chapter, is that 1 Peter has not been as silent on the matter of supersessionism as has been purported (see chapter 1).

## Guiding Assumptions of This Study

To clear room for the development of the argument of this book, I need to clarify a few assumptions that undergird, animate, inform, and in some cases limit this study. First, a word about the *authorship* and *date of composition* of 1 Peter is in order. Judgments concerning who wrote the letter and when it was written are integrally related, and they are also shaped by questions regarding the literary craftmanship and integrity of the letter as well as the historical setting in which it was composed.[14] Generally, scholars have argued either that 1 Peter was written by the apostle Peter (whether directly or by means of an amanuensis, Silvanus [1 Pet 5:12]), or that 1 Peter is a pseudonymous document, perhaps written by someone within a "Petrine circle" of disciples in Rome.[15] Much in keeping with the argumentation of Paul Achtemeier, I find it difficult if not impossible to situate 1 Peter within a precise historical setting, which makes adjudicating between the two positions extremely difficult if not impossible.[16] If one is persuaded that Peter authored the letter in some way (whether independently or with the help of Silvanus), then the letter was most likely completed prior to or just after his martyrdom (ca. 64–65 CE). Perhaps the most challenging evidence against this position, however, is the "Babylon" reference in 1 Pet 5:13. Ever since the seminal article by Hunzinger (*Babylon als Deckname für Rom und die Datierung des 1. Petrusbriefes*), many scholars have concluded that 1 Peter must have been written after

---

14. For the complexity of the issues pertaining to authorship and date of composition and how they are related to literary integrity and 1 Peter's historical setting see, for example, Williams and Horrell, *1 Peter*, 99–189; Michaels, *1 Peter*, lv–lxvii; Achtemeier, *1 Peter*, 39–50; and Elliott, *1 Peter*, 118–31, 134–38.

15. For a helpful analysis of the arguments of these positions, see Williams and Horrell, *1 Peter*, 116–62. See also Elliott, *1 Peter*, 118–30.

16. Achtemeier, *1 Peter*, 39–50. He concludes his survey by commenting, "Evidence to solve definitively the question of the authorship of 1 Peter remains unavailable" (42).

70 CE (and thus after Peter's death), since "Babylon" (1 Pet 5:13) only became a reference to Rome in extant Jewish and Christian literature after the destruction of the temple in Jerusalem. Recently, however, Lutz Doering has suggested that Hunzinger's conclusions at times have been misappropriated by those who have used his research to argue for a post-70 CE date for 1 Peter. First, he notes that evidence for the identification of Rome as Babylon is "sparser and less unambiguous than sometimes claimed by those relying on Hunzinger."[17] Second, he suggests that the force of the Babylon reference in 1 Peter is more likely a qualification of Rome as ultimately responsible for the persecution and dispersion of God's people, akin to the Babylonian exile—and not a reference to Rome as the temple destroyer *per se*.[18] This means that it is possible that the reference to "Babylon" in 1 Pet 5:13 is not used in the same way that it was in extant Christian and Jewish literature (highlighted by Hunzinger) after the fall of the Jerusalem temple in 70 CE.[19]

For the aims of this volume, it would be helpful to know precisely why the author chose the term "Babylon" to refer to Rome and if the letter was written before or after the destruction of the temple. But in my judgment, we do not have enough data within the text and beyond to make such a determination with any degree of confidence. Having said that, it is important to underscore what has not been appreciated by those who use "Babylon" for dating purposes: if a pseudonymous author does indeed draw upon the term "Babylon" to vilify Rome precisely for the fact that it was responsible for destroying the temple in Jerusalem, then this would strongly suggest that he regarded the action as lamentable and unwelcomed. Yet such an attitude toward the destruction of the temple would seem to contradict purported supersessionist claims that the same author makes in 1 Pet 2:5 regarding the temple, the priesthood, and sacrifices (see chapter 5). Decrying Rome's destruction of the temple with the term "Babylon" would run contrary to the kind of supersessionist sentiments that were expressed less than a century after the destruction of the temple, when gentile followers of Jesus *rejoiced* at the destruction of the temple and the city because they saw it as a definitive sign of God's

---

17. Doering, "First Peter as Early Christian Diaspora Letter," 233.

18. Doering, "First Peter as Early Christian Diaspora Letter," 233. It is important to note that he makes this observation *en route* to arguing that 1 Peter is a Christian diaspora letter.

19. Though see Williams and Horrell, *1 Peter*, 112–14, who use the Babylon reference to establish the letter's *terminous a quo* as 70 CE.

revocation of Israel's priestly role to the nations.[20] As Wilken underscores, "For centuries Christians appealed to the visible evidence of the ruins of the Jewish temple as certain proof that Christianity has triumphed over Judaism. One reason Christians went on pilgrimage to Jerusalem was to see with their own eyes the place where the famous Jewish temple had once stood. . . . Only by actually visiting Jerusalem could one see that the city of the Jews was no more. This sight comforted and reassured Christians."[21] Or, as Kinzer concludes, for many Christians "the stones of the Temple Mount bore witness that the Jews had been rejected by God, and that the *ekklēsia* now constituted God's beloved people."[22]

If one judges that the letter is pseudonymous, following the argumentation of Elliott, it was most likely composed no later than 92 CE.[23] In my judgment, given the paucity of evidence, I am unable to make a definitive judgment regarding the authorship and date of composition of 1 Peter, except to place it within the second half of the first century CE.[24] Thus, in the present study, I proceed assuming that the letter represents either the very words of the apostle Peter or, at the very least, is regarded to be the authoritative apostolic voice of the "bridge-builder" as he was remembered within the second half of the first century.[25] Thus, exegetical considerations will be discerned from within the wider cultural, theological, and historical realities that encompassed early followers of Jesus between 64–92 CE, including those that pertain to the way in which Peter was remembered within that timeframe. In part for convenience, henceforth, I will refer to the author of 1 Peter as Peter, as he has identified himself at the beginning of the letter (1 Pet 1:1). But, as I have already revealed, this should not be confused with a claim that the historical Simon Peter was himself the author. Nevertheless, what it does assume is that in

---

20. Kinzer, *Jerusalem Crucified*, 1–2.
21. Wilken, *Land Called Holy*, 143.
22. Kinzer, *Jerusalem Crucified*, 25.

23. Elliott, *1 Peter*, 134–38. See also Williams and Horrell, *1 Peter*, 99–103, who argue that the latest date at which the letter could have been written was 95–96 CE.

24. Not everyone gives due force to the fact that the paucity of evidence can work both ways in either confirming or denying Petrine authorship. As Michaels has commented, "the traditional view that the living Peter was personally responsible for the letter as it stands had not been, and probably in the nature of the case cannot be, decisively shaken" (*1 Peter*, lxvii).

25. For more on the "remembered Peter," see Bockmuehl, *Simon Peter in Scripture and Memory*. For more on Peter as a "bridge builder" see pages 57–59. See Williams and Horrell, *1 Peter*, 149–89, for a thorough discussion of pseudonymity.

one manner or another, the voice, or better said the authority of Peter, the Jewish apostle of Jesus Christ (1 Pet 1:1), stands behind the letter.

A second assumption that grounds and animates this study is that the kind of identity formation that is happening in Asia Minor during the second half of the first century CE through the discourse of New Testament texts such as 1 Peter is best understood, at least in part, as *intra*-Jewish debate about whether the God of Israel regards Jesus to be the appointed Messiah of Israel, and if so, what implications this has for a variety of beliefs and practices, including whether and to what extent gentiles ought to be included.[26] In other words, it is important to call attention to the fact that in contemporary parlance we might call what is happening in a text like 1 Peter something like "Christian identity formation." But to faithfully attend to 1 Peter in its socio-historical milieu, it is more accurate to regard Peter as an authoritative voice, representing a distinct *Jewish* community, tasked with shaping the addressees' self-understanding within a form of *Jewish* identity—and all because he was commissioned to do so by the Jewish Messiah.[27] This presumes that Judaism in the first century was pluriform. It also presupposes that in the second half of the first century CE we still do not have a "parting of the ways" between Christianity and Judaism.[28] And it also means that the god referenced in texts like 1 Peter is more precisely the God of Israel, and that we should presume *continuity* between this particular God's promises and interactions with Israel and these new interactions with the addressees who have faithfully aligned themselves with the Jewish Messiah Jesus—unless something within the text presses us to do otherwise.[29]

Finally, a brief word is in order regarding a term that I will be using throughout this study, namely "Israelhood." It is derived from an important essay written by theologian George Lindbeck, who calls for the elimination of the belief that the church replaces Israel even as an understanding of the church as Israel is regained. This might seem like

---

26. Skarsaune and Hvalvik, *Jewish Believers in Jesus*. For a representation of this field of Pauline studies, see Rudolph, *Jew to the Jews*; Nanos and Zetterholm, *Paul Within Judaism*; Eisenbaum, *Paul Was Not a Christian*; Johnson Hodge, *If Sons, Then Heirs*; Thiessen, *Jewish Paul*; Bird et al., *Paul Within Judaism*. See also the work of Tucker, Windsor, and Zoccali in the New Testament After Supersessionism series for a more nuanced picture of Paul, his relationship to the law, and his understanding of ongoing Jewish identity in Christ.

27. Paget, "Jewish Christianity"; Segal, "Jewish Christianity"; *Paul the Convert*.

28. Boyarin, *Border Lines*; Yoder, *The Jewish-Christian Schism*.

29. So also Burnhope, *Atonement and the New Perspective*, xxvi, 127–50.

an oxymoronic task, but as Lindbeck develops his argument, he proposes that there is a way for the church to "appropriate Israelhood" without replacing Israel.[30] I have adopted this term, not because I support all the ways Lindbeck defines it, but rather because I think it helpfully characterizes the posture and tension we find in 1 Peter.[31] As we will see, on the one hand, the addressees of 1 Peter are *not* Israel. But on the other hand, they have been incorporated or emplaced within the people of the God of Israel. As we attend to the letter, both these claims need to be held in tension, and in my mind "Israelhood" does that work in a concise manner.[32]

---

30. Lindbeck, "What of the Future?," 358–60.

31. See Rudolph's important study of Lindbeck's terminology as compared to Ephesians 2–3 ("Describing the Church in Relation to Israel"). Rudolph notes both the way Lindbeck's terminology helpful attunes us to an enlarged Israel ecclesiology, but also how his language at times goes beyond the biblical witness (e.g., "the church *is* Israel" or "the church *as* Israel"). As the study progresses, I will clarify what I mean by "Israelhood."

32. For a survey of the argument of this book, see the first section of the conclusion, 214–20.

# 1

# *The Problem(s) of Reading 1 Peter After Supersessionism*

> *In a way virtually unique among Christian canonical writings, 1 Peter has appropriated the language of Israel for the church in such a way that Israel as a totality has become for this letter the controlling metaphor in terms of which its theology is expressed. . . . In 1 Peter, the language and hence the reality of Israel pass without remainder into the language and hence the reality of the new people of God. As a result, that language is more than simply illustrative—it is foundational and constitutive for the Christian community in a way that has not always been recognized by those who have studied this epistle.*[1]

## The Problematic Identity-Formation Strategy of 1 Peter

THE ONCE-MARGINALIZED LETTER OF 1 Peter now has become a popular place to explore the social dimensions of early Christianity, and in particular the way in which Christian identity was shaped in the early church.[2] Concomitant with this recent interest in the identity-formation strategy of 1 Peter is a renewed appreciation for the way in which Second Temple Judaism is a determinative context for understanding the writings of the New Testament, and, as a result, recent studies in 1 Peter have revealed the manner in which the identity-formation strategy of the

---

1. Achtemeier, *1 Peter*, 69.

2. I wish to express my profound gratitude to David Horrell, Edward Glenny, and Ralph Korner for their thoroughness, insight, and critical engagement on an earlier draft of this chapter. This does not inculpate them, however, for any of its present shortcomings.

letter is deeply dependent upon the Hebrew scriptures, Israel's vocation, Jewish identity markers, and Jewish restoration ideology.³ In particular, Primopetrine scholars have noted the way in which Israel categories, privileges, and concepts are appropriated in order to educate and exhort newly formed followers of Jesus Christ who are trying to figure out what it looks like to be faithful to God in the midst of social alienation and persecution, and how to engage with their unsympathetic neighbors and the polytheistic Greco-Roman culture around them. What is more, in light of the scholarly attention the letter has received of late, theologians, pastors, and practitioners increasingly have been drawn to 1 Peter in order to better understand the church's mission in and for the world, especially where Christians find themselves trying to live out their ecclesial vocation in a post-Christian or even anti-Christian context.⁴

For some, these recent studies in 1 Peter helpfully have highlighted an often-underappreciated letter that is abundant with resources and creative strategies to aid in Christian identity formation and mission. But for others, the way the author of 1 Peter grounds and forms Christian identity is perplexing, and some would even say deeply troubling. The problem arises when we bring to the fore two key features of the letter. First, there seem to be convincing indications that the original recipients of 1 Peter were predominantly if not exclusively gentile in makeup (see, for example, 1 Pet 1:18, 21; 2:9–10; 4:3–4).⁵ Second, as I have already

---

3. For example, Schutter, *Hermeneutic and Composition in 1 Peter*; Bosetti, *Cristo E La Chiesa Nella Prima Lettera Di Pietro*; Dubis, *Messianic Woes in 1 Peter*; Mbuvi, *Temple, Exile, and Identity in 1 Peter*; Horrell, "'Race,' 'Nation,' 'People'"; Liebengood, *Eschatology of 1 Peter*; Sargent, *Written to Serve*; Horrell, *Becoming Christian*; Doering, "Chosen Stock"; Egan, *Ecclesiology and the Scriptural Narrative of 1 Peter*; Hockey, *Role of Emotion in 1 Peter*; Botner, "Essence of a Spiritual House"; Ok, *Constructing Ethnic Identity*; Schultz, *Estrategia misionera de la Primera carta de Pedro*; Marcar, *Divine Regeneration and Ethnic Identity in 1 Peter*.

4. E.g., Volf, "Soft Difference"; de Silva, "1 Peter: Strategies for Counseling Individuals"; Fagbemi, *Who Are the Elect in 1 Peter?*; Chester and Timmis, *Everyday Church*; Sun, *This Is True Grace*.

5. There is currently a strong consensus among 1 Peter scholars that the letter was written to a predominantly if not exclusively gentile audience in Asia Minor. To trace this modern consensus, see Michaels, *1 Peter*, xlv–xlvi; Achtemeier, *1 Peter*, 50–51; Elliott, *1 Peter*, 94–97, who emphasizes a mixed audience; and Dubis, *Messianic Woes*, 204–5. For the two most comprehensive studies on the audience of 1 Peter to date, see Williams, *Persecution in 1 Peter*, 91–127, who concludes that "it seems best, therefore, along with the majority of commentators, to posit a primarily Gentile-Christian readership as the intended audience of 1 Peter" (95), and Williams and Horrell, *1 Peter*, 207–17, who conclude that most interpreters are convinced that 1 Peter's readers are

stated in brief, the foundational strategy by which Peter seeks to develop a missional identity is to appropriate Israel categories, prerogatives, and privileges and then apply them to this predominantly or exclusively gentile audience. This can be seen most readily in a few examples in the first two chapters of 1 Peter: the recipients are introduced as "elect sojourners of the Diaspora" (1:1)[6] to whom the prophets have prophesied (1:10–12); they are exhorted to be holy as God is holy (1:15–16; applied from Lev 11:44; 19:2; 20:7, 26), and given the privilege of being a "chosen race, a royal priesthood, and a holy nation" (2:9; drawn from Isa 43:20 and Exod 19:6) who bear the vocation of offering acceptable spiritual sacrifices to God (2:5) and proclaiming the mighty acts of the one who has called them out of darkness into his marvelous light (2:9; appropriated from Isa 42:12, which is an allusion to the event of the exodus from Egypt).

Granting these two features of the letter, and in light of our post-Holocaust, postcolonial, globalized world, which has fostered a growing awareness of the way in which religious texts can be used to inculcate prejudice and discrimination in a variety of forms, some have raised concern that the message of 1 Peter promotes a supersessionist posture towards Israel; that is to say that the letter appears to suggest that the church replaces Israel as the new(er) and true(r) people of God.

Surprisingly, until recently, in the modern era of 1 Peter studies, there has been almost no reflection on or discussion of the apparent supersessionism in 1 Peter and to what degree this might be problematic as an identity-formation strategy.[7] Instead, commentators and scholars have tended to ignore this feature of the letter, or to be indifferent, ambiguous, or implicitly (and sometimes explicitly) triumphalist regarding the way in which the church relates to "Israel in the flesh." As one scholar has put it, "The supersessionism of 1 Peter has largely been ignored, downplayed or denied, but rarely discussed."[8]

There may be some explanations for this lack of discussion and/or concern regarding the way in which Peter seems to transfer Israel's

---

portrayed as mostly gentile Christians who have converted out of a pagan background. We will address the question of the ethnic makeup of the addressees more thoroughly in chapters 2 and 3, including a reassessment of the modern consensus.

6. Translation mine.

7. Three notable exceptions to this trend will be discussed below. See also Harink, *1 & 2 Peter*; Botner, "Essence of a Spiritual House."

8. Bauman-Martin, "Speaking Jewish," 150.

identity and privileges over to gentile followers of Jesus.[9] It may be the case that particular scholars do not accept that there was a sharp distinction between Judaism and Christianity in the time in which the letter was written, and that early rhetoric, like that found in 1 Peter, was part of a larger dialogue about what it meant to be a faithful Israelite. What we find in a text like 1 Peter, such might argue, is an intra-Jewish struggle to define who the true Israel of God is. As such, a charge of supersessionism would be considered anachronistic and thus irrelevant.[10]

Another way in which some have downplayed any charge of supersessionism is to argue that although Israel becomes "the controlling metaphor for the letter," there is no evidence of anti-Semitism or any sense in the letter that the Jews have been rejected by God.[11] But this is an argument made from silence and raises more questions than solutions. For example, might the metaphor itself, taken to its logical conclusion, imply a replacement of Israel? Or, might the silence be interpreted as a subtle and subversive demotion of Israel in favor of the gentile church?[12] Or, might the metaphor be regarded in a diminutive sense as a "mere analogy" that is not meant to communicate what is "real" or "true" about the audience?[13]

Additionally, one might disregard supersessionism in 1 Peter on the theological and hermeneutical grounds that such a posture towards Israel is in fact the proper way of reading not only the text of 1 Peter but also the Christian canon as a whole. Simply put, rather than reject or avoid the idea that Israel has been replaced by the church, this "replacement theology" may be seen as the correct interpretation of God's plan as revealed in scripture.[14] As we will see, this has been the predominant way in which the silence of 1 Peter has been filled in the history of interpretation of the New Testament, and 1 Peter in particular.

---

9. See Bauman-Martin, "Speaking Jewish," 150–56, for a critique of some of these possible reasons for downplaying or ignoring the apparent supersessionism of the text.

10. Levering, *Jewish-Christian Dialogue*, 12.

11. Achtemeier, *1 Peter*, 23.

12. See Michaels, *1 Peter*, 107, who questions whether there is anti-Jewish polemic that is expressed by pretending that Israel does not exist.

13. For two significant discussions on how metaphors work in identity formation, especially in 1 Peter, see Horrell "Ethnic Identity-Construction in 1 Peter 2:9," 135–43; Marcar, *Divine Regeneration and Ethnic Identity in 1 Peter*, 24–51. See also Horrell, *Ethnicity and Inclusion*.

14. E.g., Marshall, *New Testament Theology*, 650.

Regardless of what the rationale may be, overall, there remains a silence and, in spite of recent attempts, a scholarly inattention to this important phenomenon of identity formation in the text.

## More on the Problematic Silence of 1 Peter

The relative silence on the apparent supersessionism in 1 Peter was broken in 2007 in an essay by Betsy Bauman-Martin, who leveraged the tools of post-colonial criticism in order to draw attention to the problematic identity-formation strategy in 1 Peter, stressing that the replacement strategies of the letter, far from being benign, set a dangerous precedent. Bauman-Martin insists that 1 Peter scholarship has downplayed the blatant appropriation of Jewish identity and heritage by minimizing it as a mere rhetorical strategy.[15] She argues that what is not readily acknowledged in 1 Peter scholarship is that this kind of appropriation is itself a kind of imperialism that degrades the integrity and identity of the culture that is being misrepresented and defined out of existence.[16] She summarizes her critique by arguing that 1 Peter

> participates in the appropriation/plundering of cultural treasures/resources of another group, rewrites the past of another group for its own benefit, endorses a hierarchy that includes the emperor, suggests, but rejects true hybridization and a real diaspora consciousness, highlights the concepts of chosenness and homeland, all through the utilization of the language of transcendence and inclusion/exclusion.[17]

So for Bauman-Martin, while 1 Peter presents itself as a letter written to an oppressed and marginalized people, the "winning strategy involves the bankrupting of a competing oppressed group, snatching their identity" in such a way that engages in totalizing discourse that creates a universal and absolute identity of superiority.[18] For her, this is deeply problematic, and should no longer be ignored.

In the following year, David Horrell offered a more nuanced assessment of the relationship between gentile followers of Jesus and Israel in 1 Peter, but not without highlighting the "ambivalent legacy" of the

---

15. Bauman-Martin, "Speaking Jewish," 163.
16. Bauman-Martin, "Speaking Jewish," 173–77.
17. Bauman-Martin, "Speaking Jewish," 156.
18. Bauman-Martin, "Speaking Jewish," 176, 169.

methods used in the letter in order to shape Christian identity.[19] For Horrell, the ambivalence is generated by silence in the text: 1 Peter neither explicitly confirms nor denies that Israel has been replaced by the church. Horrell is not alone in pointing out the ambiguity in the letter.[20] In a 2016 essay, Lutz Doering offers a thorough assessment of the way in which 1 Peter appropriates Israel epithets and concludes that:

> In view of the thoroughgoing adoption of Israel epithets, it is significant that 1 Peter does not deploy any form of the term Ἰσραήλ for the addresses. While they take on the status, role, and function of Israel, the addressees *do not become Israel*—as either an accrual to the people of Israel, a "new" Israel, or even the "Israel of God" (cf. Gal 6:16). Neither, however, are they explicitly *likened to* Israel, which would expressly distinguish them from Israel. "Israel" simply does not feature in this letter. It seems that the constitution of the new people through divine begetting would not be appropriately expressed by reference to "Israel." . . . If not "Israel" or "Jews," what else are the addressees? Apart from applying Israel epithets to the new people constituted by divine rebegetting, the letter does not give us an answer.[21]

He further underscores that:

> Israel is appropriated without being expropriated. The confirmation to the addressees to be an elect people of God is carried out without a corresponding announcement of the rejection of the "first" people. The addressees somehow stand in connection with Israel. However, the precise relation to Israel of those addressed as elect remains open precisely because of the situative focus of the letter that is entirely concentrated on strengthening the addressees in distress.[22]

For Doering this ambiguity generated by silence in the text means that drawing on 1 Peter for Christian-Jewish dialogue is "extremely difficult."[23] He suggests that those who wish to draw any conclusions regarding the relationship between the church and Israel from 1 Peter need to acknowledge that to do so "requires us to fill aspects not actually covered by the

---

19. Horrell, *1 Peter*, 102–5.
20. See also Achtemeier, *1 Peter*, 69–70.
21. Doering, "Chosen Stock," 272.
22. Doering, "Chosen Stock," 276.
23. Doering, "Chosen Stock," 276.

situative focus of the text, or at least to read the text alongside other New Testament witnesses that are more explicit on the matter."[24]

In a similar vein, Horrell suggests that the silence in 1 Peter creates hermeneutical and theological space for readers and communities either to allow for Israel to continue as the people of God on the basis of their original covenant with God, or to deny Israel its special place as the people of God. But he also highlights that a supersessionist reading of the silence in 1 Peter is problematic, in part, because it raises a theological inconsistency: "What has become of God's faithfulness to the covenant?"[25] In the end Horrell urges readers to fill in the silence of 1 Peter "within a wider theology which constructs a positive place both for the Church and for Israel."[26] And he challenges Christian theologians with this question: "Can the identity of the Church be claimed and sustained without at the same time implying that the Jews have lost their status as God's people?"[27]

What is important to note for the purposes of this study is that for both Horrell and Doering, the problematic silence of 1 Peter requires readers to go outside of the text itself if they wish to resolve what could be interpreted as a problematic supersessionist strategy of identity formation in the letter.[28]

## How the "Standard Canonical Narrative" Problematizes the Silence of 1 Peter

But this suggestion to go outside of the text is complicated by the fact that the predominant reading strategy that has been employed for centuries problematizes the silence of 1 Peter. In his 1996 monograph, *The God of Israel and Christian Theology*, one of the primary arguments that Kendall Soulen advances is that the problem of the doctrine of supersessionism is more foundationally a canonical narrative problem.[29] Soulen defines a canonical narrative as "an interpretive instrument that provides a

24. Doering, "Chosen Stock," 276.
25. Horrell, *1 Peter*, 104.
26. Horrell, *1 Peter*, 105.
27. Horrell, *1 Peter*, 102.
28. It is also important to underscore that both Horrell and Doering, in their own ways, offer a reading of 1 Peter that does not support Bauman-Martin's claim that the letter uses imperial and colonizing strategies for identity formation.
29. Soulen, *God of Israel and Christian Theology*, 13.

framework for reading the Christian Bible as a theological and narrative unity."[30] A canonical narrative reflects both theological as well as hermeneutical decisions about how the Christian Bible, that is the Old and New Testament, fits together as a whole. For Soulen, it is simply not enough to repudiate supersessionism and re-affirm God's covenant fidelity with Israel. Rather, since Christian doctrine presupposes a storied account of God's relations with humankind, and since this storied account forms the bedrock of the church's convictions, practices (including hermeneutical strategies), and postures, the church must engage in a thoroughgoing reassessment of its standard canonical narrative.[31]

In his analysis of the writings of Justin and Irenaeus, whom he contends laid the foundation for this standard canonical reading, Soulen identifies three kinds of supersessionism that he argues have been passed down to the present. First, the standard canonical narrative contains an *economic supersessionism* that tells the canonical story about God designing carnal Israel from the very beginning to become obsolete with the coming of Jesus Christ and the creation of the church. Everything that was covenanted to Israel is made redundant by its ecclesial equivalent: "The written law of Moses is replaced by the spiritual law of Christ, circumcision by baptism, natural descent by faith as criterion of membership in the people of God, and so forth."[32] Soulen refers to this telling of how the canon fits together as *economic* supersessionism because the obsolescence of carnal Israel is an essential feature of God's overarching economy of redemption for the world. Israel is transient because its role in the economy of redemption was always only to prepare salvation for its spiritual and universal form.[33] The hermeneutical and theological framework of economic supersessionism is encapsulated by the following comment from Melito of Sardis:

> The people [Israel] was precious before the church arose, and the law was marvelous before the gospel was elucidated. But when the church arose and the gospel took precedence the model was made void, conceding its power to the reality. . . . The people was made void when the church arose.[34]

---

30. Soulen, *God of Israel and Christian Theology*, 13.
31. Soulen, *God of Israel and Christian Theology*, 13–14.
32. Soulen, *God of Israel and Christian Theology*, 29.
33. Soulen, *God of Israel and Christian Theology*, 29.
34. Soulen, *God of Israel and Christian Theology*, 29.

As Soulen notes, economic supersessionism is often accompanied by a second type that he calls *punitive supersessionism*—the notion that God abrogates his covenant with Israel because Israel has chosen to reject Jesus Christ and the gospel message. For this reason, God turns his back on and punishes the Jews.

Soulen also identifies a third type of supersessionism, which he considers to be implicit and thus more profoundly problematic. *Structural supersessionism*, Soulen argues, undergirds the standard canonical narrative, in which the Christian canon implicitly is unified in a manner that renders the Hebrew scriptures largely indecisive for shaping conclusions about how God's purposes engage creation in universal and enduring ways.[35] That is to say, God's history with Israel does not contribute much of anything to the essential narrative of God's redemption and consummation. Instead, if God's interactions with Israel were to be completely omitted from an account of Christian faith, this would not disturb the logic of the standard canonical narrative.[36] For Soulen, the absence of any explicit mention of Israel in the church's foundational creeds illustrates the existence and influence of *structural supersessionism*. It appears, he argues, that the Christian conception of God, salvation, and life is minimally impacted by God's identity as the God of Israel. As a result, the prophets are reduced to finding prophecies that point to the coming of the Messiah; the Pentateuch is only as valuable as it helps us understand sin, forgiveness, sacrifice, and our inability to keep God's commands. Soulen underscores that in the standard canonical narrative, redemption supersedes consummation as the hinge on which the canonical narrative turns. As a result, the catastrophe and remedy of sin becomes the *telos* of God's interaction with the world rather than consummation, the eternal fellowship between God and his people.[37]

One reason for highlighting the work of Soulen is to show that the standard canonical narrative exerts significant hermeneutical and theological influence (often unknowingly), especially for those who read New Testament texts with a canon consciousness—because that consciousness

---

35. Soulen, *God of Israel and Christian Theology*, 31–33.

36. Soulen, *God of Israel and Christian Theology*, 32.

37. Soulen has modified his critique of the standard canonical narrative since: "I no longer think that supersessionism is an essential or necessary feature of the standard canonical narrative. I think of it rather as a deformation of that narrative, which can be overcome from within, by making it truer to the canon's witness to Jesus Christ and to the Holy Trinity revealed in him" ("Standard Canonical Narrative," 285).

brings with it an inherited reading strategy. The reality is that the vast majority of those who read and study 1 Peter do so within the framework of this inherited reading strategy, which offers an (often unexamined) way of understanding how Israel relates to the church. Soulen has convincingly shown that the problem of supersessionism in Christian theology goes beyond the explicit teaching that the church has displaced Israel as God's people in the economy of salvation and *missio Dei*; rather, the problem is a result of the way in which Christians (scholars, theologians, pastors, and practitioners) have traditionally understood the theological and narrative unity of the Christian canon as a whole.[38] Put bluntly, while the vast majority of Christian traditions have been engaged in debates about virtually every aspect of Christian theology for centuries, these debates have occurred largely within the hermeneutical and theological parameters established and relatively unchanged by the standard canonical narrative.[39] Soulen's work highlights that for most of its existence, the church has not sought to understand nor articulate itself in light of God's fidelity to the people of Israel. Instead, it has proclaimed itself to have replaced Israel as the true, spiritual people of God, comprising the faithful of all nations, in relation to which the old carnal Israel existed merely as a temporary foreshadowing.

But more foundationally, the point of reflecting on the standard canonical narrative is to underscore that it problematizes the suggestion that we go outside of 1 Peter to resolve the silence of the text regarding the relationship between the church and Israel. Horrell and Doering have encouraged readers to fill the silence of 1 Peter from outside, theologically and canonically, respectively. But Soulen's work shows that this approach to ameliorate the silence of 1 Peter is likely to be problematic because the doctrine and hermeneutical posture of supersessionism originates as a theological and canonical problem of misreading the narrative unity of scripture. Stated plainly, the standard Christian canonical narrative, which is on the one hand a theological construct and on the other hand a hermeneutical framework, conditions many readers, especially those reading within the confines of the Christian tradition and canon, to be blind to the tension that is present in 1 Peter, which is generated by Peter's application of Jewish identity, prerogatives, and privileges to gentile followers of Jesus. This may offer one explanation for why much of modern

---

38. Soulen, *God of Israel and Christian Theology*, 33.
39. Soulen, *God of Israel and Christian Theology*, 16.

1 Peter scholarship has tended to downplay, disregard, or ignore supersessionism in the text: 1 Peter has been seen to cohere with and affirm the "standard canonical narrative" in which the earliest Christian communities are seen as fulfilling Israel's promised destiny, as inheriting Israel's privileges and identity, and in effect replacing Israel as God's people. In short, the problem is that many have not seen this as a problem.[40]

## The Textual Pressure to Solve the Problem(s) of 1 Peter

But in spite of this strong hermeneutical influence, in what follows I will demonstrate that attentiveness to the text of 1 Peter actually confronts and challenges the standard canonical reading strategy described by Soulen, pushes against the purported silence, and raises questions about its supposed supersessionist posture. I will show that 1 Peter provides, on its own terms, a way for gentile followers of Jesus to situate themselves within the story of the God of Israel and his interaction with the people of Israel. I will do this by highlighting two features of 1 Peter that exert pressure on the reader to "appropriate Israelhood" without at the same time replacing Israel.[41]

I will begin by focusing on the way in which "god" is described in 1 Peter, and how this particular God is incomprehensible outside of an implicit narrative that is unique to Israel's account of the world. Second, I will attend more carefully to the way in which the identity of the addressees is re-oriented such that they are to find a new way of life in a kind of "Israelhood" that cannot be understood in a supersessionist manner. As we will see, this reading will press against some of the concerns that Bauman-Martin has raised from her postcolonial criticism perspective, and it will offer a way of beginning to reimagine from within the text itself the relationship between Israel and gentiles who loyally align themselves with Jesus.

### "God" and the Implicit Narrative of 1 Peter

We begin with the question, *which god is Peter referring to in the letter?* In what follows, I want to briefly attend to the implicit, and in some cases

---

40. With the exception of scholars such as Bauman-Martin, Horrell, and Doering mentioned above.

41. See the introduction for the choice of this term.

explicit, ways in which god is referred to and described in 1 Peter. As we attend to these references to God in 1 Peter, we will see that Peter appeals to Israel's scriptures, epithets, privileges, and prerogatives in order to draw the readers into an implicit narrative that is organically connected to both the God of Israel as well as to the hopes and expectations of the people of Israel. That is to say that Peter is not merely using Israel as a metaphor for identify formation but instead is grounding all claims about reality in terms of God's self-revelation and promises to Israel.

The God who is blessed, trusted in, and hoped for in 1 Peter is far from being a generic supreme higher power. Instead, Peter identifies this particular God as the creator (1 Pet 1:20; 4:19), as the one who made a covenant with Abraham and his descendants (implicit in 1 Pet 3:5, and more generally with the reference to the prophets found 1 Pet 1:10–12), as the one who delivered these descendants from Egypt through the Passover (implied in 1 Pet 1:19), and as the one who has promised to once again deliver them from their self-inflicted exile (implied in the usage of Isa 40; Ezek 34; Isa 43:20/Exod 19:5–6; Isa 28:16/Ps 118:22/Isa 8:14; Hos 1:6, 9, 10; 2:23; Isa 53).[42]

It is this particular God who is also said to have raised Jesus Christ from the dead, a hope unique to the people of Israel.[43] As Peter details the accomplishments of this particular God that raised Jesus Christ from the dead, he does so in terms that are unique to Israel's way of understanding what God is up to in the world and what he has promised for his people. For example, the salvation that the God of 1 Peter accomplishes through Jesus Christ is said to conform to the programmatic new-exodus prologue of Isa 40 (1 Pet 1:24–25), the covenantal renewal promises of Hos 1:6, 9–10/2:23 (1 Pet 2:10), and Israel's national hopes for redemption from exile found in Isa 53 (1 Pet 2:22–25).[44] Jesus himself, the agent of God's redemption in the letter, is also characterized in terms that only make sense in a Jewish framework—as the lamb without blemish (1 Pet 1:19), the rejected cornerstone, who is nevertheless esteemed and chosen

---

42. For more details on the way in which these particular Old Testament scriptures are used in 1 Peter, see chapters 4 and 5, and Liebengood, *Eschatology of 1 Peter*, 97–103, 175–99.

43. I am not here claiming that everyone in Israel hoped for resurrection, but that it was nevertheless a unique, confident expectation for many, as demonstrated in Levenson, *Resurrection and the Restoration of Israel*.

44. See chapter 4 as well as Liebengood, *Eschatology of 1 Peter*, 79–104, for further development.

by God (1 Pet 2:6–8; Isa 28:16; Ps 118:22; Isa 8:14), and as the chief shepherd who heals and cares for the flock of God (1 Pet 2:25; 5:4; Jer 23; Ezek 34; Zech 13:7; Ps 23).[45] According to Peter, to trust in Jesus is to put one's hope in this particular God, the God of Israel (1:21); this hope involves seeing the world the way an Israelite would see the world, embracing the metanarrative of Israelite self-understanding.[46] Foundational to this metanarrative of hope is the expectation that this God of Israel is going to judge not only his people, but the entire world, vindicating those who remain loyal to the one true God and his Messiah (1 Pet 2:4–10; 2:12; 4:18/ Ezek 9:6). This coming judgment and vindication are said to be executed by Jesus Christ at his "revelation," and for this reason Peter urges the addressees to place their hope completely in the grace that will be brought to them on that day (1 Pet 1:13).

Additionally, the people who place their hope in this particular God are said to have been "ransomed" (a concept that originates in Israel's exodus narratives) from the futile ways of their forefathers (1 Pet 1:18); they are exhorted to live in keeping with the foundational covenant stipulation established by the God of Israel in the wilderness: "You shall be holy, for I am holy" (1 Pet 1:15–16; Lev 11:44); and their vocation, or mission, is described in terms that echo both God's call for elect Israel as they were delivered from Egypt and also God's promises of redemption for exiled Israel in Isaiah: "You are a chosen race, a royal priesthood, a holy nation, God's own people, in order that you may proclaim the mighty acts of him who called you out of darkness into his marvelous light" (1 Pet 2:9; Exod 19:5–6; Isa 43:20–21).[47]

I bring these implicit (and at times explicit) assumptions about God in 1 Peter to the surface to make three points. First, this is a uniquely Israel-centric way of telling the story of the world, of talking about who God is, and of describing what this God is up to in the world. It is important to underscore that the addressees are being asked to do more than think of Israel as an analogy; rather, they are being called to embrace a uniquely Israelite way of conceiving of and being in the world.

Second, the addressees are organically connected to and included in this story because of their association with Jesus. While it is true, as some

---

45. In this regard, even the addressees' allegiance to Jesus must be understood on Israel's terms.

46. Albeit a contested identity characterized by intra-Jewish debate on how, when, and through whom this redemption would be accomplished.

47. All scripture citations are from the NRSV unless otherwise noted.

have pointed out, that the addressees are not said to become Israel, they are nevertheless seamlessly placed within the story of God's redemption of Israel through the Christ and incorporated into the hopes of Isaiah, Hosea, Ezekiel, and the Psalmists. In this regard, the text seems to necessitate that the addressees "appropriate Israelhood," that is, to embrace an Israelite understanding of the problem of the world and the way in which this one true God of the world intends to resolve the problem. In short, he calls them to orient their lives around a particular hope (1 Pet 1:13; 3:15) that would prove to be utterly meaningless were Israel to be expropriated. To be a new people (1 Pet 2:9–10), they must see themselves as a part of a new story, belonging to a people and a history that has preceded them.

Finally, the claims that Peter makes about God and what this God has accomplished through Jesus make supersessionism deeply problematic because such a posture towards Israel is internally incoherent in the text. For example, Peter's assumption is that the God of Israel—who is characterized as the creator of the world and the one who formed, covenanted, and remains faithful to Israel (and not some generic notion of deity)—has acted decisively in and through Jesus to bring to culmination the promises he made to Israel for the sake of the whole world. To be more specific, Peter states that the God and Father of the Lord Jesus Christ (1 Pet 1:3) is in fact the God of Israel; that what this particular God has revealed about himself in Jesus is to be understood *within the context of* and *in continuity with* what he has revealed about himself through his covenant and history with Israel (e.g., 1 Pet 1:10–12). This covenantal history with Israel has been inscripturated in the Hebrew Bible (or what Christians refer to as the Old Testament), and when Peter appeals to the Hebrew scriptures to establish a point about, for example, Christology or the mission of the people of God, he is more foundationally appealing to the reliability and trustworthiness of this God of Israel. If we were to read 1 Peter in such a way that Peter replaces the privileges and mission of Israel with "the church," then this calls into question just how reliable and faithful this God is that Peter refers to fundamentally in his letter.[48] In this regard, the implicit narrative of 1 Peter forces gentile followers of Jesus to understand and articulate their own identity in light of God's

---

48. I place "the church" in quotations because it is important to note that the term ἐκκλησία never appears in 1 Peter. Despite this, scholars often refer anachronistically to the addressees as "the church," which is a historically and theological loaded term. This move subtly contributes to the problematic reading strategy I am seeking to highlight in this study.

ongoing fidelity to the people of Israel. Additionally, the way in which Peter narrates the story of God in the letter underscores the *telos* of God's dealings with Israel (as expressed in the Abrahamic covenant), namely the blessing of eternal fellowship with God through Israel for all the nations. That is, the goal of God's interactions with Israel is consummation and communion, and not merely redemption.

If we are to read 1 Peter with a posture of supersessionism that renders the Jewish people a matter of indifference to the God of Israel, this seems to be inconsistent with the foundational assumptions of Peter and his usage of the Hebrew scriptures in the letter. It also raises vexing questions such as, if the God of Israel is indifferent to a people to whom he once promised an inheritance, then how seriously can we take promises he is said to make to other peoples at other times? Or, if the God of Israel is capable of raising up a people only to abandon them for another, how sure can we be that he will not do the same to his new chosen people? In view of these foundational claims about the God of 1 Peter, the text of 1 Peter seems to necessitate that a gentile follower of Jesus "appropriate Israelhood" *without denying it to Israel*.

## Embracing a Non-Gentile Way of Life

More can be said about the "Israelhood" posture that the addressees are called to embrace by looking briefly at a particular way in which the addressees are described in 1 Peter:

> Conduct yourselves honorably among the Gentiles, so that, though they malign you as evildoers, they may see your honorable deeds and glorify God when he comes to judge. (1 Pet 2:12)

> You have already spent enough time in doing what the Gentiles like to do, . . . they are surprised that you no longer join them in the same excesses of dissipation, and so they blaspheme. (1 Pet 4:3–4)

These two references are particularly striking because, as we have already seen, there is a consensus within Primopetrine scholarship that the addressees are a predominantly if not exclusively gentile audience. So, what is Peter doing with this move in which he seems to *distinguish* his predominantly gentile addressees from "the gentiles"? Contemporary 1 Peter scholars tend to explain this move as Peter's way of distinguishing believers in Jesus from non-believers, or more specifically non-Christians. For example, regarding 1 Pet 4:3, Joel Green asserts that "this emphasizes, yet again, the distinction between believers and unbelievers";[49] Michaels states that "the term traditionally applied by Jews and Christians alike to non-Jews is transferred to non-Christians, so as to become the equivalent of such English words as 'heathen' or 'pagan'";[50] Elliott claims that "in most of its NT occurrences, the term *ta ethnē* continues to denote non-Israelites in contrast to Israelites. However, in some cases, as here in 1 Peter, when *ta ethnē /hoi ethnikoi* is a foil to followers of Jesus, it becomes a designation for all non-Christians who disobey (2:7; 3:1), who have rejected Jesus as Messiah and malign his followers, including pagans and mainstream Israel alike";[51] and Jobes insists that "both Peter and Paul, following Jewish thought, use the designation *ethnē* to refer to those outside the community of Christian faith."[52]

But I contend that this reading of those two references of "gentile" demands more care. First, it seems to me that commentators are unduly anachronistic when they claim that the author is creating a third category, "Christian," that is distinguishable from Jew and gentile. Recent scholarship on the term Χριστιανός, which appears in 1 Pet 4:16 (as well as Acts 11:26; 26:28), shows that the grain runs the opposite direction. Rather than identify or create a third entity, the word is used to designate a sub-group that includes Jews and non-Jews who have aligned themselves with Jesus.[53] In other words, Χριστιανός does not constitute a new religious category, nor is it meant to imply that the addressees were no longer viewed as Jews. What is more, Korner has observed that when the term Χριστιανός occurs in Acts, it is when "other ethnicities are depicted as being allowed entrance into a Jewish sub-group of Christ followers

---

49. Green, *1 Peter*, 138.

50. Michaels, *1 Peter*, 117.

51. Elliott, *1 Peter*, 466.

52. Jobes, *1 Peter* [1st ed.], 169–70. Ok is more nuanced than most, noting that "in 2:11–12 and 4:3–4, Peter makes the sharpest distinction between these two groups when contrasting the exceptional and holy people of God with those whom he refers to in one sweeping, opposing category, 'the Gentiles' (τὰ ἔθνη), i.e., the people *not* of God." Additionally, she notes that "rather than make a Jew/Gentile dichotomy, Peter first broadens the identification of Israel as a γένος ἐκλεκτόν, βασίλειον ἱεράτευμα, ἔθνος ἅγιον, λαὸς εἰς περιποίησιν, and λαὸς θεοῦ (2:9–10) to include his addressees and then contrasts this exceptional and holy people with the 'Gentiles' (τὰ ἔθνη), i.e., the people *not* of God (2:12)" (Ok, *Constructing Ethnic Identity*, 66–67).

53. Trebilco, *Self-Designations and Group Identity*, 272–97.

whose apostolic loyalty lies with the apostles in Jerusalem."[54] This observation fits well with reading that I have put forth in 1 Peter. All this is to say that at this stage in history, it is more accurate to see what is going on in 1 Peter as *intra*-Jewish debate about who the true people of God are (and how gentiles fit into that corporate entity), and about how God has been faithful to his covenant and his promises, rather than as Peter creating a new category ("Christian") that can be clearly delineated from Israel and its God. In other words, the text of 1 Peter itself does not give us warrant to create a new entity, Christian, that is mutually exclusive from Israel and Jewish followers of Jesus.[55]

Second, if we read 1 Pet 2:12 and 4:3–4 with the grain of the implicit narrative that I have highlighted in 1 Peter, it seems to be the case that Peter is not taking Israel's identity, prerogatives, and mission and transferring them to the gentiles (as has often been the assumption or claim); rather, Peter is exhorting gentiles to distance themselves from their gentile culture with its assumptions, values, practices, and hopes.[56] To be more specific, Peter is exhorting his readers to orient themselves *as gentiles* to a particularly *Jewish* way of life that is patterned after the life of Jesus (e.g., 1 Pet 2:21–23 mimicked in 1 Pet 3:9–12) and built upon the hopes and expectations of Israel. We see this in the fact that, as Doering as already underscored, these readers are never called a new Israel. Their identity as gentiles is in one sense preserved. But in another sense their identity as gentiles is disoriented or dislocated because they are called to a new ἀναστροφή ("way of life" or "conduct") that is on the one hand a rejection of what they have inherited (1 Pet 1:18), and on the other what they are learning as new followers of Jesus (1 Pet 1:15, 17; 2:12). Seven times in key exhortative passages in the letter Peter uses either the verb ἀναστρέφω or the noun ἀναστροφή to explain the full implications of aligning one's life with the Jewish Messiah, Jesus (1 Pet 1:15, 17, 18; 2:12; 3:1, 2). This reading helps explain, in part, why Peter employs the unique

---

54. Korner, *Reading Revelation After Supersessionsim*, 20. See also Korner, *Origin and Meaning of Ekklēsia*, 152.

55. See Trebilco, *Outsider Designations*, 270.

56. Here it is important to underscore that the Greek word τὰ ἔθνη, which is often translated "gentiles," is not meant to convey a monolithic, solitary cultural alternative to Jewish ethnicity. Instead, from a Jewish perspective, it is a catch-all term that includes and/or refers to a *variety* of ethnicities that are not Jewish. As I will argue in chapter 4, what "gentiles" have in common in Asia Minor in the first century is the pervasive and influential worldview of Roman imperial ideology, which impacts the way these various ethnicities understand themselves.

image of "newborns" to his readers (1 Pet 1:3, 23: 2:2) who now must learn to "grow into salvation" (1 Pet 2:2). To say it another way, in 1 Peter, the gentiles who have been born-anew as a result of the resurrection of Jesus Christ (1 Pet 1:3) are ransomed from their former way of life (1 Pet 1:18) and called to learn a new culture patterned after the Messiah of Israel and shaped by the God of Israel's expectations for Israel's corporate life, but distinctly as gentiles. Their new way of life in Jesus Christ is to be understood as the culmination of the promises to and hopes of Israel (e.g., 1 Pet 1:3, 13; 2:4, 25) for the sake of the world.[57] Read in this way, it is not that Israel has been superseded by gentile followers of Jesus. Quite the contrary; if the audience is in fact made up of an exclusive or even predominantly gentile audience, it appears that Peter is claiming that their gentile heritage (narrative self-understanding, hopes, way of life, values, etc.) has been replaced with that of "Israelhood." Or to borrow from Willie Jennings, these gentile-followers of Jesus, as a new-born people, have been displaced and now must learn to participate in Israel's story as guests.[58]

As we have seen, much of the discussion regarding Israel and "the church" has insinuated that Peter is appropriating Israel's identity in such a way that he gives it over to the gentiles, that the gentiles are exhorted to take Israel's vocation, prerogatives, etc., as their own in such a way that replaces Israel. But I have made the case that the pressure of the text moves in the exact opposite direction; that is, it seems that what the text is actually doing is demanding non-Jewish followers of Jesus Christ to no longer orient themselves around the inherited way of life of the "gentiles" but rather to find their heritage as part of the house or commonwealth of the Davidic king, Jesus, who is the hope of Israel and the nations (1 Pet 2:4–10, 25).[59]

This does not yet answer all the questions we may have about the relationship between Israel and the church in 1 Peter, or more accurately Israel and gentile followers of Jesus.[60] What is important to note is that

---

57. It is important to note that Israel's own self-understanding is also re-oriented by Jesus Christ as well.

58. Jennings, *Christian Imagination*, 250–88.

59. For the development of the eschatological Davidic shepherd ideology in 1 Peter see Liebengood, *Eschatology of 1 Peter*, 79–104, 156–214, as well as chapters 4 and 6.

60. While many scholars have noted that gentile followers of Jesus are never called or likened to Israel in 1 Peter, it is also the case that gentile followers of Jesus are never referred to as "the church" either. See chapter 6, 197–99, for a rationale for this move.

Peter does not care to explain all that makes these two entities different but rather seeks to emphasize what these newborn gentiles share with Israel. So, while their new birth does not make them Israel, it does connect them to Israel's God, Israel's call to be holy, and Israel's hope, all shaped by Jesus Christ, the God of Israel's cornerstone and shepherd (1 Pet 2:4, 25).

This is by no means an exhaustive survey of all the ways in which 1 Peter displaces, emplaces, and reorients the implied readers to inhabit the story of Israel. More can and will be said about how Peter places the readers into a new exodus wilderness of testing (1 Pet 1:5—2:10), how the readers are to conceptualize being living stones who are built into a spiritual house (1 Pet 2:4-10), how the readers are to be a royal priesthood, and how they are to receive promises that seem to have been given exclusively to Israel (e.g., Hos 1:6, 9–10; 2:23 in 1 Pet 2:10) without at the same time replacing Israel. But for the purposes of this chapter, our brief survey above has highlighted that there is enough pressure in the text to question the concerns of Bauman-Martin as well as the suggestion by Horrell and Doering that we must go outside of 1 Peter to resolve the seemingly problematic identify-formation strategy of the letter.

## Conclusions

The primary point of this chapter is to underscore that it is not only postcolonial criticism that exposes problems with reading 1 Peter as a text that puts forth a supersessionist identity-formation strategy. Some have tried to ameliorate this problem by pointing to silence in the letter, which creates hermeneutical space to go outside of the text itself to resolve the tension. I have shown that this move can create its own problems because of the influential standard canonical narrative, which exerts tremendous pressure to replace Israel with the church.

Instead, I have sought to demonstrate in brief that *the text of 1 Peter itself* pushes against a supersessionist posture, in part because such a reading is inconsistent with the claims made about God in the letter, raising serious questions about the trustworthiness of this God, but also because the grain of text—with the implicit narrative and the exhortation to distance oneself from a gentile way of life—seems to necessitate that the addressees "appropriate Israelhood" without expropriating Israel. The most basic observation that I have made by attuning to two non-exhaustive features of the letter is that Peter seeks to make sense of both Jesus as well as the new reality of the implied readers within the ongoing story of the God of Israel's interactions with Israel. Said in another way, the addressees are not to understand their allegiance to Jesus apart from their belonging to the hopes and expectations of Israel. First Peter compels an Israel-centric way of understanding the world and one's place in it. What is more, I have noted how a close examination of 1 Peter challenges the standard canonical reading strategy described by Soulen and, in turn, provides on its own terms a way for gentile readers to situate themselves within the story of the God of Israel and his interaction with his people.

This being the case, I contend that fresh research on the identity-formation strategy of 1 Peter is in order, which requires more attentiveness to the complex and comprehensive way that 1 Peter draws on Israel's privileges, prerogatives, and scriptures to invite gentiles to inhabit the hopes, expectations, and mission of Israel, and more inquiry into the assumptions that lead to supersessionist interpretations in the letter. In short, I maintain that reading 1 Peter after supersessionism is a problem in search of a comprehensive solution, which is what I seek to provide in the following chapters.

# 2

# *The Problem of Identifying the Ethnic Identity of the Addressees of 1 Peter*

## Part 1: Reconsidering Foundational Assumptions of the Consensus[1]

*The best explanation of the data is that 1 Peter was written primarily to Gentile Christians in Asia Minor, but that the author, for his own reasons, has chosen to address them as if they were Jews.*[2]

AS WE SAW IN chapter 1, one of the features of 1 Peter that generates concerns regarding the identity-formation strategy of the letter is the audience's ethnic makeup. If 1 Peter is written to an exclusively or predominantly gentile audience, then what are we to make of Peter's appropriation of Israel's scriptures, privileges, hope, and mission? But if the letter was written to an exclusively, if not predominantly, Jewish audience, then many of the supposed problems that thus far have been highlighted disappear. As we will see below, there are compelling reasons to question the established modern consensus.

---

1. An earlier version of this chapter was presented at ISBL in Rome and IBR in San Diego. I am grateful for the feedback I received from both these sessions.
2. Michaels, *1 Peter*, xlvi.

## Reexamining the Consensus

For at least the past seventy years there has been near-universal consensus among Primopetrine scholars that 1 Peter was written for a predominantly (if not exclusively) gentile audience in Asia Minor—this in spite of a number of features in the letter that seem to indicate a Jewish audience was in view. The opening greeting, for example, which is directed to the ἐκλεκτοῖς παρεπιδήμοις διασπορᾶς, would seem to be an indisputable reference to Jews scattered throughout Asia Minor. Even Michaels, who is one of the most persuasive advocates of the current consensus position, concedes that in this opening address "the *clear* impression is that the readers of the epistle are Jewish Christians."[3] This "clear" initial impression seems to be confirmed further by several other features in the letter. First, there is the reference in 1 Pet 2:12 in which gentiles (τὰ ἔθνη) seem to be regarded as the out-group ("Conduct yourselves honorably among the Gentiles, so that, though they malign you as evildoers, they may see your honorable deeds and glorify God when he comes to judge"). Second, an abundance of Old Testament citations and allusions, which are often appropriated in keeping with Jewish hermeneutical assumptions and techniques, would seem to favor a Jewish audience (or at least a mixed audience with a significant quantity of Christian Jews).[4] Third, not only does Peter lavishly appropriate from the Hebrew scriptures in order to persuade his recipients, he also draws attention to patriarchal heroes as paradigmatic figures for his exhortations.[5] This kind of rhetorical strategy, it could be argued, would seem to be most effective in seeking to persuade Christian Jews, who were intimately familiar with Jewish tradition, exegetical practices, and patriarchal heroes, and who were perhaps feeling pressure from their non-Christian compeers (i.e., fellow-Jews)

---

3. Michaels, *1 Peter*, xlv (emphasis mine). See also his comments in *1 Peter*, 6.

4. See, for example, Michaels, *1 Peter*, xlv; Elliott, *1 Peter*, 95; Achtemeier, *1 Peter*, 50. For a discussion of the complex nature of the use of the Old Testament in 1 Peter see Schutter, *Hermeneutic and Composition in 1 Peter*; Liebengood, *Eschatology of 1 Peter*; Sargent, *Written to Serve*; Egan, *Ecclesiology and the Scriptural Narrative of 1 Peter*.

5. For example, in 1 Pet 3:1–6, he supports his exhortation that wives are to be subject to their husbands and so win them over to the faith by appealing to Sarah's conduct before Abraham. Similarly, he alludes to the trials of Noah (1 Pet 3:20–21), who faced the jeering of his fellow countrymen, in order to encourage his readers to remain faithful to God.

to renounce their new-found allegiance to Jesus.[6] Fourth, genre considerations might seem to point to a predominantly Jewish readership. Michaels has proposed that 1 Peter is best considered an "apocalyptic diaspora letter."[7] Several scholars have followed him, noting similarities between 1 Peter and extant correspondence amongst Jews in the Diaspora (2 Bar 78:1–87:1; Epistle of Jer; Jer 29:4–23; Baruch; and 2 Macc 1:1–10a; 1:10b–2:18; cf. Jas 1:1).[8] Both Horrell and Doering have highlighted that these Jewish letters frequently focus on the theme of exile, and are not necessarily only sent from Jerusalem (Baruch, for example, emanated from Babylon).[9] Horrell notes a parallel here with 1 Peter, which is also "a kind of circular letter, sent to encourage the faithful scattered over a wide geographical area, and sent, so the letter says, from Babylon (5:13) to the Diaspora (1:1)."[10] Dunn, who suggests that the letter is probably written primarily for Jewish believers, highlights Doering's research on the genre of Jewish diaspora letters, arguing that it demonstrates that 1 Peter fits comfortably within the milieu of intra-Jewish diaspora communication and is closely modeled on the analogy of Jewish diaspora experience.[11]

---

6. Michaels (*1 Peter*, l) creatively postulates that Peter's appeal to Noah is "what convinced many Gentile Christians that all the other stories—and more—were theirs as well. The Jewish past became their past. If they began to see themselves as 'honorary Jews' (Krister Stendahls's term), they also began to see the heroes and heroines of the Jewish stories they loved as honorary Christians." This, however, seems impossible to adjudicate from the text itself, and is very likely a conclusion that one would arrive at after having determined the ethnic make-up of the audience. For a discussion of and references to Jewish hostility and persecution towards Jesus-following Jews, see Aune, *Revelation 1–5*, 162–63. The point I make about the Old Testament usage, Jewish exegetical practices, and patriarchal heroes in 1 Peter is not meant to suggest that this kind of rhetorical strategy can *only* be used for a Jewish audience. We can, of course, see similar features in Paul's letters as well, many of which were written to a mixed audience.

7. Michaels, *1 Peter*, xlvi–xlix.

8. Michaels *1 Peter*, xlvi–ii; Horrell, *1 Peter*, 8–9; Green, *1 Peter*, 5. For the most extensive work on reading 1 Peter as an early Christian diaspora letter, see Doering, "Early Christian Diaspora Letter," 215–36, 441–57; *Ancient Jewish Letters and the Beginnings of Christian Epistolography*.

9. Horrell, *1 Peter*, 8; Doering, "Early Christian Diaspora Letter," 225.

10. Horrell, *1 Peter*, 9. He concludes, however, that "the author of 1 Peter draws on Jewish language and tradition, but he is applying these terms to Christian believers," which seems to mean largely, but not exclusively, gentile Christian believers (48).

11. Dunn, *Beginning from Jerusalem*, 1158. It is important to underscore that Doering himself does not make this conclusion but instead considers the letter to have been written to a gentile audience.

We have indications that the early church understood 1 Peter to be addressed to a Jewish readership. In *Ecclesiastical History* (HE 3.1.2), Eusebius reports that Origen regarded 1 Peter to be a genuine letter from Peter written to the Jews of the dispersion. Eusebius's own conclusion regarding the ethnic make-up of the addressees is in keeping with Origen, and he appears to have arrived at his conclusion in a similar manner—by reading the letter itself: Peter "preached Christ and taught the doctrine of the new covenant to those of the circumcision" as "*is clear from his own words in his epistle* . . . in which he writes to the Hebrews of the dispersion in Pontus, Galatia, Cappadocia, Asia and Bithynia" (HE 3.4.2).[12] Jerome, Didymus, Epiphanus, Erasmus, Wycliffe, Calvin, Beza, and Wesley arrive at similar conclusions.[13] All indications are that the predominant position of the early church fathers was picked up by many of the Reformers and became the "traditional" view.[14]

These "Jewish" features of 1 Peter, however, have not persuaded the overwhelming majority of modern 1 Peter interpreters, who, having duly analyzed the evidence, consistently have pointed to several references in the letter that would seem to make a principally Jewish audience nearly impossible: in 1 Pet 1:14 the recipients are urged to no longer be conformed to the desires they formerly had in ignorance; in 1 Pet 1:18 they are said to have been redeemed from the futile way of life inherited from their fathers (πατροπαράδοτος); in 1 Pet 1:21 they are told that in trusting in Jesus they have now put their faith and hope in God; in 1 Pet 2:10 they are portrayed as those who once were not a people (of God), but now are a people of God (1 Pet 2:10); and finally, in 1 Pet 4:3–4 they are characterized as once having participated in "living in licentiousness, passions, drunkenness, revels, carousing, and lawless idolatry," blasphemed in the present because they no longer "run" with the gentiles in such behavior.

In considering the audience of 1 Peter, it is important to re-engage the foundational assumptions upon which the present consensus is built. Far from being a full discussion of all the pertinent issues, this section will

---

12. Emphasis mine. Michaels's response to this testimony is revealing in a number of ways: "So successful was the author of 1 Peter in appearing to write to Jews that the Christian historian Eusebius . . . *took him at his word*" (*1 Peter*, xlvi [emphasis mine]).

13. Jerome and Wycliffe seem to have opted for both positions over the course of their lives. According to Selwyn, *First Epistle of St. Peter*, 42, the Greek fathers follow Origen and Eusebius and assume a Jewish audience, while the Latin fathers tend to follow Jerome and Augustine, who understood the recipients of 1 Peter to be a mixed group

14. So Elliott, *1 Peter*, 96.

focus attention on the cluster of references found in 1 Peter 1:13—2:10, which have been determinant for arguing that 1 Peter's addressees are predominantly (if not exclusively) gentile in makeup. In my view, these references have been examined in isolation from the larger literary context of 1 Peter and without consideration of a prominent Jewish tradition in which the fathers are regularly critiqued for the life they have passed down to their children.

## Foundational Assumptions Regarding the Ethnic Makeup of the 1 Peter Recipients

We begin with 1 Pet 1:18, which is regularly presented as one of the most decisive references in the letter, indicating that Peter must be writing to a gentile audience. E. G. Selwyn, for example, argues that while the reference to the futility of the recipients' former way of life (1 Pet 1:18) could perhaps be directed to lapsed Jews, "the description of it as 'handed down by the tradition from your fathers' *could hardly have been used of any but Gentiles.*"[15] Most Primopetrine scholars have followed Selwyn's assumption. Steven Bechtler, for example, argues that "μάταιος (in 1:18; cf. LXX Jer 2:5) and ἄγνοια (in 1:14), used to characterize the former way of life of the intended readers and their forebears [sic], reflect the typical Jewish condemnation of gentile idolatry found in the LXX (e.g., Wis 14:22; Hos 5:11; Isa 2:20; Jer 10:25) and later adapted for Christian missionary propaganda (see Acts 14:15; 17:30; Eph 4:18; 1 Thess 4:5)."[16] Michaels concludes his even-handed appraisal of the ethnic profile of the 1 Peter addressees by noting that "such words [1 Pet 1:14, 18, 21; 2:10; 4:2–4] are scarcely intelligible in relation to a Jewish Christian audience. They describe how Jews as well as Christians regarded the Gentile world, not how Christians (or anyone else) ever regarded Jews."[17] More recently, Joel Green has reasoned that

> repeated references to the pagan character of their background strongly intimate that most of those in the audience assumed by the letter were Gentile (see 1:14, 18; 2:10, 25; 4:3–4). The

---

15. Selwyn, *1 Peter*, 43 (emphasis mine).

16. Bechtler, *Following in His Steps*, 63. In further comments on this page, Bechtler perceives 1 Peter to be an *intragentile* conflict—nonbelieving gentiles reviling gentiles because of the latter's strange new lifestyle.

17. Michaels, *1 Peter*, xlvi. So also Davids, *First Peter*, 8

comment that, prior to their conversion, the readers of 1 Peter had neither faith nor hope in God likewise urges their identification as Gentiles (1:21). These considerations speak *decisively* in favor of our identifying the first audience of 1 Peter as communities of Christians in which person of Gentile background would have predominated.[18]

These representative samples encapsulate one of the foundational assumptions of the consensus. Stated plainly, a Jew would never critique the ways or traditions of his ancestors the way that Peter does in 1:14 and 18, and he would certainly not find it remarkable that his fellow Jews have now put their hope and trust in God the way that Peter would seem to do in 1 Pet 1:21. In short, Jews just don't speak to other Jews in this manner. Therefore, these references must be addressed to gentiles.

## Intra-Jewish Critique of the Fathers:
## A Representative Sample

But is it accurate to say that Jews could hardly have ever described other Jews as needing to be redeemed from the futile traditions handed down to them by their fathers (1 Pet 1:18), or that Peter would not likely characterize his compeers as living in keeping with their "ignorant passions" (1 Pet 1:14)? Are we right to assume that since Peter describes his readers as those who have now put their faith and hope in God (1:21) that he must, then, be addressing gentiles, since Jews didn't talk to other Jews in such a manner? A representative survey from the New Testament, the Hebrew Bible, and Jewish Second Temple literature will illustrate that the kind of rhetoric expressed in 1 Pet 1:14, 18, and 21 is in no way uncommon in intra-Jewish exhortation, and is in fact quite typical, especially in times (like exile) when certain Jews are readying people for fresh expressions of Yhwh's redemptive favor. We turn first to the New Testament, where, chronologically, we find the nearest parallels.

### Intra-Jewish Critique in the New Testament

Beginning with the Synoptic Gospels, I draw attention to two illuminating examples of intra-Jewish debate in which the traditions of the ancestors are repudiated, and where Jewish fidelity to Yhwh is called into question.

18. Green, *1 Peter*, 5.

Having been accused of teaching his disciples to break the traditions of the elders, Matthew's Jesus (Matt 15:1–19; cf. Mark 7:1–13) responds by chiding his accusers, the Pharisees and the scribes, because they invalidate God's word for the sake of *their* traditions. In responding to the Jewish leaders, Jesus draws on the Hebrew scriptures, where he finds a fitting critique of contemporary Jewish devotion to Yhwh, charging that "Isaiah prophesied rightly about you when he said: 'This people honors me with their lips, but their hearts are far from me; in vain do they worship me, teaching human precepts as doctrines' [Isa 29:13]."

In Matt 23:13–36 (cf. Luke 11:39–52), Jesus, with his seven "woes," offers a similar but more scathing and detailed account of the ways in which certain Jews, in his view, have invalidated God's justice, mercy, and faith with their contradictory traditions, which he regards as having been passed down by their fathers. He calls the Pharisees and scribes blind guides, whitewashed tombs, who are full of hypocrisy and lawlessness, and concludes by exhorting them to fill up the full measure of the guilt of their fathers (23:32), charging that "you testify against yourselves that you are descendants of those who murdered the prophets" (23:31). Matthew's Jesus caps off these seven woes with a lament over Jerusalem (a synecdoche for the people of Israel), whose impending judgment is the result of repeated failures to trust in Yhwh and his chosen agents who have been sent to express God's longsuffering covenant mercy (Matt 23:37–39).

Other examples of this kind of intra-Jewish critique in the Synoptic Gospels could be highlighted.[19] Here, I will only mention that a number of Jesus' parables are intended (and often perceived) to be critiques against certain Jewish expressions of leadership as well as Israel as a whole's repeated tendency to reject Yhwh and his messengers. The parable of the vine-growers is one such example, and is significant because the Hebrew scriptures are once again availed (Ps 118; cf. 1 Pet 2:6–8) in order to provide a rationale for Jewish opposition to Yhwh's plans. We could also point to the Lukan Jesus who, in instructing his fellow Jews who have allied themselves to him, warns: "Woe *to you* when all men speak well of you, for their fathers used to treat the false prophets in the same way" (Luke 6:26).

The intra-Jewish rhetoric in Acts in not unlike that which we have highlighted in the Synoptic Gospels. The Peter of Acts inculpates his

19. E.g., Matt 10:16–23; 11:7–19, 20–24; 21:33–46; Mark 6:1–6; 12:1–12, 38–40; Luke 4:16–30; 13:31–35.

compatriots for crucifying Jesus, charging that their actions, along with those of their leaders, were in keeping with their ignorance of God's ways (Acts 3:17, 27; cf. 1 Pet 1:14); he urges his Jewish hearers to save themselves from "this corrupt generation" (Acts 2:40); and he characterizes the resurrection of Jesus as the means by which God will "bless you by turning each of you from your wicked ways" (Acts 3:26). Additionally, for the Peter of Acts, a failure to believe in Jesus is a failure to believe in YHWH: "Repent therefore, and turn to God so that your sins may be wiped out, so that times of refreshing may come from the presence of the Lord, and that he may send the Messiah appointed for you, that is, Jesus, who must remain in heaven until the time of universal restoration that God announced long ago through his holy prophets" (Acts 3:19–21; cf. 1 Pet 1:21).

Stephen's speech in Acts 7 betrays similar sentiments, asserting that Israel's rejection of Jesus is in keeping with a long-standing pattern of failing to rightly respond to the God of Israel's saving actions. He culminates his survey of Israel's history with a critique that echoes YHWH's accusation of Israel in the wilderness: "You stiff-necked people, uncircumcised in heart and ears, you are forever opposing the Holy Spirit, just as your ancestors (lit. οἱ πατέρες) used to do. Which of the prophets did your fathers not persecute? They killed those who foretold the coming of the Righteous One, and now you have become his betrayers and murderers. You are the ones that received the law as ordained by angels, and yet you have not kept it" (Acts 7:51–53; cf. Exod 32:9; Deut 10:16). In both the Synoptic Gospels and in Acts, contemporary Jewish infidelity is linked to the infidelity of the fathers of the Hebrew scriptures, whether in the wilderness or the exile. As we will soon see, this will also be the case in the Psalms, the Prophets, and Baruch—suggesting, perhaps, that there exists some sort of tradition, or at least a shared recognition of a pattern within the history of Israel's dealings with God.

Two final examples in the New Testament highlight that, as far as some early Jewish followers of Jesus were concerned, ethnic Israel was no different from the gentiles in their failure to believe in and obey God. In Eph 2:3, the author, addressing Jewish followers of Jesus, asserts that "all of us once lived among them in the passions of our flesh, following the desires of flesh and senses, and we were by nature children of wrath, like everyone else [cf. 1 Pet 1:14]." Finally, in Rom 3:9–18 Paul underscores that both Jew and gentile are "under the power of sin" and characterized by a total failure to seek God.[20]

This representative survey serves as a reminder that during the time in which the New Testament was being composed, Jewish self-understanding was in no way monolithic or uncontested. Jewish sects, such as the early Jewish followers of Jesus, the Qumran community, and the Pharisees, regarded themselves to be the true expression of Jewish fidelity to Yhwh and had no reservations in issuing scathing critiques of their fellow Jews who did not share the same view of things. First Peter may be best regarded as yet another example of this phenomenon.

## Intra-Jewish Critique in the Hebrew Bible and Second Temple Literature

The intra-Jewish critique we have highlighted is not unique to the New Testament. In the following samples from the Hebrew Bible and Second Temple literature we find rhetoric that parallels that which appears in 1 Peter. We turn first to the Psalms, and more specifically to two of the four psalms that offer a historical narrative of Yhwh's dealings with Israel, Psalm 78 and Psalm 106.

The bulk of Psalm 78 catalogues Israel's repeated inability to remain faithful to Yhwh in the wilderness—this in spite of Yhwh's miraculous provision and unrelenting mercy (Ps 78:9-72). The point of the psalm, however, is not to merely highlight the failures of the fathers; instead, the wilderness "testings" (78:41, 56) are recounted in order to frame in a contrasting manner the exhortations of the opening eight verses (Ps 78:1-8), where the psalmist urges the next generation of Israel to put their confidence in God, and "to not be like their fathers, a stubborn and rebellious generation" whose "spirit was not faithful to God" (Ps 78:7-8).[21] Whereas the wilderness generation did not believe in God, and did not trust in Yhwh's saving power (78:22), this new generation is exhorted to not hide God's mighty deeds from their children (78:3-4), to teach

---

20. The point is underscored by the fact that Paul cites from the Psalms, Proverbs, and Isaiah to make this claim.

21. Psalms scholar Kraus notes that "the drift of the teaching developed in Ps 78 is clearly recognizable in v. 8: the present generation should not be so contrary and stubborn over against Yahweh as their fathers were" (*Psalms 60-150*, 126). This kind of critique against the fathers echoes similar critiques found in early Jewish writings (Exod 32:9; Deut 32:5; 2 Kgs 17:14) and perhaps reflects a recognized tradition.

the next generation to set their hope in God (78:7). The implication of the psalm is clear: Israel's fathers have failed the present generation. To borrow from the language of 1 Peter, we might even say that Israel has inherited the futile ways of their fathers. A new generation must respond differently than their fathers did.

In Psalm 106, Israel's wilderness failures are again recounted, this time from the vantage point of the exile: "Save us, O Lord our God, and gather us from among the nations" (106:47).[22] What is significant about this psalm is that a direct line is drawn from the sins of the wilderness fathers to Israel's exilic state: the fathers did not trust in Yhwh's promise to bring them into "the pleasant land," and for that reason their offspring have been scattered (106:24–27). Psalms scholar Kraus similarly underscores that

> it is now eminently worth noting how far the line extends from the guilt to the judgment. The lamenting community knows it is solidly allied to the fathers, who in the years of origin sinned against Yahweh (cf. Exod 34:7; Deut 7:9). The present judgment finds its cause in the first encounter between Yahweh and the fathers. From the very beginning the chosen people scorned God's חֶסֶד and did what was wrong.[23]

The psalm, however, does not end in a note of despair. Instead, while the psalmist (and presumably those who recite the psalm) places blame on the fathers for their current predicament, they do not perceive that their punishment is irrevocable. Instead, they confess their sins which they have inherited from their fathers and await the same mercy that was repeatedly manifested to their ancestors in the desert. It should be noted that a very similar response to exile is found in Nehemiah 9, yet another narrative account of God's dealings with Israel. While the literary setting of Nehemiah places Yhwh's people back in the "pleasant land," they nevertheless still regard themselves as slaves (Neh 9:36), since they have yet to experience the fullness of the restoration promises made by the prophets (i.e., Jeremiah, Isaiah, Ezekiel). What is noteworthy in this historical narrative is that their enslavement in the land is framed by recounting the wilderness failures, which function in the narrative as an

---

22. "The historical situation into which the psalm is to be placed emerges very clearly in vv. 27 and 47. God's people are scattered to all lands, have suffered the Babylonian exile, and pray for 'being gathered from among the nations.' Here the prayers of repentance and petition have their 'setting'" (Kraus, *Psalms 60–150*, 317, 322).

23. Kraus, *Psalms 60–150*, 318.

epitome of Israel's pattern of turning its back on Yhwh (Neh 9:16, 26, 28, 29). This pattern of disobedience is contrasted with God's unwillingness to forsake his people (Neh 9:17, 19, 30–33). Like the response in Psalm 106, the people confess that their fathers have forsaken Yhwh's commands and refused to turn from their wicked ways (Neh 9:34–35). This confession is coupled with a new covenant drawn up by Israel's leaders, which included new obligations for the people—an expression of the assumption that if Israel will rightly align itself to Yhwh he will not forsake his people and will indeed bring them full restoration. Once again, then, Israel's predicament (exile) is understood as being rooted in the wilderness failures of the fathers, which was passed on to subsequent generations, and which was not beyond the scope of Yhwh's redemption should his people respond differently. Yhwh's people must distance themselves from the ways of their fathers if they wish to see restoration.

The prophets share a similar understanding of Israel's exile and admonish Yhwh's people in a manner that is in keeping with what we have surveyed in the Psalms and Nehemiah. In Ezekiel 20, certain leaders of Israel come to the prophet to inquire of Yhwh. Ezekiel, speaking on Yhwh's behalf, makes it clear that unless Israel and her leaders forsake the ways of their fathers, characterized by idolatry and rebellion in the wilderness, they will find only wrath (Ezek 20:4–17). The entire discourse of Ezekiel 20 implies that these unfaithful ways of the fathers have been passed down to the exiled generation: "I said to their children in the wilderness, do not follow the statutes of your fathers, nor observe their ordinances, nor defile yourselves with their idols" (Ezek 20:18). Nevertheless, even the children rebelled, and Yhwh responded to their repeated disobedience by scattering Israel among the nations—precisely because they failed to forsake the ways of their wilderness fathers (Ezek 20:24). Here, again, a line is drawn from Israel's wilderness fathers to their present state of exile in Babylon. In spite of this, Yhwh refuses to forsake his people and promises to restore Israel. The question remains, however: "Will you defile yourselves after the manner of your fathers and go whoring after their detestable things" (Ezek 20:30)? According to Ezekiel, the answer to this probing question will be determined in a new desert setting, a second exodus: "As I entered into judgment with your fathers in the wilderness of the land of Egypt, so I will enter into judgment with you, says the Lord God" (Ezek 20:36).

Jeremiah also links Israel's impending exile to the failure of the desert fathers who "went after worthlessness" and in turn became "worthless"

(Jer 2:5). "Has a nation changed its gods, even though they are no gods? But my people have changed their glory for that which does not profit," declares Yhwh in Jer 2:11. The kind of language that Jeremiah uses to characterize his compatriots is similar to the way in which the readers are addressed in 1 Pet 1:18, 21. In fact, the word translated "worthless" in LXX Jer 2:5 and the word translated "futile" in 1 Pet 1:18 are the same Greek word, μάταιος. Additionally, a text like Jeremiah 2, in which Israel is characterized as having forsaken, even changed, gods, illuminates ways in which the exhortation to put your faith and hope in God in 1 Pet 1:21 could be intelligible as intra-Jewish debate. To be clear, I am not suggesting literary dependence but merely indicating that the kind of dialogue displayed in 1 Pet 1:18, 21 is not inconceivable within intra-Jewish dialogue.

Zechariah offers one of the most detailed eschatological programs of restoration in the Old Testament, which has yet to be experienced since the return from Babylon.[24] For our purposes it is significant to note that this detailed if not also perplexing restoration program is framed with the now familiar refrain: "Do not be like your fathers" (Zech 1:4). Zechariah's readers are challenged to distance themselves from their fathers and return to Yhwh.[25] This theme is repeated again in chapters 7–8, but this time with the reminder that in "these days" Yhwh will "do good" to Israel if it will only respond accordingly.

We conclude our survey of intra-Jewish critique of the fathers with a brief mention of Baruch, which as we have noted, bears some resemblance to 1 Peter. For our specific purposes, one point will be highlighted. Israel's condition of exile is directly related to the futile ways of the fathers: "We are today in our exile where you have scattered us, to be reproached and cursed and punished *for all the iniquities of our fathers, who forsook the Lord our God*" (Bar 3:8).

---

24. For a summary of the eschatological program of Zechariah 9–14 and its reception, see Liebengood, *Eschatology of 1 Peter*, 23–77.

25. Commenting on the phrase "return to me and I will return to you," Petersen notes that "one may infer that the author of Zech 1:4 has viewed such texts as Jer 11:8; 25:5; 35:15; Ezek 33:11 as typical of pre-586 prophetic language and has appropriated it as the sort of things such prophets said" (*Zechariah 9–14*, 132–33).

## Conclusions Regarding Intra-Jewish Critique of the Fathers

Although this representative survey of intra-Jewish critique of the fathers in no way proves that 1 Pet 1:14, 18, and 21 are addressed to Jews, it does nevertheless dispel (one of) the foundational assumption(s) of the consensus position, which asserts that Jews would never use such language when speaking to their compeers. As we have now seen, Peter would not be acting out of place when he characterized his Jewish fathers and his own compeers as idolatrous, unbelieving, and ignorant of Yhwh's purposes—especially not while in exile.[26] Additionally, this survey demonstrates that for many Jews, their condition of exile was perceived to be directly linked to the infidelity of their fathers. Restoration, then, at its very core was, in part, a turning away from the foolish ways of their fathers.

With this in view, the foundation assumption of the consensus position could be turned completely on its head. The rhetoric of 1 Pet 1:14, 18, and 21 could be yet another "clear" indication that Peter, in keeping with the other "Jewish" features already highlighted in the letter, is addressing fellow Jews—and in a manner that is very much in keeping with how Jews exhorted one another throughout their history.

Having traced the way in which Jews critiqued the way of life handed down by their fathers, we now turn to an analysis of 1 Pet 1:14, 18, 21, and 2:10 in their literary context.

## 1 Peter's Wilderness Sojourners

Several recent studies helpfully have rooted 1 Peter firmly within existing eschatological restoration expectations of first-century Judaism.[27] These

---

26. Dunn, who argues for a predominantly Jewish audience, makes this point in passing: "But this [that is, the references found in 1:14, 18; 2:9–10; and 4:2–3] is all consistent with the in-house character of prophetic exhortation and rebuke, or expressive of a conviction that the realization of eschatological hope highlights the ignorance, futility and darkness of the old age" (*Beginning in Jerusalem*, 1159). In a similar vein, as we will discuss in further detail in chapter 3, Witherington wonders whether the futile ways of the wilderness-wandering generation is in view, commenting that "if our author views the audience as being in some ways like many of the exilic Jews of the Babylonian period, this language then becomes understandable" (*1–2 Peter*, 31).

27. See, for example, Dubis, *Messianic Woes in 1 Peter*; Mbuvi, *Temple, Exile and Identity in 1 Peter*; Liebengood, *Eschatology of 1 Peter*; Green, *1 Peter*; Egan, *Ecclesiology and the Narrative of 1 Peter*; Sargent, *Written to Serve*; Pierce, *Spirits and the Proclamation of Christ*; Marcar, *Divine Regeneration and Ethnic Identity*.

studies have highlighted that, in keeping with the Old Testament prophets and Jewish Second Temple literature, 1 Peter envisions a re-gathering of the diaspora Jews, a future judgment, the universal reign of Yhwh through his appointed agent, birth pangs, the restoration of the temple, gentile incorporation and national resurrection—but re-imagined through the death and resurrection of Jesus. While these studies rightly have placed 1 Peter in its first-century ideological context, they have, in my estimation, wrongly placed 1 Peter's readers as still living in exile.[28] In what follows, I will briefly argue that Peter envisions his readers emerging from exile, placing them (theologically) in a new wilderness, journeying towards an incorruptible inheritance—this because through Jesus, God's covenant with Israel has been restored. As we will see, this observation will shed light on the kind of rhetoric we find in 1 Pet 1:14, 18, 21, and 2:9–10—language that not only echoes the intra-Jewish critique of the fathers that we have just highlighted, but that also shares a similar setting, the wilderness.

As many scholars have observed, the letter prescript functions paradigmatically, orienting the readers and their precarious situation with the initially ambiguous epithet ἐκλεκτοί παρεπίδημοι.[29] I contend that this epithet is meant to be understood in harmony with the narrative that is developed throughout the letter, especially in the exordium (1:3–12) and the first *argumentatio* (1:13—2:10).[30]

---

28. E.g., Mark Dubis and Joel Green. So do translations such as the NRSV, ESV, and NIV.

29. E.g., Achtemeier notes that "the opening two verses set the stage for what is to follow in the letter in terms of content and themes" (*1 Peter*, 80). For several decades now Primopetrine scholars have been debating the meaning of the phrase ἐκλεκτοί παρεπίδημοι. As helpful as the word studies and socio-historical reconstructions have been, it is my assessment that the literary context and the argument of the text itself have not been given proper weight in determining the meaning of these words.

30. Although most Primopetrine scholars are in agreement with respect to the overall structure of the letter, there is some disagreement with regard to how the letter-body is best divided. Troy Martin, for example, parses the letter-body into three sections, which, in his view, correspond to three particular metaphor clusters: elect people of God (1:14—2:10); strangers and aliens (2:11—3:12); sufferers in the Diaspora (3:12—5:11). Campbell, drawing on classical rhetorical categories, divides the letter-body in the following manner: first *argumentatio* (2:11—3:12); second *argumentatio* 2:11—3:12; third *argumentatio* 3:13—4:11; *peroratio* 4:12—5:14. Campbell's outline of the letter-body has been modified by Witherington to include five arguments: *proposito* (1:13-16); argument 1 (1:17—2:10); argument 2 (2:11—3:12); argument 3 (3:13—4:11); argument 4 (4:12–19); argument 5 (5:1–5); *peroratio* (5:6–9); doxology (5:10-11). I have adopted the basic contours of Martin's overall schema, but

In the exordium, Peter explains that the resurrection of Jesus Christ has radical implications for how his readers are to conceptualize their lives. These implications are described in terms that echo the exodus and wilderness journey of Israel. Like the people of Israel after they were ransomed from Egypt, followers of Jesus are now a newly formed people (1:3, 23; cf. 2:10; Exod 19:6; Isa 43:21; Hos 2:23), who find themselves in a new wilderness experience, journeying towards a new, incorruptible inheritance (1:4).[31] As did the fathers, this newly formed people can expect to encounter a variety of πειρασμοί along the way (1:5–7), in which their allegiance to God will be tested. These "fiery" trials will be met with God's sustaining power and faithfulness (1:5–7). All of this, according to Peter, is in keeping with prophets, who bore witness beforehand not only to the glory that is to come but also to the present sufferings that must be endured until the Christ's return (1:10–12).

This second-exodus narrative that has been initiated in the exordium is more fully developed in the letter's first *argumentatio* (1:13—2:10). Drawing on Passover language, Peter exhorts his readers to "gird up the loins" (Exod 12:11) of their mind and to conduct themselves with fear during the time of their wilderness sojourning (1:17), since they have been redeemed with the precious blood of the lamb who was without defect or blemish, Jesus (1:19).

Within this narrative, Peter draws attention to the admonishment given to the original wilderness sojourners, in which they were urged to "be holy in all you do" (1 Pet 1:15). He follows this exhortation by quoting the often-repeated refrain from Leviticus, a foundational wilderness text, "Be holy, for I am holy" (1 Pet 1:16; Lev 11:44, 45; 19:2; 20:7).

Several other significant Old Testament texts are drawn on in this first *argumentatio*, which confirm that Peter understands his readers to be participating in a new exodus/wilderness journey. Their new birth (1:3, 23) is said to be in keeping with the word that was announced in Isa 40:6–8, a passage that many scholars have noted serves as the prologue to

---

have elected to divide the letter-body into three parts: 1:13—2:10; 2:11—4:11; and 4:12—5:11. See Martin, *Metaphor and Composition in 1 Peter*, 3–39, 135–267; Campbell, *Honor, Shame, and the Rhetoric of 1 Peter*, 58–198; Witherington, *1–2 Peter*, 49.

31. In passing, Goppelt notes that "Peter views the church as being on the march, like Israel in the wilderness" (*Typos*, 152). For κληρονομία as a circumlocution arriving and possessing the promised land, see Num 34:2; 36:2; Deut 12:9; Josh 1:15; 13:1; Judg 2:6; 18:1; 21:23; 2 Chr 6:27; 31:1; Pss 134:12; 135:21, 22; Jer 2:7; 3:19; 16:18; Ezek 11:15; 25:4, 10. For the use of κληρονομία in conjunction with the promise of restoration, see Isa 49:8; Jer 12:25; Pss 2:8; 67:10; 110:6; Ezek 45:1.

Isaiah 40–55 and its program of covenant restoration, regularly described in terms of a second exodus. This is followed by an allusion in 1 Pet 2:3 to Ps 34:8, "Taste and see that the Lord is good." It is likely that Psalm 34 has become operative here and in 1 Pet 3:10–12 because it models behavior that is fitting for sojourning righteous sufferers who are facing opposition while they wait for the fullness of what Yhwh has promised. The variant reading in LXX Psalm 33 (MT 34) seems to confirm this: whereas the righteous sufferer in the Hebrew text is delivered from all his fears, in the Greek variant he exclaims, "I sought the Lord, and he heard me and rescued me from all of my sojournings" (LXX Ps 33:4; ἐξεζήτησα τὸν κύριον, καὶ ἐπήκουσέν μου καὶ ἐκ πασῶν τῶν παροικιῶν μου ἐρρύσατό με).

The priesthood imagery of 1 Pet 2:4–10, perhaps counter-intuitively, reiterates and even intensifies what Peter has been developing thus far in the letter. This can be seen in 1 Pet 2:9, where there is a conflation of terms that are derived from Exod 19:5–6 and Isa 43:20–21: "You are a chosen people [Isa 43:20], a royal priesthood [Exod 19:6], a holy nation [Exod 19:6], a people belonging to God [Exod 19:5], that you may declare the praises of him [Isa 43:21] who called you out of darkness into his wonderful light." In the literary setting of Exod 19:1–6, Yhwh has gathered his freshly redeemed and newly formed people in the wilderness at the foot of Mount Sinai and has commissioned them to be a kingdom of priests who have a communal vocation to reflect Yhwh's character and will. It appears that Peter's appropriation of Exod 19:5–6, then, is intended to evoke in his readers the call of recapitulating the wilderness journey of their fathers, this time in fidelity to Yhwh.

This recapitulating call is confirmed by Peter's use of Isaiah 43 in 1 Pet 2:9, where he draws his readers not to the first exodus but rather to the promise of a second exodus found throughout Isaiah 40–55.[32] It is within this section of Isaiah that Yhwh speaks of a new day to come, one in which he will ransom his exiled people, renew his covenant with them, and make a way in the desert for them to journey to their inheritance (cf. 1 Pet 1:3–4). That Peter envisions his readers as already redeemed (from exile) and benefiting from covenant restoration is further confirmed by his allusion to Isa 43:21 and 42:12 in the latter part of 1 Pet 2:9 (ὅπως τὰς ἀρετὰς ἐξαγγείλητε τοῦ ἐκ σκότους ὑμᾶς καλέσαντος εἰς τὸ θαυμαστὸν αὐτοῦ φῶς). In its original literary context, this text charges Yhwh's people to proclaim his saving wonders once they have been redeemed

---

32. Anderson, "Exodus Typology in Second Isaiah"; Fishbane, *Biblical Interpretation in Ancient Israel*.

from Babylonian exile.³³ This appropriation of Isa 43:20–21 betrays that Peter understands this promised second-exodus covenant restoration to have been actualized in Jesus, who, as we learn later in 1 Pet 2:23–25, has redeemed (healed) and gathered his scattered, straying sheep through his sacrificial death.³⁴

The first *argumentatio* concludes in 1 Pet 2:10 with an allusion drawn from Hos 2:25 (also Hos 1:6, 9). This refrain from Hosea is the climax of a prophetic oracle in which Yhwh declares that he will deliver Israel in spite of her idolatry and radical infidelity, alluring her to the wilderness where "she will respond as in the days of her youth, as at the time when she came out of the land of Egypt" (Hos 2:15). According to Hosea 2, it is here, in the desert, having been redeemed from Babylonian exile, that Yhwh will proclaim that those who once were not a people are now a people of God; those who once had not received mercy, have now received mercy. For the purposes of this study, it is important to underscore that in the Old Testament more often than not the term "mercy" is shorthand for covenant restoration.³⁵ Clearly for Peter that prophetic oracle concerning God's restoration of Israel is regarded as actualized through Jesus and is extended to these addressees.

This brief survey of 1 Pet 1:1—2:10 fills out the picture Peter wishes to paint when he opens his letter with the epithet ἐκλεκτοί παρεπίδημοι διασπορᾶς. The term ἐκλεκτός reminds his readers that they too have been chosen to be a nation of priests who orient their lives around the propagation of Yhwh's will.³⁶ That they are elect παρεπίδημοι highlights that, for now, their allegiance is to be expressed in the wilderness, where, like their fathers, they will be tested until they reach their inheritance (1 Pet 2:12).³⁷ In light of the discussion in which I have argued that

---

33. The word ἀρετή is used in the LXX to speak of God's saving acts in the first exodus, and his future saving acts in the new exodus of Isaiah.

34. For further discussion regarding the way in which the shepherd imagery of 1 Pet 2:24–25 finds its place within wider new exodus themes in the Old Testament, see Liebengood, *Eschatology of 1 Peter*, 79–104.

35. See, for example, Deut 30:3; LXX Pss 76:9; 84:8, 11; 97:3; 105:45; 129:7; 135:23; Isa 12:1–6; 14:1–3; 30:18–19; 33:2; 44:22–23; 45:8; 49:10, 13; 54:7–8, 10; 55:7; 56:1; 60:10; 63:7, 15; Jer 12:15; 30:18; Lam 3:32; Ezek 39:25; Mic 7:18–20; Ezra 9:9; Amos 5:15; Zech 1:12–17; Dan 9:9, 18.

36. Schrenk underscores that "1 Pet is the only NT work in which *eklektos* has from the very outset thematic significance. Here everything is worked out in terms of this controlling concept" (Elliott, *1 Peter*, 446).

37. Laniak develops a similar line of thought: "Peter encourages these churches

Peter envisions his readers as already redeemed and journeying in the wilderness, it might be more appropriate to read διασπορᾶς as a *genitivus separationis*, indicating from where (theologically or metaphorically) the elect sojourners have been called.[38] In other words, just as the first fathers were elect sojourners of (redeemed from) Egypt, so too the addressees of 1 Peter are portrayed as elect sojourners of (redeemed from) the diaspora (understood to mean exile).[39]

## Conclusion

It remains now to simply underscore that it is within this new wilderness narrative that Peter exhorts his readers to no longer be conformed to their former passions in ignorance (1:14), and where he declares that his elect sojourners have been redeemed from the futile ways handed down to them by their fathers (1:18). For Peter, faithfully aligning oneself to Jesus is the new expression of putting one's faith and hope in the God of Israel (1:21). When these exhortations are read in their literary context, and in light of what we have surveyed in the Hebrew scriptures, they run with the grain of a text that has throughout given the clear impression that it was intended for fellow Jews. For, as we have seen, it was the desert that exposed Israel's infidelity; so too it would be the new desert where Israel's faithfulness would be tested. These elect sojourners are urged, then, to not be like their fathers, to turn and trust in God, to be children of obedience (1 Pet 1:14; cf. Isa 1:2 "I reared children and brought them up but

---

as 'aliens and sojourners,' understanding their identity as God's renewed covenant community, freshly formed in a new wilderness of testing, and anticipating glory in their future home" (*Shepherds After My Own Heart*, 225). See also Deterding, "Exodus Motifs in 1 Peter."

38. This would perhaps explain the difference between Jas 1:1 and 1 Pet 1:1. Whereas James is addressing diasporic Jewish believers in a literal and/or geographic manner (ἐν τῇ διασπορᾷ; i.e., those who live outside of Israel), Peter is making the more nuanced theological point that his addressees are being called out of, or separated from, the Diaspora (as a connotation for exile) in order to journey towards their inheritance.

39. Doering, "Chosen Stock," contends that I have forced this meaning of διασπορᾶς to fit an interpretation of the eschatological program of Zech 9–14. This is a misrepresentation of the argument I have presented in Liebengood, *Eschatology of 1 Peter*, 130–40, 156–64, 176–85, which is similar to the argument I have made in this book. Here I simply underscore that methodologically I have not predetermined what διασπορᾶς means based upon genre presumptions or available traditio-historical examples; rather, I have discerned the syntactical function of the genitive based upon a careful reading of the text in its literary context (esp. 1 Pet 1:3—2:10).

they have rebelled against me"), who in contrast to their fathers, faithfully journey toward the inheritance that awaits them. In the meantime, they are exhorted, as πάροικοι and παρεπίδημοι, to maintain good conduct among the gentiles so that they, those deemed gentiles, will glorify God on the day of his visitation—a notion that is very much in keeping with Jewish restoration ideology (1 Pet 2:12; e.g., Zech 14:16). And they are also reminded, through the catena of stone passages from Isa 28:16, Ps 118:22, and Isa 8:14 (1 Pet 2:6–8) that when their compeers reject the cornerstone and thus are unwilling to trust God in the new wilderness of testing, this too was foreseen by God.[40]

With this chapter I do not presume to offer a comprehensive argument for a predominantly (if not exclusively) Jewish audience, but I do contend that in light of the material presented, there is sufficient warrant to reassess the audience question in 1 Peter, not least because one of the foundations upon which the consensus is built has been shown to be misleading and inaccurate: it turns out that Jews actually did talk to other Jews with the kind of language we find in 1 Peter. I would suggest, then, that more work needs to be done in order to establish the ethnic makeup of the 1 Peter addressees, a task to which we now turn.

But perhaps more importantly, in the course of exploring the ethnic identity of the addressees, as we examined how Peter's critique of the futile ways of the fathers (1 Pet 1:18) coheres with similar examples of intra-Jewish debate, we learned that Peter presumes that God's covenant restoration promises are applicable to the recipients of this letter. The new exodus/wilderness imagery is both implicitly as well as explicitly drawn from the Old Testament with an assumption of continuity and serves to incorporate the addressees into God's ongoing commitment to Israel.

---

40. If a Jewish audience is in view, these texts are being used in 1 Peter in the same fashion they are employed in Matt 21:42, Acts 4:11, and Rom 9:31–33—as scriptural explanations for why some fellow-Jews have rejected Jesus as their messiah.

# 3

# *The Problem of Identifying the Addressees of 1 Peter*

## Part 2: Situating the "Elect Sojourners"

> *Whether Peter's original audience was Jewish or Gentile is an interesting historical question, but it ultimately makes no difference. Both spiritual systems [paganism and Judaism] were empty in that in themselves they offered no redemption, and both groups were equally guilty in God's sight. Whether converts from paganism or Judaism, the letter's recipients need to understand their new covenant relationship with God in Christ.*[1]

## Reconsidering 1 Peter 4:3–4

IN CHAPTER 2, I highlighted a pattern within modern 1 Peter studies in which scholars point to a set of key passages or we might even say "proof texts" (1 Pet 1:14, 18, 21; 2:10) and proceed with the assumption that since a Jew would never speak to another Jew in the manner in which Peter speaks to these addressees, it is best to conclude that the letter was written to gentiles. I have shown, however, that this foundational assumption about intra-Jewish dialogue is inaccurate. What is more, I have demonstrated that the kind of rhetoric we find in these proof texts could be leveraged to flip the argument on its head and posit that it points to an exclusively Jewish audience.

---

1. Jobes, *1 Peter* [2nd ed.], 24.

We have yet to look at all the evidence, however. The key proof text that remains for discussion is 1 Pet 4:3–4:

> 3 You have already spent enough time in doing what the gentiles like to do, living in debauchery, passions, drunkenness, revels, carousing, and lawless idolatry. 4 They are surprised that you no longer join them in the same excesses of dissipation, and so they blaspheme.

What we often see in the consensus is that the assumptions and decisions already made about 1:14, 18, 21, and 2:10 are carried over to 1 Pet 4:3–4 and exert tremendous influence on how it is read. The standard argument put forth is that the readers are portrayed as having once participated in the vices listed in the passage—sensuality, passions, drunkenness, orgies, drinking parties, and lawless idolatry; that it is unlikely that Jews would or could be characterized as living in this manner in Asia Minor. Therefore, this is one more piece of evidence to support the conclusion that Peter is writing to a predominantly or even exclusively gentile audience.

Some scholars, most of whom are either ambivalent or ultimately regard the audience as mixed or predominantly gentile, grant that the vices mentioned in 1 Pet 4:3 need not apply only to gentiles. Jobes, for example, suggests that "the inference that Jewish people would never participate in such unbridled practices reflects perhaps an idealized and romanticized view of Jewish devotion and piety rather than historical and sociological possibility."[2] Marshall notes that Jews were capable of practicing the kind of behavior outlined in 1 Pet 4:3.[3] And Selwyn concedes that "no doubt the moral condition here described would have been applicable to many lapsed Jews in Asia Minor."[4] But those who make these important observations cease to follow up this *possibility* with further examination or argumentation for why it *must* be a gentile audience. In many cases, it seems that the conclusions made about the prior proof texts have the cumulative effect of stifling curiosity and further exploration for a *plausible* scenario in which a Jewish audience fits with the description.

---

2. Jobes, *1 Peter* [2nd ed.], 264.
3. Marshall, *1 Peter*, 135.
4. Selwyn, *1 Peter*, 210.

## 1 Peter 4:3–4 and "Hellenized Jews"

One scholar who has gone against this trend is Ben Witherington. He has concluded that the letter was written to a predominantly Jewish audience, which he supports with a provocative reading of 1 Pet 4:3–4.[5] Witherington outlines the support for his thesis by pointing to the opening of the letter as the first clear indication that it is written to a Jewish audience.[6] Drawing on John Elliott's work on the sociological context of 1 Peter,[7] Witherington insists that the key terms παρεπίδημος, πάροικος, and διασπορά must be understood as indicating real, concrete social situations rather than as metaphors that spiritualize the foreignness of the readers.[8] But whereas Elliott regarded these terms to refer to the literal socio-political status of gentile readers who were either permanent or temporary residents aliens (foreigners prior to their conversion) in the five Roman provinces,[9] Witherington argues that πάροικος and παρεπίδημος are best understood to refer to actual Jewish resident aliens living in exile in Asia Minor.[10] To support this literal reading of these descriptors, he appeals to the "coded language" of 1 Pet 5:13, suggesting that the author calls his locale "Babylon" in order to indicate to his Jewish audience that "he shares their resident alien and exilic condition where

---

5. Some assume that Jobes's provocative theory regarding the historical background of the 1 Peter recipients (*1 Peter* [2nd ed.], 22–45) also includes a conclusion about the ethnic makeup of the letter addressees. This assumption is nevertheless unwarranted because Jobes never makes a final judgment on the matter except to say, "Whether Peter's audience was Jewish or Gentile is an interesting historical question, but it ultimately makes little difference. Both spiritual systems were empty" (*1 Peter* [2nd ed.], 24). For another example of her ambiguity regarding ethnic makeup, see Jobes, *1 Peter*, 264. Regarding her hypothesis that the foreigners and resident aliens of 1 Peter had previously lived in Rome, where, most likely, they first became associated with Peter, but then moved to Asia Minor, either by force or choice, as part of a colonization program (perhaps associated with Claudius), has in my opinion been sufficiently rendered implausible by the critiques of Horrell, "Aliens and Strangers," 187–88, and Williams, *Persecution in 1 Peter*, 74–90. What is more, Jobes's colonization theory runs the risk of undercutting the reason given in the letter for why the addresses were treated as outsiders, namely because of their new birth and new way of life in Jesus Christ (1 Pet 1:3–7, 17; 2:11–12).

6. Witherington, *1–2 Peter*, 22–39.

7. Elliott, *Home for the Homeless*; *1 Peter*.

8. Witherington, *1–2 Peter*, 22–24.

9. Elliott, *Home for the Homeless*, 42–49.

10. Witherington, *1–2 Peter*, 24.

he is."[11] He also notes that the language of 1 Pet 2:12, ἐν τοῖς ἔθνεσιν, indicates that the readers are the out-group: "It would be rather strange to say to an audience of Gentiles, or largely Gentiles, to live like Christians among the 'Gentiles.' This is Jewish language, and it best suits the theory that the audience itself is Jewish, in this case Jewish Christian."[12]

At the core of his argument, Witherington contends that Peter, like Paul, offered the gospel of salvation to Hellenized Jews but without the restrictions of the law that hindered them from full participation in Greco-Roman life.[13] "Christianity offered such Hellenized Jews a form of ethical monotheism that did not set up the same barriers to participation in the wider culture that came from the full practice of Judaism itself."[14] He suggests there is both literary as well as archeological evidence that show the extent to which Jews were well-integrated in society in Asia Minor, and that while the degree of Hellenization of such Jews would have been troubling to Judean or Galilean Jews, that is was the reality of most Jews in Asia Minor "should no longer be disputed."[15] As a result, Witherington argues that we must discern questions about audience in light of the reality of a "highly Hellenized backdrop of Diaspora Jews in this particular region."[16]

Building upon the initial indicators (πάροικος, παρεπίδημος, and διασπορά) and the claim that the Peter is writing to highly Hellenized Jews, Witherington rehearses the fact that many of the earliest commentators concluded that 1 Peter was written to a Jewish audience.[17] How then, he queries, did we get to this modern consensus? His conclusion is that modern readers have mischaracterized the rhetoric of 1 Pet 1:14, 18; 2:10; and 4:3–4: Hos 1:9–10 is being used in 1 Pet 2:10 to address Jews—just as it was in the first instance; 1 Pet 1:14 makes sense when we understand it is directed to highly Hellenized Jews of the Diaspora; and Peter's comments about being ransomed from the futile ways of your ancestors is best understood as a commentary on either the "the ineffecious or inadequate sacrificial practices (like the author of Hebrews)," or

---

11. Witherington, *1–2 Peter*, 24.
12. Witherington, *1–2 Peter*, 25.
13. Witherington, *1–2 Peter*, 25–28.
14. Witherington, *1–2 Peter*, 27.
15. Witherington, *1–2 Peter*, 27.
16. Witherington, *1–2 Peter*, 27.
17. Witherington, *1–2 Peter*, 28.

the futile ways of the wilderness-wandering generation.[18] Here, Witherington reveals that he regards the letter to be written by a "completionist" or supersessionist with regard to the earlier history of Israel, and that he thinks Peter is

> taking up the language of the Hebrew Scriptures and applying it now to Christians engaged in a very different sort of worship, the worship of Jesus as Lord. Whether we call this completionist or supersessionist rhetoric, clearly enough our author feels that he can make such a hermeneutical leap in the way he handles the Hebrew Scriptures, and he is comfortable in applying terms previously reserved for non-Christian Israel to his audience.[19]

Witherington leverages all these assumptions and claims to be able to address the most challenging text for those who argue for a Jewish audience, 1 Pet 4:3–4. He explains how this could be written to a Jewish audience with four quick moves. First, he posits that the author never refers to the addressees as gentile, which is a term reserved for the group that they are joining no longer. Second, this text exhibits typical Jewish polemical rhetoric directed against gentile idolatry and immorality which often culminated at feasts, akin to what we see in 1 Corinthians 8–10. Third, he asserts that Hellenized Jews "might have" participated in temple feasts as a way of climbing the social ladder and cultivating business partnerships. It is unlikely, however, that they would have been present for the sacrifice; and the sharing of a meal afterward would not necessarily be seen as an idolatrous act because these Hellenized Jews would have been laxer with respect to dietary requirements of the Torah. And finally, he makes the observation that nowhere in this passage does the author rebuke the audience for not keeping kosher. Instead, the author warns Christian Jews to not go back to their gentile-like behavior, for to do so would "ruin their Christian witness."[20]

In addition to his comments on the common proof texts for adjudicating audience makeup, Witherington raises two additional reasons to

---

18. Witherington, *1–2 Peter*, 31. It should be noted that we independently came to similar conclusions about 1 Pet 1:14, 18; 2:10 and what it might reveal about the ethnic identity of the addressees.

19. Witherington, *1–2 Peter*, 31. Earlier, Witherington claims that Peter "writes with a conversionist and sectarian mentality, assuming that those who are outside the Christian circle are to one degree or another religiously dark, whether they are formerly Jews or formerly Gentiles" (*1–2 Peter*, 30).

20. Witherington, *1–2 Peter*, 30.

suspect a Jewish audience. First, the mention of Sarah as a paradigmatic figure for wives best makes sense if it is directed to Jewish spouses.[21] And second, a Jewish audience helps explain why Peter is writing to congregations in regions where Paul has apostolic authority. Since, Witherington argues, there was a division of labor between Paul, who targeted gentiles, and Peter, James, and John, who oversaw mostly Jewish congregations, this division of labor eventually led to separate Christian communities in various cities in Asia Minor, some predominantly gentile and some predominantly Jewish. Why would Peter be writing to communities in areas in Asia Minor that are clearly under Paul's authority? For Witherington, it has to do with target audience and not region: Peter is addressing largely Christian Jews (perhaps with some God-fearers), not gentile communities founded by Paul or his coworkers.[22]

In the end, the picture that Witherington paints is one in which the addressees of 1 Peter are not only literal resident aliens because they are Jews in the Diaspora, they also now have a profound sense of foreignness because they have left their Hellenized Jewish way of life and now no longer fit in with their gentile neighbors. "Hence, they are double aliens from both non-Christian Jews and from Gentiles. Thus, the sectarian nature of this discourse becomes even more clear, as Peter seeks to carve out a unique niche for his Jewish Christian audience in their social settings."[23]

## A Critique of the "Hellenized Jew" Proposal

Witherington's proposal has not persuaded interpreters of 1 Peter. To my knowledge, Travis Williams offers the most extensive critique of Witherington's Jewish audience proposal.[24] He contends that Witherington's case depends upon two foundational arguments: (1) that language that is reserved for Israel in the Hebrew Bible must necessarily refer to Jews when it is used in the NT and (2) the term ἐν τοῖς ἔθνεσιν (2:12) indicates that the readers are not gentiles.[25] Williams shows that these two claims do not stand under examination. On the first claim, Williams states that

---

21. Witherington, *1–2 Peter*, 32.
22. Witherington, *1–2 Peter*, 34. We will circle back to the question of why Peter wrote to the places he did in a later section of this chapter.
23. Witherington, *1–2 Peter*, 37.
24. Williams, *Persecution in 1 Peter*, 91–95.
25. Williams, *Persecution in 1 Peter*, 92–93.

the assumption is "highly questionable" and chides Witherington for seemingly not engaging in the secondary literature that has demonstrated that Israelite language is in fact appropriated for the "NT Church."[26] In a footnote to this point, he makes an important insight: Witherington's contention that the author holds a supersessionist view of Israelite history "annuls any notion that language which is reserved for Israel in the OT must necessarily refer to Jews when it is employed in the NT."[27] On the second claim, Williams shows that the phrase ἐν τοῖς ἔθνεσιν is used in letters written to gentile Christian audiences in an effort to describe unbelieving gentiles outside of the community of faith (e.g., 1 Cor 5:1; 12:2).

But perhaps Williams most penetrating critique of Witherington's proposal comes in the form of a question: "Why would conversion from Judaism to Christianity suddenly alter the audience's propensity to dine at temples and partake of sacrificial meat?"[28] Put in the form of a statement, Williams argues that the following historical variables would need to all come together in order for Witherington's Jewish audience proposal to be plausible: (1) a large number of Jews across Asia Minor had been converted to the Christian faith, enough to create congregations in all of the regions addressed in the epistle; (2) the vast majority of these Jewish readers were highly Hellenized and had formerly been participating in the gentile-like activities repudiated in 1 Pet 4:3–4; and (3) for some reason, the audience's conversion from Judaism to Christianity compelled them to no longer partake of these gentile-like behaviors delineated in 1 Pet 4:3–4. "It is highly questionable that all three of these possibilities materialized *together*—especially given that 1 Peter would be our only source for this assumption."[29] For Williams, in light of these critiques, there is no compelling reason to abandon the modern consensus position of a gentile audience until one can adequately address these issues.

While the critique offered by Williams is compelling, there is more that can and needs to be said. First, Witherington's characterization of Paul offering a "law-free" gospel that is appealing to "highly Hellenized Jews," which is integral to the social setting that he constructs for the letter, is no longer sustainable as an assumption and instead must be argued

---

26. Williams, *Persecution in 1 Peter*, 92.
27. Williams, *Persecution in 1 Peter*, 93.
28. Williams, *Persecution in 1 Peter*, 94.
29. Williams, *Persecution in 1 Peter*, 95.

for. This is in part because we have no literary evidence of the kind of scenario that he constructs for 1 Peter, as Williams has noted.[30] But more significantly, in the past fifteen years or so, there has been a significant number of studies in the emerging field known as "Paul within Judaism" that undercuts this pillar of Witherington's argument.[31] Additionally, Witherington's assertions about Peter—both that he was tasked with preaching to Jews (only) and that he also targeted "law-free," "Hellenized Jews"—do not seem to match the more complex way that Peter is characterized as he is remembered in the New Testament.[32] Martin Hengel, for example, examines the New Testament portrayal of Peter and puts forth the following more nuanced and robust picture of the relationship between Peter and Paul and their division of labor to Jews and gentiles, underscoring Peter's role as bridge builder:

> One the one hand, Peter plays a decisive role in Jerusalem in the opening of the new messianic movement for the "peoples," since Jesus' work of salvation broke down the national Jewish barriers and fulfilled the prophetic promises for all peoples. From the time of persecution under Agrippa and afterward (ca. AD 43), he was increasingly the leading missionary for the Jews outside of Eretz Israel and thus addressed Godfearers in the synagogues as well, who were actual Gentiles. On the other hand, Peter wanted to pay careful attention to the Jewish Christian community in Jerusalem. It was being increasingly oppressed and, from about AD 43, when Peter had to flee, was under the leadership of the Lord's brother James. Peter sought to avoid any activity that would provoke an accusation of apostasy by Judaism, as was

---

30. For example, it would be an overstatement and a mischaracterization of the evidence to say that Acts 13:13—14:20; 17:1–15; and 18:1–17 present Paul as preaching a "law-free" gospel that is appealing to "highly Hellenized Jews."

31. For a representation of this field of Pauline studies see Rudolph, *Jew to the Jews*; Nanos and Zetterholm, *Paul Within Judaism*; Eisenbaum, *Paul Was Not a Christian*; Johnson Hodge, *If Sons, Then Heirs*; Thiessen, *Jewish Paul*; Bird et al., *Paul Within Judaism*. see also the work of Tucker, Windsor, and Zoccali in the New Testament After Supersessionism series for a more nuanced picture of Paul, his relationship to the law, and his understanding of ongoing Jewish identity in Christ. For recent critical engagement of this approach, see Van Maaren, "How Can the New Testament Writings be Within Judaism?"; Runesson, "What Does It Mean to Read New Testament Texts 'Within Judaism'?"

32. For a compelling critique of the way in which Acts 10 has been leveraged to argue that Peter's vision undermines Torah observance, see Kinzer, *Jerusalem Crucified*, 210–20; *Post-Missionary Messianic Judaism*, 65–71. Kinzer's work calls to question the assumption that Peter would have presented a "law-free" gospel to Jews.

raised against Paul. For this reason, at the Apostolic Council in Jerusalem, Peter specifically called for the Gentile mission to be released from any requirement for circumcision.... Peter himself had increasingly become a missionary to the Jews *and* to the Gentiles. In this regard, as the onetime disciple of Jesus and as the authoritative representative of the Jesus tradition, including communities that were primarily Gentile Christian, he stood in high regard.[33]

This point becomes even more important for those who argue that 1 Peter is a pseudepigraphal letter that appeals to Petrine tradition and authority.[34] In other words, if the author is not Peter, but is instead appealing to the authority of the remembered Peter, then it would make sense to find him building a bridge between Jews and gentiles in Christ, since this was what he was remembered for.[35]

In addition to this, to extend William's questioning a bit further, if these "highly Hellenized" Jews were engaged in the activities described in 1 Pet 4:3—passions, drunkenness, revels, carousing, and lawless idolatry, which is what the text presumes—then what about a "law-free, ethical" monotheism would be appealing to them?[36] It would seem, rather, that even the ethical restrictions for gentile followers of Jesus (per the letter from the Jerusalem Assembly in Acts 15) would be too inconvenient for a ladder-climbing Hellenized Jew of the sort that Witherington imagines. Additionally, if there is no longer any Torah observance for these new Jewish followers of Jesus, what is the ground on which the author warns them to not go back to the gentile behavior they practiced before? What is more, at the end of the letter the author encourages his addressees to remain steadfast in their allegiance to Jesus because "you know that your brothers and sisters in all the world are undergoing the same kinds of

---

33. Hengel, *Saint Peter*, 100–101. For the full development of his conclusions, see *Saint Peter*, 48–79.

34. Hengel suggests that "it is possible that those who were associated with Peter later considered him to be the actual 'founder' of the mission to the Gentiles on the basis of the narrative about Cornelius" (*Saint Peter*, 57).

35. Witherington seems to build his picture of Peter and "the division of labor" entirely from Acts 15 and Galatians 2. For a more nuanced way of sorting through the portrayal of the labor between Paul and Peter, see Hengel, *Saint Peter*, 52–57.

36. As Witherington develops his claim that the addressees are "highly Hellenized Jews" twice he alludes to literary and archeological evidence but offers nothing substantial apart from his own experiences in Asia Minor, and his commentary on 1 Corinthians, none of which provide more than anecdotal evidence.

suffering" (1 Pet 5:9). If we are to take this reference seriously, are we to imagine that the Jews in Judea and Galilee suffer in the same way that these highly Hellenized Jews do—because they no longer participate in gentile debauchery and have thus been rejected by their gentile surroundings? Perhaps all these factors explain precisely why Peter did not repudiate his addressees for not keeping kosher!

Before moving on, one final point needs to be made that pertains to both the Jewish audience proposal and the critique. Both Witherington and Williams, in seeking to construct the social setting of 1 Peter, at times use anachronistic language that ultimately obscures the discernment process regarding the identification of the addressees. As we have already seen, it is historically inaccurate to say that Jewish followers of Jesus "converted" from Judaism to Christianity. And claiming that "Christianity offered such Hellenized Jews a form of ethical monotheism that did not set up the same barriers to participation in the wider culture that came from the full practice of Judaism itself" is wrong on a number of fronts, not least because it assumes that at the time that this letter was written and read there was a distinct and well-developed religious tradition to choose from known as Christianity.[37] The social reality of the first century needs more nuance than is offered in the usage of those terms, especially since it seems that the word Χριστιανός, at least in the early stage of the Jesus movement, was used to identify a *sub-group within* Judaism.[38] So when Witherington says that the readers are exhorted to not go back to their gentile-like practices for the sake of their "Christian witness," this seems to entail that we must imagine that there is a new religion that has been formed with a clear set of beliefs and practices that must be preserved and that differs from Judaism. This kind of retrojection caused by historically inaccurate terms distorts our ability to properly analyze the social setting of 1 Peter.

We run into a similar problem when we say things like "Israelite language is appropriated for the NT Church." This assumes there is a clear common notion of what we all mean when we talk about the "NT church." Many, if not most, assume that the NT church is synonymous with "Christians" or "Christianity," but recent scholarship on "the church" in the New Testament underscores our need for more precision and clarity. For example, Ralph Korner, in his extensive work on the term

37. See Korner, *Reading Revelation After Supersessionism*, 14–26, for more on the problem with the terms "religion," "Judaism," and "Christianity."

38. See chapter 1, 26–27.

ἐκκλησία in the early Jesus movement,[39] argues that Paul uses the term because it "would have allowed him to keep his multi-ethnic Christ-followers socio-religiously connected to the Jewish roots of Jerusalem-loyal Christ-followers, while at the same time implicitly tying them to his apostolic authority and to the fulfillment of his divinely mandated mission to those of non-Jewish ethnicity."[40] In other words,

> If gentiles could not collectively assume the designation "Israel," but yet, through faith in the Jewish Christos, could share in historic Israel's covenantal benefits, then Paul's designations of his multi-ethnic communities as *ekklēsiai* provided them with an inherently Jewish collective identity other than "Israel" by which he could institutionally integrate gentiles *qua* gentiles into theological continuity with Torah-observant Jews *qua* Jews.[41]

What is more, as we have already seen, 1 Peter does not use the word ἐκκλησία to refer to those who have aligned themselves with Jesus. The significance of this will be explored further in chapter 6. The ultimate takeaway from this is that the term ἐκκλησία, when used in the New Testament, was a designation that was tethered to Jewish communal identity.

When we attend to this familiar terminology (i.e., "law-free gospel," "conversion," "Christian," and "church") with greater precision and historical accuracy, then "the appropriation of Israel language" becomes language of welcome from the host, rather than language of "appropriation," borrowing, stealing, completing, or superseding from an outsider. But it also makes lines less clear and calls for more exploration regarding the ethnic makeup of the addressees.

## Suffering and the Ethnic Makeup of the 1 Peter Addressees

If the best extant proposal for a Jewish audience in 1 Peter is insufficient and ultimately unsatisfying, are there other clues within the text that might give us clarity on the identity of the addressees? One helpful way forward is to consider more carefully the *Leitmotif* of suffering in 1 Peter. From beginning to end, and in every chapter in between, the letter suggests that

---

39. Korner, *Origin and Meaning of Ekklēsia*, 156–73; *Reading Revelation After Supersessionism*, 19–26.

40. Korner, *Reading Revelation After Supersessionism*, 20.

41. Korner, *Reading Revelation After Supersessionism*, 25.

suffering permeates the everyday experiences of the addressees. For this reason, Peter encourages these "elect sojourners" (1:1) with the claim that it is commendable to do good and suffer unjustly (2:19, 20), he reminds them that they will be blessed if they suffer for doing what is right (3:14), that it is better to suffer for doing good, if it is God's will (3:17); he exhorts them to rejoice as they share in Christ's sufferings (4:13), to not consider it a disgrace if they suffer as a Christian (4:15), and to entrust their lives to the faithful Creator as they suffer while doing good in accordance with God's will (4:19). He goes so far to say that suffering is their calling because Christ also suffered (2:21; 3:18; 4:1), and acknowledges that their "brothers and sisters in all the world are undergoing the same kinds of suffering" (5:9). Pastorally, Peter reframes suffering as necessary trials that test their faithfulness (1:6), or as a "fiery ordeal" that is taking place to test them (4:12). And he reminds them not only that their suffering is not a result of sin or of God's displeasure with them but also that just as Christ suffered and was vindicated, they too will be vindicated if they are willing to share in Christ's suffering (4:13; 5:10). In short, the letter seeks to address what we might call *Christian* suffering, that is suffering that is the result of faithful allegiance to Jesus Christ, and which is characterized as predictable and inevitable for followers of Jesus, a sign of fidelity, a calling, and a necessary pathway towards vindication or glory.

The most extensive study to date on the causes and kinds of suffering we find in 1 Peter comes from Travis Williams. He builds his comprehensive examination on the fact that 1 Peter is written to gentiles:

> It seems best, therefore, along with the majority of commentators, to posit a primarily Gentile-Christian readership as the intended audience of 1 Peter. What this means for our understanding of suffering in the epistle is that . . . our focus can be placed on the problems caused by Gentile conversion to the Christian faith.[42]

In what follows, I will be drawing on his groundbreaking work but turning it on its head. Williams's comprehensive study of the context in which suffering would have been experienced for gentiles who aligned themselves with Jesus Christ in Asia Minor, coupled with careful analysis of the way in which suffering is described in the letter itself, can also be a helpful way of ruling out certain possibilities and gaining clarity on the

---

42. Williams, *Persecution in 1 Peter*, 95.

situation that the 1 Peter addressees faced.[43] In other words, one need not yet make a conclusion regarding audience makeup in 1 Peter in order to use the findings of Williams. That is, when we pay attention to what has led to the addressees being maligned and ridiculed, and perhaps even harmed physically, we come to see more clearly that it is very unlikely that this kind of suffering would have been experienced by a predominantly Jewish audience or even a mixed audience.

In what follows, I highlight the findings of Williams, especially as they pertain to our aims for this chapter.[44] Williams begins his examination by affirming what most commentators have concluded: the cause or source of suffering in 1 Peter is generated because of one's allegiance to Jesus Christ and the way of life that this allegiance entails (e.g., 1 Pet 2:20; 3:14; 16; 4:3–4).[45] Generally, commentators agree that this way of life led to disassociation with family, friends, and neighbors, but it also led to practices that would have agitated their compeers. Williams highlights that most discussions of persecution do not move much beyond this general observation however, and his study seeks to bring detail to the kind of behaviors and practices that would have been plausible in Asia Minor.

## Withdrawal

For Williams, 1 Pet 4:3–4 offers an important window into the source of suffering for the addressees. It is important to note that this text does more than offer stock polemical rhetoric about gentile behavior; instead, it charges that the addressees once participated in these behaviors and that the *reason* they are being maligned is because they no longer participate in these activities with others.[46] His extensive description of the social setting of Roman Asia Minor around the time of the composition of 1 Peter amplifies our imagination for the kinds of social institutions

---

43. To be clear, I am not suggesting that Williams's argumentation is flawed in any way, but rather am noting that his conclusions (enabled by the way he argued his thesis) can be taken on their own and then used (in reverse order) to better discern the identity of the addressees.

44. Williams, *Persecution in 1 Peter*, 239–97.

45. Williams uses the language of "Christian conversion," which, for reasons that should be apparent now, I will avoid.

46. *Pace* Witherington, who highlights the polemical aspect of the text but insists that the text does not necessarily inculpate the addressees as having practiced such things (Witherington, *1–2 Peter*, 196).

that were available and that included the kinds of behaviors that these addressees might have participated in.

Voluntarily associations, for example, provided a context for friends, family, neighborhoods, business partners, or members of the same profession to gather to share meals and honor their earthly and divine benefactors. The kind of practices within voluntary associations would have varied considerably. They were criticized by both Jews and later by Christians for fostering drunkenness, idolatry, and immorality, but the literary and inscriptional evidence show that this could at times be a misrepresentation. It is nevertheless the case that some voluntary associations promoted the worship of Greco-Roman gods and facilitated drunkenness and sexual immorality. And for some, these groups were their only access to employment and thus were essential for survival. Given the prevalence of these groups, along with the social stratification that was represented in many of the associations, it is quite likely that some of those addressed in 1 Peter would have been members of these guilds prior to their allegiance to Jesus, and their withdrawal from the group would have raised suspicion and ire.[47]

Another institution that provided a context for participation in the kinds of behaviors delineated in 1 Pet 4:3 and from which withdrawal would have caused consternation and hostility was the imperial cult.[48] As Williams demonstrates, it is hard to overstate the pervasive influence of the imperial cult, for it was not just official provincial cults that perpetuated Roman imperial ideology. Rather, the cult extended to every aspect of life. Roman imperial ideology permeated civic space through the design of city structures and even city design as a whole.[49] Public institutions such as the agora, the bouleuterion, the gymnasium, and the baths tended to be associated with the imperial cult. Imperial honorary inscriptions were placed through the city landscape. What is more, imperial ideology was expressed through entertainment—the theater, festivals, and games all promoted Roman imperial worship, and some of the events would have lasted from several days to a week or more. In chapter 4 we will highlight the implicit narrative of Roman imperial ideology and the way 1 Peter offers a different way for the addressees to

---

47. See also Harland, *Associations, Synagogues, and Congregations*.

48. As we will see in chapter 4, the imperial cult was part of a larger complex known as Roman imperial ideology that functioned as what we might call today a worldview for those living in Asia Minor.

49. Wan, *Context for Time and Space*, 131–55.

understand their place in the world. For now, the important point that Williams makes is that the influence of the imperial cult was nearly inescapable, and non-participation would have required withdrawal from nearly all public forms of celebration, entertainment, leisure, and community pride. What is more, withdrawal would have been interpreted by the addressees' neighbors as a hostile act against the gods that threatened family, neighbors, and city.

The final institution that Williams highlights is the worship of traditional gods. Family, friends, and compeers regarded gentile followers of Jesus as "atheists," that is, they refused to acknowledge the traditional gods and give them their due respect. Their atheism was considered to be a threat not only to social cohesion but also to the well-being of the community because such disrespect might provoke the wrath of one of the gods in the form of flood, drought, pestilence, famine, or earthquake.[50]

## "Good Works"

Withdrawal was but one cause for hostility; 1 Peter also indicates that the addressees suffered (or in some cases would go on to suffer) for what Peter calls "good works" or "doing good."[51] As Williams notes, this expression is vague and enigmatic, and at times it has left scholars to conjecture what kind of "good works" Peter had in mind. During the modern period of 1 Peter interpretation there has been a strong consensus that whatever Peter meant, it was an exhortation to engage in activities that were valued and perceived to be honorable and beneficial within the wider community. Williams rightfully challenges this consensus view, in part by showing that it obscures rather than clarifies several key texts.[52] For example, in 1 Pet 2:20, slaves are told to endure harsh treatment from their masters if they "suffer for doing good." But if, as the consensus view would have it, "doing good" was viewed as "good" by the wider community, then why

---

50. As we will see in chapter 4, withdrawal from Roman imperial worship was also regarded as a breaking of the *pax deorum*, which opened the door to all kinds of natural disasters that were interpreted as the wrath of the gods.

51. 1 Pet 2:20; 3:6, 14, 16, 17; 4:19. The following is a sample of the terms in 1 Peter which point to the theme of "good works"/"doing good" in 1 Peter: τὴν ἀναστροφὴν καλήν (2:12); καλῶν ἔργων (2:12); ἀγαθοποιός (2:14); ἀγαθοποιέω (2:15, 20; 3:6, 17); ποιησάτω ἀγαθόν (3:11); τὴν ἀγαθὴν ἐν Χριστῷ ἀναστροφήν (3:16); ἀγαθοποιΐα (4:19).

52. Williams, *Persecution in 1 Peter*, 260–75.

would masters respond with harshness? This is especially the case if "doing good" is a technical term for *euergetism*, which is what some have tried to argue. But the fundamental problem with the consensus view is that it assumes that "good works" are exhorted as a *response* to the hostility the addressees are experiencing. In contrast, 1 Peter indicates that it is precisely these "good works" that *cause* the hostility in the first place. For example, 1 Pet 3:16 seems to indicate that the addressees will be maligned *because of* their "good works," and in 1 Pet 2:12 Peter seems to make a link between honorable conduct and being maligned as an evildoer.[53]

What, then, are the "good works" spoken of in 1 Peter? Williams puts forth a "new perspective,"[54] suggesting that we look to the letter itself, and in particular the ethical exhortations, in order to gain clarity:

> When this paraenesis is collected, there are a number of behaviors which could be classified as "good." The letter is filled with personal virtues or traits which the author expected would be developed and fostered within the Christian communities: self-discipline (1:13; 4:7; 5:8); holiness (1:15); fear of (or reverence for) God (1:17; 2:17); righteousness (2:24; 3:12, 14; 4:18); inner purity (3:2–4); sympathy and tender-heartedness (3:8); and humility (3:8; 5:5–7). Along with the individual aspects of the Christian life, he also encourages his audience to display interpersonal "goodness": loving one another (1:22; 2:17; 3:8; 4:8); submitting to proper authorities (2:13–14, 18; 3:1; 5:5); showing honor to everyone and in particular the emperor (2:17); endurance under unjust suffering (2:19–20); living with one's wife according to knowledge (3:7); maintaining unity (3:8); non-retaliation (3:9–11); hospitality (4:9); ministering to one another through spiritual gifts (4:10–11); and shepherding the flock of God (5:2). But the good works of 1 Peter were not merely pursuits in which Christians actively participated. In some cases, the "good" which the author expects is simply abstinence (e.g., 1:14; 2:1, 11; 3:3, 6, 9, 14; 4:1–3, 15). By avoiding the sinful behaviors which previously consumed their lives and which presently tested their faithfulness, they were actually doing good. As such, it is somewhat difficult to drive a wedge between the two behavioral causes of persecution.[55]

---

53. See Williams, *Persecution in 1 Peter*, 267–69, for full argumentation.
54. Williams, *Persecution in 1 Peter*, 269–75.
55. Williams, *Persecution in 1 Peter*, 273–74.

Williams last point is important to underscore. "Good works" were as much about what the addressees *did not do* as they were about what the recipients did. In other words, it is likely that the "good works" of withdrawal are what often led to hostility. For it is hard to imagine that submitting to authorities, being humble, or being self-disciplined would have perturbed their neighbors. But when withdrawal, which often produced hostility, was combined with such active "good works" as mutual love, hospitality, and ministering to others through spiritual gifts (which would have been perceived as ingroup promotion), we can see how "the ethical system as a whole would have resulted in a progression of hostility."[56]

Williams puts us on the right path by directing our attention to the letter itself as a way to better understand what the "good works" were and whose opinion determined whether an act was good/honorable or not. But, as we will see in the next chapter, there are two important omissions to the list included above, the significance of which will be explored in detail: (1) the first ethical exhortation of the letter is "to set all your hope on the grace that Jesus Christ will bring you when he is revealed" (1 Pet 1:13); and (2) Jesus Christ himself is the grounds for learning what it looks like to live in this manner (2:21–25; 3:8–12).[57]

## Legal Causes

We turn now to what may be the most significant piece of evidence in helping us to determine the ethnic makeup of the 1 Peter addressees. According to 1 Pet 4:15–16, we learn that the addressees may find themselves in a situation in which they suffer "as a Christian":

> 15 But let none of you suffer as a murderer, a thief, a criminal, or even as a mischief maker. 16 Yet if any of you suffers as a Christian (ὡς Χριστιανός), do not consider it a disgrace, but glorify God because you bear this name.

There are two ways to read the phrase ὡς Χριστιανός. Most modern 1 Peter commentators are adamant that this phrase in no way suggests that the addressees suffered because being considered a "Christian" was illegal. Instead, they suggest that it was the way of life that resulted from

---

56. Williams, *Persecution in 1 Peter*, 274.

57. Williams offers a helpful detailed expansion of this "new perspective" in a full-length monograph, *Good Works in 1 Peter*, but these omissions remain.

loyal allegiance to Jesus that led to suffering. Against this stalwart modern consensus, Williams provocatively argues that 1 Pet 4:16 indicates that at the time of composition, Christianity had become criminalized and that the addressees could have been punished for their profession of the Christian faith.[58] He points to three features of the passage that would support this claim. First, it seems clear that the label Χριστιανός is outsider language meant to be derogatory (or perhaps even accusatory), partly because it is a clear derivative of Latin but also because it is associated with shame.[59] Second, the term is associated with a list of other punishable offenses (e.g., murderer, thief, or criminal). And finally, suffering "as a Christian" is juxtaposed with God's eschatological judgment in 1 Pet 4:17, giving the impression that Peter links the persecution of 1 Pet 4:16 with the precursor events to God's eschatological judgment as detailed in the Synoptic Gospels (Mark 13:3–13/Matt 24:3–14/Luke 21:7–19), which include being brought to trial.[60]

Williams puts forth an impressively detailed argument showing how the modern consensus came to be so firmly opposed to the criminalization of being "Christian" during the time of 1 Peter's composition, concluding that most of the argumentation is outdated and misinformed.[61] One way to get at the heart of Williams's analysis is to note that modern 1 Peter scholarship has mischaracterized the term "illegal." Most assume or assert that being "Christian" is only "illegal" in the sense that one can show that there is "official" Roman proscription. Without an "official" state edict against Christianity, we cannot say that being a Christian is "illegal" until the reign of Decius (249–251 CE), so the argument goes. Those who take this line, stress that until the official imperial Roman proscription in the mid-third century, persecution of Christians was "unofficial," not because it was "illegal," but instead for any number of reasons that pertained to local issues and concerns that flared up sporadically but had nothing to do with official Roman policy. For this reason, the modern consensus sustains, ὡς Χριστιανός in 1 Pet 4:16 must not be read as a term of accusation that points to the illegality of being a Christian; instead, we should read the reference as a derogatory epithet cast at

---

58. Williams, *Persecution in 1 Peter*, 281.

59. So also Horrell, "Label Χριστιανός," 369–70. Trebilco argues that the passage "implies that outsiders are using these labels in an accusatory way, and that the accusation ... would lead to suffering" (*Self-Designations*, 283).

60. Williams, *Persecution in 1 Peter*, 284–91.

61. See Williams, *Persecution in 1 Peter*, 131–236, 278.

the addressees because of their dishonorable and offensive "Christian" lifestyle.

Williams challenges this assumption by seeking to answer with more precision when it became illegal to be a "Christian." Sifting through evidence from the time of Decius, second- and third-century Christian martyr accounts, Pliny's letter to Trajan, a rescript between Hadrian and the proconsul in Asia, documents that recount Christian persecution under Domitian (late first century), and data pertaining to the Neronian persecution of Christians, Williams yields several significant findings:

1. Decius did not outlaw Christianity *per se*. That is, he did not single out Christians and declare Christianity illegal. Instead, he obligated all to participate in traditional Roman worship. Christians failed to comply with imperial orders, and as a result suffered the consequences. This is notably different from what most Primopetrine scholars have defined as "official" persecution.[62]

2. Pliny's letter to Trajan was not written to clarify the legal status of Christians in the early second century, as has often been purported. In fact, Pliny's letter to Trajan demonstrates that there was already a precedent that established professing the name "Christian" to be illegal. Instead, the real issue that Pliny was trying to sort out was what to do with those who once professed to being Christian but have since denied it.[63]

3. Evidence from the reign of Domitian (late first century) does not provide any indication that the legal status of Christians had been altered from an earlier period. Thus, the precedent followed by Pliny was likely already in place during the time of Domitian.[64]

4. Prior to the Neronian persecution (64 CE), there is no evidence that being a "Christian" was considered a criminal act. In fact, when Christians such as Paul and his associates are brought before local magistrates or provincial governors and accused of violating Roman customs, each time they were exonerated (Acts 16:16–40; 17:1–9; 18:12–17; 23:25–30; 24–26). Instead, in terms of Roman law, "Christianity" was considered to be a tolerable alternative within Judaism.[65]

---

62. Williams, *Persecution in 1 Peter*, 185–86.
63. Williams, *Persecution in 1 Peter*, 205–6.
64. Williams, *Persecution in 1 Peter*, 217.
65. Williams, *Persecution in 1 Peter*, 222–23.

5. Between Paul's missionary journeys (and trials) and Pliny's letter to Trajan, the legal status of being a "Christian" took a negative turn.

6. During the time of Nero, "Christianity" went from being a tolerable alternative within Judaism to "effectively illegal,"[66] and this was sparked by Nero blaming and persecuting the Christians for starting the catastrophic fire that burned ten districts of Rome.[67] While Nero never issued an official decree outlawing "Christianity," his pogrom was the turning point for the legal status of Christians, effectively criminalizing them across the empire moving forward.[68]

7. The legal process described in Pliny's letter to Trajan is comparable with the legal process that was put in place during the mid- to late-first century CE in Asia Minor, making it "effectively illegal" to be a "Christian." The Roman provincial courts recognized that being a "Christian" was illegal. The process was initiated by a third-party accusation, which for a variety of reasons was sporadic, in which Christians were brought to trial and punished to the discretion of the provincial governor.[69] This was never done through a Roman edict that outlawed Christianity. Instead, it was the result of stigmatization which came from what were perceived to be a variety of deviant practices against the Roman way of life.

If Williams is correct, then being called a "Christian" would have been much more than a derogatory insult; instead, it was a charge that posed a serious risk for the addressees living within the kind of accusatorial legal system that was in place in Asia Minor during the time in which the addressees would have lived.[70]

---

66. Williams, drawing on the work of David Horrell, uses the term "effectively illegal" as a way of avoiding the false dichotomy in 1 Peter studies between "official" and "unofficial" persecution, but also to say that although there was no "official" Roman proscription that outlawed "Christianity," at the time of the composition of 1 Peter until the third century, the profession of being a "Christian" was treated as a punishable offense if one was charged so through an accusatorial process that was then brought before the governor's tribunal (*Persecution in 1 Peter*, 179).

67. Williams, *Persecution in 1 Peter*, 220.

68. See Williams, *Persecution in 1 Peter*, 221–26, for a compelling argument regarding how Nero's pogrom would have affected the legal status of Christians in the provinces.

69. See Williams, *Persecution in 1 Peter*, 226–34, for a helpful discussion of why the enforcement of the illegal status of Christians was sporadic.

70. See Williams, *Persecution in 1 Peter*, 138–78, for a detailed description.

Williams's study is compelling and significant for reorienting the way we understand the social setting for the letter. It turns out that withdrawal and good works that are rooted in allegiance to Jesus might not only produce contempt from family, friends, and neighbors, and social ostracization; it might even result in criminal punishment, possibly even execution. But his examination also raises a vexing question for the aim of this chapter. Does his work suggest that being accused of being a "Christian" was something that Jewish followers of Jesus would *not* have faced? Does the term Χριστιανός point to a break, a recognized distinction between Jewish and gentile followers of Jesus, a "parting of the ways" if you will? By the time 1 Peter is composed, is the term Χριστιανός synonymous with "non-Jewish follower of the Christ"? Williams is unclear on this but seems to lean in that direction when he claims that the Neronian persecution "clearly distinguished Christianity from Judaism and marked the Christians out as recognized deviants by the Roman authorities."[71] Or when he writes, "Whereas, in the eyes of the Romans, the confession of Christianity was once viewed as a tolerable alternative within Judaism, it later served as sufficient grounds for accusation and condemnation with a Roman court."[72] Do these comments suggest that to be a "Christian" meant one could not be considered a "Jew" any longer? Or does it suggest that to be a "Christian," Jews would have to renounce their "Judaism"? In this regard, Williams's study is significant in ways even perhaps he has not anticipated. For in the emerging field of reading the New Testament within Judaism, much has been made about there not being a parting of the ways until at the earliest the early second century, and that Χριστιανός is not a technical term that points to a distinct religion or that delineates Christianity as a religion from the religion of Judaism. Williams's study could call this claim into question.

## A Closer Look at Χριστιανός and the Identity of the 1 Peter Addressees

In the same year that Williams published *Persecution in 1 Peter*, Paul Trebilco published *Self-Designations and Group Identity in the New Testament*.[73] Whereas Williams attended to the word Χριστιανός as it per-

---

71. Williams, *Persecution in 1 Peter*, 220.
72. Williams, *Persecution in 1 Peter*, 224.
73. Trebilco, *Self-Designations and Group Identity*.

tained to legal standing in Roman provinces in the first three centuries CE, Trebilco sought to understand its origin and what it might reveal about group identity in the early Jesus movement. We look to Trebilco's work because it will broaden our understanding the term Χριστιανός beyond its legal context, and, more importantly for the aims of this chapter, will enable us to better discern the ethnic makeup of the recipients of 1 Peter.

According to the author of Acts (Acts 11:26), the term Χριστιανός originated in Antioch: "It was in Antioch that the disciples were first called Christians." Trebilco's analysis complements Williams's observation when he notes that there are two features of this reference that seem to indicate that it was likely originally coined by outsiders. First, the verb χρηματίσαι, "to take and bear a title or name," could carry either an active or a passive sense. If it was the latter, then "to be called" indicates that they were designated "Christians" by others. Second, Χριστιανός does not derive from Greek or Aramaic, but instead is a Latinism.[74] This suggests that the term originated in a Latin-speaking context, which would seem to confirm a passive sense of the verb χρηματίσαι.[75]

Drawing on the work of David Horrell, Trebilco concludes that the outsider term likely arose in response to the notable formation of a new group in Antioch that was comprised of both Jews and gentiles who adapted practices that were distinct from a more traditional Jewish way of life. Some scholars have taken it one step further and claimed that the term was likely coined by members of the Roman administration as a result of their encounter with this sub-group of Jews and gentiles.[76] Whether that is the case, Trebilco proposes that Χριστιανός was coined by "Gentile non-Christians, since Jews would not develop a designation that would indicate acceptance of the belief that Jesus was the Messiah."[77]

Trebilco's next move is to seek an explanation for why the term was coined by outsiders. Here, his comments are worth including in full, in part for how he nuances the implications of the Neronian persecution of Christians vis-à-vis Jewish identity:

---

74. Trebilco, *Self-Designations and Group Identity*, 277; Horrell, "Label Χριστιανός," 362–64.

75. Trebilco points out that we have examples in Josephus and Philo where χρηματίσαι means "to be called" by others (*Self-Designations and Group Identity*, 277).

76. Trebilco notes that some point to the verb χρηματίσαι as indicating official rather than informal naming (*Self-Designations and Group Identity*, 278).

77. Trebilco, *Self-Designations and Group Identity*, 278.

> The earlier Christians were, of course, Jews, and the earliest Christian groups, even those with Gentile members, would be seen by outsiders as groups within Judaism. But if Gentile outsiders wished to distinguish "Christians" from (non-Chrisitan) "Jews" for legal reasons or because actions by some "Christians" were becoming problematic, then a name for the Christians would be necessary. The creation of a name by non-Christian Gentiles would thus suggest that the Christian community had formed a sufficiently large and cohesive group for them to be recognized as a distinct movement or entity by outsiders and that they were a group which was sufficiently distinguishable within the Jewish community for them to be given a different name. It is important, then, to recognize that the name implies the group is distinguishable as a movement, but that it does *not* necessarily imply that they were no longer viewed by outsiders as Jews. Even the incident in 64 CE when "Christians" were blamed for the fire, and "Jews" were not does not mean that "Christians" were no longer seen as "Jews," but rather that they were seen as a sufficiently distinguishable group, even within the group known as "Jews," to be singled out.[78]

The hypothesis that the name may have emerged by Roman administrators for "legal reasons," that is, as a result of trouble making from within this distinct mixed group of Jews and gentiles who believed in Jesus as the Christ aligns with the analysis that Williams has offered, but Trebilco does not overstate the evidence, as Williams appears to do when he says that "the Neronian persecution *clearly* distinguished Christianity from Judaism."[79] But the assertion of Williams considered together with Trebilco's modest postulation that "it does *not* necessarily imply that they were no longer viewed by outsiders as Jews" does point to a curious lacuna in the evidence. When the term originates, and as it is used early on, it seems to describe a sub-group of Judaism made of gentiles and ethnically Jewish Christ-followers who had ties with the (Jewish) apostles in Jerusalem. But there does not seem to be enough evidence available to determine whether by mid- to late-first century CE the term Χριστιανός could be understood to mean something distinct from Judaism, and/or whether it was a term that indicated an exclusive gentile makeup.[80] As

---

78. Trebilco, *Self-Designations and Group Identity*, 279.

79. Williams, *Persecution in 1 Peter*, 220 (emphasis mine).

80. Trebilco, *Self-Designations and Group Identity*, 280–82, posits six reasons for why the term was most likely coined before 64 CE, perhaps in the mid 50s.

Williams has shown, in terms of legal status, there was a distinction between the Judaism protected under *religio licita* status, and what was practiced by "Christians" after 64 CE. But as unclear as the non-legal distinction between Jew and Christian might have been during the time of Nero, it seems that, given Tacitus's (116 CE) use of the term *Christianus* in his account of the fire of Rome in 64 CE (*Ann.* 15.44), we can conclude that the term was known by the Roman populace prior to the fire, and that it was used to distinguish Christians from both non-Jesus-following Jews and from non-Jesus-following gentiles.[81] Thus, by the beginning of the second century, Tacitus seems to indicate, at least from a Roman perspective, that "Christians" were no longer seen as a particular type of Jew, but instead as separate group. For example, rather than say that "Nero had those Jews arrested that were called Christians," which is what you would expect if "Christians" were perceived to be linked with Judaism, Tacitus simply names the group without any qualifiers.[82]

## Conclusions

What is the significance of this analysis on the causes of suffering in 1 Peter in relation to the aim of this chapter, which is to determine whether there is enough evidence in the letter to discern the ethnic makeup of the addressees? It seems that at least five conclusions can be made with varying levels of confidence:

First, having exposed the significant deficiencies of the Jewish-audience proposal, we can rule out a predominantly or exclusively idealized or imagined Jewish audience.

Second, considering the analysis regarding the cause of suffering instigated by the addressees' withdrawal and "good works," it seems best to conclude that the *intended* or *imagined* audience was made up of gentiles who suffered because faithful allegiance to Jesus entailed a new way of life that was seen as offensive and even hostile to their gentile family, friends, and neighbors. It is important to underscore that this is not the same as saying that there were no Jews in the congregations in which this letter was first read. But what we have seen from the letter, especially 1 Pet 4:3–4, is that Peter speaks to addressees whom he *characterizes* as *full participants*

---

81. See Trebilco, *Self-Designations and Group Identity*, 273–74, for Trebilco's analysis of Tacitus's comments.

82. Trebilco, *Self-Designations and Group Identity*, 274.

in the behaviors that were on offer within voluntary associations, the imperial cult and its many permeations in the lived experience in Asia Minor, and the worship of traditional gods. According to what is written, their withdrawal from the practices associated with these foundational gentile institutions is partly what led to the hostility they experienced. So, for the purposes of this study, it is important to make a distinction: there is a difference between who might have been present when this letter was read, and the kind of reader, or perhaps better said hearer, that Peter imagined when he wrote the letter. Based upon the evidence examined above, I am suggesting that, from a rhetorical standpoint, the imagined, intended, or "ideal" recipient of the letter was a gentile follower of Jesus. So, even if in actuality at the time of reading the audience was a mixed group, the "target audience," we might say today, was exclusively gentile.[83] We suggest this for two reasons. First, as we have seen, it is hard to explain how such a large group of highly Hellenized Jews from all over Asia Minor and the known world would have (A) been so fully participatory in the behaviors described, and (B) would have turned to Jesus and been compelled to disassociate (1 Pet 5:9). And second, there is, nothing in the letter that evidences the characteristic tensions that arose when Jews and gentiles who were seeking to align themselves with Jesus Christ got together (e.g., concerns about food, Sabbath observance, or other matters pertaining to Torah faithfulness and *halakah*). This silence, coupled with the evidence that has been put forth, suggests that Peter is intending to address gentiles and *their particular challenges* as gentiles.

Third, while we acknowledged that the term Χριστιανός originated from outside in order to indicate a distinct mixed group of Jews and gentiles seen as being *within* Judaism, it seems best to conclude that the particular "Christians" that Peter is addressing are gentiles (for the reasons mentioned above). But it is important to stress that this is not the same as saying that the term Χριστιανός means something like "exclusively gentile followers of Jesus" at all times and in all places in the first century CE. Nevertheless, given the findings of Williams on the legal status of "Christians" in the first century CE in Asia Minor, and what we have concluded above, it seems that in this particular letter with its unique setting, this term is being used both as a criminal charge against gentile

---

83. Ok draws on similar language, concluding that "while it is impossible to know the precise ethnic-religious makeup of Peter's actual audience, the author gives us clues to his *imagined* audience and writes to them as if they are Gentiles" (*Constructing Ethnic Identity*, 10–11 [emphasis mine]).

addressees as well as a name that Peter is seeking to rehabilitate. What is more, Williams's demonstration of how the term Χριστιανός deemed those who bore that name "effectively illegal" across the Roman Empire makes more sense of 1 Pet 5:9 ("you know that your brothers and sisters in all the world are undergoing the same kinds of suffering"). In other words, anyone at anytime, anywhere in the empire is at risk of being accused, being brought to trail, and suffering the consequences for being a "Christian."

Fourth, these gentile addressees, in professing allegiance to Jesus Christ and in engaging in the practices (withdrawal and "good works") that displayed their fidelity, were cut off in a number of ways from their traditional networks of support and belonging. If we are right that the ideal or imagined addressees were gentiles, in part because there are no signs of Jew-gentile tensions or debate over Torah practice, then this means that, at its core, what we witness in this letter are gentiles (compeers, coworkers, neighbors, fellow-citizens, and family members) telling other gentiles (i.e., Christ-following gentiles) that they no longer belong. There are two important implications of this reality. First, the traditional sources and institutions that provided meaning, purpose, and belonging were no longer available to these addressees, unless they deviated from their new way of life as followers of Jesus. As a result, along with the underlying disorienting effect of not belonging,[84] they experienced "a variety of trials," which tested their allegiances (1 Pet 1:6): verbal assault (2:12; 4:4, 14; 3:9), physical abuse (2:20), the threat of legal action (1 Pet 2:11–17; 3:14–16; 4:12–19), spousal tensions (1 Pet 3:1–6), and economic oppression (for withdrawing from trade associations).[85] And second, we should expect 1 Peter to focus on matters that pertain, not to the Jew/gentile dichotomy, but instead the dynamics *between gentiles*. In other words, 1 Peter's focus on gentiles is not meant to exclude Jews, especially not Jewish followers of Jesus. Instead, because the problem(s) that Peter addresses is intragentile in nature—that is, because it is gentiles that are reviling these gentile followers of Jesus and telling them they do not belong—we should anticipate that Peter may not answer all our questions about how this pertains to Israel in the flesh.[86]

---

84. See Holloway, *Coping with Prejudice*, 21–73, for a detailed account of the disorienting psychological effects the 1 Peter addressees would have experienced.

85. See Williams, *Persecution in 1 Peter*, 299–326, for a detailed explanation of each of these "trials."

86. Bechtler, *Following in His Steps*, 63.

And finally, our consideration of the term Χριστιανός has potentially cast a light on the tenuous and ambiguous status of gentile followers of Jesus with respect to their place within Jewish identity. This is one way to make sense of the lacuna of information about the way the term developed between its initial usage before the time of Nero and how it was used by the time we get to Tacitus and Pliny: the term originates in a context in which gentiles are welcomed into the people of the God of Israel by this distinct expression of Jewish identity.[87] But as time goes on, gentile followers of Jesus within this mixed group increase while the population of Jewish followers of Jesus does not keep pace. Concomitant with this demographic change is the development of the term Χριστιανός as an indicator of criminal status. Within this scenario, we can imagine that these gentile followers of Jesus are not only facing the threat of criminal punishment, not only are they being ostracized by their own people, but they may also be experiencing an erosion of their sense of belonging within their new host family. In other words, the development of the meaning of "Christian" may point to the fact that the addressees' new roots in Jewish identity are also being questioned at the time of the composition of 1 Peter—either by the addressees themselves, by other gentiles, or by Jews. While the letter itself seems to indicate that it is gentiles who are bringing charges against these "Christian" addressees, especially given what we have rehearsed about the basis for hostility, we might also suspect that this is not the only source of hostility. For example, if the pattern that we find in Acts is representative in any way, we can also imagine scenarios in which the gentile followers of Jesus are accused not only by gentile compeers, but perhaps also at times by non-Jesus-following Jews. In fact, it could even be the case that at times these non-Jesus-following Jews incite both Jews and pagan gentiles to harass and persecute these deviant gentiles.[88] Regardless of whether this is the case, if some form

---

87. Though certainly not without said hospitality being contested at times both by non-Jesus-following Jews as well as Jesus-following Jews.

88. E.g., Acts 13:13–14:20; 17:1–15; 18:1–17. In these accounts, we encounter Jews "inciting women of high standing and the leading men of the city" (13:50); "unbelieving Jews stirring up the Gentiles" (14:2); "jealous" Jews forming mobs and setting the city in an uproar (17:5), and even accusing the gentiles of acting contrary to the decrees of the emperor (17:7); and Jews bringing Paul before the proconsul of Achaia (18:12–13). These accounts happened at the initial stages of the Jesus movement. Whether this pattern continued later in the development of the movement in Asia Minor is difficult to say, but it is a reminder that "Christian" persecution could come from both Jews and gentiles. If the term "Christian" had illegal status during the time

of erosion is happening, then Peter, in addressing this imagined gentile audience, is not only seeking to help them navigate the threat of being accused as a Χριστιανός, he is not only seeking to reorient gentiles who have been cut off from their friends, family, city, culture, and heritage, but it is perhaps also the case that he is speaking to a group who once, after forsaking the ways of their forefathers (1:18), found a home within the people of the God of Israel but now struggle, in part, because their legitimacy of belonging to this new community is being questioned (whether by themselves or by others). In short, it could be that they are caught in a liminal state: feeling that they do not belong to their gentile heritage, nor to the people of the God of Israel. In other words, is it perhaps the case that 1 Peter seeks to rehabilitate the name Χριστιανός in more ways than one (i.e., in terms of its legal sense and the shame that is associated with the charge, but also as it relates to the addressees' legitimacy as members of the people of the God of Israel)? One way to confirm this hypothesis is to consider the genre and rhetorical purpose for this letter addressed to an intended gentile audience. This is the subject we turn to in the final section of this chapter.

## On "Belonging" and the Purpose of 1 Peter

### The Genre of 1 Peter

We begin our discussion of the purpose of 1 Peter by reflecting briefly upon its genre. Lutz Doering has done extensive work showing that "1 Peter engages with Jewish epistolary tradition," in part by its creative use of the term "Diaspora," its usage of a salvation-historical meta-narrative for the purpose of character formation, its characterization of Rome as Babylon, and its application of the verb πληθυνθείη in the salutation, which links with encyclical letters in the biblical Jewish tradition.[89] He has persuasively argued not only that Diaspora letters constitute a discrete genre or letter type[90] but also that 1 Peter ought to be considered an early Christian Diaspora letter.[91] As we will see, something as basic

---

in which the letter was written, this could provide even more impetus for non-Jesus-following Jews to persecute the addressees.

    89. Doering, *Ancient Jewish Letters*, 429–52. See also Doering, "First Peter as Early Christian Diaspora Letter."

    90. Doering, "First Peter as Early Christian Diaspora Letter," 225–26.

    91. Doering is careful with his usage of the term "Christian," highlighting that

as reflecting on the classification of 1 Peter in terms of genre enables us to understand more clearly the purpose for which the letter was written.

Having analyzed the extant body of Jewish Diaspora communication, Doering makes the following observations:

1. Jewish Diaspora letters contain an authoritative addresser (whether factual or fictitious).
2. The addressees are Judeans or Jews resident outside of the Land of Israel or on its fringes.
3. The letters are "quasi-official," having more in common with official rather than private letters.
4. Some of the letters are circular, addressing more than one community or area.
5. The letters usually focus on instruction and exhortation that is aimed at character formation, often in relation to Torah practice.
6. The main concern of the letters is the cohesion and unity of the people of God.
7. This cohesion is often developed through reference to a common salvific metanarrative, or a "brothers" address.

Doering then notes the way in which the author of 1 Peter adapts the characteristics of Jewish Diaspora letters for his own purposes, at times in creative fashion.[92] First, the "Diaspora" mentioned in 1 Peter is not in reference to a people that have been displaced physically or historically from their homeland, but rather those who have been made "resident aliens" because of their rebirth.[93] Doering stresses that even though we might call this usage of Diaspora metaphorical, it is modeled on the analogy with Jewish Diaspora experience.[94]

---

"it should be evident from recent debate that 'Jewish' and 'Christian' do not denote firm entities and clear-cut oppositions in the second half of the first century. . . . It is therefore best, in my view, to use 'Christian' as a low-key modifier here: these letters are adaptations of the (originally Jewish) Diaspora letter type for Christian readers by Christian authors; it is probable that these authors have their origin in Judaism, and this is possible also for some of the addressees" ("First Peter as Early Christian Diaspora Letter," 226).

92. Doering, "First Peter as Early Christian Diaspora Letter," 229–36.
93. Doering, "First Peter as Early Christian Diaspora Letter," 231.
94. Doering, "First Peter as Early Christian Diaspora Letter," 231.

Second, while 1 Peter exhibits paraenesis which is characteristic of Jewish Diaspora letters (an affirmation of their election [1:1; 2:9–10]; the call to holiness [1:14–16]; the reminder of brotherhood [5:9; 1:22; 3:8; 4:8]), one major difference is that the author replaces Torah paraenesis with a blend of christological and soteriological statements.[95] Doering also notes that in contrast to the Greco-Roman paraenesis tradition, 1 Peter shows indebtedness to the Jewish Diaspora tradition as it points to a metanarrative in order to build cohesion.[96] Importantly, Doering also underscores that there is no indication that the addressees' Diaspora existence is a form of punishment for wrongdoing.[97]

Finally, Doering makes the observation that it is fitting for apostolic figures associated with Jerusalem to send quasi-official encyclical Diaspora letters, often addressed to regions, for this would be an anticipated way for them to exercise their authority and leadership (James and Acts 15:23–29 being other examples).[98] Doering, who considers 1 Peter to be pseudonymous,[99] argues that the letter form fits with the image of the apostle Peter,

> who, according to early Christian tradition, was initially the leading figure of the Jewish Christian community of Jerusalem and Judea; then, after a period of imprisonment under Agrippa I, left Jerusalem for "another place" (Acts 12:17), probably taking up a more itinerant lifestyle (cf. 1 Cor 9:5); at some point began to accept Gentiles into the church (cf. Acts 10:1—11:18) and was involved in the mission to Gentiles (cf. 1 Cor 1:12); and finally suffered and was crucified (cf. John 21:18–19) in Rome (cf. *1 Clem.* 5:3–4; Ign. *Rom.* 4:3; *Ascen. Isa.* 4:2–3)—a Diaspora letter to suffering Christians of largely Gentile provenance, purportedly written not from Jerusalem but from "Babylon," may be considered nothing less than what is to be expected.[100]

With this helpful study, we can see that by attending to the nature of the genre and the image of Peter (purported, remembered, or otherwise), we arrive at similar conclusions about 1 Peter: it is written to gentiles, and it

---

95. Doering, "First Peter as Early Christian Diaspora Letter," 232.
96. Doering, "First Peter as Early Christian Diaspora Letter," 232.
97. Doering, "First Peter as Early Christian Diaspora Letter," 232.
98. Doering, "First Peter as Early Christian Diaspora Letter," 235. For further development of this thesis, see Doering, *Ancient Jewish Letters*, 469–71.
99. Doering, "First Peter as Early Christian Diaspora Letter," 230.
100. Doering, "First Peter as Early Christian Diaspora Letter," 232, 236.

has as its primary aim the development of cohesion and unity within the people of God.

## The "Rhetorical Exigence" of 1 Peter

Troy Martin, in a recent essay, expands our understanding of the authoritative nature of this "quasi-official" Diaspora communication as well as the intent of the letter as he considers afresh the "rhetorical exigence" of 1 Peter.[101] Whereas Doering asks what *kind* of letter 1 Peter is, Martin seeks to discern what the *purpose* of the letter is. What is the author seeking to accomplish? What need is he seeking to address? What is the thing that is other than it should be?[102] What is the foundational situation that needs attention and clarity? Martin notes the wide range of opinions about the exigence of 1 Peter—suffering, persecution, prejudice, social identity, social distinctiveness, or social assimilation—but also that there does not appear to be "one controlling exigence which functions as the organizing principle."[103] His essay proposes just that, a controlling exigence that gives more clarity regarding the purpose for the letter.

He builds his case by comparing 1 Peter with Acts 15:23–29, which he refers to as the letter from the Jerusalem Assembly.[104] He starts his comparison by noting the most obvious thing both letters have in common: Silas or Silvanus. In the case of the letter from the Jerusalem Assembly, Silas is one of the letter carriers (Acts 15:27); and in the case of 1 Peter, he is the "faithful brother" through whom the letter is written (1 Pet 5:12), whether that was also as a letter carrier or an amanuensis—or both—is not clear.[105] From here, he seeks to demonstrate that both letters, while very different, address a similar rhetorical exigence.

He looks first at the Assembly letter and the circumstances surrounding it. According to the narrative in which the letter is embedded, Jewish followers of Jesus have come from Jerusalem to tell gentile followers of Jesus in Antioch that they cannot be saved unless they are

---

101. Martin, "Peter and the Expansion of Early Christianity," 87–99.
102. Martin, "Peter and the Expansion of Early Christianity," 88.
103. Martin, "Peter and the Expansion of Early Christianity," 92.
104. Martin shows awareness of Doering, *Ancient Jewish Letters*, but does not engage with his genre implications for his own proposal.
105. See Achtemeier, *1 Peter*, 350–51, for a discussion of why Silas and Silvanus are likely the same person.

circumcised. In other words, these gentiles are being told that they do not fully belong to the people of the God of Israel unless they comply with Torah all the way. This is unsettling to the gentile contingency, and in response Paul is sent to Jerusalem for an official apostolic determination on the matter. As Martin notes, "The narrative assumes that Paul does not have apostolic standing to resolve this controversy over circumcision, although he is allowed to speak at the Jerusalem Assembly."[106] In the end, Peter persuades the assembly to welcome gentiles as legitimate members of God's people without needing to be circumcised. James "specifically ignores what Paul says but picks up on Peter's speech and articulates the official apostolic ruling."[107] James then recommends sending a letter to the gentile followers of Jesus as an apostolic decree that confirms that uncircumcised gentiles are legitimate members of God's people.

Martin notes that the letter itself presents those that unsettled the gentiles as unauthorized representatives "with no instructions from us" (Acts 15:24). He also notes that the letter does not refer to these unauthorized representatives as "brothers." In contrast, both the senders and the recipients are identified as "brothers." Martin considers this to be significant for understanding the rhetorical exigence of the letter:

> Thus, the designation of both the senders and the recipients of this letter as brothers . . . is significant and expresses a very truncated enthymeme of only a single title that states the minor premise of the enthymeme while the key assumption and the conclusion remain unstated. The recipients must supply the major premise that legitimate members of this faith community are called brothers. . . . The designation of the apostles and elders who send this letter as brothers implies and reinforces the truth of this major premise but does not state it explicitly. Furthermore, the suppression of the term *brothers* in reference to the unspecified, unauthorized persons who went out from the apostles and elders to trouble the recipients and to force circumcision on them also points to this major premise (Acts 15:24). . . . The unpacked enthymeme reads as follows: (major premise) legitimate members of our faith community are called brothers; (minor premise) we call you brothers; (conclusion) you are legitimate members of our faith community.[108]

---

106. Martin, "Peter and the Expansion of Early Christianity," 89. So also Doering, *Ancient Jewish Letters*, 89.

107. Martin, "Peter and the Expansion of Early Christianity," 89.

108. Martin, "Peter and the Expansion of Early Christianity," 92.

82   READING 1 PETER AFTER SUPERSESSIONISM

For Martin, this analysis gets at the heart of the rhetorical exigence of the letter from the Jerusalem Assembly: what is lacking in the situation of Acts 15 is an *apostolic determination* of the *status of these gentile followers of Jesus* who have been unsettled by this unauthorized group from Jerusalem. Apostolic confirmation of the legitimacy of uncircumcised gentile followers of Jesus within the people of God is the ultimate need that is being addressed.

Turning to 1 Peter, Martin suggests that one clue for understanding the rhetorical exigence of the letter is by considering its stated destinations. Why has the author left out Cilicia, Lycia, and Pamphylia? And why is there some overlap with Paul's letters?[109] Martin suggests a comparison with the letter from the Jerusalem Assembly might be illuminating: "It is curious that First Peter picks up geographically precisely where the letter from Jerusalem leaves off."[110] He suggests this because the Assembly letter provides apostolic confirmation to Syria and Cilicia (Acts 15:23), and this probably extends to Pamphylia because it is often regarded as a unit together with Cilicia (Acts 27:5). In addition to this, in 43 CE Claudius joined Lycia and Pamphylia as one political entity, and it is likely that this extends apostolic confirmation to Lycia. Martin proposes that 1 Peter, then, seeks to expand the apostolic confirmation of the legitimacy of gentiles within the people of God by extending the apostolic decision west and north of the Taurus mountains into the rest of Asia Minor.[111] Since Silas (or Silvanus) was one of the letter carriers for the apostolic decree sent to Syria and Cilicia, perhaps this explains why he is connected with 1 Peter.[112] And perhaps this explains the controlling exigence of the letter—gentiles living in Asia Minor who were not specifically addressed or officially legitimated by the letter from the Jewish Assembly needed apostolic confirmation.[113]

Martin points to several features in 1 Peter that support this hypothesis. First, the letter opens with the anarthous ἀπόστολος, which, Martin convincingly demonstrates, further underscores (rather than minimizes) Peter's official role as apostle who delivers apostolic legitimacy to its

---

109. As we saw, this is also a question that Witherington raised in his Jewish audience proposal.

110. Martin, "Peter and the Expansion of Early Christianity," 93.

111. Martin, "Peter and the Expansion of Early Christianity," 93.

112. This point holds even if one maintains that 1 Peter is pseudonymous, and perhaps even more so if Silas is also pseudonymous.

113. Martin, "Peter and the Expansion of Early Christianity," 93.

recipients.[114] Here, Martin recalls that the remembered Peter is perhaps best noted for his legitimizing of gentiles in the household of Cornelius (Acts 10:44–45) and at the Jerusalem Assembly (Acts 15:7–11). He also notes that the rhetorical function of the letter is characterized at the end: "I have written this letter to encourage you and testify that this is the true grace of God. Stand fast in it" (1 Pet 5:12). Peter writes in order to confirm and legitimize the addressees place within the people of God.

Silvanus is given special mention (1 Pet 5:12) because he is an extension of Peter's apostolic authority: Peter reckons (λογίζομαι) him as a faithful or trustworthy brother. In other words, with apostolic authority, Peter determines that Silvanus is a legitimate member of God's people ("brother") who is also a reliable (πιστός) representative of the apostolic confirmation.[115] But rather than address the recipients of the letter as brothers, Peter refers to them as "chosen exiles" (ἐκλεκτοῖς παρεπιδήμοις). Martin highlights that it is often in response to the problem of legitimacy in a foreign land that Jewish writers would often describe exiles as the "chosen" people of God. This intensified articulation of the recipients' legitimacy is echoed with additional titles such as "obedient children" (1 Pet 1:14), "believers in God" (1:21), "a chosen race" (2:9), "a royal priesthood" (2:9), and a "holy nation" (2:9). Additionally, the conclusion of the enthymeme is stated explicitly: "Now you are God's people" (1 Pet 2:10). Martin puts forth the following syllogism for the overall message of the letter:

> (Major premise) legitimate members of the people of God are called chosen exiles; (minor premise) Peter calls these recipients chosen exiles; (conclusion) the recipients are legitimate members of the people of God.[116]

While the situations that generated questions of legitimacy differ, like the letter from the Jerusalem Assembly, 1 Peter seeks to provide apostolic affirmation regarding the full legitimacy of gentiles within the people of the God of Israel. This hypothesis would explain why the destinations of 1 Peter overlap with Paul: Paul, whose apostleship is contested (e.g., 1 Cor 9:1–3; Acts 15:2), is unable to substantiate the legitimacy of the brothers in these five provinces mentioned in 1 Pet 1:1 on his own authority.

---

114. Martin, "Peter and the Expansion of Early Christianity," 94.
115. So also Achtemeier, *1 Peter*, 352.
116. Martin, "Peter and the Expansion of Early Christianity," 98.

If Martin is right, as a result of this letter, including its reliable transmission through Silas, gentiles who are suffering because of their allegiance to Jesus, who are being told by other gentiles that they no longer belong, and who perhaps are losing connections with their new host family are given apostolic confirmation that they indeed belong to the people of the God of Israel.

Thus, considerations about the genre and the rhetorical exigence of 1 Peter confirm earlier conclusions made in this chapter, namely that the intended or imagined addressees are indeed gentiles, and that they need to know that (and how) they belong to the people of the God of Israel *as gentiles*.

## Conclusions

As we saw in chapter 1, identifying the ethnic makeup of the addressees is of critical importance because it leads to certain assumptions (often unexamined) about the identify-formation strategy of the letter and its consequent meaning, both for what it says about God and also what it claims about the people of God. If we conclude that the letter was written to a gentile audience, then reading 1 Peter becomes problematic in ways that have not always been recognized in modern scholarship.

But perhaps the uncomfortable problems of 1 Peter can be resolved quite simply by concurring with early interpreters of 1 Peter, who regarded the letter to be written to a Jewish audience. In chapter 2 we explored this possibility, demonstrating that several of the common proof texts (1 Pet 1:18, 21; 2:9–10) appealed to by the modern consensus to determine the ethnic makeup of the addressees of 1 Peter are unable to give us definitive conclusions, exposing the inaccurate assumptions made by many modern interpreters who argue for a gentile audience. Additionally, we showed that these proof texts could be leveraged to argue for both an exclusively gentile as well as an exclusively Jewish audience.

In this chapter, then, we sought other ways we might discern the ethnic makeup of the addressees, and in the course of our examination we have also been able to gain further clarity on the situation that the original recipients faced. Having looked more closely at 1 Pet 4:3–4, we concluded that it is unlikely that it could pertain to "highly Hellenized Jews," as some would have us imagine. We reached this conclusion, in part, because the text doesn't merely critique "gentile debauchery" in standard Jewish polemical fashion, but instead also inculpates the addressees as having participated in the vices listed. To date there is yet to be a plausible explanation for all the variables that would have needed to come together in order for 1 Pet 4:3–4 to pertain to a Jewish audience.

Drawing on the incisive work of Williams regarding the context and causes of persecution in 1 Peter, we proposed that a better way forward in terms of determining the makeup of the addressees is to look more carefully at the causes of suffering. Having looked at the institutions from which the addressees might withdraw, at the way 1 Peter characterizes "good works," and the potential legal causes of suffering for being a "Christian," we concluded that, combined with what we had already seen in the chapter, we are able to rule out an exclusively or predominantly Jewish audience with a high degree of confidence. That is not to say that there were no Jews in any of the congregations in which the letter was first read; it is to say that the "ideal" or "imagined" people being addressed in the letter are gentile followers of Jesus with their particular challenges, which are unique to their being gentiles.

In the course of our examination of the sources of suffering, we gained some additional insights into the situation that they faced: first, these gentile followers of Jesus, because of their allegiance to Jesus and the concomitant way of life that it generated, were being told by other gentiles (their fellow-citizens, friends, and family) that they no longer belonged. In following Jesus, they lost access to the traditional institutions from which they derived a sense of belonging, purpose, and meaning. And they experienced these losses in very tangible ways: verbal abuse and slander, economic hardship, physical abuse, spousal tensions, and social ostracization. In the examination of the criminality of the term Χριστιανός, we suggested that the text along with what we know about the social setting of Asia Minor in the mid- to late-first century suggests a setting in which gentile followers of Jesus are not only being rejected by their compeers, but that perhaps their legitimacy within their new host family, the God of Israel and the people of God, might also be questioned—either by the addressees themselves or by others. This mean that the situation that these addressees were facings, at its core, was one in which their legitimacy or sense of belonging is in a state of limbo: Who are their people? And do *they* belong to the people of the God of Israel?

We finished our chapter by proposing that there are compelling reasons to contend that 1 Peter is a "Christian" Diaspora letter written to extend apostolic affirmation to gentile Jesus-followers in Asia Minor, declaring that they belong to the people of the God of Israel as gentiles.

Therefore, having ruled out a Jewish audience, and having established with a high degree of certainty that the "ideal" or "imagined" addressees were exclusively gentile, we find ourselves where we ended in chapter 1: What are we to make of the identity-formation strategy of the letter in which the prerogatives, privileges, and promises of Israel are extended to these gentile addressees? In the next three chapters, we turn to examine more carefully the way in which Peter shapes identity and belonging for these *gentile* recipients, incorporating what we have already learned about the letter from chapters 1 and 2, but expanding our examination to include a more detailed analysis of the implicit narrative of the letter set against the predominant gentile narrative of Roman imperial ideology (chapter 4) as well as an inquiry into the perplexing language of "spiritual house," "priesthood," "nation," and "race" that appears in 1 Pet 2:4–10. Through this fresh examination, we will be in a place to determine whether the letter encourages or even demands a supersessionist hermeneutic in order to make sense of the identity-formation strategy.

4

# The Problem of Empire
## Exploring the Jewish Restoration Ideology of 1 Peter

*If we are to understand the stance the author of 1 Peter takes toward the social context of his readers we must therefore pay attention not only to the situation of the readers within the Roman Empire but also to the scriptural tradition within which the author encourages his readers to interpret and respond to the situation. ... There is room ... for a more careful examination of the way in which scriptural tradition contributes to the interpretation of empire within 1 Peter.*[1]

## Introduction

ALONG THE WAY OF discerning the ethnic makeup of the addressees of 1 Peter, we became more attuned to the way in which the Roman Empire, and what we might call Roman imperial ideology, had a significant hand in the negative response toward gentile allegiance to Jesus. In this chapter, we turn our attention to "the fact of empire," which permeated and impacted every aspect of life in Asia Minor (especially for the new gentile followers of Jesus), and an overlooked way in which 1 Peter addresses this reality. In particular, we will focus on the manner in which 1 Peter draws upon Jewish restoration ideology developed in the Hebrew scriptures, interpreted through the lens of the life, death, resurrection, and ascension of Jesus Christ, in order to reorient his addressees to a uniquely Jewish way of telling time. In the process of this reconfiguring what "time" it is, Peter also conveys a new sense of belonging for these beleaguered gentile

1. Starling, "1 Peter and the Hermeneutics of Empire," 113, 115.

followers of Jesus that is rooted in their welcomed participation in the Jewish hope for a restored Davidic kingdom.

## The Roman Empire in 1 Peter Studies

The directive to "honor the emperor" (1 Pet 2:17) would seem to be a clear indication that 1 Peter is a text that promotes an accommodating strategy in negotiating the claims of Jesus Christ and the demands of Rome. It is perhaps unsurprising, then, that in an important study that compares the place of diverse associations, synagogues, and assemblies under Roman rule in Asia Minor, Philip Harland points to 1 Peter as one example of literary evidence that Christian assemblies in Asia Minor could participate positively in certain imperial practices, such as erecting inscriptions ("doing good"; 1 Pet 2:12) to honor the emperor.[2] He further argues that 1 Peter reflects a clearly positive view regarding the position of the emperor and other imperial officials within God's ordained order of existence.[3]

There is, however, reason to suspect that 1 Peter is more nuanced than Harland has suggested. For example, even in 1 Pet 2:17, the passage that many scholars appeal to as evidence for an assimilating posture towards the Roman Empire, the injunction to honor the emperor is framed by other directives that generate at least two subversive effects: "Honor everyone. Love the family of believers. Fear God. Honor the emperor." First, the honor that is due to the emperor is equalized such that it is in no way more unique than what is owed to everyone else (including slaves; 1 Pet 2:18). Second, the meaning of "honor" has been subtly nuanced with the result that it cannot refer to "worship" (as it often did in the East). Instead, a distinctively Jewish notion of worship (φοβέω; "fear") is to be exclusively offered to God alone.[4]

Harland is not the first to suggest that 1 Peter encourages an accommodating approach to culture. In the early 1980s, David Balch offered a study of the household code (1 Pet 2:11—3:12), in which he argued that the pastoral strategy of 1 Peter is to urge Christians to assimilate to social

---

2. Harland, *Associations, Synagogues, and Congregations*, 229–35. For a thorough analysis of the social context of Christian suffering in 1 Peter, see Williams, *Persecution in 1 Peter*, especially his critique of the claim that "good works" in 1 Peter is a reference to the accommodating strategy of setting up imperial honorary inscriptions.

3. Harland, *Associations, Synagogues, and Congregations*, 234.

4. Horrell, "Between Conformity and Resistance," 135.

norms as much as possible in order to minimize conflict and hostility.[5] His study sparked a sustained conversation within 1 Peter studies, in which a second, contrary appraisal emerged, epitomized by the work of John Elliot. Drawing on sociological studies of religious sects, Elliott contends that the pastoral strategy of 1 Peter is to develop a strong sense of internal cohesion within the Christian community and to encourage the community to resist conforming to social norms.[6] Subsequent attempts at advancing the contrasting proposals of Balch and Elliott have tended to further entrench the discussion such that only an either/or solution is envisioned: either the pastoral strategy is assimilation or it is resistance.

David Horrell helpfully has moved the conversation beyond the impasse by suggesting the need for a different methodology for making sense of what likely is a more nuanced approach between allegiance to Christ and culture than has been previously recognized.[7] Perhaps most importantly, he points out that the assimilation/resistance debate has either overlooked or underemphasized "the central fact about the particular world in which the addressees lived and which most fundamentally determines their difficult relationship with it: *the fact of empire.*"[8]

With that in view, Horrell suggests that the insights from postcolonial criticism can illuminate the complex and subtle ways in which dominated peoples seek to negotiate their identity and existence. I call attention to two observations that he highlights from postcolonial studies that help orient what we might expect from subordinates as they seek to express resistance in a context of cultural dominance. First, dominated people rarely resort to outright physical and/or verbal resistance as a way of confronting dominance since that strategy is certain to be short-lived and thus ineffective in the long haul. Second, subordinates make use of a variety of hidden and subversive forms of resistance that are generally concealed from the dominator's gaze. Here, Horrell draws

5. Balch, *Let Wives Be Submissive.*

6. Elliott, *Home for the Homeless.* For a concise survey of what has been deemed "the Balch-Elliott debate," see Horrell, "Between Conformity and Resistance," 111–17.

7. Horrell, "Between Conformity and Resistance," 114–17.

8. Horrell, "Between Conformity and Resistance," 117 (emphasis mine). In his seminal work on imperial cult, Price concludes that "The imperial cult stabilized the religions of the world. The system of ritual was carefully structured; the symbolism evoked a picture of the relationship between the emperor and the gods. The ritual was also structuring; it imposed a definition of the world. The imperial cult, along with politics and diplomacy, constructed the reality of the Roman empire" (*Ritual and Power,* 248).

particular attention to the work of James Scott, a political scientist who has dedicated much of his research to studying ways in which subordinated people resist their dominators in "everyday" life. A number of biblical scholars have found Scott's insights to be relevant for understanding the way in which the Gospel material, the Pauline letters, and the Book of Revelation express resistance to various aspects of Roman imperial ideology.[9] According to Scott, since subordinate groups "confront elaborate ideologies [which he refers to as the 'public transcript'] that justify inequality, bondage, monarchy, caste, and so on, . . . resistance to ideological domination requires a counter-ideology—a negation—that will effectively provide a general normative form to the host of resistant practices invented in self-defense by any subordinate group."[10] Scott refers to this counter-ideology as "hidden transcripts," the critique of power that goes on backstage, beyond the observation of power-holders.[11] Often hidden transcripts take the form of "symbolic inversion," where the social ordering maintained in the public transcript is turned upside down, and in which an alternative social structure can be imagined.[12]

David Starling has been critical of what he refers to as "1 Peter among the Postcolonials."[13] His primary critique is that these recent attempts to understand 1 Peter's response to the Roman Empire fail to attend adequately to the manner in which the author draws upon scripture. For example, Starling contends that Warren Carter "draws attention to the absence of any explicit reference to scriptural prohibitions of idolatry within the letter, but has little to say about the ways in which Scripture is cited and echoed";[14] Betsy Bauman-Martin "pays more attention to the role played by scriptural language and categories within the letter, but her interest is more in the way that the writer exploits Scripture as a source for rhetorical power than the way that the understanding of the writer himself is shaped by Scripture";[15] Jennifer Bird "includes a brief

---

9. See especially Horsley, *Paul and the Imperial Order* and the bibliography therein.

10. Scott, *Domination and the Art of Resistance*, 118.

11. See Barclay, *Pauline Churches and Diaspora Jews*, 379–83, for a critique of the application of Scott's "hidden transcripts" to New Testament epistles.

12. Scott, *Domination and the Art of Resistance*, 166–82, 27.

13. Starling, "1 Peter and the Hermeneutics of Empire," 113–15. Here Starling offers brief critiques of extant (at the time of publication) studies of the Roman Empire in 1 Peter from Warren Carter, Betsy Bauman-Martin, Jennifer Bird, and David Horrell.

14. Starling, "1 Peter and the Hermeneutics of Empire," 113.

15. Starling, "1 Peter and the Hermeneutics of Empire," 113.

discussion on how the scriptural metaphors of 'immigrants and refugees' and 'royal priesthood' function within the letter, . . . but does not attempt any sort of systematic investigation of the hermeneutics of the letter";[16] and David Horrell "pays somewhat more attention to the role played by Scripture in shaping the rhetoric and understanding of the author, . . . but the account that Horrell offers . . . still shows a certain one-sidedness."[17] Starling maintains that while Horrell examines the influence of scripture with respect to the "resistant" elements within the letter, he does not explore the ways in which the scriptural tradition has shaped the more conformist dimensions of the letter: "The picture that emerges is a kind of half-way house between Balch's reading of the letter and Elliott's, which is a stance toward the empire that Horrell characterizes as one of 'polite resistance,' in which the 'resistance' derives (in part, at least) from a scripturally-grounded identity narrative and the 'politeness' derives from the survival instincts of the author."[18] Instead, Starling argues that both the resistant as well as the conformist injunctions in the letter find their source in the author's multi-dimensional usage of scripture. Because of this lacuna among the postcolonialists, he insists that "a more careful examination of the way in which scriptural tradition contributes to the interpretation of empire within 1 Peter" is in order.[19]

In response, Starling offers a "sketch" of how an examination of the scriptural traditions in 1 Peter might proceed through the lens of three themes: fear, patronage, and honor.[20] He suggests that these "forces" were crucial dimensions of the imperial context that shaped the social experience of the addressees.[21] His outline offers some unique and helpful insights. For example, he shows how references to fear in 1 Peter can point to both deference (1:17; 2:18; 3:2) as well as resistance (2:17): "Fear, it seems, is both a prescribed and a prohibited feature of the social relationships of the readers, sometimes within almost the same breath." As important as this observation is, Starling's attempt to show the "Old Testament roots that undergird the exhortations" feels more like his own work of Old Testament biblical theology than it does a demonstration of

---

16. Starling, "1 Peter and the Hermeneutics of Empire," 114.
17. Starling, "1 Peter and the Hermeneutics of Empire," 114.
18. Starling, "1 Peter and the Hermeneutics of Empire," 114.
19. Starling, "1 Peter and the Hermeneutics of Empire," 115.
20. Starling, "1 Peter and the Hermeneutics of Empire," 115.
21. Starling, "1 Peter and the Hermeneutics of Empire," 115.

the way in which the author himself engages scripture. In other words, while he has done a helpful job at showing the way in which Peter himself puts forth deference and defiance as concomitant faithful expressions of loyalty to Jesus, his claim that it is generated from the "deep scriptural well" is weakened because he essentially (creatively) constructs a theology of fear from scriptural traditions that are not found within the letter itself (with the exception of his initial reflection on Ps 34).

His discussion on grace and benefaction is only slightly better in this regard. Starling points to Isa 40 in 1 Pet 1:24–25, makes the generic observation that the letter draws on the "resources of the Old Testament" as per 1 Pet 1:10–12, and suggests allusions to Ps 34:9 in 1 Pet 2:3 and LXX Prov 3:34 in 1 Pet 5:5 respectively. Along the way he makes insightful observations, such as "the purpose of the whole letter ... is best taken as urging in the generosity and faithfulness of God as against trust in earthly resources and defenders"; that 1 Pet 2:11—4:11 "calls on believers to imitate and participate in the generosity of God by acting as benefactors themselves, both within and beyond the community of the church"; and that "faithfulness to Christ may alienate them from patronage networks that might otherwise have offered them some degree of advancement or protection, but the church's own practice of hospitality and benefaction offered an alternative source of security, as a present and visible expression of the kindness of God."[22] But he offers little in terms of demonstrating that Peter develops these themes from the "deep wells of scriptural tradition."[23] Much of the same can be said regarding his reflections on glory. In the end, Starling's approach of analyzing 1 Peter through the prism of the three themes, creative as it is, limits what he can see in the letter and stunts a full discovery of the Peter's scriptural dependence. Along the same lines, as insightful as some of his observations about the message of 1 Peter are, when he does engage with scriptural traditions within the letter, his analysis in not only underdeveloped but it is also done in isolation from the other scriptural traditions found in the text. This move debilitates him from discovering coherence that derives from the many citations and allusions in 1 Peter that together tell a story, a *scripture-rooted* story, that shapes Peter's response not only to empire but also, and perhaps more importantly, to the addressees' social alienation. So, while Starling offers an important challenge—to

22. Starling, "1 Peter and the Hermeneutics of Empire," 122.
23. Starling, "1 Peter and the Hermeneutics of Empire," 124.

attend more carefully to the scriptural traditions that shape the author of 1 Peter's response to empire—in my estimation, he falls short of his own critiques. Ultimately, his sketch does not adequately demonstrate how Peter himself was shaped by the very scripture he draws upon in the letter, and he does not succeed in putting forth a systematic investigation of the hermeneutics of the letter. It is my contention, then, that there is still room for more careful examination of the way in which scripture has shaped 1 Peter's response to the impact of the Roman Empire.

One final study on 1 Peter and empire should be mentioned before moving on to the primary task of this chapter. Wei Hsien Wan's *The Contest for Time and Space in the Roman Imperial Cults and 1 Peter: Reconfiguring the Universe* is the first book-length examination of the way in which the letter engages the claims of Rome and the formation of its subjects. The most important contribution of this study is Wan's creative approach of analyzing and comparing the ideology of 1 Peter and Roman hegemony through the categories of *time* and *space*, showing how temporal and spatial constructions function as truth claims and prescriptions for social and moral ordering. He is careful to make the important point that while we cannot know whether or not the author of 1 Peter intentionally has set out to confront Roman imperial ideology, nevertheless, the notions of time and space developed in the letter collide with, confront, and generate dissonance with the cosmology of Rome, and for that reason the letter can and should be considered to express ideological resistance with respect to Roman imperial claims.

The strength of Wan's study is his analysis of time, both in the construction of Roman imperial ideology in Asia Minor and in 1 Peter. Synthesizing reflections on the new calendar (sometimes called the "Priene inscription") inaugurated in Asia to celebrate the birth of Augustus, the move to attach the political cycles of the local cities to that calendar, and the development and proliferation of imperial festivals, Wan shows that time in Anatolia had become "Roman." The daily, weekly, and monthly rhythms of life, work, rest, and celebration were permeated by the emperor's presence. And this new construction of time gave new occasions for cities in Asia Minor to relate to one another, engendering a shared outlook that "there could be no moment more glorious for the world than the present."[24] In contrast, Wan illuminatingly shows how 1 Peter orients time (present, past, and future) around the revelation of Jesus Christ. For

---

24. Wan, *Contest for Time and Space*, 89.

example, suffering in the present is explained, in part, as a result of the gentiles having not yet "caught up to God's time." And faithfulness in the present is characterized as "knowing what time it is." With respect to the past, Wan shows how 1 Peter claims that the only way to make sense of history itself is to understand it in light of the arrival of Jesus (e.g., 1 Pet 1:10–12); time itself is "christological," and the past is charged with the "now" of Jesus. In showing how in 1 Peter "the past only has meaning relative to the present, illumined as it were by Christ's entrance into the world," Wan underscores that the letter effectively tells a revisionist story of history that excludes the Roman Empire from having any role.[25] First Peter's conception of the future, Wan suggests, is built upon a complex interplay between the hiddenness and permanence of God's reign—both of which confront Roman imperial ideological claims by emphasizing that no human mechanisms (including imperial accomplishments) can secure outcomes outside of God's will, nor can they survive decay.

Wan's exploration of time in 1 Peter is insightful, but could have been enhanced by further exploration of the narrative of 1 Peter, especially the way in which time is constructed in dependence upon the Hebrew Bible, and in particular Jewish restoration ideology.[26] Curiously, in a footnote, he admits that there is a connection between time and narrative, but for an unknown reason chooses not to pursue this observation.[27] In the end, Wan's insights are limited by the same problem that we have seen above—inattention to the way in which the author draws upon scripture. Despite this concern, Wan extends an important invitation for further exploration regarding the identity-formation strategy of 1 Peter by attending more carefully to the letter's construction of time. In a sense, this chapter is a response to this invitation, and in particular how Peter is a tradent for the eschatological Davidic shepherd tradition of the Hebrew Bible.[28]

But before we turn to 1 Peter and its use of scripture, we will need to consider how the claims and demands of Rome are oriented by time. This will not only enable us to see the nuanced and subversive response in 1 Peter but also the way in which it is built on a non-supersessionist

---

25. Wan, *Contest for Time and Space*, 116.

26. For narrative approaches in 1 Peter, see notes 101–5.

27. Wan, *Contest for Time and Space*, 168n43.

28. Though it should be noted that my work on time in Rome imperial ideology and 1 Peter appeared in print before Wan's book-length study. Thus, while I am interacting with Wan in this present chapter, my original investigation was not dependent upon his work.

narrative. In particular, I will underscore that expressions of resistance are not discerned *primarily* in terminology that can be interpreted as having an antithetical relationship to Rome (such as *lord, savior, gospel,* or *kingdom*), but rather that a more profound confrontation can be ascertained at the level of the implied narrative of 1 Peter. That is to say, I will show the manner in which an implicit narrative in 1 Peter turns the public transcript of Roman imperial ideology upside down ("symbolic inversion"). I will develop this, first, by drawing attention to the realized eschatology (or hope) characteristic of Roman imperial ideology, and then by underscoring the way in which 1 Peter defers hope to the *eschaton* by anchoring it within the unfolding narrative of the eschatological Davidic shepherd.

## The "Public Transcript" of Rome's Realized Eschatology

In the past four decades classical historians have produced a wellspring of research that has detailed, to use Scott's terminology, the "public transcripts" of Roman hegemony in the first century CE and the ways in which Rome's message was communicated across the empire. Given the scope and aims of this study, I am only able to highlight three key findings that have emerged from these studies, which will help illuminate the way in which the implicit narrative of 1 Peter confronts and subverts Roman imperial claims by symbolically inverting the public transcripts.

I begin first by calling attention to one of the more remarkable facts about the Roman Empire in the first century CE, namely that it did not maintain imperial order in Asia Minor through military conquest or even military presence.[29] Instead, as a number of classics scholars have thoroughly demonstrated in their own ways,[30] in Asia Minor, Roman imperial order was maintained "through the symbolic arrangement of public space, the presence of images, and the performance of rituals."[31] Said in another way, beginning with Augustus, rather than conquering through military might, Rome mounted an intentional and unprecedented propaganda campaign, especially in Asia Minor, as the means by

---

29. Price notes: "No Roman legion was stationed in the province of Asia during the first three centuries" (*Ritual and Power*, 54).

30. Price, *Ritual and Power*; Ando, *Imperial Ideology and Provincial Loyalty*; Zanker, *Power of Images*; Galinsky, *Augustan Culture*; *Cambridge Companion to the Age of Augustus*; Severy, *Augustus and the Family*.

31. Horsley, *Paul and the Roman Imperial Order*, 6.

which it would extend and secure its dominion.³² In his research on the innovative use of imperial imagery in the age of Augustus, Zanker concludes that "through visual imagery a new mythology of Rome and, for the emperor, a new ritual of power were created. Built on relatively simple foundations, the myth perpetuated itself and transcended the realities of everyday life to project onto future generations the impression that they lived in the best of all possible worlds in the best of all times."³³

Ando has compellingly highlighted the way in which Rome exerted this "soft power" in order to maintain imperial order, in particular by explaining the bi-directional nature of Roman hegemony; that is to say that imperial loyalty was not imposed from some hierarchy in Rome but rather was initiated by local communities, especially in the East, who wished to get in on the prosperity and social recognition that went along with honoring the emperor and the Roman way of life. The responsibility of the empire was to provide peace, security, economic prosperity, social status, and communal honor. In exchange, communities offered loyal allegiance to the emperor, expressed in a variety of forms, not least through the imperial cult, but also in attending imperial festivals, erecting honorary inscriptions, and more generally by upholding the Roman way of life in the provinces.³⁴ As Ando argues, "It was Rome that supplied the initial articulation of the values to which residents of the empire oriented themselves as members of its community, and it was the belief that others shared those values that legitimized Rome's representation of social order. Acquiescence and, ultimately, loyalty to Rome thus required recognition that the Roman construction of society, in relations between provinces, cities, individuals, emperors, and empire, adequately mapped the collective value commitments of its residents."³⁵ Similarly, Galinsky has shown that each community in the empire had something invested in its relationship with Rome. One result of this arrangement, which is

32. Wan, *Contest for Time and Space*, 73–96, 131–55, has arrived at a similar conclusion regarding the scholarship on Roman imperial influence in Asia Minor.

33. Zanker, *Power of Images*, 4.

34. In an otherwise excellent analysis of "time" in Roman imperial ideology in Asia Minor, this is one place, in my estimation, where Wan's study (89–96) could have benefited from the insights of Ando. Wan is right to underscore Price's "ideology of imperial victory," that this, the claim that Rome's rule was predestined, and its future success is inevitable. But what is important to underscore is how that "realized eschatology" is maintained through loyal allegiance to the emperor, the high priest who mediates life to the empire.

35. Ando, *Imperial Ideology and Provincial Loyalty*, 5.

significant for understanding the nature of suffering in 1 Peter, is the fact that anyone who was seen as deviating from this new construct of Roman life, anyone who did not express loyalty to the emperor in the proper way, was seen as a threat to the stability of the community, a stability secured by Rome. "Leadership," Galinsky notes, "is thus inseparable from followers' needs and goals."[36] All this to say that Roman imperial order was sustained, in grand measure, because the adherents—local communities—were convinced that Rome helped them meet their needs and realize their hopes and dreams.

A second significant (and related) conclusion that has emerged from four decades of research on the Roman Empire in the first century CE is a more acute awareness that the symbolization of dominance was undergirded by a *narrative* that professed realized hope for those who loyally aligned themselves with Rome and all that it represented (or at least promised). Through this complex ideological program that included imperial temples, festivals, statues, shrines and monuments, coins, theater, and literature, first-century inhabitants of Asia Minor were, in a variety of manners, unrelentingly told that they were fortunate to live in a unique moment in history, a time of restoration, peace, and prosperity. Although imperial worship was expressed in a number of ways, as the archaeological, epigraphic, and literary evidence bears witness, Rome's narrative remained constant: thanks to one man, a man sent by god (or the gods), a new age had dawned. No longer were Romans being punished for their impiety and their disregard for the ways of their forefathers. For, through this one man, the enemy had been defeated, *pax deorum* (peace with the gods) had been restored, and prosperity awaited all who proved themselves loyal to the new lord and savior of the universe. Two important inscriptions illustrate the consistency of this narrative of realized hope: the *Res Gestae* and the Priene calendar inscription.[37]

Zanker and Ramage independently have argued that the *Res Gestae* is perhaps the most important artifact to help us understand the ideology of the Roman Empire in the first century CE.[38] The inscription, which tells the story of how Augustus restored peace and prosperity to the world, was distributed throughout the empire. It is certainly significant for our discussion that our only extant remains of the *Res Gestae* are from Asia

36. Galinsky, *Cambridge Companion to the Age of Augustus*, 6.

37. Wan has an excellent discussion of both in *Contest of Time and Space*, 74–82, 143–49.

38. Zanker, *Power of Images*; Ramage, *Nature and Purpose of Res Gestae*.

Minor (Ancyra, Apollonia, and Pisidian Antioch). The Priene calendar inscription narrates a more condensed version of this narrative: providence has given the world Augustus, sending him as a savior, who has established a dynasty that brings peace and order to the world. According to Price, all of Asia Minor instituted a calendar that began the New Year on Augustus's birthday with similar inscriptions that declared that a new epoch, a golden age, was initiated with Augustus.[39]

Finally, classics historians have demonstrated that the aggressive propaganda program along with its consistent narrative of realized eschatology, which was initiated by Augustus, was foundational for the rest of the Julio-Claudian and Flavian lines and was appropriated in order to establish a narrative of imperial dynasty.[40] That is to say that all of the emperors that followed Augustus in the first century, in one way or another, appealed to the dawning of the Golden Age initiated by Augustus as a way of legitimizing their own rule and in an effort to compel loyalty that would in turn generate peace, security, and prosperity for all.[41]

## Conclusion

For the aims of this chapter, it is important to underscore four implications of this reflection on the "public script" of Roman imperial realized eschatology. First, as Wan has pointed out, the conception of time shaped the daily, weekly, and monthly rhythms of life, work, rest, and celebration for all in Asia Minor (to varying degrees no doubt), and this time was permeated by the emperor's presence. Second, this new construction of time gave new occasions for cities in Asia Minor to relate to one another, engendering a shared outlook that "there could be no moment more glorious for the world than the present."[42] Third, this shared outlook regarding the realized eschatology of Roman imperial ideology *unified* Asia Minor in ways it had never been before; it *provided a context for*

39. See Wan, *Contest of Time and Space*, 76–88, for the way in which this calendar was implemented in local governance and imperial festivals.

40. See especially Severy, *Augustus and the Family*; Millar, "Ovid and the Domus Augusta"; Crossan and Reed, *In Search of Paul*, 142–52.

41. Galinsky, *Cambridge Companion to the Age of Augustus*, argues that under Augustus a foundation was laid for a system of belief that lasted for more than two hundred years, which would also include the Flavian dynasty. According to scholarly consensus, 1 Peter was written sometime between 64–92 CE.

42. Wan, *Contest for Time and Space*, 89.

*membership and belonging* for inhabitants spread across thousands of miles that did not exist prior.[43] Finally, this membership enabled Roman citizens of all kinds living in the provinces of Asia Minor *to participate in the maintenance of peace, security, economic prosperity, social status, and communal honor.* In this regard, Roman imperial ideology *empowered* Asia Minor's inhabitants to be privileged mediators of the promises and power of Rome. This dynamic of belonging and maintenance helps us to understand more fully (1) why gentiles in Asia Minor could become so hostile to fellow gentile compatriots who, by professing allegiance to Jesus, were at the same time seen to be dishonoring the emperor and thus threatening the peace and prosperity of the community; and (2) the profound sense of disorientation and alienation gentile Jesus-followers would have felt as they were excluded from the Golden Age and all that it promised.

## The Davidic Imperial Narrative of Hope in 1 Peter

This narrative of belonging to Rome's Golden Age is the setting in which Peter seeks to help Anatolian followers of Jesus negotiate their professed loyalty to Jesus Christ and its concomitant consequences. As we will see, in a variety of manners, one of the strategies of 1 Peter is to encourage the addressees to distance themselves from the false (realized) hopes of the Roman Empire and instead to inhabit a different way of life that is grounded in a different narrative with a different *telos*.

Horrell has demonstrated the way in which the letter-frame sets the tone for the manner in which the readers ought to understand their circumstances and identity.[44] In the opening of the letter, Peter strategically refers to the recipients as "elect sojourners [i.e., chosen refugees] of the Diaspora" (1 Pet 1:1). Here Peter draws on the Jewish experience of being exiled and exported to foreign lands (the Diaspora or dispersion) in order to depict the addressees, who seem to be native to Asia Minor, as those who must now think of themselves as outsiders, foreigners in their own land.[45] Horrell encourages us to read this opening depiction of the addressees along with the closing verses of the letter, in which Peter sends

43. Wan, *Contest for Time and Space*, 61–62.
44. Horrell, "Between Conformity and Resistance," 124–29.
45. See Horrell, "Between Conformity and Resistance," 127, for a condensed argument regarding the alienation of the addressees which is a result of their conversion.

greetings to the Anatolian followers of Jesus from "Babylon" (1 Pet 5:13). There is a strong consensus that 1 Peter was written in Rome and that the Babylon reference is meant to characterize Rome in a particularly negative light. Since the book of Daniel, Babylon was used by Jews as a symbolic name for the world power that oppressed and displaced God's people. It is likely that Peter refers to Rome as Babylon in order to align himself and his readers to a different narrative about Rome, one that claims that this seemingly invincible, universal power, whose influence upon the world seems to negate the very claims that Peter is making in his letter (i.e., that restoration has begun in Jesus Christ), will in fact be judged and destroyed because it has oppressed the people of God and opposed God's ways. In other words, what lies behind the Babylon reference is a call to interpret Rome's rule as fleeting, its judgment and destruction as pending. Thus, while to some the reference to Babylon might work to conceal the identity of Rome, for those who have ears to hear, the term "Babylon" does not actually conceal but rather reveals the real nature of Rome's alluring and tenuous reign.[46] Doering advances a similar point: "If Rome were indeed meant here [1 Pet 5:13], it would be more likely a *qualification* of Rome as ultimately responsible for persecution and dispersion, than an oblique reference by code name."[47] As Horrell has noted, this "view of the empire as godless power, scattering and displacing the people of God, stands in stark contrast to the narrative promoted by the architects of empire, for whom their divinely appointed vocation is to bring peace to warring tribes and civilization to uncultured barbarians."[48] This is yet another example of Peter encouraging his addressees to adopt an Israel-centric perspective in order to understand their uniquely gentile circumstances.

## Hope Deferred

But what perhaps is most significant about the manner in which the letter seeks to orient the readers, especially in light of Rome's public script of realized eschatology, is the fact that real, enduring hope is deferred to

---

46. It should be noted that the Book of Revelation also appropriates apocalyptic imagery and refers to Rome as Babylon with a similar aim in view.

47. Doering, *First Peter as Early Christian Diaspora Letter*, 233. For further comments on Babylon, see pages 7–8, 77–80, in this volume. See also Williams and Horrell, *1 Peter*, 112–14, 639–46.

48. Horrell, "Between Conformity and Resistance," 126–27.

the *eschaton*. We can see this most immediately in the opening section of the letter (1 Pet 1:3-9), where the readers are reminded that God is to be praised for a variety of reasons, all which center around a hope that is to be fully actualized at the return of Jesus Christ. Those who align themselves with the resurrected and ascended Jesus Christ, Peter writes, are born anew to a living hope, to an inheritance that will not perish, to a prepared salvation that will be revealed in the last time (1:3-5). Furthermore, Peter explains, those who love and believe in Jesus Christ rejoice with inexpressible joy because the outcome of their faithfulness will result in the salvation of their souls (1:8-9).

After providing his readers with an orientation that is foundationally eschatological in nature, Peter then offers his first exhortation in what most consider to be the opening line of the body of the letter: "Set all your hope on the grace that Jesus Christ will bring you when he is revealed [i.e., 'when he returns']" (1:13). The importance of having a legitimate, enduring hope seems to be a primary concern of Peter elsewhere in the letter as well. In 1 Pet 1:21, he reminds his readers that the resurrection of Jesus from the dead means that their faith and hope are in God; in 1 Pet 2:11, his exhortation to abstain from the passions of the flesh is based, in part, on the fact that God will vindicate their good behavior on the day of his visitation; in 1 Pet 3:15, addressees who are undergoing hardship because of their loyalty to Jesus Christ are exhorted to be prepared to make a defense for the *hope* that they share among one another; and finally, the letter-body ends with one final word of hope: readers are encouraged to endure suffering "for a little while" because the God of all grace will restore and establish them in due course (1 Pet 5:10).

This optimism, however, is tempered with the reminder that this living hope, this incorruptible inheritance, this already-prepared salvation is yet to dawn; instead, it will be realized through fiery trials that will test one's true loyalty (1 Pet 1:6-7; 4:12-17). In other words, Peter portrays his readers as living in a period of transition, or liminality. And this in-between period is characterized as a time in which faithful followers of the Christ must (δεῖ; "it is necessary") pass through various trials (1 Pet 1:6), though not without God's protection (1 Pet 1:5). In 1 Pet 1:7 this transition period of various trials is further characterized as a time in which their "proven faithfulness" (τὸ δοκίμιον ὑμῶν τῆς πίστεως) will result in them being honored at the revelation (return) of Jesus Christ.[49]

49. The genitive τῆς πίστεως in the phrase τὸ δοκίμιον ὑμῶν τῆς πίστεως is best understood as an attributed genitive. As such, the head noun, τὸ δοκίμιον (understood

In light of this brief survey, it is not difficult to perceive a rudimentary narrative of deferred hope that undergirds the discourse of 1 Peter, nor is it too much to say that the schema of deferred hope in 1 Peter competes with, even subverts, the public transcript of the realized Golden Age of the Roman Empire. In recent years a number of scholars have underscored (some more explicitly than others) that a narrative underlies the theological orientation that Peter offers.[50] Bechtler, for example, demonstrates that a foundational element of Peter's strategy for helping the addressees deal with their alienation and suffering is essentially narrative in character.[51] In particular, Bechtler reveals the manner in which Peter constructs, as he calls it, a "symbolic universe" of temporal liminality:[52] "1 Peter presupposes a temporal context for Christian life that is liminal in the literal sense; the addressees are living in that ambiguous time between Christ's death and resurrection on the one hand and the imminent manifestation of the fullness of his glory on the other."[53]

In his work on the paraenetic strategies of 1 Peter, Dryden is much more explicit about the narrative aspects within the letter:

> The author's aim in 1 Peter is to encourage young Anatolian churches to live out their beliefs in the midst of social hostility.... Before giving them moral instructions, he gives them a moral vision that places them within a moral universe. He does this by depicting not simply a theological worldview, but a *narrative* theological worldview. He is not giving simply ontological statements about how the world is, but weaving together a *story* of how the world is; and this becomes the context for their own

---

as "genuineness as result of a test") functions as the adjective, and the genitive, τῆς πίστεως, syntactically speaking, functions as the head noun; the phrase, then, should be translated "proven faithfulness." Read in this way, 1 Pet 1:7 highlights confidence that Peter has in the proven fidelity of the readers with respect to their allegiance to Jesus in the midst of trials. Thus, the basis for rejoicing is not because of the inherent value of trials (e.g., Jas 1:2–4), but rather because of the certainty of salvation for those who maintain faithfulness.

50. For a helpful survey of narrative approaches to 1 Peter, see Joseph, *Narratological Reading of 1 Peter*, 13–25.

51. Bechtler, *Following in His Steps*. He does not, however, use the terminology "narrative."

52. "1 Peter's depiction of the temporal liminality of Christian existence provides part of the letter's answer" to their social liminality (Bechtler, *Following in His Steps*, 126). To be clear, Bechtler does not grant Petrine authorship and would thus not attribute this strategy to the historical Peter.

53. Bechtler, *Following in His Steps*, 126.

> stories as individuals and as a community. This is the sense in which the narrative world of 1 Peter contextualizes the lives of the readers and their moral choices. It places their lives within a story of the world conceived on the largest possible canvas—a story of creation, fall, redemption, and consummation. What God is doing in their midst is part of the grand narrative of his plan to redeem his creation and a people for himself. Thus, the world is not spinning aimlessly, but headed toward a goal. In this context, daily choices, as the means by which they appropriate their salvation in the present, take on truly cosmic significance.[54]

He further underscores that

> the author only refers to key elements of the story of salvation to evoke an entire narrative worldview that is familiar to both author and readers. This sort of shorthand description of key elements is, as we have noted before, typical of paraenesis, where only a few key points need to be reviewed and emphasized. Thus, what we have access to in the epistle is that portion of the entire presupposed narrative theological worldview that the author found it useful to highlight.[55]

Eugene Boring has shown that even though it is an epistle, 1 Peter nevertheless "projects a narrative world composed of all events it assumes to be real—compelling serious readers/hearers to examine their own understanding of reality, and indirectly inviting them to live their lives in the world projected by the letter."[56] In evaluating his mapping of the narrative world of 1 Peter, he concludes that when we pay attention to what is highlighted regarding the past, present, and future of the epistle, it enables us to see how the author challenges the addressees with an alternative vision of reality rather than a list of commands.[57]

This recognition that there is a narrative within the epistle of 1 Peter is significant for the aims of this chapter (and the overall thesis of the book), in part because confrontation or subversion is often best discerned at the level of competing narratives, but more importantly because of what that narrative implies about God's ongoing commitment to Israel—as we will see in due course. Although my own reading of 1 Peter resonates with many of the observations made by Bechtler, Dryden, and Boring, I regard

---

54. Dryden, *Theology and Ethics in 1 Peter*, 64.
55. Dryden, *Theology and Ethics in 1 Peter*, 66.
56. Boring, "Narrative Dynamics in First Peter," 8.
57. Boring, "Narrative Dynamics in First Peter," 36.

each account in its own way to be too generic: that is, each describes in a one-dimensional fashion a narrative that has more texture and depth than has been indicated or allowed for. Defining the narrative projected in 1 Peter with generic terms like creation, fall, redemption, and consummation (as Dryden has) is akin to identifying the kingdom and perhaps the phylum of a living creature, but electing to say nothing about its class, order, family, genus, or species when such an identification can be made. In particular, narrative approaches to 1 Peter at times have neglected to connect the surface narrative to its dependence upon Israel's scriptures and, more specifically, to the prominent expectations of Jewish restoration eschatology[58]—this in spite of the predominance of Hebrew Bible citations in the letter.[59] One recent study on narrative in 1 Peter has been better in this regard. Joseph's *A Narratological Reading of 1 Peter* aims at employing narratology to the letter in order to "bring to light the significance of 1 Peter's christological understanding of God's actions on behalf of Israel for its audience."[60] In his study, Joseph attends more carefully to 1 Peter's dependence upon scripture, concluding that "the author's extensive use of the Old Testament assumes a narrative substructure in the epistle which undergirds the message conveyed therein."[61] Joseph argues that this narrative substructure of the letter is held together by a "fabula" that consists of four elements: election, suffering, faithful response, and vindication.[62] While he has moved us in the right direction, pointing us to one important layer of the narrative, in my estimation, Joseph has not discerned the way in which at a more profound level the narrative in 1 Peter is driven, undergirded, and animated by scripture itself and not something else. In other words, instead of discerning a story in 1 Peter that derives from the scripture cited or alluded to in the letter, Joseph seems to regard 1 Peter's engagement with scripture to be more like proof

---

58. Regarding this point, Boring contends, "There is no connected 'story of Israel' implied by the discourse," but he reaches this conclusion because he insists that "the interpreter should not suppose that references to a biblical figure or event implies the larger narrative of which it is a part, and that these supposed narrative lines are all connected into one grand story" ("Narrative Dynamics in First Peter," 27–28).

59. My point is not to minimize Bechtler, Dryden, and Boring or their work but rather to show where their work, helpful as it is, can be taken further. For a survey of the study of the use of scripture in 1 Peter in the modern era, see Sargent, *Written to Serve*, 7–16.

60. Joseph, *Narratological Reading of 1 Peter*, 1, 178.

61. Joseph, *Narratological Reading of 1 Peter*, 179.

62. Joseph, *Narratological Reading of 1 Peter*, 180.

texting in order to support a "pattern" of events: "An inquiry into 1 Peter has shown that the pattern of events that the audience is experiencing, including what the author urges them to look forward to, was similar, though not identical, to a pattern of events that occurred in the lives of Israel and Jesus."[63] In this regard, scripture in 1 Peter has a secondary role. For, according to Joseph's account, it is the "pattern of experiences" of the addressees that generates the fabula which has been constructed by the author. The author then seeks to show how these patterns correspond to the pattern of events that occurred in the lives of Israel and Jesus respectively.[64] In this the next section, I hope to show that the narrative of 1 Peter is more derivative of scripture than Joseph has discerned and that the personal narratives of the addressees projected at times within the letter are enveloped by a larger narrative. For ultimately, this authoritative apostolic correspondence invites, or we might even say welcomes, the addressees to participate in the continuation of God's faithfulness to Israel.[65]

---

63. Joseph, *Narratological Reading of 1 Peter*, 180.

64. For further critiques of Joseph's methodology and argumentation, see Darian Lockett, "Review of *A Narratological Reading of 1 Peter*."

65. On this theme of continuity, Benjamin Sargent has offered an extensive discussion of the way in which 1 Pet 1:10–12 offers insight into how scripture is interpreted in the letter. His most important contribution, developed through a meticulous analysis of 1 Pet 1:10–12 and fresh engagement with all the citations and allusions in the letter, is to show that "the kerygmatic function of Scripture is subordinated to its paraenetic function" (Sargent, *Written to Serve*, 48). In other words, Sargent argues that "the primary function of Scripture is to justify, or simply provide, paraenesis since the Prophets spoke to serve the very communities to whom Peter writes" (49). But in developing this important observation that scripture in 1 Peter serves ecclesiological ends, he also contends that 1 Pet 1:10–12 posits the discontinuity between the communities being served by 1 Peter and the communities to which these Old Testament texts were written to (and with no reflection on the implications of this in terms of ecclesiology). Said in another way, he suggests that the narrative substructure of 1 Peter does not place the addressees within God's ongoing dealings with Israel. This conclusion, however, is puzzling, not least because it is not warranted by the exegesis of 1 Pet 1:10–12 and is not demanded by his analysis of the way in which scripture is presented in 1 Peter. What is more, in chapter 1, 22–25, I've shown that in order to make sense of the way in which God is referred to in 1 Peter, one must attend to a rudimentary implicit narrative. See Egan, *Ecclesiology and the Scriptural Narrative of 1 Peter*, who, like Sargent, analyzes 1 Pet 1:10–12 in order to discern the hermeneutical implications for scripture usage in the letter, and who also underscores the ecclesiological ends of the use of the Old Testament in 1 Peter, but who shows that the text projects continuity between the addressees and God's dealing with Israel.

## A New Exodus/Wilderness Journey with the God of Israel

In the course of discussing the problems with reading 1 Peter (or, we might say, exploring the potentially problematic identify-formation strategies in the letter), and in the process of reexamining the foundational assumptions of the consensus position regarding the ethnic identity of 1 Peter's addressees, we caught glimpses of the way in which the implicit narrative of 1 Peter connects the addressees to the God of Israel's ongoing covenant fidelity with Israel. Rather than rehearse what we have already considered, I will highlight the main findings.

First, as we pay attention to the assumptions made about God and the way in which God is (directly and implicitly) referred to in the letter, we see that the author grounds all claims about reality in terms of God's self-revelation and promises to Israel. We are also attuned to the fact that the particular God of 1 Peter is said to have raised Jesus Christ from the dead, a hope that is unique to the people of Israel. Our brief survey of some of the Old Testament citations, allusions, and imagery in the letter revealed that the accomplishments of this particular God that raised Jesus Christ from the dead are stated in terms that are unique to Israel's way of understanding what God is up to in the world and what he has promised for his people. We also were reminded that to trust in Jesus is to put one's hope in the God of Israel (1:21), and that this hope involves seeing the world the way a Jew would see the world, embracing the metanarrative of Israelite self-understanding. The addressees are seamlessly placed within the story of God's redemption of Israel through the Christ and incorporated into the hopes of Isaiah, Hosea, Ezekiel, and the Psalmists. In short, they are called to orient their lives around a particular hope (1 Pet 1:13; 3:15) that would prove to be utterly meaningless were Israel to be expropriated. Foundational to this metanarrative of hope is the expectation that this God of Israel is going to judge not only his people but the entire world, vindicating those who remain loyal to the one true God and his Messiah. Additionally, we discovered that the God of Israel—who is characterized as the creator of the world and the one who formed, covenanted, and remains faithful to Israel—has acted decisively in and through Jesus to bring to culmination the promises he made to Israel for the sake of the whole world. In other words, what this particular God has revealed about himself in Jesus is to be understood within the context of and in continuity with what he has revealed about himself through his covenant and history with Israel (e.g., 1 Pet 1:10–12).

What is more, this covenantal history with Israel has been inscripturated in the Hebrew Bible (or what Christians refer to as the Old Testament), and when the author of 1 Peter appeals to the Hebrew scriptures to establish a point about, for example, Christology or the mission of the people of God, he is more foundationally appealing to the reliability and trustworthiness of this God of Israel. To be a new people (1 Pet 2:9–10), they must see themselves as a part of a new story, belonging to a people and a history that has preceded them. Importantly, the way in which the author of 1 Peter narrates the story of God in the letter underscores the *telos* of God's dealings with Israel (as expressed in the Abrahamic covenant), namely the blessing of eternal fellowship with God through Israel for all the nations. Ultimately, this is a uniquely Israel-centric way of telling the story of the world, of talking about who God is, and of describing what this God is up to in the world. The addressees are being called to embrace a uniquely Israel-centric way of conceiving of and being in the world. Or we might say, the implicit narrative of 1 Peter forces gentile followers of Jesus to understand and articulate their own identity in light of God's ongoing fidelity to the people of Israel.

Second, as we questioned the validity of one of the foundational assumptions of the consensus regarding the ethnic identity of 1 Peter, I offered an analysis of 1 Pet 1:14, 18, 21, and 2:10 in their literary context. I showed how these passages contained eschatological restoration expectations common within first-century Judaism. In particular, I highlighted how Peter describes the addressees as being gathered in order to undertake a new exodus/wilderness journey towards their promised inheritance, but that this journey will include a variety of trials that will test their fidelity to Jesus. The appropriation of Passover lamb imagery (1:19), the call to "be holy" (1:15), and the appeal to LXX Ps 33 and Exod 19:5–6, read through the lens of Isa 40 and 43, and Hos 2, all serve to emplace these ἐκλεκτοί παρεπίδημοι διασπορᾶς (1 Pet 1:1) within God's ongoing faithfulness to Israel, again, drawing on terminology that is unique to Israel's way of understanding what God is up to in the world, what he has promised for his people, and what he is accomplishing through Jesus.[66]

---

66. Scholars of 1 Peter often have wondered whether the gentile addressees could have comprehended Peter's complex usage of Israel's history and scripture. This in turn has raised questions about whether this strategy was the best, given the audience. Perhaps Peter is committed to the language of the Hebrew Bible (events, citations, allusions, etc.) neither for its poetic merit nor because it is beneficial for making analogies, but precisely because it is the *most accurate account* of what God is doing presently in the world and with these addressees.

We will return to this theme of new exodus briefly, because, as we will see, the gathering of these "elect sojourners" for the wilderness journey is said to have been accomplished by the "shepherd and guardian" of their souls (1 Pet 2:25).

## Following the Footsteps of 1 Peter's Eschatological Davidic Shepherd-King

In what remains, I will sketch the manner in which the competing narrative of 1 Peter is Davidic at its core.[67] That is to say that the accomplishments of Jesus Christ (whether past or future), the identity of the Jesus-followers in Asia Minor, and the rationale for "Christian" suffering (that is, suffering because of one's allegiance to Jesus Christ) are all explained in relation to the eschatological Davidic shepherd tradition, especially as it is mediated through Zechariah 9–14.[68]

When tuned to this prominent tradition within the prophetic material of the Old Testament, there is a sense in which the eschatological Davidic shepherd program is in one sense nowhere explicitly mentioned and yet everywhere present in 1 Peter. For example, in the central section of the letter (1 Pet 2:4–10), which many scholars have noted is where the foundational indicatives of the letter are found, Jesus is presented as

67. It is important to underscore that in this section, I will not say everything that there is to say about the narrative of 1 Peter. Instead, I will be highlighting one aspect of a more comprehensive narrative that has too often been neglected.

68. Given the letter's situational focus (chapter 3) and the fact that we have very limited knowledge of the social setting, it is unclear precisely how the 1 Peter addressees would have gained access to Israel's scriptural tradition. The argument I put forth in chapter 3 for an exclusively gentile (ideal or imagined) audience does not exclude the possibility that these addressees where in some way connected to a synagogue, though again, we lack evidence of any of the common disputes that arose when gentiles gathered with Jews (probably because of the purpose of the letter). Whatever the precise setting may be, given the proliferation of Old Testament citations and uncontested allusions in the letter, it seems likely that Peter assumed that his addressees would have access to these traditions and perhaps also to interpreters with varying levels of familiarity with such texts as Zechariah 9–14. What is more, as I demonstrated in an earlier study (*Eschatology of 1 Peter*, 23–78), given the familiarity of the Passion Narratives in the early church and the variety of ways in which Zechariah is appropriated therein, it is likely that followers of Jesus in the middle-to-late first century not only would have been familiar with Zechariah 9–14, but also that they would have looked to it to make sense of suffering. For a helpful exploration of the socio-locals available to gentiles in which they might learn about the Hebrew Bible, and especially the eschatological pilgrimage tradition, see Tucker and Cirafesi, "Paul's Segmentary Grammar of Identity."

the chosen and precious stone of stumbling, which the builders have rejected. These references, sometimes referred to as the "stone catena" (Isa 28:16; Ps 118:22; Isa 8:14), have an interpretive history in certain forms of Judaism and in the early Jesus movement that are associated with God's promise to restore his people through an eschatological Davidic king.[69] Additionally, the "house" language of 1 Pet 2:5 (and 4:14-17), while often regarded to be temple imagery, can also be understood as a reference to the re-establishment of the Davidic house (or dynasty) in keeping with the promises found in such places as 2 Sam 7, Ps 132, and Zech 12:9-10.[70] But it is the author's identification of Jesus as the "shepherd" who "returns" straying sheep by giving up his life that is the most direct reference to the eschatological Davidic shepherd tradition (1 Pet 2:25). Prior to Jesus, no Jewish leader ever bore the title "shepherd," which as we will soon see, was exclusively reserved for the eschatological Davidic king. In order to discern the manner in which these eschatological Davidic shepherd themes in 1 Peter are brought together in a coherent pattern, we must first briefly consider the development of the eschatological Davidic shepherd tradition in the prophets and the way in which it was received, especially in the Passion Narratives, and briefly in the Book of Revelation.

*The eschatological Davidic shepherd tradition and its reception*

In the historical books of the Old Testament and in the Psalms, the title "shepherd" is reserved for YHWH alone, and although Israel's leadership (most notably that of Moses and David) was periodically described with shepherding terminology, the title of shepherd seems to have been intentionally avoided.[71] In the prophetic material the term "shepherd" has three distinct reference points that are all integrally connected to Israel's restoration from exile, often depicted in terms of a new exodus and accomplished in conjunction with the rule of a Davidic shepherd-king.[72]

69. See, for example, Kim, "Role of Zechariah in the Self-Identification of Jesus."

70. See Hillyer, "Spiritual Milk"; Liebengood, *Eschatology of 1 Peter*, 164-70. See also chapter 6 for further development of this theme.

71. For references of YHWH as the shepherd of Israel, see Gen 48:15; 49:24; Pss 23; 28:9; 74:1; 77:20; 78:52-55; 79:13; 80:1; 95:7. For shepherding terminology used to describe Moses' leadership, see Ps 77:20; Hos 12:13. For shepherding terminology to describe David's leadership, see, e.g., 2 Sam 7:8; Ps 78:70-71.

72. For a full development of this, see Laniak, *Shepherds After My Own Heart*,

The prophets announce that (1) Yhwh is the good shepherd[73] who will judge the (2) bad shepherds (unnamed and unfaithful Jewish leadership), return the straying sheep of Israel, renew his covenant, and appoint for his people (3) a new shepherd (king) from the house of David, who will bring about healing and restoration, and usher in the new age of universal peace. It can be shown that the shepherd tradition of the prophets, with its eschatological framework, is first developed in Jeremiah 23, elaborated in Ezekiel 34,[74] and then is significantly expanded in Zechariah 9–14, where Yhwh not only affirms the unworthiness of the "bad shepherds," but also reveals that the people themselves share responsibility for the deterioration of the community (11:7–9). In what appears to be a reversal of the shepherd tradition of Jeremiah 23/Ezekiel 34, the coming of Yhwh's appointed good shepherd does not bring immediate restoration and renewal; instead, the shepherd will be rejected by not only the leaders but also by the people (11:4–14) and struck by a sword (13:7). His affliction will bring about a time of trouble, described as "fiery trials"—even for those who are faithful. The remnant "one-third" that makes it through the time of trouble will be re-established with Yhwh through covenant renewal (13:8–9; cf. 1 Pet 2:9–10) and will worship him in purity as a renewed "house" (14:3–20; cf. 1 Pet 2:4–5; 4:14–17).

Reception of the eschatological Davidic shepherd program of Zechariah 9–14 in the Jewish Second Temple period was sparse, though there is enough evidence to suggest that it was known and available for theological reflection, but without any uniform approach for interpreting and appropriating the eschatological program.[75] In contrast, in the early Jesus movement, Zechariah 9–14 became a prominent and integral source in the Passion Narratives for reflection on Jesus' rejection, suffering, and death.[76] For example, a number of key events in the week leading up to the crucifixion of Jesus are linked to Zechariah 9–14: "the

---

115–70. For a full development of the Davidic shepherd-king tradition, see Willitts, *Matthew's Messianic Shepherd-King*, 58–67; Chae, *Jesus and the Eschatological Davidic Shepherd*, 32–94.

73. For Yhwh as shepherd in the prophetic material, see Mic 2:12–13; 4:6–8; 7:14–15; Isa 40:10–11; 49:9–13; Jer 23:2; 31:10; 50:19; Ezek 34:31; implied in Zech 9:16; 10:8–10.

74. Echoes of the Jeremiah 23/Ezekiel 34 tradition can be found in Isa 40:1–11 and Mic 4:14—5:5.

75. See Liebengood, *Eschatology of 1 Peter*, 52–61.

76. For a detailed analysis of the reception of Zechariah 9–14 in the Passion Narratives, see Liebengood, *Eschatology of 1 Peter*, 61–78.

triumphal entry" (Mark 11:1-11; Matt 21:5; Luke 19:29-40; John 12:15—Zech 9:9-10), the thirty silver pieces, Judas' betrayal, and the rejection of Jesus by the Jewish leaders (Matt 27:9-10; 26:15—Zech 11:12-13), the prediction of Jesus' death (Mark 14:27-28; Matt 26:31-32; John 10:11; 15:17—Zech 13:7), the prediction of the disciples' desertion (Mark 14:27-28; Matt 26:31-32; John 16:32-33—Zech 13:7-9), the piercing of Jesus' side (John 19:34-37—Zech 12:10), the mourning at the crucifixion (Luke 23:27—Zech 12:11-14), the flowing of living waters (i.e., forgiveness of sins; John 19:34—Zech 13:1; 14:8), and Jesus' actions in the temple (Mark 11:15-17; Matt 21:12-13; John 2:16) all find scriptural antecedents in Zechariah 9-14.

A detailed analysis of the use of Zechariah 9-14 in the Passion Narratives yields several other important conclusions for the argument I will make below. First, although each Evangelist looked to Zechariah 9-14 in order to explain and provide scriptural warrant for the events surrounding the death of Jesus, they each did so in slightly different ways.[77] There was not, in other words, a monolithic approach to interpreting Zechariah 9-14. What they held in common, however, was the tendency to read Zechariah 9-14 as a foundational narrative that offered an eschatological program. Each Evangelist, however, connected different dots in that narrative. Mark, for example, connected the figures of Zech 9:9 and 13:7 to Jesus' entry into Jerusalem and his betrayal and death. Matthew and John went one step further and interpreted the figures of Zech 9:9; 12:10; and 13:7 as representing the same figure in the narrative of Zechariah 9-14; this figure, they argue, points to Jesus.[78] Second, all indications are that the early followers of Jesus perceived in Zechariah 9-14 an eschatological program that included the advent of the Messiah on a donkey, his betrayal and rejection, his tragic death, the scattering of his followers, a tribulation period prior to restoration, and forgiveness of sins that would enable Israel's restoration.[79] Third, Zechariah 9-14 was read alongside

77. In my view, this point is not emphasized enough in the studies of Dodd, *According to the Scriptures*, and Black, "Rejected and Slain Messiah." They, instead, tend to present an aggregate reading of Zechariah 9-14 based upon all of the constituent parts found in Matthew, Mark, Luke, and John (e.g., Black's comment that "the early church read Zech 9-14 as a whole" ["Rejected and Slain Messiah," 98]).

78. Moo, *Old Testament in the Passion Narratives*, 173. Such a reading of 9:9; 12:10; and 13:7 likely demonstrates dependence upon the Hebrew text-plot, since it would difficult (though not impossible) to arrive at such a conclusion by reading the LXX or the Targum of Zechariah.

79. Dodd, *According to the Scriptures*, 64-67; Black, "Rejected and Slain Messiah," 239; Mitchell, *Message of the Psalter*, 237.

several other Old Testament passages—most notably Isaiah 40–66, the Psalms, and Daniel. Thus, although the eschatological program of Zechariah 9–14 is foundational to the Passion Narratives, it did not exclude other relevant passages in the Old Testament, and in fact appeared to encourage input from them. Together then, Zechariah 9–14 and other key Old Testament passages provided mutual interpretation of Jesus' suffering and death. Finally, in the Passion Narratives, shepherd imagery, and especially the designation of Jesus as the shepherd, are integrally related to the eschatological Davidic shepherd program of Zechariah 9–14. Given the familiarity of these Passion Narratives amongst the early followers of Jesus and the variety of ways in which Zechariah 9–14 is appropriated by these narratives, it is likely that: (a) many would readily hear allusions to Zechariah 9–14 when they were made;[80] (b) some teachers (such as the author of 1 Peter) in the early Jesus movement would look to Zechariah 9–14 as an aid in explaining the meaning of Christ's suffering and death; and (c) those familiar with the Passion Narratives might be inclined to associate shepherd imagery with the eschatological program of Zechariah 9–14.

While Zechariah 9–14 is appropriated in the Passion Narratives almost exclusively in order to understand the events leading up to the death of Jesus and how they could be a part of God's plan of restoration, in the Book of Revelation, Zechariah 9–14 is seen to speak beyond the death of Jesus, to the culmination of restoration, that is, to things that have yet to come.[81]

### The "shepherd" of 1 Peter 2:25 and Zechariah 9–14

Primopetrine scholars consider 1 Peter 2:21–25 to be one of the most significant passages for understanding the letter as a whole.[82] Some have gone as far as regarding it as "the heart of 1 Peter's Christology,"[83] and

---

80. See Thompson's helpful study on early epistolary usage of the Jesus Tradition (JT), which includes the Passion Narratives (*Clothed with Christ*, 37–63). Thompson concludes his survey of the usage of JT in non-Pauline epistles and the early church fathers by noting that "the readers' knowledge of JT was assumed as fundamental to their Christian instruction" (63).

81. See Jauhiainen, *Use of Zechariah in Revelation*, for how Zechariah 9–14 is drawn upon in the Book of Revelation.

82. Brox, *1. Petrusbrief*, 128.

83. Jobes, *1 Peter* [1st ed.], 192.

the place where "all the literary characteristics of the letter converge."[84] The passage begins by exhorting followers of Jesus[85] to endure unjust suffering, since "Christ also suffered for you" (2:21). This exhortation is followed by an appropriation of Isaiah 53, which is used to present Jesus' innocent suffering and subsequent death (2:22-23) as a means of "healing" (2:24). It concludes by describing Anatolian Christians as straying sheep who have now been returned to the shepherd and overseer of their souls (2:25).

Scholarly inquiry of this passage has almost exclusively focused on issues pertaining to the appropriation of Isaiah 53 and its relation to Jesus.[86] While there is certainly warrant for this fruitful line of research, other important features in the passage have been neglected. In particular, there has been very little attention given to the shepherd imagery found in 2:25, and even less reflection on why this imagery has been combined with the imagery of the "suffering servant" of Isaiah 53.[87] To date, the most tenable proposal for this combination of images is found in the works of Elena Bosetti, Mark Dubis, John Elliott, and Karen Jobes. They suggest that the suffering servant of Isaiah 53 is intentionally conflated with the shepherd imagery of Ezekiel 34.[88] This approach has a number of strengths. First, it rightly points out that ἐπεστράφητε (2:25) is best translated with the passive voice ("have been returned") rather than as a passive deponent ("have turned").[89] Second, it notes a link between the motif of restoration found both in Isaiah 53 and Ezekiel 34 with a similar

---

84. Cervantes, *La Pasión de Jesucristo Primera de Primera de Pedro*, 108: "donde todas las características literarias de la carta convergen."

85. While the passage specifically addresses slaves, most commentators agree with Elliott, *1 Peter*, 540-42, who writes that "this passage has in view not simply servants/slaves but the entire community. The former are held up here as paradigmatic of the condition and vocation of the brotherhood as a whole" (542). See also Achtemeier, *1 Peter*, 192; Michaels, *1 Peter*, 135.

86. This includes whether it comes from a hymn or as a midrash, what it reveals about atonement theory, etc.

87. Elliott, *1 Peter*, 538-39, notes that it is not immediately clear whether the term "shepherd" refers to God or to Jesus, but points to a number of reasons why he, along with the majority of 1 Peter scholars, concludes it is best understood as referring to Jesus.

88. Bosetti, *Pastore*; Elliott, *1 Peter*, 537-38, 541; Jobes, *1 Peter* [2nd ed.], 192-202; Dubis, *Messianic Woes in 1 Peter*, 56-58.

89. Elliott, *1 Peter*, 539; Dubis, *Messianic Woes in 1 Peter*, 57.

motif found in 1 Peter (i.e., 1:19; 2:10).[90] And finally, it recognizes that both Ezekiel 34 and 1 Pet 2:25 share the same or similar words: πρόβατα, πλανάω, ἐπιστρέφω, ποιμήν, and cognates of ἐπίσκοπος.[91] The presence of such verbal parallels leads Dubis to conclude, "Since Ezekiel 34 is the only chapter in the LXX in which all these Greek terms come together, the argument that Ezekiel influences 1 Pet 2:25 is especially strong."[92]

While this proposed linkage of Isaiah 53 and Ezekiel 34 has helpfully illuminated the way in which 1 Pet 2:21–25 connects Isaiah 53 with the eschatological Davidic shepherd tradition found in the prophets, in my view it has not gone far enough. In a previous monograph, I show why it makes more sense that the author links Isaiah 53 to the eschatological Davidic shepherd tradition through Zechariah 9–14 instead—a text of particular significance since it is widely agreed that Zechariah 9–14 interacts with and even reworks the shepherd tradition of Ezekiel 34.[93] In particular, I argue that in 1 Pet 2:24–25 the author employs the

90. Elliott, 1 Peter, 537–38; Dubis, Messianic Woes in 1 Peter, 57–58; Bosetti, Pastore, 117–58.

91. Dubis, Messianic Woes in 1 Peter, 57–58; Bosetti, Pastore, 117–58.

92. Dubis, Messianic Woes in 1 Peter, 57n21. Dubis also writes: "Evidence that 1 Peter 2:25 does indeed allude to Ezekiel 34 appears in the common use of a number of Greek terms. Like 1 Pet 2:25, Ezekiel 34 describes Israel as God's 'sheep' (πρόβατα, nineteen times in this chapter) who have 'gone astray' (πλανώμενον in Ezek 34:4, 16; cf. πλανώμενοι in 1 Pet 2:25). Ἐπιστρέφω adds a further verbal parallel. In Ezekiel 34, God rebukes the leaders of Israel: 'the strayed you have not brought back' (τὸ πλανώμενον οὐκ ἐπεστρέψατε; Ezek 34:4). God himself, then, vows to do himself what the leaders have failed to do: 'I will bring back the strayed' (τὸ πλανώμενον ἐπιστρέψω; Ezek 34:16). First Peter 2:25 sees God's promise in Ezekiel 34 as now fulfilled: although previously 'straying,' the readers have now been 'brought back' (ἦτε ... πλανώμενοι, ἀλλὰ ἐπεστράφητε νῦν). First Peter 2:25's 'shepherd and overseer' (ποιμένα καὶ ἐπίσκοπον) exhibits yet further verbal parallels to Ezekiel 34. First, ἐπίσκοπος in 1 Peter 2:25 echoes God [sic] resolution to care for the scattered flock (ἐπισκέψομαι αὐτά in Ezek 34:11). Ποιμήν is also a prominent term in Ezekiel 34 ... God will raise up a faithful shepherd of the line of David. So says Ezek 34:23: 'I will set up over them one shepherd (ποιμήν), my servant David, and he shall feed them: he shall feed them and be their shepherd (ποιμήν)'" (57–58). Elliott similarly notes verbal parallels between Ezekiel 34 and 1 Pet 2:25, writing: "The verb epestraphēte ... and the image of the return of straying sheep do not occur in Isa 53. It appears to be derived from Ezekiel (34:4–11, 16), where mention is made of sheep (probata, 34:5, 6, 8 10, 11), straying (planōmenon, 34:4), return (apostrophō, 34:4, 6, 10); epistrephō, 34:16 [God's returning the strayed sheep]; and episkeptō, 34:11, the verb related to the noun episkopos ... in 1 Peter)" (1 Peter, 537).

93. Coggins regards the shepherd theme in Zechariah 9–14 as "the beginnings of a tradition of biblical commentary, applying to the contemporary situation (whatever

Jewish exegetical technique known as *gezerah shavah*, linking LXX[94] Isa 53:5-6 with LXX Zech 10:2 via the catchwords ὡς πρόβατα and ἰάθημεν/ ἴασις so that the two texts and their wider text plots mutually interpret each other.[95] This observation becomes even more significant when we consider the literary context in which that exegetical technique is employed, namely 1 Pet 2:21-25.

Many 1 Peter scholars rightly characterize 1 Pet 2:21-25 as an early "Christian midrash."[96] What is not always seen is that (1) 2:21 ("because Christ also suffered on your behalf," ὅτι καὶ Χριστὸς ἔπαθεν ὑπὲρ ὑμῶν) functions as the theme verse for the midrash (2:21-25) and that (2) the Old Testament citations and commentary that follow it (2:22-25) serve to develop this primary theme. Bauckham has demonstrated a similar structure in 1 Pet 2:4-10, where "vv. 4-5 briefly state the theme which is then both supported and expanded by Old Testament citations and their interpretation in vv. 6-10."[97]

Peter's deliberate choice of ἔπαθεν in 1 Pet 2:21 instead of the more common creedal formulation of ἀπέθανεν found in 1 Cor 15:3 and elsewhere[98] can be explained on the grounds that he wanted to refer to more

---

that may have been) the warnings against false shepherds which are found particularly in Jeremiah 23 and Ezekiel 34" (*Haggai, Zechariah, Malachi*, 71). So also Meyers and Meyers, *Zechariah 9-14*, 35-45; Duguid, "Messianic Themes in Zechariah 9-14," 266, 272-75; Larkin, *Eschatology of Second Zechariah*; Tigchelaar, *Prophets of Old*; Laniak, *Shepherds After My Own Heart*, 162. In an otherwise comprehensive study of shepherd imagery in 1 Peter, Bosetti, *Pastore*, notably does not trace the progress of the shepherd tradition through to Zechariah 9-14.

94. From this point on in the book, the term LXX refers to the critically reconstructed text of Rhalfs's *Septuaginta*. I acknowledge that the Greek OT was in a state of flux in the first century. The *Septuaginta* offers a working hypothesis for what Peter and the Anatolian Christians were likely reading, one that will be maintained unless there is good reason to adopt another reading. It should be noted that in a recent survey regarding the Septuagint textual tradition in 1 Peter, Jobes concluded: "The author of 1 Peter seems to be . . . familiar with a Greek form that is . . . the same as the critically-reconstructed Septuagint text" ("Septuagint Textual Tradition in 1 Peter," 332).

95. See Liebengood, *Eschatology of 1 Peter*, 81-103 for the full argumentation.

96. Michaels, *1 Peter*, 136-37; Schutter, *Hermeneutic and Composition in 1 Peter*, 138-44, 168.

97. Bauckham, "James, 1 and 2 Peter, Jude," 310.

98. See Rom 5:6, 8; 2 Cor 5:14, for similar formulations. Regarding 1 Cor 15:3, see Conzelmann, *1 Corinthians*, 251. Fee writes, "It is generally agreed that . . . Paul is repeating a very early creedal formulation that was common to the entire church" (*1 Corinthians*, 718).

than just Jesus' death.⁹⁹ In his scope was the entire narrative surrounding his death—his unjust trail, how he responded to this unjust treatment, and his subsequent crucifixion.¹⁰⁰ This initial appraisal of ἔπαθεν is strengthened when consideration is given to why the Isaiah 53 citations do not appear in 1 Peter in the same order in which they occur in Isaiah 53.¹⁰¹ In this regard, several scholars have helpfully proposed that Peter arranges Isaiah 53 in this fashion in order to "reflect fundamental aspects of the Passion narrative."¹⁰² Accordingly, 2:22-23 allude to Jesus' trial, and 2:24 refers to his crucifixion.¹⁰³

If 1 Pet 2:21 is an intentional modification of the more traditional creedal formulation, this may explain why the "midrash" on the passion of Jesus begins with Isaiah 53. There is consensus that Isaiah 53 stands behind the early confession (i.e., 1 Cor 15:3, etc.), though not all agree about which text (i.e., Greek, Hebrew, Aramaic) informs the idea of vicarious death.¹⁰⁴ The point in all of this is that, rather than being simply a "Christian midrash," 1 Pet 2:21-25 more specifically functions as a *Passion* midrash. Portions of Isaiah 53 have been selected and modified not only to represent key aspects of the Passion Narrative but also in order to elaborate on the main theme of the passage—"Christ suffered on your behalf." Given what we know about the aims of 1 Pet 2:21-25, then, and the prominence of Zechariah 9-14 in explaining Christ's death in the Passion Narratives, we have good reason to suspect, perhaps even expect, an allusion to something in Zechariah 9-14.

---

99. Some manuscripts have ἀπέθανεν instead of ἔπαθεν. It is likely that a scribe wrote ἀπέθανεν instead of the original ἔπαθεν because it was more in keeping with both the oral tradition and the early textual form found in 1 Cor 15:3 and elsewhere. The fact that the two words look alike may have also influenced the scribe's reading.

100. Cervantes, *La Pasión de Jesucristo*, 167: "El uso de este verbo en relación con Cristo en el NT se encuentra también en los Sinópticos, Hechos, Hebreos y 1 Pedro, y se refiere a la Pasión y Muerte de Cristo, considerados como un todo, como un único acontecimiento, pero al mismo tiempo pone de relieve los sufrimientos que precedieron a la muerte de Jesús." He notes the following texts as significant: Luke 22:15; 24:26, 46; Acts 1:3; 3:18; 17:3; Heb 9:26; 13:12.

101. I do not find warrant in the assertion that an early Christian hymn is the source behind 1 Pet 2:22-24 for the reasons laid out in Elliott, *1 Peter*, 548-50.

102. Goppelt, *Commentary on 1 Peter*, 211. See also Achtemeier, *1 Peter*, 180; Jobes, *1 Peter* [1st ed.], 194; Schutter, *Hermeneutic and Composition in 1 Peter*, 40.

103. Achtemeier, *1 Peter*, 180.

104. Conzelmann, *1 Corinthians*, 251-55; Fee, *1 Corinthians*, 722-25.

For the reasons above, I have proposed that the best way to understand the shepherd imagery in 1 Peter is as an allusion to the eschatological Davidic shepherd tradition of Zechariah 9–14. This approach is more satisfying than the Ezekiel 34 proposal (which, it should be noted, also affirms an allusion to the eschatological Davidic shepherd tradition) for at least three reasons: (1) Zechariah 9–14 was not just available for use but also was preferred by prominent exegetes in the early Jesus movement who sought to interpret the meaning behind Jesus' unjust suffering and crucifixion (we do not find a similar phenomenon with Ezekiel 34); (2) Isaiah 53 and the shepherd tradition of Zechariah 9–14 share a more specific conceptual link than do Ezekiel 34 and Isaiah 53—restoration through the affliction of YHWH's chosen agent; and finally, (3) Peter's selection of LXX Zech 10:2, "They were driven away like sheep and were afflicted, since there was no *healing*," best explains why Peter chose to culminate his appropriation of Isaiah 53 with "by his wounds you have been *healed*" (οὗ τῷ μώλωπι ἰάθητε; 2:24) and to then link it with shepherd imagery. Two important points now become clear. First, Peter interprets healing in Isaiah 53 to mean Israel's restoration from exile.[105] Second, what these two texts have in common (Isaiah 53 and Zechariah 9–14) is not simply the theme of restoration but more specifically restoration that is accomplished *by the affliction of* YHWH's *chosen agent*.[106]

The kind of exegetical activity that I have suggested in 1 Pet 2:21–25 concords well with what others have noticed in 1 Peter. For example, Schutter, in his comprehensive analysis of Primopetrine hermeneutics observes that "nothing is quite so significant as the variety of ways [that Old Testament] materials have been handled"; Peter conflates OT texts, gathers OT texts around a single idea, assumes that readers will pick up on the wider text-plot cited, and interacts with exegetical traditions in existence.[107] Both Bauckham and Elliott have also demonstrated that in 1 Pet 2:4–10 Peter not only creatively uses the OT but builds on early Christian tradition in order to "create a midrash specifically designed

---

105. Healing terminology is often, though not exclusively, used in the OT as a metaphor for forgiveness of sins and/or restoration from punishment, affliction, or exile (LXX: Deut 30:3–5; Jer 33:6; Isa 30:26; 53:5; 57:18–19; 61:1; Ps 59:4; 102:3; 106:20; 146:3. For healing and national restoration outside of the OT, see Jub. 23:29, T. Zeb. 9:8; 2 Bar. 73:2; 4 Ezra 13:50; 4Q521).

106. This also likely explains why Peter would want to link the two texts together with the phrase ὡς πρόβατα, since in the shepherd tradition straying, wandering, or cast out "sheep" is a metaphor for YHWH's people in need of restoration.

107. Schutter, *Hermeneutic and Composition in 1 Peter*, 43.

for its context."[108] Similarly, Ceslas Spicq asserts that 1 Peter "peut être caractérisée comme une 'Épître de la Tradition,'" drawing upon creedal formulas, Jesus' own teachings, and midrash from the Old Testament in order to craft his message.[109]

### The Eschatological Davidic Shepherd and the Narrative Substructure of 1 Peter's Eschatology

There are a number of unique parallels between 1 Peter and Zechariah 9–14 that strongly suggest that the latter functions as the substructure for 1 Peter's eschatological program.[110] What is significant for our purposes is that the eschatological program of Zechariah 9–14 is foundationally a Davidic program that 1 Peter draws on to explain why Jesus was rejected, and why his loyal followers should expect the same if they are to follow in his footsteps.[111] Given the limited scope of this chapter, I will simply highlight a few of these parallels, which give texture and dimension to the narrative of deferred hope that I have already highlighted. In both 1 Peter and Zechariah 9–14:

1. The community that aligns themselves with God's royal figure is described as "the house of God" (Zech 12:8/1 Pet 2:4; 4:17);[112]

2. The royal/messianic agent is described variously as a slain shepherd (Zech 13:7/1 Pet 2:23–35), a stone (Zech 10:3/1 Pet 2:6–8), and the shoot of David (implied in Zechariah 9–14 from Zech 3:8; 6:12, and in 1 Pet 4:14 from Isa 11:2);

---

108. Bauckham, "James, 1 and 2 Peter, Jude," 312; Elliott, *Elect and the Holy*, 16–49; *1 Peter*, 405–49.

109. Spicq, *Les Épitres de Saint Pierre*, 15.

110. On occasion I have been understood to be suggesting that Zechariah 9–14 is the substructure for the narrative of 1 Peter as a whole, and that it explains all of the Old Testament imagery in the letter. This is not, however, what I have argued in *Eschatology of 1 Peter*. Instead, I limit my claim to the eschatological program of 1 Peter.

111. For a comprehensive development of the Davidic contours of the eschatological program of Zechariah 9–14, see Liebengood, *Eschatology of 1 Peter*, 23–52. Here I will simply note that the coming king (Zech 9:9–10), the pierced one (12:10), and the slain shepherd (13:7) are all depicted in terms of an eschatological Davidic king.

112. In 183–204, I explore further the polyvalent language of "house of God" in 1 Pet 2:5.

3. The house of God will undergo a period of fiery trials that are likened to a wilderness/new exodus journey and that is designed to test fidelity towards God (Zech 10:4-12; 1 Pet 1:3—2:10);

4. The Spirit will be poured out/now rests upon the house of God (Zech 12:10; 1 Pet 4:14; "spiritual" house in 2:5);

5. Restoration is described in terms of scattered/straying sheep being gathered from exile and returned to the shepherd-king (Zech 9:16; 10:8-12; 1 Pet 1:1; 2:24-25);

6. Metallurgy imagery is used to describe trials in terms of an assaying/sifting process rather than as mere purgation (Zech 13:7-9; 1 Pet 1:5-7; 4:12-19);

7. God declares "You are my people" to his ingathered/remnant sheep who are called to endure the fiery trials (Zech 13:7-9; 1 Pet 2:10; both Zechariah and 1 Peter drawn on Hos 2:23 to make this point).

8. There is an optimism concerning those who have aligned themselves with God's appointed agent/shepherd; they will journey faithfully through the fiery trials/second exodus on to their salvation/inheritance/glory through God's enabling (Zech 10:6-12; 13:7-9; 1 Pet 1:5-7; 4:12-19; 5:10).

9. God, through his agent, will restore a rightly functioning royal house/temple where acceptable offerings are presented to God (Zech 14; 1 Pet 2:4-10/2:23-24).

What is most significant, perhaps even determinative, when the implicit narrative of 1 Peter is read in light of Zechariah 9-14 is that only 1 Peter and Zechariah 9-14 offer an eschatological program that develops the notion of a transition (or liminal) period subsequent to the coming of YHWH's redemptive agent and prior to consummation that is described both as a period of fiery trials as well as a new exodus/wilderness journey.[113] In other words, Zechariah 9-14 offers the unique solution to one of the issues with which Peter and his addressees are concerned: If Jesus is in fact the Christ, the agent appointed to bring about restoration, then why are we suffering *after* his coming?

---

113. Isaiah 40-55, for example, cannot account for shepherd imagery in 1 Peter or the transition period of suffering which comes after the suffering servant has suffered and died and prior to consummation. And while Ezekiel shares the shepherd imagery that is found in both 1 Peter and Zechariah 9-14, as I have sketched above, Zechariah 9-14 develops the Ezekiel program in a unique fashion, underscoring a transition period of fiery trials prior to consummation.

Often, in 1 Peter scholarship, Peter's appropriation of Hebrew Bible texts and early Jesus movement traditions is characterized as being eclectic (often a euphemism for "lacking a coherent rationale") in nature. However, when we analyze Peter's appropriation in light of the eschatological program of Zechariah 9–14, a coherent pattern can be discerned. Peter has drawn on particular Hebrew Bible passages and themes such as fiery trials, stone, house, new exodus, and shepherd in order to support and affirm the substructure provided by Zechariah 9–14. Said in another way, Peter uses a variety of Old Testament passages and images, sayings from the Jesus tradition (1 Pet 2:11–12), and early traditions within the Jesus movement (e.g., stone catena in 1 Pet 2:4–8) in order to fortify, explain, illustrate, and corroborate the very substructure that undergirds and generates his eschatological program of deferred hope. In this regard, we could say that Zechariah 9–14 functions as the frame upon which the bricks of Old Testament citations and early Jesus movement traditions have been laid. Additionally, Peter's fragmentary allusions and echoes derive coherence from their relation to the eschatological program of Zechariah 9–14: they are allusive recollections of the foundational eschatological narrative. The eschatological program of Zechariah 9–14 is thus a springboard for his understanding and presentation of the outworking of God's restoration, in which he feels the freedom to draw upon texts from the Hebrew Bible which concord with his reading of Zechariah 9–14.

What this means, especially for the aim of this chapter, is that the narrative of deferred hope found in 1 Peter, which stands in contrast to the narrative of Rome's realized hope, is more specifically a narrative about Israel's promised Davidic king, and the way in which this king's people ought to faithfully orient themselves while living under foreign (and alluring) rule. Said in another way, Jewish restoration ideology, and more specifically the eschatological Davidic shepherd tradition, is Peter's way of helping *gentile* followers of Jesus from Asia Minor learn how to negotiate their allegiance to Jesus in a social context that, for a number of reasons, is antagonistic to such a commitment. Peter seeks to encourage his addressees to interpret their suffering and social alienation in light of the fact that they have been invited to participate in the Davidic shepherd's program of restoration, in part, by faithfully enduring "various trials" (1 Pet 1:6) in the present wilderness of testing as they journey to their inheritance (1 Pet 1:3).

Within this narrative of the eschatological Davidic shepherd, it is important to point out the way in which 1 Peter frames suffering and faithful allegiance to Jesus: the primary enemy with whom Jesus-followers struggle is not Rome or its loyal citizens. Instead, the author paints the narrative of deferred hope and faithful allegiance upon a much wider canvas, the cosmic struggle between the God of Israel and the devil.[114] The addressees are called to be on the lookout for an enemy more powerful than Rome, namely the devil, who roams all over the world seeking for someone to devour (1 Pet 5:8–9). Identifying the devil as the true source behind the addressees' social alienation and suffering actually functions to deflate Rome's over-exalted and totalizing self-understanding as the divinely appointed agent through whom the world is blessed with peace, prosperity, and justice. It minimizes Rome by depicting it as just another fleeting manifestation of the devil's schemes against God and his people. What is more, in 1 Peter, loyal allegiance to the true king in this in-between time of deferred hope is most fully and faithfully expressed by following the eschatological Davidic king's pattern of enemy-love, who, when he suffered, did not threaten in return, and who, when he was reviled, did not return revile in return but instead entrusted himself to the one who judges justly (1 Pet 2:23). Likewise, Jesus followers are exhorted to not repay evil for evil but instead to bless those who revile them (1 Pet 3:9) and to entrust themselves to the faithful creator while continuing to do good (1 Pet 4:19). This way of life that is rooted in enemy-love is one of the ways in which the addressees participate in this eschatological Davidic shepherd program, establishing an alternative social structure that runs counter to the fundamental way in which *pax romana* was administered.

### The "For-You-ness" of the Eschatological David Shepherd

There is one final point to be made about the eschatological Davidic shepherd tradition in 1 Peter, and it relates to our discussion about the purpose of the letter.[115] If we are right about the rhetorical exigence of 1 Peter, namely that it was written to give (Jewish) apostolic legitimacy to gentile followers of Jesus, then perhaps more should be made of the second person plural pronouns in 1 Peter, especially in 1 Pet 2:24–25. I am

114. This yet another unique Jewish understanding of the way the world is.
115. See pages 77–84.

not the first to suggest this, though I am highlighting a different sense for why it is emphatic. In reflecting on 1 Pet 1:4, John Elliott has highlighted what he calls the "for-you-ness" of the letter:

> At this point the focus shifts from the inclusive "our" (3a), "us" (3b) to the addressees as the specific recipients of and responders to God's saving action, and *this focus dominates throughout the remainder of the letter*. . . . This consistent stress upon the "for-you-ness" of the letter's good news is one of the most typical and noteworthy features of its encouragement and exhortation.[116]

He reiterates this point as he comments on 1 Pet 1:10–12, which stresses that "the prophets prophesied of the grace intended *for you*," and that they were "serving not themselves but *you*, in regard to the things that have now been announced to *you*." "The addressees," Elliott remarks, "are constantly assured that they are the direct recipients of the good news about all that God has accomplished through Jesus Christ."[117] This notion of "for-you-ness" again is reiterated in 1 Pet 1:20–21, where Peter underscores that Jesus "was revealed at the end of the ages *for your sake*," and that as a result "*your* trust and hope are in God." In keeping with what we saw in chapter 1, the "god" in reference here is none other than the God of Israel. In stressing that the addressees are included in the God of Israel's building project/household, Peter seems to put an emphasis on the second person plural: καὶ αὐτοὶ ὡς λίθοι ζῶντες οἰκοδομεῖσθε οἶκος πνευματικὸς (1 Pet 2:5).[118] And then there is the emphatic statements in 1 Pet 2:9–10:

> But *you* are a chosen people, a royal priesthood, a holy nation, God's own people, in order that *you* may proclaim the excellence of him who called *you* out of darkness into his marvelous light. Once *you* were not a people, but now *you* are God's people; once *you* had not received mercy, but now *you* have received mercy.[119]

---

116. Elliott, *1 Peter*, 336 (emphasis mine). Elliott notes that *you* as object appears twenty-nine times; *you* as subject two times; *your* twenty-one times; and second person plural verbs and participles appear ninety-one times.

117. Elliott, *1 Peter*, 353.

118. So Williams and Horrell, *1 Peter*, 611. For a discussion of the meaning of οἶκος, see pages 131–48, 183–99.

119. Williams and Horrell, *1 Peter*, 661, note the emphatic and contrastive ὑμεῖς δὲ of 1 Pet 2:9.

We will discuss this passage in more detail in the following chapter. For now, I wish to highlight, as Martin has helped us see, that this message is precisely the "explicit conclusion" of the rhetorical exigence of 1 Peter—"gentiles, *you* belong to the people of God." Additionally, these statements found in 1 Pet 2:9–10 are made up of a number of Old Testament passages that were originally directed to Israel. I would suggest that the "for-you-ness" of 1 Pet 2:9–10 has a layer that is not always perceived, namely because the "you" referred to are gentiles that were not anticipated as beneficiaries of the claims made in these texts and their wider text plots. This, I suggest, is also happening in 1 Pet 2:24–25: "By his wounds *you* have been healed. For *you* were going astray like sheep, but now have returned to the shepherd." As we have already seen, here Peter draws together pieces from Isaiah 53 and Zechariah 10, texts written to respond to Israel's predicament of exile. The shocking twist, or we might say the punchline, of this passage in 1 Pet 2:24–25, in light of the eschatological Davidic shepherd tradition that has been detailed above, is that this shepherd has not only come to restore Israel *but also* the wayward sheep of the *gentiles*.[120] If discerning the use of the Old Testament in the New Testament is at times a bit like understanding the punchline to a joke, in my reading of 1 Peter, I perceive a punchline regarding 1 Peter's development of the eschatological Davidic shepherd program through Zechariah 9–14 that underscores the purpose of the letter.[121] In one sense, saying that *Jesus* is "the *shepherd* and *overseer* of your souls" is the punchline to a long story, the twists and turns of the eschatological Davidic shepherd tradition. But as audacious as that claim is, it seems even more audacious that he is shepherd and overseer of *your* souls (gentiles). Elliott is right to note the "for-you-ness" of 1 Peter, but I would contend that part of the encouragement is an affirmation that "you gentiles" also share in what God is doing in and through Jesus Christ. It is, in other words, an affirmation that they (the gentile addressees of 1 Peter) have been welcomed into the people of God and are in fact participating in God's ongoing work through the eschatological Davidic shepherd, Jesus.

---

120. It is perhaps not a coincidence that when the Johannine Jesus connects himself to the shepherd tradition (in John 10), he remarks, "I have other sheep that are not of this fold. I must bring them also, and they will listen to my voice. So there will be one flock, one shepherd" (John 10:16–17).

121. For more on how intertextuality, especially how the New Testament draws upon the Hebrew Bible, works like the punchline of a joke, see Leithart, *Deep Exegesis*, 109–39.

## Conclusion

The main point of this chapter has been to show that Peter confronts the challenges of Roman imperial ideology and its claims of realized eschatology by pointing to a distinctively Jewish way of understanding what God is up to in the world; namely, he appeals to the inaugurated but deferred hope of the eschatological Davidic shepherd. In other words, Peter's solution to the addressees' problem of empire and the way in which it has alienated these newly formed gentile followers of Jesus is to welcome them into what the God of Israel is doing in and through the Davidic king, Jesus. In the end, the solution is "Israelhood," that is, for gentile followers of Jesus to inhabit, even participate in, a uniquely Jewish way of being in the world by following in the footsteps of the radical and transforming pattern of enemy-love embodied by the eschatological Davidic king Jesus, who it should be noted also confronts and reshapes Jewish self-understanding.

5

# The Problem of Temple and Priesthood in 1 Peter

*It is in this section of 1 Peter (2:4–10) that the contrast is sharpest between the conception of the "new Israel"—the new "Temple-Community"—and the Israel of old with its physical temple. The Christians are now the "elect and holy nation" (1:2), and in contrast to the letter to the Hebrews where Christ is the High Priest, here there is a corporate priesthood which is both "holy" (2:5) and "royal" (2:9). . . . It is difficult not to see a hint of a polemic with first-century Judaism, especially the Jerusalem temple and its priesthood.*[1]

## Temple and Priesthood as Polemic and Replacement

CONTEMPORARY PRIMOPETRINE SCHOLARSHIP HAS emphasized the important role that 1 Pet 2:4–10 plays in terms of executing the identity-formation strategy of the letter. Elliott, for example, underscores how this literary unit connects all the way back to the letter opening, calling attention to how "these verses bring to a resounding climax the line of thought begun in 1:3."[2] He also notes that "here [1 Pet 2:4–10], the fundamental indicative for the entire epistle has been spoken."[3] In summarizing their exegesis of the passage, Williams and Horrell conclude that "these rich and complex verses are crucial to the overall message and

---

1. Mbuvi, *Temple, Exile and Identity in 1 Peter*, 91.

2. Elliott, *1 Peter*, 407.

3. Elliott, *Elect and the Holy*, 217. As we highlighted in 80–84 of chapter 3, Martin came to the same conclusion in his investigation of the rhetorical exigence of 1 Peter.

strategy of 1 Peter, as well as to our understanding of its achievements in terms of the *making* of Christian identity."[4] And Green underscores that 1 Pet 2:4–10 draws together major threads "into a climax that is focused on both the *identity* and the *vocation* of Peter's audience."[5] He further notes that these threads sketch "an interpretive canopy" under which the addressees are to make sense of their suffering. However, as Williams and Horrell have observed, 1 Pet 2:4–10 serves not only as a culmination of what has been said thus far but also as the "foundation for the instruction that is to follow in the second major section of the letter (2:11—4:11)."[6] All this is to illustrate that a careful reading of 1 Pet 2:4–10 is essential to understanding the overarching message of the entire letter.

But the strategic importance of 1 Pet 2:4–10 becomes problematic when we consider that many scholars have detected, for a variety of reasons, polemic against the Jerusalem temple and its priesthood, and by extension perceive that Israel is being replaced by the church. For example, Andrew Mbuvi, in his work on temple imagery and identity formation in 1 Peter, contends that "in this section of 1 Peter (2:4–10) . . . it is difficult not to see a hint of a polemic with first-century Judaism, especially the Jerusalem temple and its priesthood."[7]

It is important to call attention to the fact that often a detection of anti-temple/priesthood polemic in these verses morphs and intensifies into claims that the "spiritual house" of 1 Pet 2:5 replaces the Jerusalem temple and the "spiritual sacrifices" supersede the Jerusalem temple priesthood. Jobes is representative of this when she claims that "the Christian community is portrayed as a temple, implying that now it—not a literal stone building—is the place of God's earthly dwelling by the Holy Spirit, a place of *true* worship and of acceptable sacrifice."[8] But Mbuvi offers perhaps the most pervasive and consistent example of replacement in a variety of forms. For example, he claims that the classification of Christians as "living stones" points to a contrast with the "*un*living" stones of the literal temple.[9] He suggests that "1 Peter has transferred

---

4. Williams and Horrell, *1 Peter*, 684 (emphasis mine).
5. Green, *1 Peter*, 55 (emphasis mine).
6. Williams and Horrell, *1 Peter*, 684.
7. Mbuvi, *Temple, Exile and Identity in 1 Peter*, 91.
8. Jobes, *1 Peter* [2nd ed.], 147 (emphasis mine).
9. Mbuvi, *Temple, Exile and Identity in 1 Peter*, 102.

the Jewish expectations of the temple to the believers through Jesus."[10] He concludes that 1 Peter redefines Israel, the temple, and the nature of restoration.[11] He asserts that "the transference that 1 Peter is making of the priesthood to the believers is not simply one of expansion of the boundaries of priesthood but of a complete reconstitution."[12] And finally, he declares that the community's identity is as the "new Israel" of God in whom are fulfilled the OT promises.[13]

It is not uncommon for claims of this sort in 1 Peter scholarship to be based, in part, upon the interpretation of πνευματικός to mean something akin to "true" or "legitimate." Thus, when Peter uses the adjective "spiritual" before house and sacrifices, it is his way of minimizing (or perhaps more accurately, denigrating) what happens (or happened) in the Jerusalem temple on the one hand, while at the same time positioning this new community as the true and legitimate replacement.[14] This modern line of interpretation for πνευματικός ultimately seems to be derivative of Selwyn's suggestion in his commentary on 1 Peter as well as Bertil Gärtner's influential study, which compared "temple-as-community" imagery in Qumran texts with that of the New Testament.[15] This is how Mbuvi reads the history of interpretation:

> Gärtner, following Selwyn, explains that "spiritual" refers to its belonging to a "new sphere," which is itself a product of the outpouring of the Holy Spirit. In that case the term "spiritual" would also suggest the meaning "true temple of God" versus a "false temple."[16]

---

10. Mbuvi, *Temple, Exile and Identity in 1 Peter*, 124.

11. Mbuvi, *Temple, Exile and Identity in 1 Peter*, 131.

12. Mbuvi, *Temple, Exile and Identity in 1 Peter*, 108.

13. Mbuvi, *Temple, Exile and Identity in 1 Peter*, 133. Mbuvi repeatedly claims that 1 Peter declares the addressees to be the "new Israel." See *Temple, Exile and Identity in 1 Peter*, 75, 77, 80, 81, 85, 91, 101, 108, 117, 126.

14. Selwyn, *1 Peter*, 160; Spicq, *Les Épitres de Saint Pierre*, 84–85; Goppelt, *1 Peter*, 145; Boring, *1 Peter*, 101; Beale, *Temple and the Church's Mission*, 331; Feldmeier, *1 Peter*, 90; Jobes, *1 Peter* [1st ed.], 148–51.

15. Selwyn, *1 Peter*, 291. Gärtner, *Temple and the Community in Qumran and the New Testament*, 73. See also Botner, "Essence of a Spiritual House," 409–16, who traces how this history of interpretation is built upon an erroneous reading of community-as-temple in the Dead Sea Scrolls. More on that below.

16. Mbuvi, *Temple, Exile, and Identity in 1 Peter*, 94.

Ultimately, Mbuvi rejects this approach, claiming that the distinction "true/false" is "too radical." Instead, he argues that in referencing the "new" temple, the author is offering a typological fulfillment of the "old" temple. Both temples, he argues, are true; but the physical temple points to the new eschatological reality, the church.[17] As we will see below, there are good reasons to reject this way of reading the adjective πνευματικός—whether as the "true" or the "legitimate" temple—but for reasons that differ from what Mbuvi has offered. In due course we will also consider whether 1 Pet 2:5 presents these gentile followers of Jesus as "the eschatological temple where God's presence rests permanently."[18] For now, I wish to highlight two other factors that have led some to suspect polemic against the Jewish leaders, if not also the supersession of Israel in 1 Pet 2:4–10.

One contributing factor has been the way some have drawn a line in 1 Pet 2:7 from the "unbelievers" who are characterized in that same verse as the builders that rejected the stone (a description that is derived from Ps 118:22 [LXX 117:22]) to the Jewish leaders who rejected Jesus as Messiah.[19] There is precedent for the use of Ps 118:22 to point the finger at Jewish leadership in Jerusalem. For example, in Acts 4:8–11 this same citation (Ps 118:22) is explicitly appropriated in order to inculpate the "rulers of the people and the elders" for crucifying Jesus: "This Jesus is the stone that was rejected by *you*, the builders" (Acts 4:11).[20] Additionally, the parable of the vineyard tenants found in all three of the Synoptic Gospels draws upon Ps 118:22 to speak against the Jewish leaders and their rejection of Jesus.[21] When these two examples of the usage of Ps 118:22 are brought into conversation with what we find in 1 Pet 2:7, some interpreters assume that Peter is following this same precedent, using the psalm once again to confront the Jewish leadership. When this assumption about 1 Pet 2:7 and Ps 118:22 is joined with other assumptions about

---

17. Mbuvi, *Temple, Exile, and Identity in 1 Peter*, 94.

18. Mbuvi, *Temple, Exile, and Identity in 1 Peter*, 94.

19. Reicke, *James, Peter, and Jude*, 92. See Horrell, "Das im Unglauben verharrende Judenvolk," 327–51, for how this line of interpretation was followed in German scholarship.

20. Emphasis mine.

21. The parable of the vineyard tenants can be found in Mark 12:1–12/Matt 21:33–46/Luke 20:9–19. Within the context of each of those stories, it is clear that the chief priest, scribes, and/or Pharisees conclude that Jesus is using this psalm citation to refer to them.

supersession in the letter, it serves to confirm yet again that 1 Peter is replacing Israel with the church.

Another factor that has contributed to a perception of polemic and replacement, as we have already seen at various points in this study, is the fact that 1 Pet 2:9–10 contains three Hebrew Bible citations that were originally addressed to Israel: Exod 19:5–6; Isa 43:20–21; and Hos 1:6, 9–10/2:23. It is assumed, given the consensus regarding the ethnic makeup of the 1 Peter addressees, that these honorary titles ("chosen people," "holy people," "a people for God's possession") and prerogatives ("royal priesthood," and "proclaim the excellencies of him who called you out of darkness") that once belonged exclusively to Israel have now been extended, or, perhaps even more ominously, transferred to the gentiles. Given that this exchange of honorary titles and prerogatives happens just after a discussion about builders who rejected Jesus, it is not difficult to see why some might have drawn the conclusion that this transfer is God's response to Israel's rejection, akin to what Jesus meant in his parable of the vineyard tenants, especially the conclusions he reaches in Matt 21:33–46 and Luke 20:9–19, when he says he will "give the vineyard to others."

## The Problem with Seeing Replacement in 1 Peter 2:4–8

But there are compelling reasons to reject polemical overtones targeted at the Jerusalem temple, its priesthood, and its leadership in 1 Pet 2:4–10.[22] And, as we will see below, interpreting "spiritual house" and "spiritual sacrifices" as Peter's way of claiming that the church replaces Israel or the temple is misguided.

Regarding the interpretive move to identify the "unbelievers" and "builders that rejected the stone" as the Jewish leadership, Williams and Horrell demonstrate that "there is no indication that the author of 1 Peter has such a specific target in mind."[23] For example, whereas in Acts 4:8–11 and the Synoptic Gospels, there is a clear reference to the "builders" being the Jewish leadership, in 1 Pet 2:4, the author broadens the reference in at least two important ways: first, by characterizing those who reject with

---

22. The focus of this chapter is on 1 Pet 2:4–8 and the temple and priesthood imagery. We will attend more comprehensively with the challenges of the "ethnic" language of 1 Pet 2:9–10 in the next chapter.

23. Williams and Horrell, *1 Peter*, 646.

the more general descriptor ὑπὸ ἀνθρώπων ("human beings"; 1 Pet 2:4). "Here in v. 4, there is no exegetical reason to see the contrast as anything other than a general one indicating the hostile reaction to Christ—which the recipients continue to experience in their social context."[24] In short, "there is no explicit mention of Jews as those who have 'failed' to believe (contrast John 8:22–44; Rom 9–11; 1 Thess 2:14–16)—the references [2:4, 7–8] in the text [of 1 Peter] are all non-specific and generic.[25] I would add to this the fact that there is no mention anywhere else in the letter of conflict between the addressees and Jewish leadership. Instead, as we have seen in the discussion in chapter 3, the conflict that the addressees of 1 Peter face comes from *gentile* compeers, neighbors, and family members. Secondly, Williams and Horrell note how the author seems to indicate a more open-ended reference to those doing the rejecting by using the anarthous ἀπιστοῦσιν in 1 Pet 2:7.[26] What is more, "the subsequent description of this group as those who reject the gospel (v. 8), may suggest that it refers to those with whom Christians [i.e., the 1 Peter addressees] are in conflict."[27]

Williams and Horrell highlight two other exegetical features of this passage that deserve consideration in regard to this discussion about polemic and replacement. First, "there is no contrast between an 'old' and 'new' Israel, or between an (inferior) old covenant and a (superior) new one, as is common in early Christian literature."[28] This is an important observation. Talk of a "new" Israel in the interpretation of 1 Peter is inferred but is nowhere stated explicitly in the text. One of the aims of this chapter is to show how this inference is unwarranted. Second, they note that the "race, nation, and people" descriptions of the addressees in 1 Pet 2:9–10 all appear without the definite article.[29] While they are hesitant to lean into this exegetical observation, they think it is nevertheless important to note, since it opens space for the ongoing status of Jews as the people of God.

In the end, Williams and Horrell contend that 1 Peter is silent about the ongoing status of non-Christian Jews, and that silence can be read

---

24. Williams and Horrell, *1 Peter*, 609.
25. Williams and Horrell, *1 Peter*, 687.
26. Williams and Horrell, *1 Peter*, 646–47.
27. Williams and Horrell, *1 Peter*, 647.
28. Williams and Horrell, *1 Peter*, 687, in which they note the follow examples: 1 Cor 10:18; Gal 4:21–31; Heb 7:18–19; 8:6–13; 9:11–15; Barn. 16:5–8.
29. Williams and Horrell, *1 Peter*, 687.

either positively or ominously.³⁰ They also believe that a contemporary theological response to the issue of supersessionism goes beyond the constraints of their exegetical work in their commentary on 1 Peter. But given the exegetical observations they have made about 1 Pet 2:4–10, they find Leonard Goppelt's claims about the author's focus in the letter to be compelling. Goppelt contends that the author of 1 Peter is not concerned with the relationship between the church and Israel but rather the church in relation to a hostile society.³¹ Williams and Horrell extend Goppelt's observation:

> In seeking to encourage his readers with a positive view of their group-identity, the author applies to them the most honourable attributes given to Israel, whose scriptures provide the main source for his identity-defining and conduct-shaping material. Yet there is no evidence of any interest on his part in denying that identity to other (Jewish) groups, nor (perhaps surprising) any indication of exactly how he regarded these other groups, of whose existence he must sure have known, nor, indeed, any clear indication of how he sees the groups of Χριστιανοί in relation to (or even as a sub-group of) Ἰουδαῖοι.³²

In chapter 6, we will further address some of the issues that Williams and Horrell have raised with these important observations, but for now, by drawing on their work, I underscore some of the significant exegetical reasons to be suspicious of the claim that polemic and even replacement can be found in 1 Pet 2:4–10. But there is more that can and needs to be said, especially about the manner in which οἶκος πνευματικός has often been interpreted in modern 1 Peter scholarship.

## Assessing the Interpretation of οἶκος πνευματικός and "Spiritual" Sacrifices in Modern 1 Peter Scholarship

Recently, Max Botner has offered an insightful essay that demonstrates how 1 Peter commentators consistently have misrepresented "community-as-temple" metaphors in the Dead Sea Scrolls and then have used those mistaken conclusions to support a reading in which οἶκος πνευματικός purportedly conveys that the Jerusalem temple has been replaced by the

30. Williams and Horrell, *1 Peter*, 688.
31. Goppelt, *1 Peter*, 147–51.
32. Williams and Horrell, *1 Peter*, 688.

"new" and "true" temple where "true" or "legitimate" sacrifices are made.[33] In particular, Botner shows how modern 1 Peter commentators tend to pass on a kind of modern interpretive tradition regarding the use of temple imagery in the Dead Sea Scrolls. Importantly, he notes that while supersessionist interpretations of 1 Pet 2:5 were a fixture of Primopetrine scholarship prior to the discovery of the Dead Sea Scrolls, the publication of these scrolls generated a new line of argument for *how* the church replaces Israel and its temple.[34] The line runs as follows:

> (1) The Jewish Scriptures contain critiques of the practices of sacrifice; (2) the Qumran sectarians marshal these critiques to establish themselves as the "new" or "true" temple, thus paving the way for Christians to do the same; and (3) 1 Peter carries the sectarians' rhetoric to its logical and inevitable conclusion by asserting that Christ's followers have superseded the Jerusalem temple.[35]

Part of what Botner uncovers for us is the manner in which the Qumran texts have served as a "missing link" between Second Temple cult and the "higher order" of worship in the New Testament.[36] In other words, as the interpretive tradition goes, the Qumran sectarians serve as "proto-Christians" who till the interpretive soil for New Testament authors to speak of the community as temple in such a way that promotes a replacement of the ineffective Jerusalem temple and its sacrifices.[37]

The problem with this interpretive tradition is that the second link in the chain is erroneous. Drawing on Jonathan Klawans's seminal work, *Purity, Sacrifice, and the Temple: Symbolism and Supersessionism in the Study of Ancient Israel*, Botner points to the fact that the Qumran community did *not* see itself as the "new" and "true" temple that offers legitimate and effective sacrifices in the place of the Jerusalem temple.[38] Instead, at best, these sectarians at Qumran saw their community as a *provisional* response to an undesired circumstance, namely the ritually

---

33. Botner, "Essence of a Spiritual House."
34. Botner, "Essence of a Spiritual House," 413.
35. Botner, "Essence of a Spiritual House," 415.
36. Botner, "Essence of a Spiritual House," 411.
37. See Botner, "Essence of a Spiritual House," 413–16, for a development of this theme.
38. So also, Regev, "Community as Temple," 606, who argues that "the Community Rule never refers directly to the temple and does not seem to replace it fully."

and morally defiled temple.³⁹ The provisional nature of this community-as-temple metaphor, then, must be understood with the awareness that there is no evidence in the Qumran texts that the community claims to be as good as or better than the temple. Given the way that 1 Peter scholarship has used the sectarian literature as the missing link to understand temple and sacrificial language in 1 Pet 2:5, and more generally the way earlier Qumran scholarship has influenced some of the supersessionist assumptions we find in New Testament scholarship, it is important to survey in more depth some of the pertinent conclusions that Klawans makes regarding the community-as-temple metaphor in the Dead Sea Scrolls.

Klawans notes that foundationally scholars have tended to perceive supersessionism within the Qumran sectarians because "they replaced the temple and its sacrificial activity with their own kinds of worship—all too often referred to as 'spiritual' sacrifices."⁴⁰ These so-called "spiritual" sacrifices included such things as prayer, righteous deeds, and even scripture exegesis. But walking through a number Dead Sea Scrolls passages, some of which have been used to support the assumption of temple and sacrifice replacement, Klawans shows that the evidence runs in a different direction. First, the Qumran sectarians' understanding of being a provisional temple is built upon the expectation of a pending future physical temple, in which animal and vegetable sacrifices would be offered once again.⁴¹ Second, the community's attitude regarding divine presence challenges the claim that they saw themselves as replacing the temple. As Klawans demonstrates, "none of the texts that are generally understood to express the notion that the community is a temple explicitly asserts that the divine presence, glory, or name now dwells among the community."⁴² He goes on to comment that "it is therefore jarring . . . that some scholars assert that the Qumran sectarians believed that the divine presence dwelt

---

39. Klawans, *Purity, Sacrifice, and Temple*, 163, 164, 166–67, stresses this point repeatedly.

40. Klawans, *Purity, Sacrifice, and Temple*, 162.

41. Klawans, *Purity, Sacrifice, and Temple*, 163–64. Regev, "Community as Temple," 613, also points to the provisional nature, concluding that "replacements recorded in the Community Rule are neither final nor absolute in eliminating sacrificial service for all times. Rather, they are interim substitutes while the Yahad awaits its eschatological validation."

42. Klawans, *Purity, Sacrifice, and Temple*, 166.

among them at Qumran at the present age."[43] Third, Klawans shows that "the sectarians did not believe they had the power to effect atonement, at least not in a very expeditious manner, which is what one would expect from a temple."[44] Fourth, Klawans underscores that priestly activities performed by the Qumran sectarians should not be regarded as anti-temple polemic: "We need not suppose that those who emulated priestly purity necessarily thought of themselves as real priests or ascribed to themselves all the obligations of the priests."[45] In other words, the sectarians did not set themselves up as an alternative cult. Rather, what we find, Klawans argues, is not a "spiritualization" of sacrifice but instead "sacrificialization" of other modes of worship that do not pertain to temple cult. This, Klawans notes, can also be extended to the temple. The temple and sacrifices, rather than being the inactive direct objects, are instead the active forces motivating imitation. In other words, to "templize" and "sacrificialize" non-cultic acts of worship—such as prayer, righteous deeds, and scripture exegesis—is to channel the sanctity that pertains to the temple and its sacrifices:[46] "The point is to make a rather straightforward statement: 'this too is divine service.'"[47] Importantly, Klawans underscores how the metaphor of "temple as community" often is treated as operating in only one direction, with the temple or sacrifices being replaced by something else. But he stresses the way the imagery flows in both directions: "Describing activities in cultic terms, the group is at the same time asserting the significance of the cult. This side of the equation has been missed in much of the scholarship, where antisacrificial, antipriestly, or antitemple biases continue to predominate."[48] In the end, Klawans contends that scholars

---

43. Klawans, *Purity, Sacrifice, and Temple*. Klawans suggests that the sectarians may have considered that the divine presence had already departed the temple, but this does not lead to the divine presence residing with the community at Qumran.

44. Klawans, *Purity, Sacrifice, and Temple*, 168.

45. Klawans, *Purity, Sacrifice, and Temple*, 171. Additionally, it should be stated that to express displeasure and disappointment in the temple and its priesthood is not the same as repudiating and thus replacing them with something else.

46. Regev similarly argues that "the comparison of prayer and righteousness to cultic actions shows that the authors greatly value, even if only in principle, the religious importance of the sacrificial service and are thus trying to copy or imitate it within the religious discipline of their community. They do not reject the essential purpose of the flesh-and-blood sacrificial service as they base the meaning of their ritual metaphors upon it" ("Community as Temple," 612).

47. Klawans, *Purity, Sacrifice, and Temple*, 171.

48. Klawans, *Purity, Sacrifice, and Temple*, 172.

who have studied the Qumran sectarians understanding of temple in relationship to their own community have not read the Dead Sea Scrolls with enough care. For Klawans, it is clear that "compared to the temple that they themselves envision in the Temple Scroll, the community offers *limited access* to the divine presence and relatively *inadequate means* of achieving atonement."[49] With this awareness in place, it is important to call attention to the fact that *temple imagery*, whether in Qumran texts or in the New Testament, *does not necessarily entail a zero-sum game.* That is, it is possible to promote community-as-temple imagery without at the same time replacing the Jerusalem temple and its sacrifices. What is more, we have seen that temple imagery that is conjoined with the mention of "spiritual" sacrifices certainly does not entail the devaluing or repudiating of the Jerusalem temple and by extension the Jewish sacrificial cult. Thus, if such a disposition exists in 1 Peter, it would need to be demonstrated with careful exegesis rather than assumed, as is all too often the case.

The foundation of the modern Primopetrine interpretive tradition of 1 Pet 2:5, which contends that οἶκος πνευματικὸς should be read in light of Qumran's supersessionist posture toward the temple and its priesthood, has been exposed, revealing substantial cracks. This in no way nullifies a replacement reading of "spiritual house" in 1 Pet 2:5, but it should caution us against making hasty conclusions about the "church" replacing Israel. Accordingly, perhaps it is best to suspend judgment about how the "temple-as-community" imagery is functioning until further examination. Botner's essay concludes with an invitation for a fresh examination of the polyvalence of the term οἶκος and whether some other temple might be in view in 1 Peter, an invitation we take up in what follows.[50]

## Exploring the Meaning of Οἶκος Πνευματικός in 1 Peter
### Lexical and Syntactical Considerations

Although most modern Primopetrine scholars refer to the οἶκος in 1 Pet 2:5 as a "temple," this is not the only, or even the most common, usage

---

49. Klawans, *Purity, Sacrifice, and the Temple*, 168 (emphasis mine).

50. Botner, "Essence of a Spiritual House," 416–24. In this chapter we will explore οἶκος as temple imagery, and in the following chapter we will explore its possible reference to household or dynasty.

of the word. In the New Testament, there are two other words that unambiguously refer to a temple, ἱερόν and ναός. If Peter wanted to make it abundantly clear that he was speaking about his addressees replacing the "no-longer legitimate" Jerusalem temple and all that happens therein (e.g., sacrifices and atonement), he would have been better off using one of those two unambiguous words, especially ἱερόν, which appears most often in the LXX and Acts to refer to the entire Jerusalem temple and its surrounding consecrated complex.[51] And if Peter wished to stress with unquestionable clarity that the community was now the (exclusive) place where God's dwells, where divine presence is encountered, he could have been more clear in making that point if he would have chosen ναός. This, of course, does not negate that he may indeed be doing both of those things in 1 Peter, but it does serve to highlight the ambiguity (perhaps strategically) of the word he has chosen.[52] Part of what makes things difficult is that at its core the word οἶκος can refer to either a building (whether that be a house, a large building such as a royal palace, or by extension a palace where God dwells), a group of people (be that a household, a people that descended from a common ancestor, or a dynastic family), or an estate (the building and what is in it).[53] Elliott calls attention to full display of the polyvalence of the term οἶκος in Acts 7, where it refers to Pharaoh's "realm" (7:10), Moses' father's "household" (7:20), the "house/extended family" of Israel and Jacob respectively (7:42, 46), and Solomon's "temple" (7:47). Thus, one of the advantages of choosing οἶκος is that it allows for some metaphorical flexibility, as we will see in chapter 6.[54]

---

51. Louw-Nida 7.16, ἱερόν.

52. I agree with Williams and Horrell, *1 Peter*, 615, who point out that the term οἶκος is sufficient to describe a temple, and at times in the LXX οἶκος θεοῦ is employed to designate the Jerusalem temple. "For this reason, the presence of οἶκος (rather than ἱερόν or ναός) in v. 5 should not be viewed as a reason to disassociate the reference from a temple." My point is simply to highlight that in choosing οἶκος, Peter is creating more space for ambiguity, which may be intentional.

53. BAGD [3rd ed.], οἶκος. Similarly, Elliott, *1 Peter,* 415, notes that οἶκος can mean (1) family or kin group, (2) the residence itself, that is the building in which persons lived, (3) an extended family, clan, tribe, realm, or lineage as in the "house of Jacob," the "house of Israel," the "house of Pharaoh," or the "house of David," and that metaphorically it can refer to a temple, shrine, or sanctuary as the "house" or "dwelling-place" of a deity.

54. So Williams and Horrell, *1 Peter*, 616; Jobes, *1 Peter* [2nd ed.], 150.

Lexically, the term πνευματικός is also challenging, not least because its translation, "spiritual," in certain Anglophone Christian traditions is often understood to mean "immaterial," "true," and/or "legitimate" as opposed to the noun that the adjective modifies. Often, "spiritual" carries Neoplatonic connotations in which the material or physical type is of lesser value than the "spiritual" form or essence. Be that as it may, in the New Testament, πνευματικός is most often used to associate the attributed noun with the Holy Spirit.[55] Thus, at its most basic level the term can mean something like "pertaining to the Spirit." This, of course, calls forth further exploration regarding how the Spirit pertains to that which is being modified by the adjective πνευματικός. Commentators seem to be at somewhat of a loss in trying to offer an explanation for a precise meaning here in 1 Pet 2:5. Many attempt almost no explanation whatsoever.[56] And those who do, often offer underwhelming conclusions. Achtemeier, for example, surmises that "the adjective πνευματικός ('spiritual') is not so much symbolic or metaphoric as it is intended to indicate its nature: it is the place where the Spirit is found."[57] After rehearsing some of the ways the adjective is used in other places in the New Testament, Williams and Horrell point to Selwyn, who suggests that "the house is spiritual because it consists of spiritual persons and exists for spiritual purposes."[58] Elliott says more about what it is not: "The function of *pneumatikos* . . . is not to identify these entities as 'figurative' or 'immaterial' (in contrast to material realities)."[59] But he also makes the most helpful observation about the adjective, which he generates from the text of 1 Peter itself, namely that πνευματικός seeks to communicate that the "house" and the "sacrifices" are controlled and/or animated by God's sanctifying Spirit.[60] At the end of this chapter, we will further demonstrate and develop this insight.

---

55. BAGD.

56. E.g., Jobes, who limits her discussion to the following three sentences: "Peter modifies both *oikos* and *thysias* (sacrifices) in 2:5 with the adjective *pneumatikos* (spiritual). In the symbolic world of these verses, the holy priesthood offers up 'spiritual' sacrifices in the 'spiritual' house (temple). In other words, it is among Christian believers that spiritual sacrifices acceptable to God will be offered (not the physical, animal sacrifices of Judaism or paganism)" (*1 Peter* [2nd ed.], 150).

57. Achtemeier, *1 Peter*, 155.

58. Williams and Horrell, *1 Peter*, 617.

59. Elliott, *1 Peter*, 418.

60. Elliott, *1 Peter*, 418.

In the end, a lexical analysis can only get us so far and ultimately does not determine for us the meaning of the elusive phrase οἶκος πνευματικός. As Elliott rightly notes, in the face of such ambiguity, "the context of its use generally determines its meaning."[61] We must look beyond this passage, then, examining the wider themes and patterns of the letter in order to discern what Peter might have meant.

But before we do that, we must consider briefly the perplexing syntax in which οἶκος πνευματικός is found. The challenges arise as we consider the syntactical function of οἶκος πνευματικός, its relationship to λίθοι ζῶντες, as well as the mood of the verb οἰκοδομεῖσθε:

καὶ αὐτοὶ ὡς λίθοι ζῶντες οἰκοδομεῖσθε οἶκος πνευματικὸς εἰς ἱεράτευμα ἅγιον. (1 Pet 2:4a)

Achtemeier, Elliott, and Williams and Horrell have the most detailed analyses regarding the syntax of this complex verse. Rather than rehearse the discussion, I will simply note that I follow Williams and Horrell, who make the following conclusions:

1. While it is possible to read οἰκοδομεῖσθε as either a middle or passive imperative, the absence of a reflexive pronoun discourages the middle interpretation. What is more, the metaphor itself, along with the literary context, which teems with indicative statements, make the imperative mood unlikely. Instead, it seems best to designate οἰκοδομεῖσθε as a passive indicative verb, in which God is the implied builder.[62]

2. While it is possible to regard οἶκος πνευματικός as being in apposition to the implied subject ὑμεῖς, it makes better sense to attribute the unusual construction to the "process of passivisation," in which case οἶκος is the complement of a double nominative subject-complement construction. The translation "you, yourselves, as living stones are being built as a spiritual house" would best reflect this syntactical analysis.[63]

With these lexical and syntactical observations registered, we are now ready to examine in greater depth the context in which we find the elusive descriptor οἶκος πνευματικός. We will begin by exploring the consensus

61. Elliott, *1 Peter*, 414.
62. Williams and Horrell, *1 Peter*, 612–13.
63. Williams and Horrell, *1 Peter*, 614.

reading of 1 Pet 2:5, namely that οἶκος πνευματικός is Peter's way of referring to his addressees as a communal temple. If this is the case, in light of the above discussion that underscores the weaknesses of assuming replacement when this imagery is employed, we will explore what kinds of claims Peter makes when he refers to the addressees throughout Asia Minor as an οἶκος πνευματικός.[64]

## Οἶκος Ρνευματικός as "Community as Temple"

For those who offer justification for οἶκος being a reference to a temple, the most common arguments are as follows:[65] (1) the phrase is surrounded by other temple imagery, namely, the offering of sacrifices, the priesthood, and the architectural terminology of ἀκρογωνιαῖος that could apply to a temple; (2) the verb οἰκοδομέω makes the most sense in reference to the construction of a building, which is being built with the "living stones" mentioned in 1 Pet 2:5. What is more, the LXX uses the verb οἰκοδομέω to refer to the building of the temple, which is described as an οἶκος; and (3) since the purpose (εἰς) of the οἶκος is to offer acceptable sacrifices to God, it makes most sense that a temple is in view.[66] In

---

64. It is beyond the scope of this study to compare the Primopetrine temple imagery with Pauline material. For that, see Kinzer, *Jerusalem Crucified*, 79–85; Regev, "Community as Temple," 624–31; Macar, *Divine Regeneration and Ethnic Identity*, 218–20.

65. One might expect that there would be more argumentation for taking οἶκος to mean temple than is actually found in modern 1 Peter scholarship. For example, in her essay "Building a Holy House," Katie Marcar asserts several times that the author of 1 Peter uses "community-as-temple" as a metaphor for identity formation but never explicitly argues for this reading (see, e.g., "Building a Holy House," 43, 49, 50). Some sort of argumentation seems called for, especially since she notes how community-as-temple is "nestled inside" the larger metaphor of ethnic identity that spans from regeneration (1:2, 23), to infancy (2:1–3), and childhood (1:14), to οἶκος (2:5). It would seem that οἶκος as household would fit much better with this other imagery, and given Elliott's proposal, which she dismisses in a brief footnote (42n7), it would require some sort of argument to adequately claim that οἶκος is functioning as temple imagery. Confusingly, she seems to suggest οἶκος means "house" (42, 50) or "household" (48), but then does not explain how this imagery morphs into "community-as-temple" language. Her explanation that the polyvalence of οἶκος (50) explains how the author smoothly transitions from a domestic metaphorical domain to a cultic one seems more like an explanation for "community-as-priesthood" than "community-as-temple." In the end, she may very well be correct in asserting that the author of 1 Peter develops a "community-as-temple metaphor." My point is that the assertion is not sufficiently *argued* for, as is the pattern in much of 1 Peter scholarship.

66. Achtemeier, *1 Peter*, 155–59, is representative of this common line of

light of this complex of temple terminology, there seems to be warrant for assuming that with the words οἶκος πνευματικός, Peter is drawing upon the architecture of a temple as well as that which happens inside the temple in order to put forth a metaphor that invites the addressees to liken their corporate life to a "spiritual" temple. This, however, is often where reflection on community as temple stops.

### In what way is the community (not) like a temple?

Perhaps, then, the most important question to ask once we encounter community-as-temple imagery is, *in what manner is the community like a temple?* Katie Marcar has helped us here with several important observations.[67] First she notes that there is no evidence in the letter itself that this notion of community as temple is developed out of dissatisfaction with the Jerusalem temple and its priesthood, as was clearly the case in Qumran. Instead, she observes that in 1 Peter, "Christ is at the centre of the community-as-temple language."[68] We might extend this important observation further by saying that in 1 Peter it is not ritual or moral defilement of the Jerusalem temple that instigates the need to become an alternative temple, but rather it is the identity, the mission, and the vindication of Jesus that enables the addressees to become "living stones" that are being built as a "spiritual house." To restate this important point more clearly, the existence of the kind of temple that Peter is talking about is entirely dependent upon the status and accomplishments of Jesus.[69]

Marcar also calls attention to the fact that in the temple as community of 1 Peter, *there is no atonement*.[70] Whatever we determine "spiritual sacrifices" to be, and we will explore that further in due course, we can say with clarity that the priesthood of 1 Peter does not achieve any kind of atonement for itself or for others through sacrifices. This is a

---

argumentation, though it should be noted that Achtemeier allows for polyvalence and considers that the author of 1 Peter is more interested in the concept of Christians as a household than a temple. See also Williams and Horrell, *1 Peter*, 616, who suggest that temple imagery is at the fore.

67. Marcar, "Building a Holy House."

68. Marcar, "Building a Holy House," 50.

69. In what follows, I also will call attention to the fact that Jesus is not the only basis for community as temple; instead, the sanctifying work of the Spirit also is shown to be integral to the temple imagery.

70. Marcar, "Building a Holy House," 50.

significant observation because it shows that Peter is not claiming nor even assuming that the addressees replace or fulfill the Aaronic priesthood, or even that they serve as a provisional alternative to the central activity of the Jerusalem temple. There is, in other words, no zero-sum game at play with respect to the priesthood mentioned in 1 Peter, which also strongly suggests the same for the temple imagery. Thus, we can see more clearly that Peter can claim that the addressees of 1 Peter are a temple without requiring him to nullify and replace the Jerusalem temple and its priesthood with "true" and "effective" worship.

*The function of the Jerusalem temple: pointing to realities beyond itself*

But there are other observations to be made about this community as temple in 1 Peter. Unlike the Qumran conception, 1 Peter's community as temple is said to be the place where "the Spirit of glory and of God rests upon" them (1 Pet 4:14). In other words, divine presence is said to reside in Anatolian communities that faithfully align themselves with Jesus Christ. Is this, then, the point at which we encounter some kind of supersessionism in 1 Peter?

Here the work of Messianic Jewish scholar Mark Kinzer is helpful. In his illuminating work in *Jerusalem Crucified, Jerusalem Risen*, Kinzer details how the temple has been a complex and unstable symbol throughout Israel's history.[71] It is a *symbol* in that it has always functioned to point to realities beyond itself—and we might also say to provide access to realities beyond itself.[72] But it is a *complex* and *unstable* symbol because, from its inception, the temple depended upon the holiness of a particular place, and sacred furniture and architecture to convey its symbolism. But over the course of Israel's history, this complex of space, furniture, and architecture proved to be unstable and fragile more often than not and would at times be significantly disrupted. Whether it was the capture of the ark, the establishment of an alternative sanctuary in Nob, the destruction of the temple in Jerusalem and the permanent disappearance of the ark of the covenant, or the establishment of the second temple with an empty holy of holies, in one sense the temple did not always function as it should; and yet, in another sense, in spite of its setbacks, it continued

---

71. See especially Kinzer, *Jerusalem Crucified*, 59–128.
72. Kinzer, *Jerusalem Crucified*, 66, 125.

to function in important ways not always appreciated. Kinzer remarks, "In those eras when the temple imperfectly incorporated its diverse components, or ceased its institutional operation entirely, the realities to which it pointed never lost their existence or their hold on the Jewish imagination."[73]

What, then, was the indefatigable symbolic function of the temple? Kinzer details four distinct realities that the temple pointed to amid its instability, fragility, and disruption. The earthly Jerusalem temple pointed *upwards* to the reality of the heavenly temple (e.g., Exod 25:9, 40; Isa 6:1–5); it pointed *outwards* to the cosmos itself as a temple (e.g., Gen 1:1—2:3); it pointed *forwards* to the eschatological temple, a notion developed during the time of Israel's exile and pending restoration (e.g., Ezek 40–48; Zech 14); and finally, the temple pointed beyond itself to a human temple, namely, the people of Israel as the place where God dwells.[74] Kinzer shows how all four of these *biblical* patterns of temple symbolism expand and deepen in extra-biblical Jewish writings, concluding:

> In combination with Jerusalem's political vulnerability and the spread of the Jewish diaspora, *this intensified symbolism heightened the significance of the Jerusalem temple in Jewish imagination while at the same time reinforcing the consciousness of its relativity and provisionality.*[75]

In other words, there has always been a sense, from the witness of the Hebrew Bible to extra-biblical reflection on the scriptures, that the Jerusalem temple itself was provisional in some sense. But provisionality never led to it being devalued or discarded. But in what sense is the temple provisional?

Kinzer shows that as far back as the construction of the tabernacle, God's aim was not ultimately to dwell *in* the temple (*betocho*) but instead that the temple was a means by which God might dwell *among* (*betocham*) the people of Israel (Exod 25:8).[76] That is to say that the tabernacle, and later the temple, were never meant to be ends in themselves but instead were instituted in order to facilitate a greater end, namely fellowship between God and the people of Israel. Kinzer suggests that the

---

73. Kinzer, *Jerusalem Crucified*, 125.

74. For the development of these four realities, see Kinzer, *Jerusalem Crucified*, 66–78.

75. Kinzer, *Jerusalem Crucified*, 78.

76. Kinzer, *Jerusalem Crucified*, 69.

implications of this foundational point in the Exodus narrative become clear during the time of Babylonian exile.

He notes the vision that the prophet Ezekiel had (Ezek 8–11) ten years before the destruction of the temple, in which he sees the "glory" (*kavod*) of God, that is, God's divine presence, depart from the temple because of sins of the people (Ezek 8:3–5, 6; 9:3; 10:1–22). Where does the *kavod* go? It moves eastward to the Mount of Olives (Ezek 10:19; 11:23). But in an earlier vision, Ezekiel learns that the *kavod* travels further east, to Babylonia, to be with the exiles (Ezek 1:1–28). Ezekiel himself tells the reader that this first vision is connected to the second vision: "And the glory of the God of Israel was there, like the vision that I had seen in the valley" (Ezek 8:4; see also 10:20). That the *kavod* of God relocated to Babylon is also implied when Ezekiel sees the glory of God coming from the east in his vision of Jerusalem's future temple (Ezek 43:2). This "exile" of the *kavod* to abide with the people of Israel is further characterized as a "sanctuary" (*mikdash*): "Thus says the Lord GOD: Though I removed them far away among the nations and though I scattered them among the countries, yet I have been a sanctuary to them for a little while in the countries where they have gone" (Ezek 11:16). The implication is that the relocation of the *kavod* means the relocation of the sanctuary.[77] In other words, "The LORD dwells among his servants, who are now in exile."[78] Kinzer notes how Isaiah 40–55 seems to be working with this same framework. As Israel learns that return and restoration are near, Isaiah also speaks about the LORD's return to Zion (see especially Isa 52:7–8, 11–12). The implication is that the return of the LORD to Zion is inseparable from the return to that place of the people of the LORD."[79]

But it is not just in the biblical material that is related to exile that we see this reality. That is, it seems that God's divine presence among the people was not limited to Babylonian exile. It is affirmed, for example, in the exodus from Egypt: "When Israel went out from Egypt, the house of Jacob from a people of strange language, Judah became God's sanctuary" (Ps 114:1–2). What is more, Kinzer points to at least three ways

---

77. One of the arguments of those who argue that the church has indeed replaced Israel is that when God's glory departed from the temple it never returned until Pentecost. In other words, the true temple of God is the Christian church because God left the Jerusalem temple, and the church is now referred to as the temple of God. Kinzer challenges this line of interpretation with his reading of Ezekiel and Isaiah.

78. Kinzer, *Jerusalem Crucified*, 70.

79. Kinzer, *Jerusalem Crucified*, 71.

in which this notion of God's presence abiding with the people beyond the temple boundaries was developed in extra-biblical Judaism. The first is somewhat contested. We find in the Qumran literature the community's self-designation as a *mikdash adam*. Many have interpreted this to mean something akin to "community as temple," leading to the translation of the phrase as "human sanctuary." But recently this view has been challenged,[80] and three other possibilities have been put forth with varying degrees of plausibility: (1) the "human-made temple," which is to be built in the future; (2) the human-made temple of the monarchic period; or (3) the ideal temple that will return humanity to the days of Adam.[81] But even if the interpretation of *mikdash adam* is disputed, what is clear is that this community described its behavior by drawing on sacrificial terms, thus extending the temple beyond its physical boundaries.[82] Secondly, Kinzer points to the Pharisaic practice of extending temple rules to non-sacrificial meals. And finally, he draws attention to a later rabbinic tradition that described the study of the Torah, prayer, and deeds of loving-kindness in terms that matched or bettered temple sacrifice. This same tradition claims that the divine presence resides with those communities that engage in such practices, wherever they may be located.[83]

What is important about all of this for our purposes is threefold. First, we learn that this concept of the God of Israel dwelling with his people and characterizing that reality as a "community as temple" is not a "Christian" innovation whereby religion finally evolves to a more universal "spiritual" plain by abandoning ritual cult with all its tangible accoutrements (i.e., dead animals, manipulation of blood, burnt grains and meat, etc.), as often is assumed. It turns out that from the inception of the building of the tabernacle and its concomitant institution, God has intended to dwell among his people in an analogous way to that of the temple. Second, we see more clearly, especially from Ezekiel, that from its inception, the temple has had as one of its functions the pointing to this fundamental reality: "Divine presence was bound to the people of Israel more closely than the building that they had constructed."[84] And third, we see a precedent in which community-as-temple imagery does

---

80. See, for example, Klawans, *Purity, Sacrifice, and the Temple*, 163–64.
81. Regev, "Community as Temple," 613–15.
82. Klawans, *Purity, Sacrifice, and the Temple*, 164.
83. Kinzer, *Jerusalem Crucified*, 77.
84. Kinzer, *Jerusalem Crucified*, 71.

not entail replacement or supersession. (This is especially the case when the people of God are in exile and when the Jerusalem temple does not stand, which, to one degree or another, is analogous to the situation of the 1 Peter addressees.)

This last point is underscored in Kinzer's provocative and persuasive work on Luke-Acts, which, if accurate, offers an important example of Jewish apostolic teaching in which temple-ecclesiology does not entail Jerusalem temple repudiation or replacement. Here, I briefly highlight his conclusions as a way of showing that 1 Peter may not be unique in apostolic teaching to draw on temple imagery without replacing Israel with the church.

Kinzer shows how "Luke does not portray daily prayer as a substitute for temple sacrifice, but instead as its essential accompaniment."[85] He does this by tracing the manner in which the daily temple liturgy known as the *tamid* features prominently in Luke and Acts in the service of developing a "temple-ecclesiology."[86] For example, he argues that in order to understand the foundational events that occur in Acts 2 (Pentecost) and Acts 10 (the conversion of Cornelius and his household), one must see the connection made between the *tamid*, the prayers of the people, and the gift of the Holy Spirit. Here Kinzer shows how in the opening chapters of Acts, Luke wants the reader to see that the apostles and the disciples gather in the upper room, that the apostles and the people pray in the temple courts (Acts 3:1), and that Cornelius prays in his house (Acts 10:3) as the priests offer the *tamid*.[87] Kinzer concludes:

> This linkage points to the temple-like character of the *ekklēsia*. Just as fire falls from heaven to consecrate the altar of the wilderness tabernacle and Solomon's temple, tongues of fire now rest on each of the disciples of Jesus gathered in prayer. After the days of Pentecost the *ekklēsia* no longer gathers in the upper room, but in the temple itself. Just as their prayer complements rather than replaces the temple sacrifices, so their corporate presence perfects the Temple Mount and structure by bringing

---

85. Kinzer, *Jerusalem Crucified*, 111.

86. Kinzer, *Jerusalem Crucified*, 111–25. The *tamid* was a twice-daily temple liturgy (Exod 29:38–42; Num 28:1–8) that involved prayer and sacrifice in the temple. The community as a whole could participate in the liturgy by praying at the time of sacrifice, either in the temple courts, or towards the temple if one was out of reach of the temple.

87. Kinzer, *Jerusalem Crucified*, 111–25, 190–95.

the foretaste of the eschatological human-temple into the precincts of the temple made with human hands.[88]

He goes on to argue further that "the temple structure points to a reality beyond itself—that is, to the *human-temple* at the heart of the *eschatological-temple*."[89] And he brings his provocative study to a conclusion by claiming that Luke-Acts intensifies this symbolic function of the Jerusalem temple by intensifying the reality of Israel as the human-temple and extending that reality to the nations:

> This intensification becomes evident on the day of Pentecost, as the Messiah pours out the Holy Spirit on his Jewish disciples in Jerusalem at the time of morning *tamid* offering and prayer. The extension of that intensified reality becomes just as evident when the gentile Cornelius in the gentile city of Caesarea receives the same Spirit at the time of the afternoon *tamid* offering and prayer. While temple-ecclesiology is intensified and extended in the present age through the work of Jesus and the gift of the Spirit, the present age remains an ambiguous time involving *both* restoration *and* exile. The *ekklēsia* points prophetically to Israel's destined future, but represents only a partial and preliminary sketch of the glorious "return of the Lord to Zion" that is yet to come.[90]

Kinzer's observations about the temple in Luke-Acts are significant because they provide evidence of at least one New Testament text in which the focus on community as temple (as well as its focus on the heavenly temple and the eschatological temple) does not derive from a critique of the Jerusalem temple as an institution but instead is a reflection of its symbolic function. In keeping with Kinzer's hypothesis, this is precisely what one would expect the temple to do—to point to realities beyond itself.[91] But his analysis of temple themes extends beyond Luke-Acts to include the writings of Paul (and the Pauline tradition), Hebrews, the Gospel of John, and the Book of Revelation.[92] He concludes his extensive examination by concluding that "New Testament expressions of this symbolism do not differ in kind from those found in Hebrew scripture or

88. Kinzer, *Jerusalem Crucified*, 112.
89. Kinzer, *Jerusalem Crucified*, 122.
90. Kinzer, *Jerusalem Crucified*, 123.
91. Kinzer, *Jerusalem Crucified*, 126.
92. Kinzer, *Jerusalem Crucified*, 79–108. Unfortunately, the temple in 1 Peter was not considered.

THE PROBLEM OF TEMPLE AND PRIESTHOOD IN 1 PETER    147

Jewish tradition.... There is no reason to assume without evidence that the New Testament is an exception to the rule."⁹³ If this is the case, then the punchline to the claim in 1 Peter that God's presence can be found among these suffering Anatolian Jesus followers (e.g., 1 Pet 2:5; 4:14) is not that they have replaced Israel but rather that they—gentiles—have been emplaced within this reality to which the temple pointed, namely fellowship with the God of Israel.

Kinzer's insight that the temple-ecclesiology of Luke-Acts is actualized in "an ambiguous time involving *both* restoration *and* exile" serves as a segue to yet another important observation about the way in which Peter characterizes the community as temple. One detail that is not always appreciated is that the οἶκος πνευματικός of 1 Peter is characterized as provisional in nature. That is, it is under construction, "being built" (1 Pet 2:5).⁹⁴ As we have already seen, read within the literary (and narrative) context of 1 Pet 1:3—2:10, this provisional "house" under construction is located in a space that is analogous to Israel's wilderness experience after the exodus from Egypt—in between redemption (1 Pet 1:18-19; 2:9-10) and inheritance (1 Pet 1:3-9)—where faithful allegiance will be tested (1 Pet 1:5-7). One feature of 1 Peter that is noteworthy but has received almost no attention, is the optimism that Peter has concerning the addressees making it through the wilderness of fiery trials (1 Pet 1:5-9; 4:12-19; 5:9-10).⁹⁵ In other words, why is Peter so confident that these "elect-sojourners" will receive praise, glory, and honor at the revelation of Jesus (1 Pet 1:7), that they will indeed reach the intended goal of their faithfulness, namely their salvation (1 Pet 1:9), or that God himself will restore, confirm, strengthen, and establish them after they have resisted the devil and suffered "a little while" (1 Pet 5:8-10)? It turns out that attending to this unique and underappreciated feature of 1 Peter as well as the provisional nature of the community-as-temple imagery in 1 Peter, especially within its new exodus/wilderness context, alerts us to the possibility that there may be another temple in view in 1 Peter.⁹⁶

---

93. Kinzer, *Jerusalem Crucified*, 126.

94. This is in keeping with the conclusion that οἰκοδομεῖσθε is a passive indicative verb, on which see above.

95. See Liebengood, *Eschatology of 1 Peter*, 155.

96. See Botner, "Essence of a Spiritual House," 421-24, who to my knowledge, is the first to make this suggestion.

*Where is Jesus and what is he doing?*

## SIX CLUES THAT THERE MAY BE ANOTHER TEMPLE IN 1 PETER[97]

Thus far, I have shown a sampling of ways in which Peter shapes the identity of his addressees by implicitly inviting them to "appropriate Israelhood," that is, to make sense of their lives in keeping with the way in which the God of Israel has revealed himself to the people of Israel. In chapter 1, for example, I underscored that the addressees are being asked to do more than think of Israel as a metaphor for their own sense of identity; rather, they are being called to embrace an Israel-centric way of telling the story of the world, of talking about who God is, and of describing what this God is up to in the world, and they are being asked to find their place within the God of Israel's ongoing work in and through Israel. In chapter 4, we saw how Peter reorients the addressees by calling them to align themselves with the expectations and hopes of Israel's Davidic shepherd king in contrast to the realized eschatology of Roman imperial ideology. In what follows, I seek to show that as a part of the identity-formation strategy of the letter, Peter draws his gentile audience into yet another mode of "appropriating Israelhood," namely by having them understand their identity and allegiance to Jesus with respect to the logic of covenant and sacrifice. There seem to be at least six pressure points, or clues, in the letter to suggest this to be the case.

Our first clue is found when we consider *where* Jesus is at this moment, according to the letter. In the "remarkable, unique, and difficult"[98] passage of 1 Pet 3:18–22, we learn that Jesus has gone into heaven and is presently "at the right hand of God."[99] His entrance into heaven is said to be the result of both his death (3:18) as well as his resurrection from the dead (1 Pet 3:21; 1:3). In other words, as Williams and Horrell

---

97. I would like to express my thanks to David Moffitt (Biblical Studies Seminar at University of St Andrews) and Carlos Gil (Theology Faculty Seminar at the Universidad de Deusto), who provided the opportunity for me to receive helpful feedback on the remaining sections of this chapter.

98. Williams and Horrell, *1 Peter*, 292.

99. This is a notoriously challenging passage to interpret for a variety of reasons. Given the scope of this project, I will limit my discussion to the clearest portions of the passage, 1 Pet 3:18 and 22. For a helpful survey of the history of the interpretation of this passage along with all its interpretive challenges, see Williams and Horrell, *1 Peter*, 185–294.

underscore, Jesus' ascension in 1 Pet 3:22 is the culmination of a concise narrative sequence that is signaled with the participles θανατωθείς, ζῳοποιηθείς, and πορευθείς.[100] What is also important to see is that these participles suggest that there is a connection to be made between the ascension of Jesus and the purpose or goal described in 1 Pet 3:18.

This leads to our second clue, or pressure point. According to Peter, the ultimate goal and/or result (ἵνα) of this journey of being at the right hand of God, or alternatively we might say, this process of death, resurrection, and ascension, is "to bring *you* to God" (1 Pet 3:18). Two important observations are in order as we consider the significance of this phrase. First, if we were to read this reference within Israel's covenantal frame of reference, as I am suggesting we do for the moment, to be "brought" (προσάγω) to God is only possible through the offering of an acceptable sacrifice through a priest in a "set-apart" space in the temple.[101] In other words, προσάγω potentially signals priestly sacrificial activity. Second, here again, as we noted in chapter 4, the "for-you-ness" of Jesus' accomplishment is stressed: ἵνα ὑμᾶς προσαγάγῃ τῷ θεῷ. As can be seen, the second person plural pronoun is placed forward in the sentence in order to emphasize that it is *you* that is being brought to God. As I have suggested in chapter 4, given the social setting of the letter, it seems best to regard the punchline of this emphasis as directed to the fact that Jesus' resurrection and ascension, that is, the God of Israel's vindication of the Jewish Messiah, pertains *even to these gentile addressees.*

Our third clue, or pressure point, can also be found in 1 Pet 3:18. The first step of this concise and interrelated narrative sequence, namely death, which ultimately results in ascension, is characterized as suffering περὶ ἁμαρτιῶν. That is, Christ is said to have suffered "on account of" the sins of others (cf. 1 Pet 2:22).[102] This means that the suffering that led to the death of Jesus was part of an intentional process to secure forgiveness of sins. In other words, the addressees need atonement in order to be brought to God. This phrase περὶ ἁμαρτιῶν is followed by an equally illustrative phrase, δίκαιος ὑπὲρ ἀδίκων. Williams and Horrell suggest that while περί and ὑπέρ can often be used interchangeably, it seems that the author wishes to make an important nuance in 1 Pet 3:18: with περί, the addressees are told that sin is the reason why Jesus' suffering

---

100. Williams and Horrell, *1 Peter*, 288, 191.

101. See LXX Lev 3:7, 12; 4:3, 14.

102. See Williams and Horrell, *1 Peter*, 196–97, for a discussion on the meaning of the preposition περί when followed by the singular and plural forms of ἁμαρτία.

was necessary; and with ὑπέρ, the author claims that the suffering was in some way vicarious, though not necessarily in a penal substitutionary sense.¹⁰³

The fourth clue, or pressure point, is that the syntax (and not just the narrative sequence) of 1 Pet 3:18-22 makes it clear that forgiveness of sins and being brought to God are dependent upon the ascension of Jesus (and not merely his death). This is because the participles θανατωθεὶς and ζωοποιηθεὶς are best regarded as the means by which the phrase ἵνα ὑμᾶς προσαγάγῃ τῷ θεῷ is accomplished.¹⁰⁴ By extension, the "being made alive" (1 Pet 3:18), which is described synonymously as the resurrection (1 Pet 3:22), also makes up part of the means by which Jesus is able to "proceed" (πορευθεὶς) into heaven (1 Pet 3:22).

Williams and Horrell briefly entertain the possibility that cultic connotations may be present in this passage, particularly as it pertains to the phrase ἵνα ὑμᾶς προσαγάγῃ τῷ θεῷ, noting that προσάγω is frequently used in the LXX of the bringing of sacrificial offerings and of the consecration of priests.¹⁰⁵ But they dismiss this possibility with no argumentation, pointing instead to others who assert that there is no significant basis for seeing sacrificial or priestly imagery in this instance.¹⁰⁶ But if, for the moment, we remove Jewish cultic connotations, then how are we to make sense of this passage? What is the logic that brings together the themes of (a) death that is characterized as part of a process for dealing with the sins of others; (b) the prospect of being presented to God in connection with this death that is "on account of sins"; and (c) a figure who is characterized as having ascended to be at God's right hand and described as having proceeded into heaven with the express purpose of presenting others before God? In other words, why is this passage concerned with making a connection between the death of Jesus *and* his being at the right hand of God? And how is this related to forgiveness of sins and being presented before God? Here I suggest that the logic of covenant and sacrifice is what holds this sequence of events together and best explains

---

103. Williams and Horrell, *1 Peter*, 199.

104. So Williams and Horrell, *1 Peter*, 202-3; Jobes, *1 Peter* [2nd ed.], 241; Dubis, *Handbook on the Greek*, 117.

105. Williams and Horrell, *1 Peter*, 201.

106. Williams and Horrell, *1 Peter*, 201. Gupta's essay on sacrificial imagery in 1 Peter, "Spiritual House of Royal Priests," does not touch upon 1 Pet 3:18-22. To the contrary, see Botner, "Essence of a Spiritual House," 221-24.

the inclusion of these elements as an integrated claim that Jesus brings the addressees to God.

Recently, a number of New Testament scholars—building on the work of Jacob Milgrom, Roy Gane, Christian Eberhart,[107] and others—have drawn attention to the ways in which the logic of covenant and sacrifice illuminates the Gospels,[108] Paul's letters,[109] and Hebrews.[110] Here, briefly, I draw attention to the helpful work of David Moffitt, summarizing several key observations about the process and logic of sacrifice that will be helpful as we further consider 1 Pet 3:18–22 and its relationship with the rest of the letter:[111]

1. Levitical sacrifice is established in response to covenant. That is, according to the narrative of the Pentateuch, the temple, the priesthood, and the sacrificial system are the *result* of God's covenant with Israel, or we might say "the realities that come after the establishment of the Mosaic covenant."[112] In this regard, the language of sacrifice is meant to be understood within the context of covenant.[113]

2. Levitical sacrifice is given, in part, in order to solve the problems of impurity and sin, which jeopardize the relationship between the God of Israel and the covenant people.[114] In other words, sacrifice is given as a means for the people of God to maintain its covenant relationship with God.[115]

3. Acceptable sacrificial atonement results in the purgation of sin and impurity, which enables God to dwell with the people and the people to dwell with and benefit from God on an ongoing basis. "Sacrifice, because it atones for sin and impurity, is therefore an essential part of maintaining the covenant relationship."[116]

---

107. E.g., Milgrom, *Leviticus*; Gane, *Cult and Character*; Eberhart, *Sacrifice of Jesus*.
108. E.g., Thiessen, *Jesus and the Forces of Death*.
109. E.g., Rillera, *Lamb of the Free*.
110. See especially Moffit, *Rethinking the Atonement*.
111. Moffitt, *Rethinking the Atonement*, 245–50.
112. Moffitt, *Rethinking the Atonement*, 54.
113. Moffitt, *Rethinking the Atonement*, 53.
114. Moffitt, *Rethinking the Atonement*, 54. This is not to say that sacrifice is only for problem solving.
115. Moffitt, *Rethinking the Atonement*, 38–39, 53–55, 147–54.
116. Moffitt, *Rethinking the Atonement*, 249.

4. Levitical sacrifice is best understood as a process. The process *begins* with the slaughter of a victim. However, the atoning benefits of forgiveness of sins and/or purification are associated more with the acts of blood manipulation and/or the burning of parts than with the slaughter of the victim.[117] In fact, in Leviticus we see that in some cases the priests have nothing to do with the slaughtering of victims (e.g., Lev. 17:3); but they have everything to do with the presentation of the sacrifice before God in the temple. In other words, for the slaughter to be acceptable and effective, its blood must be presented to God in the temple at an altar by a priest. This is to emphasize that the slaughter or death of a victim in no way encapsulates the sacrificial process. To reduce blood sacrifice to the death of the victim is a conceptual mistake.[118]

5. The center of blood sacrifice is drawing near to God and conveying the material of the sacrifice into his presence.[119]

6. One cannot offer a ritual (atoning) sacrifice in order to inaugurate a covenant or to restore a broken covenant.[120] When the temple is defiled or destroyed, or when covenant infidelity becomes irreparable through covenant maintenance, (atoning) sacrifice is no longer possible. Instead, redemption and reconciliation are needed.[121]

7. Levitical sacrifices are never described as objects of God's wrath.[122] Instead, they are presented to God as gifts.[123]

I would maintain that attending to the logic of covenant and sacrifice helps to explain why the suffering and death of Jesus "for sins" have been joined with the events of Jesus' resurrection and ascension to the right hand of God. In other words, this logic offers a compelling rationale for

---

117. Moffitt, *Rethinking the Atonement*, 246. Eberhart, *Sacrifice of Jesus*, 95, 97, makes the important point that in order to understand the logic of sacrifice, we must take into account all sacrificial substances (not just animals). Since we are dealing explicitly with atonement in our discussion of sacrifice, I have focused on such sacrifices that are said to effect such an outcome.

118. Moffitt, *Rethinking the Atonement*, 249.

119. Moffitt, *Rethinking the Atonement*, 247.

120. Moffitt, *Rethinking the Atonement*, 39, 54.

121. See Moffitt, *Rethinking the Atonement*, 29–71, for more development of this claim.

122. Moffitt, *Rethinking the Atonement*, 52.

123. See also Eberhart, *Sacrifice of Jesus*, 70–71.

why the ascension of Jesus to the right hand of God is framed as the culmination, the ultimate mechanism if you will, that enables the addressees to be presented to God. To put it as clearly as possible, working within the framework of Levitical cultic worship, *death, in and of itself, is not a sacrifice and cannot achieve atonement.* Purification and forgiveness of sins, which is necessary to be in the presence of God, is only achieved when the life of the victim (i.e., the blood) is brought before God on the altar by a priest. Working from within this logic, it seems at least plausible to assume that at the right hand of God, Jesus performs his priestly ministry in the heavenly temple.[124]

But we can anticipate at least three potential objections to this claim that Peter locates Jesus in the heavenly temple, serving as a priest, offering himself as a sacrifice for atonement. First, there is no explicit mention that Jesus is in the heavenly temple before the heavenly altar, like what we find in Hebrews (e.g., Heb 8:1–2; 9:24–28). Instead, Peter seems to stress Jesus' ascension for the purpose of emphasizing his vindication. Second, there seems to be no explicit signal in 1 Peter that Jesus is to be regarded as a priest. And third, notably absent from 1 Pet 3:18–22 is any mention of the manipulation of blood, which is essential to the process of sacrifice for the purpose of achieving atonement (e.g., Heb 9:13–14).[125]

Regarding the observation that the ascension in 1 Peter seems to be about the vindication of Jesus, this certainly seems to be the case. But I see no reason why this would entail that the "being at the right hand of God" is *only* about vindication.[126] That Jesus is vindicated at his ascension is not mutually exclusive with other functions that the ascension imagery might be serving (see, for example, Heb 1:3–4; 10:12–13). What is more, if one were to take away the heavenly temple dimension of Jesus' ascension, one still needs to explain why Peter joins the ascension imagery with suffering and death for the sake of forgiveness of sins—especially given that death itself does not constitute a sacrifice or effect atonement. Additionally, one would need to explain the redundant and unnecessary inclusion of the phrase "has gone into heaven" (πορευθεὶς εἰς οὐρανὸν) that is appended to the mention of Jesus being at the right hand of God in 1 Pet 3:22 if the point is exclusively about vindication.[127]

---

124. For a discussion of the heavenly temple, see Himmelfarb, *Ascent to Heaven in Jewish and Christian Apocalypses*; Kinzer, *Jerusalem Crucified*, 73–74.

125. Lev 4:1—5:13; 16:1–34; Eberhart, *Sacrifice of Jesus*, 82–88, 97–101.

126. See Heb 1:3–4, where the themes of vindication and priestly service are joined.

127. See especially the word order in Greek: ὅς ἐστιν ἐν δεξιᾷ [τοῦ] θεοῦ πορευθεὶς εἰς οὐρανὸν.

The objection that Jesus is not depicted as a priest elsewhere in 1 Peter leads us to the fifth clue or pressure point in 1 Peter, namely the overlooked and suggestive prepositional phrase in 1 Pet 2:5 that seems to offer a window into where Jesus is presently:

ὡς λίθοι ζῶντες οἰκοδομεῖσθε οἶκος πνευματικὸς εἰς ἱεράτευμα ἅγιον ἀνενέγκαι πνευματικὰς θυσίας εὐπροσδέκτους [τῷ] θεῷ **διὰ** Ἰησοῦ Χριστοῦ.

Here, Jesus is presented as the agent *through whom* the "spiritual house" offers "acceptable" spiritual sacrifices to God. The proliferation of cultic language in 1 Pet 2:5, together with what we have discussed regarding 1 Pet 3:18, 22, seems to necessitate that Jesus be considered a priest serving in a different temple. And it is not just the accumulation of priestly imagery (i.e., temple, priesthood, "to offer," "acceptable sacrifice") in 1 Pet 2:5 that fosters the implicit reference to Jesus as priest; there is also a consistent pattern in 1 Peter in which the addressees share in the identity and mission of Jesus. Jesus is elect (1 Pet 2:4), they are elect (1:1); Jesus is a living stone (2:4), they are living stones (2:5); Jesus is rejected (2:23), they will be rejected (2:12; 3:9–17; 4:12–19); Jesus suffered (3:18; 4:1), they suffer (3:17; 4:1); Jesus is vindicated (1:3; 3:22), they will be vindicated (5:10). It follows then, that if the addressees are identified as a priesthood (2:5, 9), then we should expect Jesus himself to be a priest.[128]

*Where is the manipulation of blood?*
*Exploring the letter prescript (1 Pet 1:1–2)*

In response to the objection that there is no evidence of blood manipulation in 1 Peter, we turn to an extensive analysis of the prescript of 1 Peter (1 Pet 1:1–2), where we find our sixth and final clue or pressure point, namely "the sprinkling of blood." It is important to underscore that the letter prescript is where Peter immediately begins to construct the identity of the addressees and how they ought to conceptualize their calling in the midst of their precarious "wilderness" situation of suffering and social alienation. This is one reason why we will spend considerable time on this important section of the letter.[129] What is more, as we attend to

---

128. Harink makes a similar observation: "Their life reflects his . . . the church is the priesthood because Christ is the original priest; the church offers acceptable sacrifices because Christ himself is the original sacrifice" (*1 & 2 Peter*, 68).

129. Achtemeier, for example, says that "the opening two verses set the stage for

the term "sprinkling of blood" in its context, we will also gain insight into what Peter means by elusive term πνευματικός and how it is related to both οἶκος as well as θυσία.

As was developed in chapter 2, the initially ambiguous epithet, ἐκλεκτοί παρεπίδημοι (see table 1) encapsulates both the privilege as well as the responsibility of these gentile followers of Jesus.

### TABLE 1. FIRST PETER 1:1B-2

| Nestle-Aland 28 |
|---|
| ἐκλεκτοῖς παρεπιδήμοις . . . |
| κατὰ πρόγνωσιν θεοῦ πατρὸς |
| ἐν ἁγιασμῷ πνεύματος |
| εἰς ὑπακοὴν καὶ ῥαντισμὸν αἵματος Ἰησοῦ Χριστοῦ |

The term ἐκλεκτός reminds the addressees that they have been chosen to orient their lives around the propagation of God's will and to mediate the life of their God to one another and to their neighbors.[130] That they are elect παρεπίδημοι highlights that for now this privileged calling is to be expressed in a kind of the wilderness liminality: their allegiance to this call will be tested until they reach their inheritance (1 Pet 1:5-7; 2:11-12; 4:12-17).

As can be seen in Table 1, Peter amplifies the foundational epithet ἐκλεκτοί παρεπίδημοι with three prepositional phrases. First, he underscores that their status as "elect-sojourners" is in keeping with the foreknowledge of God the Father (κατὰ πρόγνωσιν θεοῦ πατρός). Given the proliferation of Hebrew Bible texts appropriated and applied to the addressees of 1 Peter, not to mention Peter's own words in 1 Pet 1:10-12 regarding the prophets, its seems best to regard this first prepositional phrase as highlighting that the Father has predetermined the inclusion and salvation of these gentile addressees, as previously has been revealed

---

what is to follow in the letter in terms of content and themes" (*1 Peter*, 80). See Tite, *Compositional Transitions in 1 Peter*; Michaels, *1 Peter*, 4, 13; Goppelt, *1 Peter*, 64. For more on why I do not regard διασπορά as the controlling metaphor of the letter, see Liebengood, *Eschatology of 1 Peter*, 156-64.

130. Schrenk underscores that "1 Pet is the only NT work in which *eklektos* has from the very outset thematic significance. Here everything is worked out in terms of this controlling concept" (Elliott, *1 Peter*, 446).

in the scriptures.¹³¹ In other words, their inclusion into this unique status and vocation that they have been given and which they must now live out is in keeping with what the Father planned and which he revealed to the prophets (cf. 1 Pet 1:10–12).

Second, Peter credits the consecrating (or "holy-fying") work of the Spirit (ἐν ἁγιασμῷ πνεύματος) as providing the means by which the "elect-sojourners" are enabled to live out this calling.¹³² What is not always appreciated about this brief reference is that already Peter seems to be "templizing" the addressees. That is, in the same way that the sanctuary and the altar had to be consecrated for divine communion, so too, by the Spirit, the addressees are being made sacred or consecrated space for God's presence to dwell in.¹³³ Thus, from the start of the letter, perhaps it is that we are alerted to anticipate that the Spirit is to be associated with the recipients becoming a kind of temple space.

Attentiveness to the development of the theme of holiness in 1 Peter fills out what Peter has in mind with respect to the "consecrating" (ἁγιασμός) activity of the Spirit. For example, as we saw in chapter 2, holiness is a foundational injunction (1 Pet 1:15–16) as these "elect-sojourners" wait for their inheritance in the wilderness. To be holy (ἅγιος) is characterized as being obedient to "the one who is holy" (1 Pet 1:14–15), and is contrasted with no longer being conformed to "the desires that you formerly had in ignorance." The imperative, "You shall be holy, for I am holy," is a citation from Lev 11:44.¹³⁴ In the literary context of Leviticus, holiness is characterized as rightly relating to God in the way that he has revealed (obedience), including but not limited to how to properly offer acceptable sacrifices (see especially Lev 17:1–9; 19:1–8). But holiness in Leviticus is also framed as not doing as they did in Egypt and Canaan (Lev 18:1–5). In other words, much like it is characterized in 1 Pet 1:14–18, in Leviticus holiness is about learning a new culture or way of life.¹³⁵ The important point is to see that the foundational injunction to be holy (ἅγιος) points readers back to 1 Pet 1:2, where they are reminded

---

131. See also Green, *1 Peter*, 19.

132. To be clear, ἐν expresses instrumentality or means, and πνεύματος is a subjective genitive and refers to the agency of the Holy Spirit.

133. Mbuvi, *Temple, Exile and Identity in 1 Peter*, 80.

134. Similar imperatives are found in Lev 19:2; 20:7, 26; 21:8.

135. This theme will be explored further in chapter 6.

that holiness is enabled by the Spirit's activity of consecration or "holy-fying" (ἁγιασμός).[136]

The final way Peter amplifies the epithet ἐκλεκτοί παρεπίδημοι is with the challenging phrase εἰς ὑπακοὴν καὶ ῥαντισμὸν αἵματος Ἰησοῦ Χριστοῦ. Because of the preposition εἰς, most commentators make "obedience *to* Jesus" the *telos* of the activities of the Father and the Spirit. While this is a possible rendition of the Greek, it notably fails to follow the pattern that Peter seems carefully to have arranged in the prescript; it does not run with the grain of what is developed in the rest of the letter, as we will see in a moment; and it either ignores or distorts the logic of covenant and sacrifice.

Regarding the pattern that Peter has arranged, in the two previous prepositional phrases the genitives are clearly subjective, which is to say that the Father and the Spirit are the subjects doing the activities described in the head nouns (predetermining and sanctifying/consecrating). Given this pattern, it seems most natural to at least consider the possibility that Ἰησοῦ Χριστοῦ is also a subjective genitive. Such a reading would alleviate the unnecessary, awkward, and confusing fragmentation of ὑπακοὴν καὶ ῥαντισμὸν αἵματος that is found in some English translations.[137] What has discouraged many from keeping with the subjective-genitive pattern is the preposition εἰς, which is frequently used to indicate purpose or goal (*for*), thus making the subjective genitive reading unintelligible. Some, however, have argued for a causal meaning of εἰς (*because*), which enables a subjective-genitive reading of Ἰησοῦ Χριστοῦ such that Jesus Christ is doing the obeying and sprinkling the blood.[138] The Common English Bible translation of 1 Pet 1:2 reflects this exegetical judgment: "To God's chosen strangers ... *because* of the faithful obedience and sacrifice of Jesus Christ." However, as attractive as this reading might be, there seems to be no lexical support for the claim that εἰς can have casual force.[139] There is, however, lexical support that at

---

136. See Green, *1 Peter*, 215, who underscores the importance of "being made holy" in the letter and that "Peter makes it clear that the agent of sanctification is the Spirit."

137. See, for example, the NRSV: "to be obedient to Jesus Christ and to be sprinkled with his blood"; or the ESV: "for obedience to Jesus Christ and for sprinkling with his blood." See also Williams and Horrell, *1 Peter*, 324–25, who argue that ὑπακοή should not be joined with the genitive Ἰησοῦ Χριστοῦ, which is only modifying ῥαντισμός.

138. E.g., Liebengood, *Eschatology of 1 Peter*, 160–61; Elliott, *1 Peter*, 319; Green, *1 Peter*, 20.

139. See Page, "Obedience and Blood-Sprinkling in 1 Peter 1:2," 294–95. While I agree with his argument regarding the causal εἰς, I think his overall argumentation against a subjective genitive reading of 1 Pet 1:2 is unconvincing.

times εἰς conveys the idea of instrumentality (*by means of*).[140] If we regard the third prepositional phrase to convey the notion of instrumentality, and that Jesus is the subject performing the action of the two head nouns, then Peter is claiming that his addressees are enabled to live out their calling as ἐκλεκτοί παρεπίδημοι *by means* of the obedience of Jesus and his activity of sprinkling blood.[141]

In an effort to determine what might be meant by the phrase "by means of the obedience and the sprinkling of the blood of Jesus Christ," I briefly will show how this "instrumental-subjective-genitive" reading of the final prepositional phrase in 1 Pet 1:2 runs with the grain of rest of the letter in compelling ways; and how it offers a clue as to why Peter is so optimistic about the addressees making it through the wilderness of testing.[142] I begin by underscoring that in 1 Peter, Jesus in never presented as the object of obedience; instead, he is held up as the model of faithfulness because of his obedience to the Father. For example, in 1 Pet 2:21, Peter asserts that his implied readers have been called for the purpose of following in the footsteps of the suffering and vindicated Jesus (εἰς τοῦτο γὰρ ἐκλήθητε ... ἵνα ἐπακολουθήσητε τοῖς ἴχνεσιν αὐτοῦ), who left them an example (or pattern of life) to emulate. In 1 Pet 2:23, the example that Jesus leaves behind to be followed is one of non-violent resistance to injustice and wrongdoing: in the face of revilement and threats, rather than respond in kind, Jesus "continued entrusting himself to the one who judges justly." Thus, in the midst of being mistreated and shamed, Jesus becomes the example of what faithful obedience to the will of the Father looks like. For this reason, later in 1 Pet 3:9, Peter draws a line back to the paradigmatic obedience of Jesus (cf. 1 Pet 2:23) by exhorting his readers to "not repay evil for evil or reviling for reviling." Additionally, in 1 Pet 4:19, he draws on Jesus' response to wrongdoing by exhorting followers of Jesus to "entrust" their souls (as Jesus did) to a faithful Creator while doing good. And in 1 Pet 4:1–2, Peter urges his readers to arm themselves with the same disposition that Jesus had—living no longer for the passions of the flesh but rather for the will of God.

---

140. See BDAG. Louw-Nida acknowledge εἰς, ἐν, and διά as "markers of the means by which one event makes another event possible" (e.g., Acts 7:53).

141. This assumes that the genitive Ἰησοῦ Χριστοῦ modifies both "obedience" and "sprinkling of blood," though see Williams and Horrell, *1 Peter*, 325.

142. This also serves as a response to Williams and Horrell, *1 Peter*, 324, who claim that an instrumental reading of εἰς should only be considered if context demanded such an uncommon use of the preposition.

Thus, if we let the letter itself help us understand what Peter might have meant by "the obedience of Jesus" in the prescript, it seems best to regard it as shorthand for Jesus' paradigmatic obedience as what it looks like to be a faithful "elect-sojourner."

It is illuminating that the theme of obedience is joined with the concept of holiness in 1 Pet 1:22, which in turn is linked to the addressees' rebirth in 1 Pet 1:23. Peter affirms that the addressees have "sanctified" or "purified" (ἁγνίζω) their lives by their obedience to the truth, and that the ground for this is their "being born again" (ἀναγεννάω). If we consider other accounts of regeneration in apostolic teaching together with what we discussed about the sanctifying work of the Spirit in 1 Pet 1:2, we might not be misguided to assume that the Spirit is behind the sanctifying obedience (John 1:13; 3:1–8; 1 John 2:29; 3:9; 4:7; 5:1, 9–10, 18; Titus 3:5) highlighted in 1 Pet 1:22. In other words, the sanctifying or consecrating work of the Spirit leads to obedience. Additionally, if we follow Peter's strategic use of the word "call" in 1 Peter (καλέω; 1 Pet 1:15; 2:21; 3:9; also 2:9; 5:10), it leads us to the two interrelated themes: the *call to pattern one's life in the footsteps of Jesus* (1 Pet 2:21; 3:9) and the *call to be holy* (1 Pet 1:15). All these interrelated themes seem to unpack and clarify what Peter means in the prescript: the sanctifying or consecrating work of the Spirit is, in part, enabling the addressees to conform their lives to the pattern of Jesus's life, which is characterized as faithful obedience to the Father. In this regard, holiness in 1 Peter is Spirit-enabled imitation of Jesus' obedience to the Father.

I contend that expanding our vision as we have by tracing these key themes above helps us determine what Peter means with the term πνευματικός as it modifies "house" and "sacrifices." As we have already discussed, the οἶκος is described as "being built" (i.e., passive voice, under construction). That is to say, there is an implied external agent who is making the house into a "holy priesthood." I would suggest that this implied agent of the passive verb οἰκοδομεῖσθε is indicated by the qualifying term πνευματικός. This, the wider context seems to suggest, is the Peter's way of pointing back to the prescript, reminding the "elect-sojourners" that they are made the space where God's presence is encountered *by the sanctifying work of the Spirit*, who empowers the addressees to conform their lives to the obedient pattern of Jesus.[143]

---

143. See Elliott, *1 Peter*, 418.

This reading gives us more of a window into what may be meant by the allusive term "spiritual sacrifices." If we follow the logic of covenant and sacrifice, then a θυσία (translated as "sacrifice" in 1 Pet 2:5) is not a reference to death or to suffering but instead points to an acceptable gift or offering that is brought into God's space as an expression of worship. Eberhart reminds us that to understand the meaning of the Levitical temple cult, we must take into consideration the variety of sacrificial rituals outlined in Leviticus.[144] Not all sacrifices involve a victim or blood, and not all sacrifices are for dealing with purification or expiation. The cereal offering (Lev 2:1–16), for example, is a way for worshippers to communicate the desire to be near to God and to please him, expressed in the phrase "pleasing aroma" (Lev 2:2, 12).[145] The Hebrew word often used to describe the character of the cereal offering is *qorban* (Lev 2:1, 4, 7, 12),[146] which conveys both a token of homage paid to a superior party, as well as the desire to draw near to God's space.[147] It is illuminating, as Eberhart has shown, that the LXX most often translates the technical term for cereal offering (*minha*) with the Greek term θυσία. This, he suggests, shows that the term θυσία had a broader meaning than slaughter and should be thought of more in terms of gift or offering.[148]

In light of what we have discussed, I would suggest that the phrase "spiritual sacrifices" is Peter's way of affirming that because of the Spirit's work of conforming the addressees to the faithfulness of Jesus, their obedience is to be regarded as an "acceptable offering," a gift of homage and an expression of being near to God. This insight aligns with the way in which some have tried to make sense of "spiritual sacrifices" in 1 Peter. For example, Regev has noted that the complex bundling of references to temple, priests, and sacrifices, rendering them as "spiritual" and connecting them to Jesus, is done in the context of the call to be holy: "The intention of the temple-priest-sacrifice imagery is to reinforce and increase the value of holiness and closeness to God to the readers so they will be scrupulous in their interpersonal relationships and instilled with a consciousness of holy community similar to the sanctity of the

---

144. Eberhart, *Sacrifice of Jesus*, 97, 60–89.

145. See Eberhart, *Sacrifice of Jesus*, 67–68, for how burning and pleasing aroma terminology points to arriving to God's space.

146. Eberhart, *Sacrifice of Jesus*, 78.

147. Eberhart, *Sacrifice of Jesus*, 69–71.

148. Eberhart, *Sacrifice of Jesus*, 78–79.

people of Israel to God."¹⁴⁹ Williams and Horrell have suggested that the "community-as-temple idea is simply the metaphor through which he wants the audience to approach their service to the divine. More than anything, this image—along with reference to priests, sacrifices, and so on—is intended to emphasise the group's holy character."¹⁵⁰

But if Jesus is presently at the right hand of God, interceding as a priest in the heavenly temple, and if it is indeed *through* this Jesus that such "spiritual sacrifices" are brought to God (1 Pet 2:5), then maybe it is better to regard these "spiritual sacrifices" as analogous rather than metaphorical.¹⁵¹ In other words, there is a fitting correspondence between the earthly temple and its activities on the one hand, and the heavenly temple and its activities on the other. In keeping with what Kinzer has highlighted about the symbolic function of the Jerusalem temple, two distinct temples with two distinct priesthoods can exist without them being mutually exclusive.¹⁵² In the end, the term "spiritual sacrifices" is Peter's way of "sacrificializing" and "templizing" Spirit-generated, Christ-conforming acts of non-violent resistance, withdrawal, hope, patience, brotherly love, "good works," and entrusting oneself to the one who judges justly in the midst of being treated wrongly. These acts of Christlike obedience are acceptable gifts because they are authorized by God—through the sanctifying work of the Spirit and by means of the ongoing priestly intercession of Jesus in the heavenly temple, to which we turn once again.

What are we to make of the phrase "the sprinkling of the blood of Jesus Christ"? Here we see some confusion in the modern interpretive tradition of 1 Peter (and beyond).¹⁵³ Most often commentators regard the "sprinkled blood" to be shorthand for talking about the sacrificial *death* of Jesus.¹⁵⁴ When this is combined with the noun "obedience," it often yields a claim that runs something along the lines of "Jesus' obedient life

---

149. Regev, "Community as Temple," 619–20. See also Doering, "Chosen Stock."

150. Williams and Horrell, *1 Peter*, 619.

151. See Moffitt, *Rethinking the Atonement*, 117–34, for a helpful discussion of the difference between metaphor and analogy.

152. See also Moffitt, *Rethinking the Atonement*, 128, who points out that a "more literal interpretation of Exod 25:40 would . . . imply that the spaces and practices carried out in the earthly tabernacle would be properly organized and composed along the lines described . . . as 'an analogy of structure.'"

153. Moffitt, *Rethinking Atonement*, 90, notes confusion in Hebrew scholarship as well.

154. I confess to making this error in Liebengood, "Participating in the Life of God," 86. See also, e.g., Achtemeier, *1 Peter*, 86; Green, *1 Peter*, 20.

is what made his death on a cross atoning." But as we have seen, this interpretation is problematic because, according to the logic of the sacrificial cult of Israel, "blood" does not represent the death or the killing of the victim; rather, it represents the life presented before God on the altar as a gift (Lev 17:11).[155] What is more, the death or slaughter of the victim has no atoning value except that it is a part of the process by which the blood is presented before God on the altar.

So, if it is not a reference to the cultic sacrificial death of Jesus, what does it point to? Williams and Horrell lead us in the right direction by contending that "ῥαντισμὸν αἵματος, is undoubtedly an image of cleansing and purification that recalls the Jewish sacrificial system."[156] In keeping with the vast majority of interpreters, they pinpoint this imagery to the covenant sacrifices made by Moses at Sinai (Exod 24:3–9), highlighting that in that context the people pledge to be obedient to God.[157] For Williams and Horrell, the point of the "sprinkling of blood" imagery is not to emphasize the shedding of Christ's own blood but rather the fact that a new-covenant community has been created, "marked out by obedience and the sprinkling of the blood of Christ."[158] This reading is certainly commendable, not least because it connects with several themes in the near and far context of both Exodus and 1 Peter. We have already noted the pledge of obedience that is found in both 1 Pet 1:2 (if we read εἰς with telic force) and Exod 24:3, 7. In both texts, a liberated people have been declared to be a royal priesthood and a holy nation (1 Pet 2:9/Exod 19:6). And finally, in both texts the events of covenant inauguration and the pledge of obedience happen as the people enter the wilderness on their way to their inheritance. So, interpreting the "sprinkling of blood" as an allusion to Exodus 24 and as Peter's way of claiming that Jesus has inaugurated the new covenant—and that these addressees are part of it—fits well with several features of the letter. However, reflecting on this interpretation of the third prepositional phrase of 1 Pet 1:2, Williams and Horrell raise an important question: Why does the author describe the "sprinkling with the blood of Jesus Christ" as the *purpose* of these "elect-sojourners" rather than the *means* which their new identity is achieved?[159]

155. Eberhart, *Sacrifice of Jesus*, 84, 96–97; Moffitt, *Rethinking the Atonement*, 95–96.
156. Williams and Horrell, *1 Peter*, 325.
157. Williams and Horrell, *1 Peter*, 326.
158. Williams and Horrell, *1 Peter*, 326.
159. Williams and Horrell, *1 Peter*, 327.

They suggest it is because being sprinkled with blood, in the end, serves as a sign of the addressees' pledge or commitment to God.[160]

But here is where I think the reading that I am proposing (that the third prepositional phrase puts forth the "sprinkling of the blood of Jesus Christ" as the means by which the addressees are able to live out their calling as "elect-sojourners" who pattern their lives after the obedience of Jesus) is more compelling. To start with, it is important to notice a distinction that Peter makes that is indebted to Pentateuchal narratival logic.[161] To state it boldly, he speaks of the death of Jesus as that which initiates covenant restoration. While this death is salvific and reconciling, it is not a ritual sacrifice.[162] But he speaks of the "sprinkling of blood" as the means by which that renewed covenant is maintained in the wilderness as the elect-sojourners wait for their inheritance. Unfortunately, all too often these two distinct (but nevertheless interrelated) acts are conflated by interpreters of 1 Peter.[163] But for this conflation to occur, Peter must intentionally ignore or distort the logic of covenant and sacrifice as it is narrated in the very texts that he appeals to for his identity-formation strategy.

For example, in 1 Pet 1:19 Jesus' death is characterized with Passover imagery: the "precious" blood of the "unblemished and spotless" lamb has ransomed the addressees from the futile ways inherited from their forefathers.[164] What is important to see here is that this imagery, understood from within its context, does not convey the notion of Levitical sacrificial atonement—even if it is often read that way by modern interpreters.[165] As Eberhart notes, Passover blood evokes concepts of deliverance and protection but is never considered to be a sacrifice of atonement.[166] In other words, this blood mentioned in 1 Pet 1:19 does not pertain to consecration or expiation; instead, it is intended to communicate God's protection and deliverance from pending judgment because of the futile ways that were inherited from the forefathers. When we read this allusion to the

---

160. Williams and Horrell, *1 Peter*, 328.

161. I am indebted to Moffitt, *Rethinking the Atonement*, 29–45, for this insight.

162. Moffitt, *Rethinking the Atonement*, 54–55.

163. See, for example, Mvubi, *Temple, Exile and Identity in 1 Peter*, 72–73.

164. See Mbuvi, *Temple, Exile and Identity*, 86–89, 133, for a helpful discussion of the term λυτρόω and how it relates to restoration from exile, or what I am calling "covenant renewal/restoration."

165. Mbuvi, *Temple, Exile and Identity in 1 Peter*, 84.

166. Eberhart, *Sacrifice of Jesus*, 120.

Passover in the larger literary context of 1 Peter, which I have already highlighted, much like the Exodus account, the Passover blood *initiates* the addressees' journey into the wilderness and toward their inheritance.

Additionally, in 1 Pet 2:24 the death of Jesus is characterized as a vicarious act in which the sins of others are placed upon him: "He himself bore our sins in his body on the tree, . . . by his wounds you have been healed." Again, it is important to see that neither of these images, bearing sins in his body, nor healing others with his wounds, are related to the Levitical sacrificial cult. Instead, they point to covenant renewal rather than covenant maintenance. In other words, 1 Pet 2:24 speaks of Jesus' earthly ministry of offering his life in exchange for others so that the covenant can be restored—and so that the covenant can then be maintained by the priestly ministry of Jesus. This is in line with how the Servant figure of Isaiah 53 is presented in Isaiah itself, as Janowski, Moffitt, and others have shown.[167] What is more, Peter's joining of Isaiah 53 with the shepherd imagery of Ezekiel 34 and Zechariah 9–14 in 1 Pet 2:25 also demonstrates that he had covenant restoration in view, and not sacrificial cult.[168] That is, the images of "healing" and "being returned," read within in their prophetic contexts, point to restoration from exile and covenant renewal.

So when these descriptors—Jesus as Passover lamb, Jesus as suffering servant who heals by bearing the sins of others, and Jesus as shepherd who returns straying sheep—are joined with other affirmations of being included in God's covenant (e.g., the Hebrew Bible citations found in 1 Pet 2:9–10), there is no doubt that the author of 1 Peter affirms what Williams and Horrell claim, namely that these gentile Anatolian addressees have been included within the community in which the covenant has been restored. But I contend that what is in view in 1 Pet 1:2 with the mention of "sprinkling of blood" is not covenant renewal but instead covenant maintenance—that is, Peter is pointing towards the means by which these addressees can live "in front of God" as a form of continuous worship, offering "spiritual sacrifices" in the midst of their wilderness testing *through* Jesus, who is presently at the right hand of God as high priest. For this reason, the "sprinkling of blood" seems to be yet another pressure point that indicates where Jesus is presently.

This "instrumental-subjective-genitive" reading of 1 Pet 1:2 has the added benefit of offering a compelling rationale for the curious and unique

---

167. Janowski, "He Bore Our Sins," 48–74; Moffitt, *Rethinking the Atonement*, 47–61.

168. See Liebengood, *Eschatology of 1 Peter*, 79–104.

optimism that Peter has concerning the addressees making it through the wilderness of fiery trials. Why is he confident that the addressees' tested faith will result in their praise, glory, and honor at the revelation of Jesus (1 Pet 1:7)? Why is he convinced that they will be faithful in the face of suffering and ultimately be restored, confirmed, strengthened, and established to God's eternal glory (1 Pet 5:10)? Why is he certain that the addressees will be guarded for a "ready-to-be-revealed" salvation (1 Pet 1:5)? I would suggest that Peter has been giving us clues all along—at least six of them! Jesus Christ, the faithful high priest, is in the heavenly temple, sprinkling his blood on the heavenly altar, enabling the addressees to *maintain* a life of continuous worship before God while they are in the wilderness of testing.[169] In other words, Jesus' continual intercession at the right hand of God enables covenant maintenance that will result in future salvation. Jesus Christ provides ongoing atonement for these addressees that enables perseverance as they wait for their hoped-for high priest and king to return with an imperishable, undefiled, and unfading inheritance kept in heaven for them (1 Pet 1:4). It is for this reason that Peter can write with confidence the shocking words, "The Spirit of glory and of God rests upon you" (1 Pet 4:14). This is not a repudiation nor a replacement of the Jerusalem temple; rather, it is an affirmation of another temple at play, the one to which the Jerusalem temple has always been pointing.

## Conclusions Regarding Identity Formation and Temple/Priesthood Imagery in 1 Peter

Temple and priesthood imagery—which commences in 1 Pet 1:2, peaks in 1 Pet 2:4–10, and then extends in varying ways all the way to at least 1 Pet 4:19 (but perhaps as far as 1 Pet 5:10)[170]—is integral to the identity-formation strategy of 1 Peter. Though there has been a tendency to read this imagery as a polemic against the Jerusalem temple (and by extension Judaism), and while such judgments often intensify into claims that constitute the church or Christians as the "new" and/or "true" Israel, in this chapter we have seen that there are no grounds for such a reading.

---

169. This thesis I have advanced may also give clarity to the elusive phrase διὰ πίστεως in 1 Pet 1:5. As Horrell, "Whose Faith(fulness) Is It in 1 Peter 1:5?," has highlighted, the syntax is ambiguous. Perhaps this is yet another clue that points to Jesus' faithful priestly ministry.

170. So Mbuvi, *Temple, Exile and Identity in 1 Peter*, 122–24.

To start with, we saw that Peter intentionally avoids pointing the finger at Jewish leadership when he draws on Psalm 118 to explain the meaning of Jesus' rejection. Additionally, we traced the trend in contemporary 1 Peter scholarship to make replacement assumptions about the temple imagery based upon mistaken conclusions about temple as community in the Dead Sea Scrolls and the Qumran sect. What is more, we saw that the priesthood of 1 Peter offers no atonement and thus does not replace the Aaronic priesthood. We also learned that the Jerusalem temple has always functioned as a complex and unstable symbol pointing to and providing access to realities beyond itself. The Jerusalem temple pointed upwards to the reality of the heavenly temple, outwards to the cosmic temple, forwards to the eschatological temple, and beyond itself to the temple as community. As a result, there is no zero-sum game at play when community as temple is mentioned in 1 Peter: to claim that the addressees are a "spiritual house" offering "acceptable spiritual sacrifices" does not entail a polemic or replacement of Israel that can be demonstrated exegetically.

In contrast to repudiating and replacing Israel with the church, I have tried to show that as we attend more carefully to the temple and priesthood imagery, we see how Peter constructs gentile "Christian" identity *in continuity with and even under the pressure of the logic of covenant and sacrifice*.[171] This logic holds together "suffering on account of sins," ascension, being at the right hand of God, and the bringing of others near to God. It also explains Peter's optimism regarding the addressees' faithful perseverance in the wilderness of testing. Through the unjust suffering and death of Jesus, which Peter characterizes in relation to the Passover lamb, the suffering servant, and the eschatological Davidic shepherd, God's covenant with Israel has been restored—and 1 Peter makes the apostolic claim (see chapter 4) that gentiles *qua* gentiles have been included in this restoration. But this account of the death of Jesus should not be confused or conflated with the ongoing covenant maintenance that Jesus presently supplies at the right hand of God in the heavenly temple, where he sprinkles his blood as an offering of atonement. It is this ongoing ministry of purification, consecration, and expiation, coordinated with the sanctifying work of the Spirit, that enables Peter to confidently claim that the Spirit of glory and of God rests upon his imagined recipients; that they are a "spiritual house" that offers up "acceptable spiritual sacrifices."

---

171. I write the term Christian in scare quotes as a hedge against anachronism.

In other words, I suggest that it is the logic of covenant and sacrifice (or better said, the reality that this logic points to) that can make these claims possible.

How so? In keeping with the logic of covenant and sacrifice, God's space is holy space. And anything that is to come into God's presence must also be holy. Israel's sacrificial system is designed to contend with this reality, to provide purification and expiation for the corrupting forces of sin and death. From the beginning of 1 Peter, we already see that the coordinated activities of the Spirit and Jesus are characterized as consecrating the space in which God dwells, namely the people whom he has chosen (1 Pet 1:2). The Spirit's "templizing" consecration of the "elect-sojourners" encourages the reader to anticipate further development of this theme. So too does the mention of Jesus and his sprinkled blood. As we read along, we see that Jesus has been foundational in inaugurating a new building project (1 Pet 2:4–8), one in which a provisional, and we might say eschatological, οἶκος is being built, not with human hands, but by God. In one sense, this provisional οἶκος is the space that functions as a kind of portal that enables Jesus to receive "spiritual sacrifices," which he then offers to God (1 Pet 2:5) in the heavenly temple (1 Pet 3:18, 22). This priestly ministry of Jesus enables the "elect sojourners" to faithfully wait for the completion of this eschatological temple that is being built. The making of this sacred space in which God dwells with his people is made possible by the *living* stone (1 Pet 2:4). I would suggest that this adjective, "living," does not merely point to Jesus' resurrection but also to his present ministry as priest at the right hand of God. Since the addressees, by the Spirit, are being conformed to the pattern of Jesus' faithful obedience to God, and since they receive the ongoing purification of Jesus by the sprinkling of his blood in the heavenly temple, these addresses are also "living stones" (1 Pet 2:5) That is, these coordinated activities of the Spirit and Jesus, both of which are characterized in sacrificial terms, are what sanctify the people and make them the space where God can be encountered, where they can be united to God. Thus, the logic of covenant and sacrifice enables Peter to say what he does in 1 Pet 4:14 ("the Spirit of glory and of God rests upon you").

What is important to note is that the claims of 1 Pet 2:5 and 1 Pet 4:14 are only possible *by means* of the activities of both the Spirit and Jesus Christ. That is, the impetus for the claim that these gentile followers of Jesus are holy space in which God is found is not derived from polemical concerns with the Jerusalem temple and Judaism more generally. Instead, these claims are pneumatologically and christologically generated. Because of the "templizing" and "sacrificializing" activities of the Spirit and Jesus, daily faithful obedience is the *place* where God is encountered. Perhaps another way of saying this is to note that, on the one hand, it is the coordinated acts of the Spirit and Jesus Christ that enable the addressees to experience fellowship with God. But on the other hand, as we attend carefully to the activities of the Spirit and Jesus together with the interlocking themes of obedience and holiness, we see that being close to God, being presented before him, is also characterized as participation in the obedience and faithfulness of Jesus. Enabled by the Spirit, these gentile "elect-sojourners" encounter God by offering "spiritual sacrifices" of Christ-patterned faithfulness *through* the ongoing priestly intercession of Jesus. This Spirit-empowered, Christ-shaped obedience and faithfulness will at times lead to suffering, rejection, alienation, and perhaps even death. But far from being a sign of God's rejection and removal, these quotidian expressions of allegiance and worship in the wilderness of testing become the means for—or perhaps better said the *space* for—divine communion. To adapt a line from Klawans, "spiritual sacrifices" imagery not only communicates that "this too is divine service," but also that "this is divinely enabled service."

This, I suggest, is a foretaste of what the Jerusalem temple was always pointing to, the day when God would be able to dwell with his people because the conditions would finally be made right for his holy presence—through the atoning blood of Jesus. Jesus, the *living* hope of this pending reality, is presently at the right hand of God, interceding for his people, keeping them safe in the wilderness, until such a salvation is revealed. It is the priestly "sprinkling of blood" that enables these Anatolian Christians to be the holy place were God's presence can be found. And it points forward to the day in which the human temple, the eschatological temple, and the heavenly temple converge.

Thus, if there is any sort of polemic going on with temple and priesthood imagery in 1 Peter, it is directed toward Rome and its realized eschatology (*pax Romana*), which is said to be maintained through faithful allegiance to the Roman emperor, who bears the title *pontificus maximus* for his priestly role in keeping the *pax deorum*. Here we see once again, as we did in the previous chapter, where Peter calls his audience to "appropriate Israelhood" in order to make sense of their social alienation, as well as their place in the liminal wilderness. Peter points to the vindicated Jesus, who is presently in the heavenly temple maintaining the peace between God and these embattled "elect-sojourners," drawing upon the logic of covenant and sacrifice in order to help them understand how their daily acts of fidelity testify to their belonging to the God of Israel and the people of God.

# 6

# The Problem of "Race, Nation, and People" in 1 Peter 2:9–10

*This [1 Pet 2:9] is the most explicitly ethnoracial description of Christian identity in the whole NT, and one that initiates an influential discourse about ethnicity and "race" in early Christian writing. These ethnic terms are . . . taken over from the language of Jewish self-identity . . . and this raises the further question about whether, and in what ways, Christian identity itself should be seen as ethnic or ethnoracial in character.*[1]

## Ethnic Identity Formation in 1 Peter

IT HAS NOT BEEN until recently that scholars have observed a distinctive attribute of 1 Peter, namely that the identity-formation strategy of the letter is in fact *ethnic* identity formation.[2] David Horrell was the first to draw attention to this overlooked feature, focusing on the cluster of

---

1. Horrell, "'Race,' 'Nation,' 'People,'" 135.

2. It is beyond the scope of this study to engage in the wider discussion of whether the New Testament comprehensively engages in ethnic reasoning as a strategy for developing Christian identity. For a survey of the debate, see Esler, "Paul's Contestation of Israel's (Ethnic) Memory of Abraham"; Horrell, "Ethnicisation"; Mason and Esler, "Judaean and Christ-Follower Identities"; Horrell, "Reply to Mason and Esler"; Horrell, *Ethnicity and Inclusion*; Esler, "Religion, Race, Whiteness in Constructions of Jewish and Christian Identities." It is notable that the discussion tends to focus on texts associated with Paul and with the Gospels. As will be demonstrated below, 1 Peter clearly employs a form of ethnic reasoning and for this reason I have adopted the terminology (but not uncritically, as will be seen).

ethnic terms found in 1 Pet 2:9.[3] Part of what makes this observation significant is that, as we have seen, the fundamental indicative of the letter is found in 1 Pet 2:4–10. Horrell perceptively highlights that while commentators rightly have drawn attention to the appropriation of Israel's identity in this strategic passage, they have tended to ignore the foundational role that ethnoracial terms play in constructing "Christian" identity, instead characterizing the move as being in the service of fortifying the corporate bond of the addressees.[4] In his generative essay, Horrell not only calls attention to the compressed proliferation of the ethnoracial terms γένος, ἔθνος, and λαός in 1 Pet 2:9[5] but also highlights that the three fundamental identity-forming designations for Israel in the Second Temple period found in texts like Jubilees (*"holy* people," *"chosen* people," and "God's *special possession"*) are the same terms found in 1 Pet 2:9.[6] "This," Horrell argues, "is the most explicitly ethnoracial description of Christian identity in the whole NT . . . and this raises the further question about whether, and in what ways, Christian identity itself should be seen as ethnic or ethnoracial in character."[7] Horrell's discerning observation unsettles the commonly held notion that Christian identity ought to be regarded as more universal and accessible because it is non-ethnic and by contrast transcends the exclusive, ethnic particularity that is inherent to Judaism.[8]

As helpful as these observations are, perhaps Horrell's most important contribution is the line that he draws between the ethnoracial terms found in 1 Pet 2:9 and recent research on ethnic identity formation.[9]

---

3. See Horrell, "'Race,' 'Nation,' 'People'"; "Ethnicisation, Marriage, and Early Christian Identity."

4. Horrell, "'Race,' 'Nation,' 'People,'" 124–25. I parenthesize the term *Christian* because, as I have already argued elsewhere, it is important to remember that this identity formation is happening in a time in which Jesus-allegiance is being worked out within competing notions of what faithful Judaism looks like in response to Jesus of Nazareth. See below for further discussion.

5. "This is the only NT text in which all three 'people' words, γένος, ἔθνος, and λαός, occur together, and the occurrence of all three here suggests an almost deliberate attempt to pack the verse with ethnic identity labels" (Horrell, "'Race,' 'Nation,' 'People,'" 129).

6. Horrell, "'Race,' 'Nation,' 'People,'" 128–29 (emphasis mine).

7. Horrell, "'Race,' 'Nation,' 'People,'" 135.

8. Horrell, "'Race,' 'Nation,' 'People,'" 135. For more discussion on this point, see Horrell, *Ethnicity and Inclusion*, 21–46.

9. Horrell, "'Race,' 'Nation,' 'People,'" 135–43.

What emerges from his study is a recognition that 1 Peter exercises a kind of ethnic reasoning that is fundamental to the pastoral strategy of the letter. In the course of his examination, he highlights three characteristics of ethnic identity and points to ways in which these are manifested in 1 Peter:

1. Ethnic identity is a social construct that is predominantly shaped through written and spoken discourse.

2. Ethnic identity is expansive and polythetic, constructed from a variety of characteristics such as (a) a common proper name, (b) a myth of common ancestry, (c) shared historical memories, (d) elements of a common culture, (e) a link with a homeland, and (f) a sense of solidarity.

3. Ethnic reasoning operates in two modes: aggregative (a strategy that seeks to incorporate all into this new people) and oppositional (a strategy that stresses what distinguishes the in-group from others).

Horrell's work has generated other important studies that develop further his observations, showing how the ethnic identity-formation strategy is not isolated to 1 Pet 2:9.[10] Janette Ok, for example, demonstrates the way in which ethnic reasoning in 1 Peter serves the purpose of fortifying a new ἀναστροφή (or "way of life") for gentile addressees, which entails that they construct clear boundaries and *disassociate* or *disidentify* from their inherited culture in order to be faithful to Jesus in their precarious setting.[11] "By ethnicizing his recipients' Christian identity in order to replace their ethnic majority status as Gentiles, he attempts to create a stronger sense of ingroup identity and solidarity for his addressees and

---

10. Ok, *Constructing Ethnic Identity*; Marcar, *Divine Regeneration and Ethnic Identity*.

11. See especially Ok, *Constructing Ethnic Identity*, 43–58, 65–74, for her exegetical demonstration of this claim. Ok defines ethic reasoning as "the way in which Peter makes metaphorical use of the vocabulary of peoplehood as a rhetorical strategy to help his addressees conceive of their communal identity as grounded in their common essence as people who share common ancestry through the blood of Christ and a (new) birth story." She further clarifies that "it refers to the way in which the language and concepts of shared blood, peoplehood, human difference, etc., serve as an important point of entry for defining what it means to be Christian and as a means for helping his addressees to define themselves in contrast to the 'other,' so that they can disidentify from their former way of life" (Ok, *Constructing Ethnic Identity*, 9).

weaken their sense of belonging to the values of the dominant culture and the values of their family and associations."[12]

Surveying key passages outside of 1 Pet 2:9, Ok concludes that 1 Peter constructs an ethnicity for its gentile audience in five ways: (1) by establishing their relationship to God and to one another through election, new birth, and the ransoming blood of Jesus; (2) by instructing them to live according to a new culture characterized by obedience and holiness; (3) by linking them with a heavenly homeland and as a people who are dislocated (diaspora) from mainstream society; (4) by drawing on Israel's identity-defining designations to describe his addressees as a rhetorical strategy to construct Christian identity as an ethnoreligious identity; and (5) by strengthening their identity as "Christians" so that when they suffer as a result of this identity, they do so for the right reasons and in the right ways.[13] "By emphasizing new birth and patrilineage, the shared blood of Christ,[14] and the common practices concomitant with being obedient children of God," Ok argues, "the letter's author urges his readers to undergo the equivalent of a transfer of ethnic membership from the broad category of 'Gentiles' to the particular and peculiar identity as God's people."[15] In short, Peter's ethnic reasoning helps *disidentify* with the past and *reidentify* as the "people of God."[16]

In the course of her analysis of 1 Peter, Ok makes three further observations, which align with what we have highlighted elsewhere in this study. First, she calls attention to the fact that the contrast in 1 Peter is not between Jew and gentile (or by anachronistic extension, as is too often the case, Judaism and "Christianity"),[17] as is often assumed, but rather between the people of God and those who do not belong to the people of God.[18] So rather than trying to distinguish this early Jesus move-

12. Ok, *Constructing Ethnic Identity*, 90.

13. Ok, *Constructing Ethnic Identity*, 90.

14. In my estimation, Ok puts more weight on "blood" as an integral component of ethnic identity formation than the text seems to bear. There are only two references to blood in 1 Peter (1:2, 19), and neither seems to pertain directly to ethnic identity construction. Instead, as I have shown in chapter 5, they relate to covenant restoration and/or covenant maintenance within the Jewish framework of sacrifice and covenant. See Ok, *Constructing Ethnic Identity*, 2, 9, 36, 48, 74, 89.

15. Ok, *Constructing Ethnic Identity*, 91.

16. Ok, *Constructing Ethnic Identity*, 92. For exegetical argumentations to support this claim, see especially 71–87.

17. Parenthetical comments mine.

18. Ok, *Constructing Ethnic Identity*, 11.

ment from Judaism, she notes instead how the author encourages the addressees to distance themselves from the values and social associations of the Greco-Roman world that are at odds with their allegiance to Jesus.[19] This is similar to what we have shown in chapters 1, 3, and 4. Drawing on insights from Shively Smith, Ok draws attention to the way in which the "diaspora condition" that the addressees suffer in 1 Peter "is a condition induced by decisive and volitional consent" and "not by divine compulsion and peremptory command." In other words, "Diaspora is a way of life resulting from the faithful response and embrace of God's people to God's action through Christ."[20] In this regard, diaspora is not a geopolitically induced social condition of displacement and estrangement (*pace* Elliott and Jobes) but rather is a *social stance* of theological displacement and estrangement for a people very much at home within the values of the dominant culture.[21] Second, she highlights that Peter's construction of a new ethnic identity for these diverse gentiles spread across Asia Minor necessitates that all other identities be subordinate to their new way of life in allegiance to Jesus.[22] This is what our study has suggested in chapters 1 and 4. And finally, Ok underscores that it is "a completely new eschatological orientation toward the world" that compels the addressees to obedience to the will of God and faithful allegiance to Christ and his pattern of life.[23] In chapter 4, this study has argued that this "completely new eschatology" is founded upon and oriented toward Israel's hope of an eschatological Davidic shepherd who will establish the God of Israel's benevolent rule which includes care for gentiles.

Katie Marcar has also expanded upon Horrell's work in a monograph that explores the way in which 1 Peter "contrasts and overwrites" the addressees' ethnic (gentile) identities inherited at birth by constructing a new ethnic identity that is animated, she argues, by the metaphor of divine regeneration, which undergirds the theology and exhortations of the letter, especially those found in 1 Pet 1:3—2:10.[24] Marcar's exploration of the letter's identity-formation terminology within the context

---

19. Ok, *Constructing Ethnic Identity*, 56.
20. Ok, *Constructing Ethnic Identity*, 57; Smith, *Strangers to Family*, 21.
21. Ok, *Constructing Ethnic Identity*, 57.
22. Ok, *Constructing Ethnic Identity*, 91–92.
23. Ok, *Constructing Ethnic Identity*, 72.
24. Marcar, *Divine Regeneration and Ethnic Identity*, 264. Macar and Ok worked independently of each other, and because both were finishing their studies around the same time, they were unable to engage with each other's work in their monographs.

of the Hebrew Bible and Second Temple Judaism helpfully complements the work that Ok has done.[25] Prior to her study, the theme of divine regeneration was a remarkable lacuna in 1 Peter studies.[26] Marcar's most important contribution is her demonstration of the way in which divine regeneration is integrally related to three other seemingly disparate themes in 1 Peter: imperishable seed (1 Pet 1:23), milk (1 Pet 2:2), and the "spiritual house" of 1 Pet 2:5.[27] She shows how each of these images contributes to the construction of group membership along ethnic lines. For example, she establishes that in some forms of Judaism it is the seed that determines the kind of thing something is. This led some strands of Judaism to believe that part of what made Israel ontologically distinct from all other peoples was the fact that they came from "holy seed."[28] First Peter, she argues, draws upon this notion of seed in order to support the claim that his gentile addressees are now a different kind of people because they have been begotten again by divine seed.[29] Because the seed that gave them new birth is imperishable (1 Pet 1:23), so too is their inheritance (1 Pet 1:4).

Additionally, she shows how milk extends the ethnic identity-formation strategy of the letter because it is commonly regarded as "kinship-forging substance."[30] In other words, in both Greco-Roman and Jewish sources, milk marked in-group membership and was associated with socialization into an ethnic identity. In 1 Peter, the fact that all the addressees feed from the same milk means that they all belong to the same family.[31] Having constructed a new ethnic identity that carries with it familial connotations by means of the imagery of divine regeneration, imperishable seed, and milk, Marcar argues that the author of 1 Peter then extends the divine regeneration metaphor complex of 1 Pet 1:1—2:3

---

25. See, for example, Marcar, *Divine Regeneration and Ethnic Identity*, 15–21, 65–73, 75–86, 119–48, 169–87, 202–20.

26. See Marcar, *Divine Regeneration and Ethnic Identity*, 2–6.

27. Her chapter on metaphor theory, in which she explores the anatomy of a metaphor, the way metaphors can constitute a narrative sequence, the false dichotomy often made between "real" and "fictive," and Metaphor Identification Procedure (MIP), is exceptional and merits the attention of biblical studies scholars. See Marcar, *Divine Regeneration and Ethnic Identity*, 24–51.

28. Marcar, *Divine Regeneration and Ethnic Identity*, 130–44, 151–68.

29. Marcar, *Divine Regeneration and Ethnic Identity*, 151–68.

30. Marcar, *Divine Regeneration and Ethnic Identity*, 169–76.

31. Marcar, *Divine Regeneration and Ethnic Identity*, 187–92.

in order to construct an "ethno-national" identity in 1 Pet 2:4–10, "the theological pinnacle toward which the divine regeneration metaphor was building."[32] She notes that the author's "expanded vision" to move from a single person to a family and then to nation is done in a "Pentateuchal fashion."[33] This perceptive insight, which she does not develop further, concurs with a pattern that we have demonstrated in 1 Peter, namely that Peter reasons from "Pentateuchal logical" in a variety of ways in order to make certain theological claims. Additionally, Marcar stresses that the author of 1 Peter has taken advantage of the polyvalency of the term οἶκος ("temple" and "house" or "household") in order to convey how divine regeneration ultimately leads to the formation of a family or household that can also be regarded as a people or nation belonging to God (1 Pet 2:10). Below, we will explore further the way Peter leverages the polyvalence of the term οἶκος, but we will argue it is for the purposes of helping them understand their place within God's ongoing commitment to Israel. Mapping the complex of divine regeneration, seed, milk, spiritual house, and people/nation metaphors in 1 Peter, Marcar concludes that "Christian" membership means being begotten anew, growing up in God's family, and belonging to a sojourning nation. God's family, therefore, is best regarded as an ethnic group.[34]

## What to Make of *Ethnic* Identity Formation in 1 Peter?

The insights of Horrell, Ok, and Marcar regarding the ethnic characteristics of identity formation in 1 Peter are a significant new contribution to our understanding of the letter. But as Horrell indicates, "The crucial question, of course, is what we should make of all this information, and how we should understand the rhetorical move made by the author of

---

32. Marcar, *Divine Regeneration and Ethnic Identity*, 270, 198–202, 220–53. Her analysis of community as temple at Qumran (*Divine Regeneration and Ethnic Identity*, 202–16) references Regev ("Community as Temple") and Botner ("The Essence of a Spiritual House") but shows no awareness of the ways in which her conclusions about Qumran conceptions regarding atonement and temple are in tension with what they have demonstrated. Notably absent from both "Building a Holy House" and her monograph is any engagement with Klawans's seminal work, *Purity, Sacrifice, and the Temple*. While I disagree with some of the comparisons she makes between Qumran and 1 Peter, her exegetical work on 1 Pet 2:4–8 is helpful, especially the way she underscores the polyvalence of the term οἶκος.

33. Marcar, *Divine Regeneration and Ethnic Identity*, 198.

34. Marcar, *Divine Regeneration and Ethnic Identity*, 274.

1 Peter."³⁵ In one sense, this is what this monograph has been trying to answer all along. And it is here, precisely on this point that Horrell raises, where it is important to press further into their exegetical observations and conclusions.

To start with, while Horrell, Ok, and Marcar have done an outstanding job of demonstrating the technique of ethnic reasoning evidenced in 1 Pet 2:9–10 and beyond, for reasons that are unclear to me, they are resistant to exploring more thoroughly the wider text plots from which most if not all of the ethnic reasoning derives.³⁶ That is, they do not attend to the multi-faceted narrative of *Jewish* restoration ideology, which key texts like Isaiah 40 and 53, Hosea 2, Psalm 118, and the shepherd imagery of Ezekiel 34/Zechariah 9–14 (to name but a few in 1 Peter) implicitly (and in some cases explicitly) develop, nor how these key Jewish restoration ideology themes, especially those of restoration from exile and new exodus, are woven together into a coherent narrative in 1 Peter, in part, through the aid of these Hebrew Bible texts, as I have tried to show already in this current study.³⁷ This reluctance leads to what I regard as a significant lacuna in their studies, namely that it is not just ethnic reasoning that is being performed in 1 Peter, but more specifically it is *Jewish* ethnic reasoning, or perhaps we could say "Israelhood" reasoning. That is, it is not just that ancillary Jewish resources are being leveraged as tools to accomplish the primary task of constructing a new "ethnic" self-understanding, which is what it seems like these studies suggest at times.³⁸ Neither is it merely the case that Peter uses the techniques of ethnic reasoning in order to accomplish particular objectives in the letter that he wouldn't be able to accomplish otherwise, which is the impression I get at times when I engage with the explanations for ethnic reasoning.³⁹ Rather, it seems more to be the case, as I have tried

---

35. Horrell, "'Race,' 'Nation,' 'People,'" 135.

36. See, for example, Ok, *Constructing Ethnic Identity*, 9, 90, who refers to the ethnic reasoning as a *rhetorical strategy*.

37. See pages 43–48, 87–124.

38. See, for example, the comment by Ok: "Israel . . . serves as the backdrop or template for Peter's understanding of what it means to be a people of God for those who cannot claim to belong to Israel by natural blood ties but can claim to be part of God's people through supernatural means" (*Constructing Ethnic Identity*, 52n107).

39. See, for example, Horrell, "'Race,' 'Nation,' 'People,'" 141, who suggests that "drawing on the specific traditions of Judaism . . . the author of Peter . . . was able to construct just such a form of identity, without a focus on specific (geophysical) territorial attachment or biological (human) kinship links. In short . . . it suited early

to demonstrate, that Peter is incorporating these gentiles addressees into a very specific, Israel-centric hope that animates their faithful allegiance in the face of suffering—which comes at the hand (or mouth) of their compeers—and that is built upon a logic that is rooted in the God of Israel's revelation to Israel but modulated through the accomplishments of the Jewish Messiah, Jesus (e.g., their perseverance is dependent upon the faithful covenant maintenance of Jesus in the heavenly temple). Thus, as I read their insights in light of what I have developed thus far in this monograph, many of their observations seem to support precisely what I have been demonstrating all along, namely that Peter emplaces gentile followers of Jesus within the God of Israel's ongoing work in and through his people Israel for the sake of the whole world. But they support the conclusions that I have made without acknowledging that this is in fact what is happening with the ethnic reasoning in 1 Peter. In fact, in varying ways, they seem to regard the opposite to be the case. Horrell, for example, claims that "it is notable that 1 Peter is simply silent about the continued existence of what Paul elsewhere called ὁ Ἰσραὴλ κατὰ σάρκα. . . . The Church, it seems, has simply become the chosen race, the holy nation."[40] Marcar is slightly more attuned to some kind of relationship between the addressees of 1 Peter and God's ongoing engagement with Israel when discussing the way in which in 1 Pet 2:9–10 the author applies epithets from Isa 43:20–21, Exod 19:6, Hos 2:23 to the gentile Jesus followers. She remarks, "Curiously, he does not explain how ethnic Israel fits into this schema. For the author, Christians are to understand themselves as the people of God and to read their personal histories into the history of Israel and God's narrative of salvation."[41] Ok, on the other hand, is more provocative:

> When Peter ascribes his beleaguered addressees with the community- and ethnic identity-forging titles and dignities of Israel in 2:9 drawn from Jewish Scriptures, he does not do so in order to replace Israel as the "people of God" (2:10) or *to incorporate them into the legacy of Israel* or to transpose the status and identity of Israel unto the Church. Rather, as Horrell explains, Peter draws on the specific traditions of Judaism because they are "a form of ethnic identity with religio-cultural practices at its

Christians to claim and describe their identity in ethnic terms, to *use* 'ethnic reasoning' as one discursive means to articulate that identity."

40. Horrell, "'Race,' 'Nation,' 'People,'" 135.
41. Marcar, *Divine Regeneration and Ethnic Identity*, 272.

heart" that make it possible for him to construct the same form of identity for his addressees "without recourse to a specific territorial attachment or to biological human kinship links." Peter thus uses ethnic reasoning in his construction of Christian identity in order to provide a new way for his Gentile Christian addressees to understand themselves in relation to God the Father and to one another as a holy people, because of divine election and new birth, share the same bloodline—that of Jesus Christ.[42]

What is more, in Ok's comments below, we see an example of how she regards the ethnic reasoning of 1 Peter to be more akin to a technique than as an invitation to join the God of Israel and his people in some way:

> Gentile converts were confronted with a unique problem and opportunity to choose or construct a new way to understand themselves, and Peter addresses this very challenge. Rather than arguing that Gentile Christians are "neither Jew nor Greek" (cf. Gal 3:28) or that they are Jews, Peter argues instead that they are no longer Gentiles. He does this by appropriating ethnic identity language ascribed to the Jews as a means to express how Gentile Christians belong to God. He constructs Christian identity using ethnic language because ethnic categories—while they are fluid enough for him to adapt and reimagine to serve his purposes—help to fix or concretize the ways in which Gentile Christians are to cohere with one another and adhere to the behavior and values that imitate Christ (2:21) and befit their status as "a chosen race, a royal priesthood, a holy nation, and a people for [God's] possession" (2:9).[43]

But if ethnic reasoning in 1 Peter primarily functions as a rhetorical feature or a kind of technique to construct communal identity, then is this not problematic? Is this not yet another example of what Bauman-Martin has called attention to—the downplaying, ignoring, or being indifferent to the cultural appropriation that the author of 1 Peter seems to be performing in the name of "rhetoric"?[44] While Horrell, Ok, and Marcar have acquitted 1 Peter of supersessionism, have they not created another problem that is just as menacing? That is, is the "winning strategy" of the

---

42. Ok, *Constructing Ethnic Identity*, 60 (emphasis mine). She also is perplexed that "while it is not entirely clear whether or not Peter intends for Jews to be included in the category 'Gentiles,' his failure to mention 'Jews' at all in his letter remains very puzzling to me" (*Constructing Ethnic Identity*, 67n23).

43. Ok, *Constructing Ethnic Identity*, 55.

44. See pages 5, 13, 15.

letter still the same: snatch the identity of another oppressed group and use it for your own purposes? It would seem to me that in future work on this subject, Ok, Marcar, and Horrell need to attend more carefully to and perhaps address the concerns raised by Bauman-Martin, especially if they see their insights as in some way improving upon previous readings of 1 Peter.

Additionally, what at times seems to obscure or conceal the conceptualization of ethnic reasoning in 1 Peter is the consistent usage of the anachronistic terms "Christian" and/or "church." When these descriptors are used to refer to the addressees (e.g., "Christians" or "church") or the identity-formation strategy of the letter (e.g., "Christian" identity formation), it (often unknowingly) tends to veil the complex and interpenetrating relationship between pluriform Judaism and the later first-century Jesus movement. That is to say that the kind of identity formation that is happening in places like Asia Minor during the second half of the first century through the discourse of New Testament documents like 1 Peter is best understood, at least in part, as a kind of *intra*-Jewish debate about whether the God of Israel regards Jesus to be the Messiah of Israel, and if so, what implications this has, not only for Israel but also for gentiles who have sought to pledge their allegiance to Jesus and the God of Israel.[45] It is, therefore, important to regard "Christian" identity formation as something that, at least in the time of the composition of 1 Peter, is a self- and communal-understanding that is being worked out from *within some form of Jewish identity*.[46]

Furthermore, as I indicated in chapter 1, one of the important features of the letter that gets lost when we use anachronistic terms like "Christian" or "church" is the very identity of the God to whom the text refers. For example, when Ok claims that the key point in 1 Peter is not that the addressees have been incorporated into the God of Israel's family/people but rather that "Gentile Christians" are no longer gentiles, or when she claims that "Gentile Christians belong to God," it is unclear to me *which god* she refers to. The same question arises when she claims that rather than understand themselves as incorporated into the people of the God of Israel in some way, instead 1 Peter urges gentile Christians to understand themselves in relation to God the Father and to one another as a holy people, because of divine election and new birth, and the fact that

---

45. No one NT text deals sufficiently or comprehensibly with the variety of questions and problems that emerge from this complex and interpenetrating interface.

46. Paget, "Jewish Christianity," 731–75; Segal, "Jewish Christianity," 326–48.

they share the same bloodline with Jesus Christ. But is not Jesus Christ Israel's Messiah? And if Jesus is Israel's Messiah, is the god referred to in Ok's statement not the God of Israel? Who is the god doing the electing and begetting, and which bloodline does Jesus share? In other words, if the addressees are indeed God's people, do they not in some way belong to the people of the God of Israel? But this important component of the letter is significantly obscured when Ok, and to a lesser degree Horrell, try to distance the ethnic reasoning from Israel and the God who elected Israel for the purposes of blessing the nations. Thus, it seems to me that one of the significant dangers of these recent studies on ethnic identity formation in 1 Peter is that in refusing to see that Peter incorporates the addressees in some way into "Israelhood," they run the risk of erasing God's own particular identity as the God of Israel, which in turn calls into question the reliability of all those resources (e.g., Hebrew scriptures, Jewish identity markers) called upon to construct identity in letter. Said in another way, if ethnic identity in 1 Peter is generic, that is, merely generated from a technique used to give the addressees a sense of purpose and belonging, then it seems to me that this entails that the god referred to in 1 Peter must also be generic.[47] Or to follow Horrell's lead, if it is a misnomer to speak of Christian identity as universal and non-ethnic, then does that not also mean that we cannot think of the "Christian God," or perhaps more accurately, the God and Father of Jesus Christ, as a non-ethnic, generic god?

As one who has been working on this project for a number of years, I am acutely aware of the delicate balance one must strike in making sense of 1 Peter's identity-formation strategy. Horrell, Ok, Marcar, and others are to be commended for their work, which demonstrates that supersessionism does not drive the ethnic reasoning in 1 Peter; or, as Doering has shown, that it is clear that Peter never says that the addressees are the new Israel, or even that they are Israel. But in affirming this, we must also be sure to acknowledge that neither does 1 Peter say that they do *not* belong to Israel. This requires careful nuance, and the text of 1 Peter is not as clear on these matters as we would like it to be, but there seems to be enough data in the text to suggest that we must hold these two realities together. As Doering helpfully has noted, 1 Peter is more concerned to tell us what these addressees have in common with the people of the God of Israel than what they hold in distinction. And as I tried to

47. Or perhaps "Christian" in an anachronistic sense. (Yes, I do see the slight irony in using the term "generic," since it comes from the Greek word *genos*!)

show at the end of chapter 3, this is most likely because of the rhetorical exigence that the letter seeks to alleviate. But having said all that, I still wonder why there is reticence to accept that Peter extends belonging to the people of the God of Israel to gentiles *qua* gentiles. Regardless of one's view about the authorship or dating of 1 Peter, as we discussed in chapter 3, the voice of the letter, in one way or another, is a Jewish apostle of the Jewish Messiah Jesus, who is remembered as continuing to be a faithful Jew (though modulated in light of Jesus), as having been commissioned by Jesus to welcome gentiles into the blessings of the God of Israel's family, as well as being a bridge-builder between gentile and Jewish followers of Jesus. It is *this* Peter who welcomes these gentile followers of Jesus in Asia Minor who are wondering whether they belong. This, along with the other points mentioned above, strongly suggests that seeing 1 Peter as a text that incorporates gentiles (in some way) into the people of the God of Israel is not an imposition on the "silence" of the text but instead runs with the grain of letter; it is the logical extension of all the clues contained therein.

In what remains of this chapter, I wish to expand upon the observations of Ok and Marcar, who each in their own way have argued that the ethnic reasoning of 1 Pet 2:9–10 (and beyond) serves as the basis for their call to a new ἀναστροφή that is to be lived among family, friends, and neighbors who consider the postures and practices of this new way of life troubling and threatening. In order to do this, we need to revisit the οἶκος πνευματικός imagery in 1 Pet 2:5 within the wider context of 1 Peter, especially 1 Pet 2:11—3:12. As we will see, as we explore term *oikos* and related themes in 1 Peter, we find striking resonance with the text-plot of Zechariah 9–14 and its eschatological Davidic program. I will argue that when we are attentive to the Zecharian eschatological program, it enables us to explain a number of curious features in the letter, ultimately revealing the depth to which Peter incorporates gentiles into God's ongoing commitment to Israel. Along the way, we will attend to two questions that have been raised through the course of this study: (1) why does Peter not use the term ἐκκλησία to describe the addressees; and (2) if gentiles have been incorporated into the people of the God of Israel *qua* gentiles, how far does this go? In other words, what parts of Jewish life are gentiles to mimic or embrace? And what parts of Israel's life are these gentiles followers of Jesus *not* to adopt?

## Οἶκος Revisited

In the previous chapter, we mentioned that οἶκος has a range of meanings (i.e., house/temple, household, or dynasty), but we only explored it as temple imagery in 1 Pet 2:5 and then considered whether it entailed supersessionist implications. While this was necessary work, to only focus on οἶκος as community-as-temple imagery ensures that we miss key dynamics at play in the letter, especially as they relate to the "people, race, and nation" language in 1 Pet 2:9-10, as we will see below. In 1 Peter scholarship, the possibility that οἶκος refers to a household (or perhaps a royal dynasty) tends to get minimal consideration, in part, because the most prominent proponent of this reading, John Elliott, put forth a proposal that had some idiosyncrasies that detracted from some of his important observations.[48] Elliott's most helpful insight was the detection of an intentional structure to 1 Pet 2:4-10, pointing to a relationship between 1 Pet 2:4-5 and 2:6-10.[49] Bauckham helpfully clarifies Elliott's insight by noting that "vv. 4-5 briefly state the theme which is then both supported and expanded by the OT citations and their interpretation in vv. 6-10."[50] Both Elliott and Bauckham note that 1 Pet 2:4-5 echoes the texts that are quoted in 1 Pet 2:6-10. They also note the way that these texts provide a framework for the interpretation of the themes introduced in 1 Pet 2:4-5.[51] For example, 1 Pet 2:4 underscores God's election of Jesus (the living stone) and his rejection by humans, and this corresponds to scriptural proofs found in 1 Pet 2:4-8, which help make sense of these claims, especially as it pertains to his rejection. And in 1 Pet 2:5, we find that the "living stones" who have aligned themselves with Jesus are described as a "spiritual house" to be a "holy priesthood that offers spiritual sacrifices." First Peter 2:9-10 corresponds to the claims of 1 Pet 2:5 in that it offers scriptural support that emphasizes the election and holiness of this "spiritual house," ultimately characterizing the addressees as a people or family-nation, as we have already seen.[52]

48. A critique of his proposal is beyond the scope of this chapter. For his argument, see Elliott, *Elect and the Holy*, 149-59; *Home for the Homeless*, 165-266. For a representative critique of some of the weaker elements of Elliott's proposal, see Horrell, *1 Peter*, 45-52, 76-85.

49. See Elliott, *1 Peter*, 407, 412-24.

50. Bauckham, "James, 1 and 2 Peter, Jude," 310.

51. Bauckham, "James, 1 and 2 Peter, Jude," 310; Elliott, *1 Peter*, 407, 412-19.

52. Elliott, *1 Peter*, 408, 415-22; *Elect and the Holy*, 156-59; *Home for the Homeless*, 167-70, 200-237, 240-41.

This exegetical observation about the structure of 1 Pet 2:4–10 is important to underscore for what we will be examining, because if 1 Pet 2:9–10 helps interpret 1 Pet 2:5, and if the scriptural support in 1 Pet 2:9–10 highlights the communal nature or "peoplehood" of the "living stones," then this ought to inform how we understand the word οἶκος. Along this line, Elliott concludes his work on 1 Pet 2:4–10 by drawing attention to the fact that "multiple honorary epithets of ancient Israel, all corporate in nature, are employed in 2:9–10 to affirm the communal identity of the believers. . . . The *communal* metaphor, 'house(hold) of the Spirit,' . . . serves as an inclusive root metaphor in the letter's description of the Christian community."[53] Williams and Horrell, however, have suggested that the structure of 1 Pet 2:4–10 has been overplayed, claiming that "not every point emphasized in vv. 6–10 finds specific resonance in vv. 4–5." For example, they point to the climactic emphasis in 1 Pet 2:9–10 on the identity of the addressees as a people, which, they note, is stressed in the terms γένος, ἔθνος, and λαός.[54] But they point out that none of the people imagery of 1 Pet 2:9–10 is captured in 1 Pet 2:5 and none of the stone or building imagery in 1 Pet 2:5 finds expression in 1 Pet 2:9–10.[55] However, for Williams and Horrell to make this claim that the communal emphasis of 1 Pet 2:9–10 does not appear in 1 Pet 2:5, it would seem that they must assume that οἶκος does not contain any communal connotation. This is at odds, however, with their exegesis of οἶκος in 1 Pet 2:5, in which they seem to support the polyvalence of the word, noting that it is difficult to exclude the community dimension of οἶκος, and that Peter likely chose the word over alternative options (i.e., ἱερόν and ναός) because it provided "semantic flexibility."[56] Additionally, they also underscore that "it is difficult to deny that the 'living stones' also constitute a community of people."[57] So, it seems that in spite of their claim that the structure of 1 Pet 2:4–10 is overplayed, their own conclusions about "living stones" and οἶκος support the helpful insights of Elliott and Bauckham.

---

53. Elliott, *1 Peter*, 444 (emphasis mine).
54. Williams and Horrell, *1 Peter*, 600.
55. Williams and Horrell, *1 Peter*, 600.
56. Williams and Horrell, *1 Peter*, 615–16.
57. Williams and Horrell, *1 Peter*, 616.

## Οἶκος and the Jewish Restoration Theology of 1 Peter

To further understand the οἶκος imagery of 1 Pet 2:5 and how it is connected to 1 Pet 2:9-10, it is important to consider the other usage of the term οἶκος in 1 Peter (i.e., 1 Pet 4:17), and as we will see, the way in which this key term fits within both the context of 1 Pet 4:12-19 and also the particular Jewish restoration ideology that Peter draws upon in this letter. With regard to 1 Pet 4:17, it has been argued that in the LXX οἶκος never refers to a community or household when joined with the genitive θεοῦ.[58] This claim, however, overlooks one significant instance in the LXX where οἶκος θεοῦ is clearly a reference to a community—namely, Zech 12:8, where the ὁ οἶκος Δαυιδ is ὡς οἶκος θεοῦ. The import of this one instance becomes clear when we look at a constellation of themes in 1 Pet 4:12-19, which are also echoed in 1 Pet 1:1—4:11, that find their coherence when attention is given to the eschatological Davidic shepherd ideology developed in Zech 9-14, which we introduced in chapter 4.

Primopetrine studies on the literary structure and rhetorical strategy of the letter have resulted in a number of scholars observing a dependent relationship between 1 Pet 1:1—4:11 and 4:12-19.[59] This is clearly the case with respect to 1 Pet 1:3-9 and 1 Pet 4:12-19, where in both passages we find a number of shared themes: fiery (πῦρ/πύρωσις) trials (πειρασμοὶ/πειρασμός) which are necessary/to be expected (1:6-7/4:12); rejoicing (χαίρω; χαρά; ἀγαλλιάω) in the midst of suffering (1:6-8/4:13); the expected revelation (ἀποκάλυψις) of Jesus (1:7/4:13); salvation (σωτηρία/σῴζω) of ψυχαὶ in the appointed time (καιρός; 1:5, 9/4:17-19); as well as confidence that the faithful, sustained by God, will survive the trials, which are a part of God's overall plan (1:5-7/4:19). These striking parallels have led a number of scholars to conclude that the fiery trials imagery that is appropriated in 1 Pet 4:12 intentionally builds upon the usage in 1 Pet 1:6-7. Elliott, for example, comments, "Since our author has already used this metaphor in 1:6-7 in speaking of faith as more precious than 'perishable gold tested by fire,' this sense of *pyrōsis* is clearly implied here

---

58. Johnson, "Fire in God's House," 291.

59. Elliott contends that "1 Peter 4:12-19 recapitulates and expands on what has already been stated on the issue of suffering. This unit does not mark a caesura or break in the line of thought but a crescendo" (*1 Peter*, 770). See also Michaels, *1 Peter*, 258; Schutter, *Hermeneutic and Composition in 1 Peter*, 74-76; Bechtler, *Following in His Steps*, 199.

as well."⁶⁰ Given the nature of an *exordium* (i.e., 1 Pet 1:3-12), one would expect the repetition of themes in the body of the letter which were introduced at the beginning. But how is this imagery being used? Some have argued that the "fiery ordeal" is to be interpreted "as a 'trial' that *purifies* faith under pain and strengthens it through preservation."⁶¹ But, as I have shown elsewhere, the notion of purification, while not entirely absent, does not appear to be the primary aim of the fire imagery in 1 Peter.⁶² Instead, in both 1 Pet 1:5-7 and 1 Pet 4:12, the emphasis is on the *inevitability* of the fiery testing, as well as its *authenticating* or *verifying* purpose: Ἀγαπητοί, μὴ ξενίζεσθε τῇ ἐν ὑμῖν πυρώσει πρὸς πειρασμὸν ὑμῖν γινομένῃ ὡς ξένου ὑμῖν συμβαίνοντος. With fresh expression, Peter here (1 Pet 4:12) is reiterating what he has already stated: they ought not to be surprised by the fiery testing which comes upon them because it is a necessary part of a larger eschatological schema, which was hinted at in 1 Pet 1:5-9 and will be outlined in greater detail in 1 Pet 4:17-19.⁶³ In keeping with the imagery of 1 Pet 1:7, what they are going through is described in terms of a process of fire (πύρωσις) which serves the primary purpose of testing or ascertaining (πρὸς πειρασμὸν) the true extent of their faithfulness.⁶⁴ Instead of being surprised, they are exhorted to rejoice (cf. 1 Pet 1:6-8) in as much as (καθό) they are partners in the "belonging-to-the-Messiah sufferings" (τοῖς τοῦ Χριστοῦ παθήμασιν; 1 Pet 4:13).⁶⁵ Since this passage highlights suffering that is experienced particularly "in the name of Christ" (εἰ ὀνειδίζεσθε ἐν ὀνόματι Χριστοῦ; 1 Pet 4:14),⁶⁶ or that

60. Elliott, *1 Peter*, 772. See also Michaels, *1 Peter*, 258, 261, who argues that 4:12-13 looks back to being tested by fire, and to final joy in 1:6-8; Selwyn, *1 Peter*, 221; Achtemeier, *1 Peter*, 304-6; Dubis, *Messianic Woes*, 79; Witherington, *1-2 Peter*, 208; Feldmeier, *1 Peter*, 224.

61. Goppelt, *1 Peter*, 314 (emphasis mine).

62. Liebengood, *Eschatology of 1 Peter*, 130-53.

63. So also Goppelt, *1 Peter*, 311; cf. Michaels, *1 Peter*, 260.

64. *Pace* Goppelt, *1 Peter*, 313, who asserts that πύρωσις ought to be understood as a "purifying fire" in keeping with is usage in the wisdom traditions of LXX Ps 65:10 and Prov 27:21. I would point out that there are other ways to conceive of fire. For example, in Daniel 3 fire does not have a purifying function but instead demonstrates the authenticity of the faithfulness of Daniel's three friends.

65. *Pace* Elliott, *1 Peter*, 774, who translates καθό as "since" or "inasmuch as." First Peter, in particular 1:5-9, places an emphasis on the ongoing faithfulness of the believers in the face of testing, which will be rewarded with praise, honor, and glory in due course. Therefore, it seems best to translate καθό in its more customary sense as a marker of degree (i.e., "in so far as," or "to the degree that"). See BDAG 493, 2.

66. Here I would agree with Achtemeier, who argues that the phrase ἐν ὀνόματι

is the result of being labeled a Χριστιανός (1 Pet 4:16), in corresponding fashion it seems best to interpret the phrase τοῖς τοῦ Χριστοῦ παθήμασιν (1 Pet 4:13) as the "of the Messiah" sufferings; that is, the sufferings that come from belonging to, or associating oneself in loyal allegiance to, the Christ.⁶⁷ This translation of 1 Pet 4:13, which aligns with the thrust of the passage, helps bring out the meaning of κοινωνέω, which is best understood in terms of being partners of or associating with a particular group. This reading also helps explain why those who partner in the "of Christ" sufferings will rejoice in the revelation of his glory (1 Pet 4:13): those who align themselves now with the shamed Christ and his people will find honor (i.e., "glory") when the Christ is honored at his return.⁶⁸

Two verses in 1 Pet 4:12-19, each of which begins with ὅτι, provide justification for the kind of assertions that Peter makes in this section of the letter. These two verses also provide us with glimpses of the substructure of his theology of suffering. For example, in 1 Pet 4:14, Peter contends that when his readers are ridiculed "in the name of Christ" then they are blessed, further explaining this assertion by alluding to Isa 11:2: ὅτι τὸ τῆς δόξης καὶ τὸ τοῦ θεοῦ πνεῦμα ἐφ᾿ ὑμᾶς ἀναπαύεται.⁶⁹ If, as

Χριστοῦ is probably to be construed as a dative of sphere (*1 Peter*, 308). Accordingly, they are ridiculed for associating themselves with the name of Christ. See Goppelt, *1 Peter*, 322-23, who suggests that ἐν ὀνόματι Χριστοῦ should be understood as synonymous with Χριστοῦ ἐστε (cf. Mark 9:41). Michaels remarks that "to suffer ridicule ... for Christ's name was to suffer because of one's allegiance to Christ" (*1 Peter*, 264). He nevertheless takes the phrase to be a dative of cause.

67. Compare this with 1 Cor 1:12 (λέγω δὲ τοῦτο ὅτι ἕκαστος ὑμῶν λέγει· ἐγὼ μέν εἰμι Παύλου, ἐγὼ δὲ Ἀπολλῶ, ἐγὼ δὲ Κηφᾶ, ἐγὼ δὲ Χριστοῦ) in which the genitive construction is used to express identification with a group that holds in high esteem a particular figure; associating with this group brought with it a certain perceived societal status. As such, the proper names represented the group with which these people associated. Achtemeier suggests that τοῦ Χριστοῦ is an objective genitive that should be translated "what is suffered for Christ" (*1 Peter*, 324n47). In the end, I want to stress that my reading of the genitive construction derives from the overall thrust of the passage (4:12-19), which, as Martin has highlighted, "is dominated by the description of the readers as partners in the sufferings of the Messiah" (*Metaphor and Composition in 1 Peter*, 256). In other words, they suffer because they have associated themselves with the Messiah.

68. Both Bechtler, *Following in His Steps*, and Campbell, *Honor, Shame, and Rhetoric of 1 Peter*, are very helpful in demonstrating how the term "glory" fits within the letter and within the honor-and-shame culture, in which 1 Peter was composed and read.

69. See Achtemeier, *1 Peter*, 307, who writes, "The εἰ with which the sentence begins, combined with a verb in the indicative mood (ὀνειδίζεσθε), emphasizes the reality of the assumption that Christians will be reproached, and hence has the force not so much of 'if' as of 'when.'" See also Elliott, *1 Peter*, 778, who suggest that if this remark

is most likely the case, Isa 11:2 is the precursor text for 1 Pet 4:14, then there are three substantial modifications that have been made:

1. ἀναπαύσεται (future, "will rest") has been changed to ἀναπαύεται (present; "rests").[70] Thus, that which was previously regarded to have a point of reference in the future, is now regarded as taking place in the present.

2. The object upon which the Spirit will rest has been changed from ἐπ' αὐτὸν (singular) to ἐφ' ὑμᾶς (plural). In other words, the object is no longer exclusively the messianic "shoot" or "root" of Jesse (Isa 11:1; a scion of David), but instead is now applied to a community that identifies with this eschatological Davidic figure.[71]

3. The genitive τῆς δόξης has been added to the phrase πνεῦμα τοῦ θεοῦ, and the word order has been changed from πνεῦμα τοῦ θεοῦ to τὸ τῆς δόξης καὶ τὸ τοῦ θεοῦ πνεῦμα. There is some debate as to whether the additional genitival phrase is intended to modify πνεῦμα (and if so, how it functions in relation to the head noun),[72] or whether it is a substantivized genitival phrase that stands on its own and that points back to the glory mentioned in 1 Pet 4:13 (ἐν τῇ ἀποκαλύψει τῆς δόξης αὐτοῦ).[73]

---

is based on the dominical sayings of Jesus that are found in Matt 5:11–12, then the temporal meaning (i.e., when) is more likely what Peter had in view. See also Michaels *1 Peter*, 263; Selwyn, *1 Peter*, 191.

70. Neither the Hebrew nor the Greek manuscript traditions help to explain this change.

71. See Gen. Rab. 2:3–4; QpIsa 8–10 iii 11–25; Pss. Sol. 17:32, 37; and the Targum on Isaiah for messianic interpretations of this passage. For messianic interpretations of Isa 11:2 in early Christianity, see Rom 15:12; 2 Thess 2:8; and John 1:32.

72. Michaels, for instance, thinks the phrase τῆς δόξης both points to 4:13 as well as modifies πνεῦμα. He renders the phrase as follows: "for the spirit of that glory (i.e. the eschatological glory of Christ mentioned in 4:13), even the spirit of God, is resting upon you" (*1 Peter*, 64–65). Elliott regards the two genitive phrases as a pleonastic hendiadys construction that is best translated "the divine spirit of glory." Elliott adds that the addition of the phrase *glory* "is consistent with the stress on *glory* in this section (4:13, 14, 16; cf. 4:11d) and throughout the letter and may also have been prompted by the desire to ground the addressees' honor (*makarioi*) explicitly in the honor of God, thus once again linking glory to suffering" (*1 Peter*, 782).

73. So Achtemeier, *1 Peter*, 309, who concludes that such a rendering of the grammar would mean that the sufferers are blessed because they already have a share in the eschatological glory yet to be revealed. Selwyn, *1 Peter*, 222–24, also regards it as a substantivized genitival phrase, and suggests that *glory* refers to the Shekinah.

What is the basis for these changes?[74] That is, what has compelled Peter to make the imaginative connection between a community that is blessed since it is reviled and the messianic promise of Isa 11:2? Additionally, what has prompted Peter to take a promise that was originally addressed to the messianic "shoot" or "branch" of Jesse (Isa 11:1) and apply it now to this gentile messianic community?[75] And finally, why has Peter added the genitival phrase τὸ τῆς δόξης to the mix? As we will see in a moment, the text-plot of Zechariah 9–14 provides a compelling rationale.[76]

The second ὅτι passage is found in 1 Pet 4:17. There Peter explains to his readers that when they suffer as Christians, they ought not be ashamed. This exhortation underscores once again that Peter regards shame, understood within the context of a Greco-Roman honor-shame society, to be a legitimate mode of suffering—perhaps the primary mode of suffering for these Anatolian Christians.[77] Instead of being ashamed, Peter's readers are exhorted to "glorify" God "in this name," turning the honor-shame paradigm on its head. In justifying this exhortation, much like he did in 1 Pet 1:5–7, he reminds them of *when* they are, or perhaps more properly *what time it is*: "For the time has come for judgment to begin with the household of God" (ὅτι ὁ καιρὸς τοῦ ἄρξασθαι τὸ κρίμα ἀπὸ τοῦ οἴκου τοῦ θεοῦ).[78] Given the way that καιρός is used elsewhere in the letter (1 Pet 1:5, 11; 5:6), it appears that Peter has in mind a fixed time that is in keeping with a foreordained eschatological program.[79] In other words, there is an appointed time for restoration and salvation (1 Pet 1:5; 5:6), as well as a time for κρίμα (1 Pet 4:17), which is all in keeping with what the "Spirit of Christ" announced beforehand to the prophets (1 Pet 1:11).

---

74. There is no evidence from the extant Hebrew or Greek manuscripts that would suggest these changes are due to a textual variant.

75. To be clear, I recognize that there was a variety of messianic visions and expectations in the first century. I do think, however, that many of the messianic hopes revolved around a coming king, appointed by Yhwh, and often (though not always) associated with the eschatological Davidic king.

76. See Liebengood, *Eschatology of 1 Peter*, 144–45, for a discussion of some unsatisfying ways in which some have tried to explain these exegetical moves.

77. Bechtler, *Following in His Steps*, 94–105; Campbell, *Honor, Shame, and the Rhetoric of 1 Peter*.

78. Michaels, *1 Peter*, 270; Achtemeier, *1 Peter*, 315.

79. See BDAG 497, 2. See also Bechtler, *Following in His Steps*, 127–35; Jobes, *1 Peter* [1st ed.], 292.

It is important to underscore that κρίμα does not necessarily imply punitive retribution for wrong behavior.[80] Although it does often carry overtones of punishment (e.g., Rom 3:8; Gal 5:10; 2 Pet 2:3; Jude 4; Rev 17), in its broadest sense κρίμα refers to the process of rightly ascertaining whether someone is innocent or guilty, a procedure of fairly evaluating whether one has remained loyal or not. Given that Peter has paradigmatically described Christian suffering as πειρασμοί (1 Pet 1:6; 4:12), and given that the addressees' suffering is framed within an honor-shame system that is determined by the group with whom one associates, this broader sense of κρίμα seems to be in view. In other words, as Green has pointed out, here in 1 Pet 4:17 "to judge" means "to evaluate," "to discern," or "to distinguish," instead of "to condemn."[81] With this in view, suffering "in the name of Christ" here (as elsewhere in the letter) is not understood to be punishment from God but instead is evidence of one's loyalty towards God and his Christ, a loyalty that will be rewarded in the last time (1 Pet 1:5–9; 5:4).[82] According to Peter, this sifting process begins with "the house of God" and will be carried forward to the eschaton.[83]

Some have argued that LXX Ezek 9:6 might stand behind 1 Pet 4:17, based in part on two lexical features shared between the two texts: (a) the phrase ἄρξασθαι ἀπό and (b) the word οἶκος.[84] Elliott and Jobes have responded aptly to this proposal principally by highlighting the fact that Ezek 9:6 and its wider context (Ezek 8–11) envision the destruction of God's temple and the punishment of God's people for their failure to abide by his covenant.[85] As Elliott has retorted, if Peter did draw from Ezek 9:6, he did so by making a point entirely different from that which is

---

80. This point is often missed in exegetical analysis of 1 Pet 4:17. See especially Dubis, *Messianic Woes in 1 Peter*, 142–46.

81. Green, *1 Peter*, 155. See also Elliott, *1 Peter*, 799. This is not to suggest that punitive punishment is entirely absent from text; those who in the end refuse to associate themselves with the Christ, as 4:17b–18 indicate, will be punished.

82. Pace Dubis, *Messianic Woes in 1 Peter*, 163–67, who unduly regards the suffering as punitive in nature. His reading runs against the entire grain of 1 Peter, which in no way suggests that the addressees are suffering as a result of their own sins.

83. Green, *1 Peter*, 155.

84. E.g., Schutter, *Hermeneutic and Composition in 1 Peter*, 156–63; Michaels, *1 Peter*, 271; Dubis, *Messianic Woes in 1 Peter*, 151–52.

85. Elliott, *1 Peter*, 798. For the full rebuttal, see Elliott, *1 Peter*, 798–900; Jobes, *1 Peter* [1st ed.], 291–92. Jobes interprets Zech 13:9 to be speaking of punitive punishment against God's people as well.

made in the proposed precursor text.[86] Thus, it seems very unlikely that Ezek 9:6 stands behind 1 Pet 4:17.[87]

Those who consider Ezek 9:6 as the precursor text for 1 Pet 4:17 also regard the term οἶκος τοῦ θεοῦ to be a reference to the temple, and thus argue for temple imagery as the primary metaphor of this passage. It seems, however, that the *letter itself* has defined οἶκος τοῦ θεοῦ for us in a different manner. There are, for example, several features in the near context (i.e., 1 Pet 4:12-19) that press us to read οἶκος τοῦ θεοῦ as a reference to a particular community of people who are associated with a royal figure (i.e., the Christ).[88] As I have already demonstrated, leading up to 1 Pet 4:17 the primary subject of the passage has been the community that associates itself with the Christ. They are variously described as those who partner in the "belonging to the Christ" sufferings (1 Pet 4:13), those who are ridiculed "in the name of Christ" (4:14), the messianic community upon which the Spirit rests (4:14), and Χριστιανοί who glorify in "this name" (4:16). It would seem, then, that the reading of οἶκος τοῦ θεοῦ that runs most naturally with the grain of the wider context is the one that regards οἶκος as a reference to the community (household or dynasty) that has associated itself with the Christ. The phrase ἀφ' ἡμῶν, which appears in the latter half of 1 Pet 4:17, and which stands in apposition to ἀπὸ τοῦ οἴκου τοῦ θεοῦ seems to corroborate this interpretation.[89]

Additionally, this reading of οἶκος τοῦ θεοῦ in 1 Pet 4:17 is further confirmed if we allow 1 Pet 2:4-10 to inform our interpretation. As I have already noted, 1 Pet 2:4-8 presents a mixed metaphorical description of the community that associates itself with the rejected cornerstone: they are living stones that are under construction, a spiritual house that now offers acceptable sacrifices to God through Jesus Christ (1 Pet 2:5). These polyvalent images are then elaborated with ethnoracial terms derived from Exodus 19, Isaiah 43, and Hosea 2, which all refer in various ways to the people of God—a chosen race, a royal priesthood, a holy nation,

---

86. Elliott, *1 Peter*, 799. Elliott has also pointed out that proponents of Ezek 9:6 in 1 Pet 4:17 have overlooked the fact that the term οἶκος is used in reference to both the temple and God's people (9:6, 7, 9). For a critique of Elliott, see Dubis, *Messianic Woes in 1 Peter*, 152-53.

87. For a more comprehensive rationale for why Ezek 9:6 is not a precursor text for 1 Pet 4:17, see Liebengood, *Eschatology of 1 Peter*, 128-30, 144-48.

88. So also Hillyer, "Spiritual Milk," 126, who argues that οἶκος refers to royal dynasty.

89. Elliott, *1 Peter*, 799.

God's own people, and those who have received mercy (1 Pet 2:9–10). In the context, then, it is best to consider the primary referent of οἶκος τοῦ θεοῦ to be the household of God, or perhaps more specifically, those who belong to the dynasty of Christ and who willingly have chosen to associated themselves with the Messiah in spite of the fact that such an association incurs shame and suffering from their compeers.[90] The addressees' faithfulness in the face of ridicule and shame is the beginning of a sifting process, the κρίμα, which serves to delineate who belongs to this house of God. Suffering, then, is not regarded as having an educational or purifying purpose but instead proves or demonstrates who in fact has remained loyal to God's royal agent (see 1 Pet 1:5–7). That the addressees are called a "spiritual house" (οἶκος πνευματικός) in 1 Pet 2:5 likely points cataphorically to the themes developed in 1 Pet 4:14 and 17, where they are described as belonging to the Davidic household or dynasty. Their belonging to this Jewish communal entity is attested to by the Spirit, which now rests even upon them (i.e., gentile followers of Jesus).[91]

Before we consider in more detail the relationship between the eschatological program of 1 Peter and the text-plot of Zechariah 9–14, it is important to consider briefly the section that immediately follows what we have just examined, namely 1 Pet 5:1–5, and how it might fit into the program of restoration developed in the letter. There, Peter exhorts elders to "shepherd" the "flock" of God under their care (ποιμάνατε τὸ ἐν ὑμῖν ποίμνιον τοῦ θεοῦ; 1 Pet 5:2). They are called to do so not under compulsion (ἀναγκαστῶς), nor for shameful gain (αἰσχροκερδῶς), nor as lording it over them (μηδ' ὡς κατακυριεύοντες τῶν κλήρων), but instead intentionally (ἑκουσίως) and willfully (προθύμως), serving as models (τύποι). The point in drawing attention to this is that it appears that Peter envisions the restoration of a second tier of leadership as a part of the eschatological program that he is unveiling. This second tier of leadership is described with shepherding imagery. He concludes this exhortation by reminding the elders that their selfless leadership will gain for them "an imperishable crown of glory" when their chief shepherd, Jesus (cf. 1 Pet

---

90. Similarly, in Heb 3:6 being a member of God's οἶκος is contingent upon loyal allegiance to Christ.

91. On this point, it seems to me that the awkward genitival construction τῆς δόξης in the phrase τῆς δόξης καὶ τὸ τοῦ θεοῦ πνεῦμα is meant to communicate that the Spirit of God is also the Spirit that establishes and recognizes (i.e., δόξα in the sense of approval, affirmation, or praise) the status of these gentile followers of Jesus as belonging to the people of the God of Israel.

5:4; Jesus is designated as the chief shepherd [ἀρχιποίμην], which points back to 1 Pet 2:25), appears.

## Οἶκος τοῦ θεοῦ and the Text-Plot of Zechariah 9–14

All of this demonstrates that the phrase οἶκος τοῦ θεοῦ, read within its epistolary context, refers to the royal messianic house, that is, a people who have aligned themselves with the God of Israel's Messiah. Further reflection on the text-plot of Zechariah 9–14 strengthens this claim. In other words, as we familiarize ourselves with this unique eschatological program of Zechariah 9–14, we find a compelling similarity with the eschatological program of 1 Peter that has been outlined above.

The first oracle (9:1–17) of Zechariah 9–14 functions paradigmatically as a miniature of what will be developed in more detail in 10:1—14:21 and introduces the predominant theme of Zechariah 9–14, Yhwh's intention to restore his people.[92] In Zech 9:8, this restoration is described in terms of the God of Israel coming as a conquering king to watch over his "house" (בֵּיתִי/τῷ οἴκῳ μου). The parallel stanza of Zech 9:8 suggests that "house" refers to the God of Israel's people or household (עֲלֵיהֶם/ἐπ' αὐτούς; cf. 9:14–15) rather than the temple itself. In Zech 9:9–10, we learn of the sudden emergence of a divinely appointed human agent who becomes integral to the God of Israel's restoration plans. Additionally, we learn that this human agent is some kind of eschatological Davidic figure. Such an expectation was prominent within some forms of postexilic Judaism, as they looked for a royal eschatological Davidic figure who would emerge as an integral part of the national and spiritual restoration of Israel. This expectation was rooted in the covenant that the God of Israel made with David, in which he promised that David's "house" (בֵּיתְךָ/οἶκος; 2 Sam 7:11–16; cf. Isa 9:7; Pss 18:50; 89:4, 29–37; 132:11–12) would be established forever. This expectation of a perpetual reign for the house of David found expression in several texts in which the future Davidic ruler is described as either a branch of David (Isa 11:1; Jer 23:5; 33:15) or a shepherd (Ezek 34:23–24; 37:24; see also Pss. Sol. 17–18). Significantly, branch and shepherd are two designations used in Zechariah to describe the God of Israel's future ruler (Zech 3:8; 6:12; 13:7). What we find, however, in Zech 9:9–10 is unexpected: the legitimacy of this

---

92. See Liebengood, *Eschatology of 1 Peter*, 27–33, for further development of the ideas in this paragraph.

coming king will be questioned by God's own people, and the coming king will require vindication from the God of Israel. But the oracle closes by indicating that this vindication of the God of Israel's king will bring forth the restoration of his people, who are climactically described as his flock and "stones of a crown"/"holy stones" (אַבְנֵי־נֵזֶר/λίθοι ἅγιοι) in Zech 9:16.

Stone imagery is picked up once again in Zech 10:4, this time however in reference to a leader who will emerge from the house of Judah, and who, unlike the unfaithful shepherds of Israel's past (Ezekiel 34; Jeremiah 23), will faithfully lead the God of Israel's people. This leader is described as both a "cornerstone" (פִּנָּה) as well as a "tent peg" (יָתֵד). The term פִּנָּה is used in Isa 28:16 and Ps 118:22 with reference to an eschatological figure, YHWH's appointed agent who will bring about restoration (cf. 1 Pet 2:6, 8).[93] This cornerstone/tent-peg figure is linked to a second exodus in Zech 10:6–12, in which the God of Israel's people will be gathered in the wilderness, the covenant will be renewed (along the lines of Hosea 2), and the people will be led to their inheritance.

But Zech 11:4–17 significantly alters the expectations about the way in which the covenant with Israel will be restored. While Zechariah 9–10 has given the impression, much in keeping with Jeremiah 23 and Ezekiel 34, that the good shepherd/cornerstone would immediately usher in liberty, peace, and prosperity, Zech 11:4–17 opaquely indicates that the good shepherd will be rejected and will provoke enmity among those in Jerusalem before restoration is finalized.[94] Zechariah 12:8–14 reveals and emphasizes that as the God of Israel's restoration unfolds, the house of David will be filled with remorse as they mourn for the death of the "pierced one" (Zech 12:10; i.e., the eschatological Davidic king), and as a result will become like the "house of God" (Zech 12:8).

The somber tone of Zech 12:10–14 is infused with hope in Zech 13:1–6. Concomitant with the death of the "pierced one" is a "day" in which a fountain will be poured upon the house of David to cleanse it from its sin and impurity (Zech 13:1). This fountain of cleansing resonates with the eschatological program of Ezek 36:20–30, in which the unclean spirit of the land (cf. Zech 13:2) will be replaced with a spirit that cleanses the people of their idolatry (Ezek 36:26–27; Zech 13:1–2).[95]

---

93. The Targum also understood פִּנָּה as an eschatological royal figure.

94. See Liebengood, *Eschatology of 1 Peter*, 38–40, for more development.

95. See Liebengood, *Eschatology of 1 Peter*, 40–42, for more development.

Zechariah 13:7–9 provides further details regarding the identity of the "pierced one" (Zech 12:10), the fate of those that have rejected the good shepherd (Zech 11:8–14), and what will happen to the house of David.[96] According to Zech 13:7, the shepherd will be struck, and the sheep will be scattered. In Zech 13:8, two-thirds of the people in the land will be cut off and perish, and one-third, presumably those who identify with the pierced one, will have to endure an unspecified period of "fiery trials" intended to test their fidelity to the God of Israel and his appointed agent. The one-third that is put into the fiery trials will participate in the renewal of the God of Israel's covenant with his people, in which he will declare, "They are my people" (Zech 13:9; cf. 10:6; Hos 2:23; Ezek 37:23). The ensuing fiery trials described in Zech 13:8–9 add texture to the second-exodus motif of Zech 10:6–12: we now are to understand the fiery trials of Zech 13:7–9 as being a part of the second-exodus journey mentioned earlier, a time, not of purification, but rather of testing. Zechariah 13:9 highlights that the one-third that are placed in the fire will emerge from the testing, protected by the God of Israel—thus a renewed community will emerge from the fire. The import of this section of Zechariah cannot be overstated. Contrary to what one might have been led to believe from the programs of Jeremiah and Ezekiel, the coming of the eschatological Davidic shepherd will not immediately usher in a time of peace and prosperity. Instead, a time of trouble, described as a period of "fiery testing," will precede final deliverance.

Zechariah 14:3–21 makes it clear, however, that the time of trouble will not be the end of Israel's story. The God of Israel will intervene, appearing first on the Mount of Olives (Zech 14:4) to defeat the nations, secure Jerusalem, and reign over all the earth (Zech 14:4–15). Those among the nations who survive (presumably by loyally aligning with the God of Israel's chosen agent) will, year after year, join Israel in worshipping the God of Israel. The eschatological program of Zechariah 9–14 culminates in a very significant fashion, especially as it relates to our study of 1 Peter. The final vision that Zechariah casts before its readers is that of a holy house offering holy sacrifices to the God of Israel (Zech 14:21).

In our discussion of the alterations of the precursor text of Isa 11:2 in 1 Pet 4:14, I raised the following questions: What has led Peter to connect (a) a persecuted community of God with (b) the promise of the Spirit resting upon a *messianic* community, and (c) why is this messianic

---

96. See Liebengood, *Eschatology of 1 Peter*, 42–46, for more development.

community described as the house of God? Additionally, (d) what has compelled Peter to alter Isa 11:2 from a text that originally spoke of a future day in which the Spirit would rest upon the messianic "shoot" to a text that now speaks of the Spirit presently resting upon a persecuted community that is defined in terms of their steadfast allegiance to the Christ? In light of our review, I would argue that the most satisfying answer can be found by considering the eschatological program of Zechariah 9–14 and the unique parallels it shares with 1 Peter. In both texts the community that aligns itself with God's royal figure is described as the house of God (Zech 12:8/1 Pet 4:17); (b) the royal/messianic agent is described variously as a slain shepherd (Zech 13:7/1 Pet 2:23–25), a stone (Zech 10:3/1 Pet 2:6–8), and the shoot of David (implied in Zechariah 9–14 from Zech 3:8; 6:12, and in 1 Pet 4:14 from Isa 11:2); (c) the house of God will undergo a period of fiery trials that are likened to a wilderness/new exodus journey and that are designed to test fidelity towards God; (d) the spirit will be poured out/now rests upon the house of God; and (e) the house of God, that is, those who align themselves with the slain shepherd, are to be characterized by holiness, in which they offer acceptable sacrifices to God (Zech 13:1–2; 14:21/1 Pet 2:5). It is remarkable to note that there is no other place in Israel's scriptures where we find these themes joined together. For this reason, I have argued elsewhere and in more detail that Zechariah 9–14 is the substructure for Peter's eschatological program. For example, read through the lens of Jesus' life, death, resurrection, and ascension, Zechariah 9–14 and its unique Jewish restoration ideology provides Peter with the theological resources for connecting a persecuted messianic community with the promise of the Spirit that was to be poured out on the shoot of David. It also helps explain why this community is referred to as the "house of God."[97] If this is the correct reading of 1 Pet 4:14, that is, if the eschatological program of Zech 9–14 undergirds Peter's alteration of Isa 11:2, then the two ὅτι clauses in 1 Pet 4:14–19 (i.e., 4:14, 17), which are both intended to provide scriptural justification for the corresponding exhortations, both display the influence of Zechariah.

---

97. Although texts such as Ezekiel 36, Joel 2, and Isaiah 11 speak of the spirit coming upon God's people, none of these texts suggests that God's people will subsequently undergo persecution; Zechariah 9–14 is unique in this regard, and it is likely that Zechariah has modified these eschatological programs with this unique feature.

## Why οἶκος instead of ἐκκλησία?

If we allow for the possibility that the eschatological program of Zechariah 9–14 may have shaped Peter's understanding of the suffering that his addressees were undergoing, then this might shed even more light on why he elected to use the term οἶκος to characterize his addressees who have aligned themselves with the Christ (1 Pet 2:5; 4:17). Primopetrine scholars have often noticed the conspicuous absence of the word ἐκκλησία in a letter that is keenly interested in identity and community formation. Elliott explains this absence in two moves. First, he argues that the bulk of the letter's addressees resided in rural areas, in which the term ἐκκλησία would be alien to their everyday experience.[98] Second, given the rural setting of the addressees, 1 Peter has adopted οἶκος terminology throughout the letter as a more contextually relevant strategy for dealing with social estrangement by showing their "at-home-ness" in the family of God.[99] He notes that "of the various ecclesial concepts employed in this letter, it is the symbolization of the community as the household of God that serves as the root metaphor and organizing ecclesial image in 1 Peter."[100]

Horrell underscores that Elliott's foundation for assembling such a social profile is an over analysis of the terms πάροικος and παρεπίδημος, which according to Elliott, provide clues to the social condition of the addressees.[101] As Horrell points out, Elliott concludes that the terms πάροικος and παρεπίδημος may indicate that the addressees were numbered among the rural populations, and that they were comprised of artisans, craftsmen, traders, and merchants traveling through villages and towns respectively. Elliott suggests that if we combine these conclusions regarding πάροικος and παρεπίδημος with the limited urbanization of much of Asia Minor then it becomes likely that the letter is directed at a predominantly rural audience.

Horrell, however, argues convincingly that the terms πάροικος and παρεπίδημος do not offer a literal socioeconomic description of 1 Peter's addressees, but instead (1) "convey something about the character of their experience," and (2) "express their alienation and estrangement in

---

98. Elliott, *Home for the Homeless*, 62–63; *1 Peter*, 84–90.
99. Elliott, *Home for the Homeless*, 165–266; *1 Peter*, 105, 112–18.
100. Elliott, *1 Peter*, 113.
101. Horrell, *1 Peter*, 179–80; 187–91. See also Williams, *Persecution in 1 Peter*, 61–90.

terms of Jewish tradition."[102] He follows this critique of Elliott's proposal by pointing out that if the addressees are not literally πάροικοι, then there is little to support the claim that they were most likely rural dwellers.[103] We can also add to this that there is little to support the claim that οἶκος terminology has been appropriated instead of ἐκκλησία because it was a more effective way of constructing identity in a rural setting.

If οἶκος has not been appropriated in order to address the rural context of the addressees, then how can we explain its usage in place of the more common term ἐκκλησία? I would suggest that the eschatological program of Zechariah 9–14 may provide us with an answer. As I have highlighted in my review above, there is an *inclusio* in Zechariah's eschatological program (i.e., Zech 9–14) built around the image of God's house. In Zech 9:8, the God of Israel announces that he is coming to his house, which, as we have seen, refers to his people. And in Zech 14:20–21, the eschatological program concludes with a rightly functioning house offering acceptable sacrifices in the God of Israel's house. Interestingly, Zech 14:20–21 seems to use "house" in a dual manner, pointing to both the household of God, as well as the temple.

In between these two bookends, in a climactic episode of the program, we see that those who have mourned the death of the "pierced one" will be cleansed from their impurity, enabling them to be called both the house of David as well as the house of God (Zech 12:8–12). If I am right about the influence of Zechariah 9–14 thus far, then it is very likely that Peter has chosen the term οἶκος τοῦ θεοῦ rather than ἐκκλησία on the one hand in order to express to these beleaguered gentile followers of Jesus that they belong to the God of Israel and the slain and vindicated Davidic shepherd, and that they are included in this restoration project. But on the other hand, the phrase also signals themes that have been developed throughout the letter, namely that as they faithfully align themselves with the rejected and vindicated Davidic shepherd, they *must* pass through fiery trials that are likened to a new wilderness journey before they experience full restoration and receive their inheritance. In other words, Peter's appropriation of the phrase οἶκος τοῦ θεοῦ, as well as οἶκος πνευματικός (1 Pet 2:5), may actually be an attempt to connect his readers to the scriptural text-plot that supports precisely the point that he has been making throughout his letter, namely that their necessary (1 Pet

102. Horrell, *1 Peter*, 189.

103. Horrell, *1 Peter*, 190. See also his brief critique of the "limited" urbanization of Asia Minor and the supposed rural metaphors in the letter.

1:6) and to-be-expected (1 Pet 4:12) suffering is part of a wider eschatological program that culminates in not only the restoration of Israel but also the inclusion of the gentiles.

### Zechariah 9-14 and the restoration of under-shepherds

One further link between 1 Peter and Zechariah 9-14 can be ascertained. It appears that from the earliest stages of its reception, scribes and scholars have puzzled over the relationship between 1 Pet 4:12-19 and 1 Pet 5:1-5. Michaels notes that the manuscript variations for 1 Pet 5:1 "reflect scribal questions about the connection of this statement [i.e., 1 Pet 5:1-5] with what immediately precedes [i.e., 1 Pet 4:12-19]."[104] An analysis of the textual tradition of 1 Pet 5:1 reveals that the majority of the later manuscripts substitute τούς for the inferential conjunction οὖν, which was most likely original to the text.[105] Michaels rightly concludes that "the effect of the substitution is to eliminate the necessity of seeking any real connection to the preceding context."[106]

Since the consensus position today is that οὖν was original to the text, many scholars have struggled to understand how these two passages are related; in other words, what is 1 Pet 5:1-5 inferring from 1 Pet 4:12-19? Green has suggested that 1 Pet 5:1-5 "particularizes 4:12-19 for relationships within the community of believers, drawing out inferences from the change of life-world documented in 4:12-19 for the particular sets of persons named in 5:1-5: elders, younger persons, and everyone."[107]

Green's proposal, however, only partially explains the connection between the two passages; it describes epiphenomenally the relationship between the two texts. Pressing further into the relationship between the two, why has Peter followed the exhortation in 1 Pet 4:12-19, in which he reminds his readers of to-be-expected trials that come to test fidelity, with an exhortation to the *elders* of the community to "shepherd"

---

104. Michaels, *1 Peter*, 276.

105. For a full discussion, see Michaels, *1 Peter*, 276. See also Elliott, *1 Peter*, 811.

106. Michaels, *1 Peter*, 276.

107. Green, *1 Peter*, 164. Achtemeier, *1 Peter*, 321, proposes that the author is repeating a pattern in the letter in which a section deals with matters external to the community, and then is followed by a discussion of matters internal to the community: 4:1-6 (external); 4:7-11 (internal); 4:12-19 (external); 5:1-5 (internal). This distinction he makes between external and internal matters, however, is blurred throughout 1 Peter 4-5, which makes it hard to see the pattern that Achtemeier describes.

the "flock" of God, eagerly watching over them without selfish motives (1 Pet 5:2; ποιμάνατε τὸ ἐν ὑμῖν ποίμνιον τοῦ θεοῦ ἐπισκοποῦντες μὴ ἀναγκαστῶς ἀλλὰ ἑκουσίως κατὰ θεόν)? Troy Martin suggests that it might have something to do with the influence of Zechariah 9–14:

> 1 Peter's connection of the ideas of God's flock being led by shepherds (5:1–5) and being tried by fire (4:12) is paralleled by the collection of ideas in Deutero-Zechariah. This collection of ideas provides part of the rationale for the connection of this subsection with the previous one.[108]

He supports this assertion by suggesting that Zechariah 9–14 has shaped the letter elsewhere:

> Deutero-Zechariah provides important background material for other notions expressed in 1 Peter. 1 Peter 1:7; 2:10; and 4:12 are paralleled by Zechariah 13:9. 1 Peter 2:25 alludes to ideas expressed in Zechariah 13:7–9.[109]

One additional parallel between Zechariah 9–14 and 1 Peter should be noted. As I briefly demonstrated above, the eschatological program of 1 Peter includes the restoration of a second tier of leadership that will watch over the flock of God that is characterized in terms that are antithetical to the bad shepherds who are chided in Ezekiel 34 (1 Pet 5:1–4). We find a similar vision for the restoration of a second tier of leadership in the eschatological program of Zechariah 9–14. For example, in Zech 10:1–5 the diagnosis and the cure for Israel's predicament, as well as the language that is used in Zechariah 10–13, is described in shepherding terms: the people wander like sheep because they lack shepherding (Zech 10:2 [MT]; LXX reads "because they lack healing"). This particular way of describing Israel's predicament (that is, with pastoral imagery) finds its antecedent in Ezekiel 34, which itself builds upon Jeremiah 23.[110] In both texts, Israel's crisis is credited to selfish and unrighteous leaders: the God of Israel's "flock" has been scattered because the "shepherds" have failed to "feed the sheep, strengthen the weak, heal the sick, bind up the injured, bring back the stray, and seek out the lost" (Ezek 34:3–4). For this reason, the God of Israel is against the "shepherds" (Ezek 34:10; Zech 10:3). In

---

108. Martin, *Metaphor and Composition in 1 Peter*, 259. It should be noted that his observation is not based on my study, since his work predates mine by two decades.

109. Martin, *Metaphor and Composition in 1 Peter*, 259n418.

110. Sweeney, *Twelve Prophets*, 668–71; Laniak, *Shepherds After My Own Heart*, 162–65.

addition to the God of Israel personally intervening, he also foretells of his plan to set up over the "sheep" "one shepherd," his servant David, who will give them the kind of leadership they need (Ezek 34:23 and again in 37:24–5). All this is said to happen on the day when the God of Israel will vindicate his name, gather in his people from the nations, cleanse them from their idolatry, give them new hearts, and put his spirit within them that they might walk in his statues (Ezek 36:25–7).

Zechariah 10–13 builds upon this program in Ezekiel by complementing the one Davidic shepherd with a second tier of leadership. The "cornerstone" (פִּנָּה) and "tent peg" (יָתֵד) is accompanied by a group of leaders who are described as overseers in the MT (lit. every overseer; כָּל־נֹגֵשׂ).[111] According to the Zechariah program, when Israel is restored there will no longer be self-serving under-shepherds who abuse the God of Israel's sheep (cf. Ezek 34). Instead, the God of Israel's new leadership will serve the people in such a way as to bring about victory for the entire nation (Zech 10:5; cf. 9:11–13).[112] Importantly, Zechariah scholar Paul Redditt highlights the restoration of leadership as a major theme in Zechariah 9–14.[113] In particular, he points to Zech 12:7—13:1, a passage that insists that restoration will only come about when the house of David becomes like the house of God (Zech 12:8).[114]

This major Zecharian theme, then, provides the distinctive link between 1 Pet 4:12–19 and 1 Pet 5:1–4. The house of God (1 Pet 4:17/ Zech 12:8)—that is, those who have aligned themselves with the God of Israel's royal agent (1 Pet 4:12–15), the pierced-one (Zech 12:10–13:1), and upon whom the Spirit now rests (1 Pet 4:14)—is now, in keeping with the Zechariah program, equipped with under-shepherds who will faithfully and selflessly lead the God of Israel's people through the necessary fiery trials until the chief shepherd returns to reign (1 Pet 5:4/Zech 14:3–21). Importantly, as Bosetti helpfully has pointed out, these elders

---

111. Meyers and Meyers, *Zechariah 9–14*, 203; Duguid, "Messianic Themes in Zechariah 9–14," 272.

112. Mason, *Use of Earlier Biblical Material*, 100; Meyers and Meyers, *Zechariah 9–14*, 203–4.

113. Redditt, *Introduction to the Prophets*, 338–39, 344.

114. Redditt has also argued that Malachi was redacted in order to be read along with Zechariah 9–14 in order to "stamp the Twelve with this word of caution: the promised restoration cannot come about until the leadership in Jerusalem repents and changes its ways" (*Introduction to the Prophets*, 344).

are to pattern their leadership (ποιμάνατε; ἐπισκοποῦντες)[115] after the ποιμήν καὶ ἐπίσκοπος τῶν ψυχῶν ὑμῶν.[116] But what is perhaps most remarkable about this interplay between Zechariah 9–14 and 1 Peter 5 is that Peter includes gentiles in this program. That is, as Israel undergoes transformation through restoration, so too do communities of gentile followers of Jesus, and this transformation is emplaced within the God of Israel's ongoing commitment to the restoration of his covenant people.

## Conclusions Regarding Οἶκος and the Jewish Restoration Ideology of 1 Peter

Further analysis of the term οἶκος, this time as it appears in 1 Pet 4:12–19, has demonstrated that it is indeed polyvalent. That is, in 1 Pet 4:12–19, οἶκος points to a people belonging to a messianic household or dynasty. Significantly, this "house of God" is said have the Spirit of God rest upon it (1 Pet 4:14). For this reason, I have suggested that the term οἶκος πνευματικός in 1 Pet 2:5, while it indeed contains connotations of community as temple (which we explored in chapter 5), points cataphorically to the messianic house of God in 1 Pet 4:14 as well. We reached this conclusion for two reasons. First, it appears that the decision to use οἶκος to describe the addressees likely has been derived from the eschatological program of Zechariah 9–14, where "house" is also polyvalent (i.e., household and temple), but the emphasis appears to be on the community that expresses allegiance to the God of Israel's Davidic shepherd. And second, as Elliott and Bauckham have observed, 1 Pet 2:9–10 helps clarify the meaning of the phrase "spiritual house" in 1 Pet 2:5, broadening the connotation beyond temple to include also the notion of a people who serve royalty. In other words, since οἶκος is polyvalent, 1 Pet 2:9–10 explains that to be part of this "spiritual house" demands a new way of life that is so radical that it can be characterized as a new ethnic identity that entails a new way of life.

As we considered the origin of the term οἶκος, and especially the phrase οἶκος τοῦ θεοῦ, we saw how 1 Peter develops an eschatological

---

115. Michaels comments that "the command to 'watch over' (ἐπισκοποῦντες) the flock is omitted in certain MSS (including ℵ* and B) but is retained in the majority of MSS (including p72 2ℵ A P Ψ the OL versions and g). It is difficult to see why scribes would have added it if it were not original since the verse reads quite smoothly without it" (*1 Peter*, 276).

116. Bosetti, *Pastore*, 194.

program that includes features that are also found in the one-of-a-kind eschatological program of Zechariah 9–14. Rather than rehearse those features, here in the conclusion I simply will underscore that, based upon our analysis, Peter welcomes his gentile addressees into what the God of Israel is doing in and through his Davidic shepherd king, Jesus. This welcome entails an entirely new way for gentiles to orient themselves to the world. This helps explain the "people, race, and nation" language of 1 Pet 2:9–10. Peter draws on such terms, not in order to suggest that these gentile followers of Jesus replace Israel, but instead to illustrate the profound change that is required for these gentile addressees to align themselves with Israel's Messiah. As Ok has developed,

> The emphasis Peter places on being an οἶκος πνευματικὸς and οἶκος τοῦ θεοῦ provides an alternative family and household *in addition* to their unbelieving families and households. Christians must manage multiple commitments (e.g., to their masters, husbands, wives, neighbors, and associates) and must navigate multiple ideologies and pressures (e.g., how to honor the emperor without worshipping him, how to live as free people within the laws of Rome, how to worship God while living under the roof of a master or husband who worships other gods). Their primary and ultimate commitment, however, is to Christ their Lord.[117]

But our analysis in this section has sought to demonstrate with more depth and texture that the ethnic reasoning of 1 Pet 2:9–10 and beyond is more than a technique or rhetorical device. We have done this by attuning to the text-plot and unique Jewish restoration ideology of Zechariah 9–14. What we have seen is that for these gentile followers of Jesus, allegiance to Israel's Davidic shepherd entails inhabiting a new story, a new way of understanding who God is and what he is up to in the world, and a concomitant new way of life that is undergirded, oriented, and animated by the logic of Israelhood. That is, hope, faith, a sense of belonging, purpose, and communal love are all shaped and maintained in an Israel-centric manner, or more specifically in a Zechariah-shaped pattern. In other words, the ethnic language not only serves as a helpful metaphor for conveying the profundity of change that this ἀναστροφή entails, but it also conveys something more profound about who these addressees are: *they belong to the people of the God of Israel.*

---

117. Ok, *Constructing Ethnic Identity*, 81.

Given the social setting of this letter, this message is important in part because, as we discussed in chapter 3, it appears that there may have been an erosion of solidarity between Jewish and gentile followers of Jesus, which would have left these addressees in a kind of no man's land: they no longer share in the unifying narrative of Roman imperial order, but they also wonder whether they belong to the people of the God of Israel. That they are οἶκος πνευματικὸς/οἶκος τοῦ θεοῦ reminds them that the Spirit has welcomed them into the household of the Davidic shepherd king, Jesus. But the οἶκος πνευματικὸς/οἶκος τοῦ θεοῦ imagery also serves to ameliorate the addressees' disorienting sense of alienation from their Greco-Roman compeers as well. The polyvalence of the descriptor οἶκος read together with other prominent themes in the letter such has "household" (1 Pet 2:18—3:7), "family/brotherhood" (e.g., 1:22; 3:8), and "God as father" (1:2, 3, 17) reconfigures yet another unique aspect of Roman imperial ideology (not explored in chapter 4) which conceives of membership in the Roman Empire as belonging to the household or family dynasty that is under the beneficent care of the "father of the fatherland" (i.e., the emperor).[118]

## Οἶκος Πνευματικός and Gentile Halakhah

There is one set of questions that were raised in this chapter that have yet to be answered: if gentiles have been incorporated into the people of the God of Israel *qua* gentiles, which parts of Jewish life are they to embrace and practice? We've already seen that these gentile followers of Jesus are expected to understand the problem and the solution of the world from an Israel-centric perspective, they are exhorted to ground their hopes and expectations in the God of Israel's ongoing fidelity to the covenant made with Israel, and they are to understand their reconciliation to God and ongoing relational maintenance with him in keeping with the logic of sacrifice and covenant. But are there more aspects of Israel's way of life that these gentile followers of Jesus are to embrace or adopt? And are there aspects of Israel's way of life that these gentiles are *not* to adopt? In an effort to respond to this set of related questions, it will be illuminating to consider the rhetorical structure that proceeds 1 Pet 2:4–10, namely the *Haustafel* or "household code" that is found within the next unit of

---

118. See especially Severy, *Augustus and the Family*; Ramage, *Nature and Purpose of Res Gestae*.

the letter (1 Pet 2:11—4:11).¹¹⁹ As Williams and Horrell indicate, 1 Pet 2:11-12 "serve as an introduction not only to the codes of instruction relating to the contexts of both empire and household but also to the whole section (1 Pet 2:11—4:11) of which these codes form a part."¹²⁰ They also note how 1 Pet 2:11-12 introduces the addressees to a new way of life that they are urged to adopt, which includes two fundamental and programmatic aspects: (a) that which they must abstain from as well as (b) "good works" that they ought to engage in.¹²¹ All these descriptors used to characterize this section of 1 Pet 2:11—4:11 (a "way of life," "codes of instruction," "fundamental and programmatic aspects" that include instruction for "good works" and what to abstain from) might also be used to explain what is meant by the Jewish concept of *halakhah*, though not without significant distinctions. In what follows, as we continue to revisit the meaning of οἶκος πνευματικός, I seek to show how the "household code" of 1 Peter functions as a kind of *halakhah* for gentile followers of Jesus, continuing this pattern of drawing upon "Israelhood logic" in order to form identity.¹²²

What is important to underscore for our purposes is that the climactic fundamental indicative of 1 Pet 2:4-10, which reorients the addressees to their new peoplehood, or more precisely to their Israelhood, is followed by a call to practice a new ἀναστροφή (1 Pet 2:12) that is to reflect this new culture, if you will, into which they have been emplaced.¹²³ It is important to appreciate that after declaring his addressees to be a "spiritual house," "a royal priesthood," "a people belonging to the God of Israel," or drawing on Horrell et al., after he uses ethnic reasoning to declare their new identity, in 1 Pet 2:13—3:12 he follows those fundamental

119. Most 1 Peter scholars consider 1 Pet 2:13—3:12 to be a kind of adaptation of the Greco-Roman "household code." It is beyond the scope of this study to enter into what is known as the "Balch-Elliott Debate." For a brief overview and critique, see Horrell, "Between Conformity and Resistance," 111-43; Christensen, "*Balch/Elliott* Debate." For reading the household code in 1 Peter within its Greco-Roman context, see Keener, *1 Peter*, 163-69.

120. Williams and Horrell, *1 Peter*, 693. To be clear, Williams and Horrell limit what they consider to be the household codes to 1 Pet 2:18—3:7 (*1 Peter*, 779).

121. Williams and Horrell, *1 Peter*, 693. Though it is the case in 1 Peter that some of the "good works" involve abstaining from certain practices.

122. Cf. Williams and Horrell, *1 Peter*, 781.

123. The term ἀναστροφή appears more frequently in 1 Peter than any other New Testament document (1 Pet 1:15, 18; 3:1, 2, 16, and as a verb in 1 Pet 1:17), so Williams and Horrell, *1 Peter*, 701.

indicatives with a kind of chiastic structure in which he bookends directives for all with instructions to sub-groups of the οἶκος πνευματικός regarding how to do the will of God within particular settings and circumstances:

Instructions for entire community (2:13–17)

    Instructions for household slaves (2:18–20)

        Jesus Christ as the paradigm to follow (2:21–25)

    Instructions for wives and husbands (3:1–7)

Instructions for the entire community (3:8–12)[124]

In other words, not unlike like the ethos of Pharisaic (and later rabbinic) *halakhah*, in this section of the letter, Peter seeks to help gentiles followers of Jesus understand how to *practice* the will of God, or we might say, how to perform their allegiance to the God of Israel and the Jewish Messiah, within their own unique context.[125] It is worth noting that in 1 Peter, the practice of Jesus-allegiance is frequently characterized as "good works" or "doing good" or "maintaining a good way of life" (1 Pet 2:12, 14, 15, 20; 3:6, 11, 16–17; 4:19). As we have already discussed in chapter 4, Peter does not exhort his addressees to do "good works" as a means of accommodating to their cultural context and thus alleviating the source of suffering. Instead, he expects this new way of life that is characterized by "good works" to at times be the very cause of misunderstanding and conflict with their compeers (1 Pet 2:20; 3:14, 16; 4:19). As Williams and Horrell have shown, "the value assigned to good deeds derives not from their congruence with the standards of the wider culture or even their benefit to society, but from the fact that such behaviour is modeled by Christ and thus represents the will of God."[126] This important observation in many ways summarizes what *governs* gentile ἀναστροφή (or *halakhah*) in 1 Peter. In other words, according to Peter, if gentiles want to know and to do the will of the God of Israel, they must *walk* in the footsteps of Jesus (1 Pet 2:20), "for to this they have been called" (1 Pet 2:21).[127]

---

124. Green, *1 Peter*, 72.

125. For an extensive study on gentile *halakhah*, see Bockmuehl, *Jewish Law in Gentile Churches*.

126. Williams and Horrell, *1 Peter*, 717. For a comprehensive development of this claim, see Williams, *Good Works*, 246–54.

127. See Windsor, *Reading Ephesians and Colossians After Supersessionism*, 177–78, for the relationship between the concept of "walk" and *halakhah*.

As we explored in detail in chapter 5, walking in the footsteps of Jesus is integrally connected to the themes of holiness/obedience and the work of the Spirit. That is, the Spirit's work of sanctification consists of enabling the members of the "spiritual house" to conform their lives to the pattern of Jesus' faithful obedience to the Father.[128] As we demonstrated, these themes of Spirit-enabled holiness and obedience converge in 1 Pet 2:5, where Peter characterizes the addressees as an οἶκος πνευματικὸς εἰς ἱεράτευμα ἅγιον ἀνενέγκαι πνευματικὰς θυσίας εὐπροσδέκτους τῷ θεῷ διὰ Ἰησοῦ Χριστοῦ. When we allow for οἶκος πνευματικός to be polyvalent, that is, when we read it as a reference to both a temple as well as a people or royal dynasty, we can see more clearly how the structure highlighted above, namely 1 Pet 2:13—3:12, offers general directives as well as specific instructions for the making of "spiritual sacrifices." Additionally, we see how 1 Pet 2:18-25 becomes the epicenter from which all gentile *halakhah* emanates.

These observations are supported by the recognition that the paradigmatic members of the οἶκος πνευματικός are the οἰκέται, or household slaves.[129] Most commentators agree that even though 1 Pet 2:21-25 falls within a passage specifically directed towards household servants, Peter nevertheless has in view his entire audience, which, as we have seen, is described as either the οἶκος πνευματικός (1 Pet 2:5) or the οἶκος τοῦ θεοῦ (1 Pet 4:17). Elliott has helpfully suggested that these slaves "are held up here as paradigmatic of the condition and vocation of the brotherhood as a whole."[130] This seems to be the case since Peter previously urges *all* of his addressees to consider themselves as "slaves of God" (1 Pet 2:16),[131] and since he draws on the pattern of Jesus' faithful obedience as outlined in 1 Pet 2:21-25 in order address the entirety of his readership in 1 Pet 3:8-12. Peter's move, then, to address household slaves (οἰκέται) who are called to submit to their owners, whether good or bad (1 Pet 2:18),

---

128. So also Ok, who concludes, "The new culture or way of life (*anastrophe*) is characterized by obedience and holiness, which as we have seen, is enabled by the Spirit and in conformity to the pattern of Jesus" (*Constructing Ethnic Identity*, 36).

129. Elliott, *1 Peter*, 540, 542.

130. Elliott, *1 Peter*, 542. See also Achtemeier, *1 Peter*, 192; Michaels, *1 Peter*, 135; Campbell, *Honor, Shame, and the Rhetoric of 1 Peter*, 143; Jobes, *1 Peter* [1st ed.], 187; Green, *1 Peter*, 78, 82.

131. Though it should be noted that he uses the term δοῦλοι in 1 Pet 2:16.

becomes the model for the opening exhortation to all the addressees to submit or be subject to every human creature or institution (1 Pet 2:13).[132]

It is important to appreciate, however, that the manner in which Peter urges both these household slaves as well as the addressees as a whole to walk is grounded on the pattern of Jesus' faithful obedience, particularly the way he responded to unjust treatment *en route* to inaugurating Israel's restoration, which, Peter argues, included even these "straying" gentile "sheep." The four γάρ clauses (1 Pet 2:19, 20, 21, 25) in this passage offer a three-tiered motivation for doing the will of the God of Israel by walking in the pattern established by Jesus. With the first two γάρ clauses (1 Pet 2:19, 20), Peter argues that the addressees will receive divine approval (χάρις)[133] when they submit to unjust suffering because they do so in awareness of and commitment to God's will (διὰ συνείδησιν θεοῦ).[134] He further reiterates that it is favorable or honorable in God's eyes (τοῦτο χάρις παρὰ θεῷ) to endure suffering for doing good rather than for some wrongdoing (1 Pet 2:20). Thus, with these first two γάρ clauses, Peter draws a straight line between right behavior that generates unjust suffering and the doing of God's will.

The third γάρ clause (1 Pet 2:21; εἰς τοῦτο γὰρ ἐκλήθητε) explains that one knows God's will by attuning to the pattern seen in Jesus' unjust suffering, whom the addressees have been called to follow. This is further explained (ὅτι) with the theme phrase for 1 Pet 2:21–25: καὶ Χριστὸς ἔπαθεν ὑπὲρ ὑμῶν.[135] There seems to be a double meaning of the phrase ὑπὲρ ὑμῶν. On the one hand, in the most immediate context it appears that Peter is gesturing towards the suffering of Christ as the paradigm for these addressees to follow (ὑμῖν ὑπολιμπάνων ὑπογραμμὸν ἵνα ἐπακολουθήσητε τοῖς ἴχνεσιν αὐτοῦ; 1 Pet 2:21). In other words, since the Christ walked this difficult path of faithful obedience, so too they are called to do the same. It is here that Peter highlights how Jesus did not use retaliatory speech when reviled (1 Pet 2:22), but instead entrusted himself to the one who judges justly (1 Pet 2:23), implying that faithful followers of Jesus are to do the same (especially when read along with

---

132. I am persuaded by Williams and Horrell that the phrase πάσῃ ἀνθρωπίνῃ κτίσει is best translated as "human creatures" (*1 Peter*, 728–35).

133. In this particular instance χάρις is to be understood within the semantic domain of honor language rather than divine enabling grace; cf. 1 Pet 2:20. See also Achtemeier, *1 Peter*, 196.

134. See Williams and Horrell, *1 Peter*, 801–2, 809.

135. See Liebengood, *Eschatology of 1 Peter*, 89–97, for argumentation on this point.

1 Pet 3:10–12).¹³⁶ Although this is certainly one aspect of what Peter has in view, 1 Pet 2:24–25 suggest there is more to say.

For instance, in 1 Pet 2:24, Peter moves away from a reflection on the paradigmatic function of Jesus' suffering to address the significance of his death. According to Peter, Jesus bore "our sins in his body upon the tree." This, according to Peter, enables "us to live to righteousness." He rearticulates this at the end of 1 Pet 2:24 by stating that by his wounds "you have been healed." This statement is followed by the final γάρ clause of this passage (1 Pet 2:25). Here we see that Peter interprets "being healed" as being returned to the eschatological Davidic shepherd. As I have shown elsewhere, here Peter links Jesus' last week, his passion, with the righteous sufferer of Isaiah 53, and then conflates that with Zech 13:7 and its wider eschatological program in order to develop the theme of covenant restoration which comes through the suffering and death of the God of Israel's appointed agent.¹³⁷ As we have already seen, Zechariah 9–14 offers a unique twist to the shepherd tradition of the prophets: the God of Israel's agent, the appointed shepherd over God's people, was rejected and suffered death before securing Israel's restoration (Zech 11:4–17; 12:10). This death would initiate the gathering of God's scattered sheep (described also as healing; LXX Zech 10:2); it would enable the "house of God" to be cleansed from its sin (Zech 12:8—13:2); but it would also bring about a transition period described as fiery trials, which are additionally likened to a new exodus. As those who have been returned to the slain shepherd-king because of his death, Peter's readers are now in the fiery trials where their fidelity to God will be tested while they undertake a new exodus journey towards their inheritance. This means that for these gentile followers of Jesus, they have been enabled to discern the will of God in the wilderness as they wait for their inheritance by conforming their lives to the pattern that Jesus left them to follow. But it also means that their fidelity in the wilderness is measured against the extent to which their lives conform to the footsteps of Jesus. In other words, Christ governs the ἀναστροφή, or to put it in Israelhood terms, he shapes gentile *halakhah*. We see this when Peter draws on the paradigm of Jesus in the instructions that follow 1 Pet 2:21–25. For example, in 1 Pet 3:1, Peter writes, "Wives, in the same way," and then makes a link between his directive to wives and the footsteps of Jesus in 1 Pet 2:21–25.

136. Though see Williams and Horrell, *1 Peter*, 826–32, for a helpful discussion regarding the *what* or *who* has been entrusted to God.

137. E.g., pages 113–21.

Similarly, in 1 Pet 3:7, he writes, "Husbands, in the same way," and then follows this with an injunction.

The *oikos* imagery initiated in 1 Pet 2:5 and then extended in the "household codes" of 1 Pet 2:13—3:12 culminates in 1 Peter 4, where Peter urges his addressees to be good οἰκονόμοι (stewards) of the manifold grace of God by serving one another with the gifts they each have received (1 Pet 4:10). The purpose of leveraging these gifts in service of the "spiritual house that is being built" (1 Pet 2:5) is that God may be glorified *through* Jesus Christ (1 Pet 4:11). This suggests once again, when read in light of what have seen in 1 Pet 2:18–25, that Jesus is the *means by which* these gentile "οἰκονόμοι" practice God's will as God's house. That is, what makes the addressees "holy" (1 Pet 1:15), "obedient children" (1 Pet 1:14) who are no longer passively conformed to the desires that were formed in them by the way of life they inherited from their forefathers (1 Pet 1:18) is their decision to disidentify with their past by walking in a new way of life patterned after the faithful obedience of Jesus.[138]

It is important to note that Peter has more to say about what this new ἀναστροφή entails. For example, as Ok has pointed out:

> Peter detaches Christian identity from those Greco-Roman values and social associations at odds with Christian values. He does this by describing their corporate identity as an ethnic identity with its own distinctive culture. This culture is characterized by the following attributes: living hope (1:3); obedience to the Father (1:14); unity of spirit; mutual love among members of the household of God (2:5, 17; 3:8; 4:17); faithful adherence to the example of Christ—who committed no sin, spoke without guile, did not reply with insults when insulted, and did not threaten revenge though he suffered (2:21–5); and humility toward one another (5:5–6).[139]

It nevertheless remains the case that this new ἀναστροφή that the "spiritual house" is called to is ultimately governed by the work of the Spirit who is conforming the addressees to the pattern of Jesus' life. This governing work generates "spiritual sacrifices" of hope, holiness, obedience, faithful endurance, unity of spirit, humility, and mutual love—a kind of pneumatological-christological *halakhah* for gentile followers of the Messiah of the God of Israel.

---

138. I am indebted to Ok, *Constructing Ethnic Identity*, 44, for this observation.
139. Ok, *Constructing Ethnic Identity*, 56.

By now it is perhaps unsurprising that this pattern of identity formation that is developed in 1 Peter—namely that an elect and redeemed people are told who they are in light of God's saving actions (1 Pet 1:1—2:10) and are then given instructions about how to live in light of this reality (2:11—4:11)—is yet another display of Pentateuchal logic that seems to drive much of the pastoral strategy of the letter. But it is equally important to call attention to the fact that instead of requiring these gentile followers of Jesus to become Torah-observant proselytes, Peter anchors their new way of life to the faithful obedience of Israel's Messiah, the Davidic king, showing how his pattern of life is to be instantiated in a variety of contexts, from the household to life under the Roman Empire. As Marcar has observed, "The author was *selective* in his application of Jewish ethnic identity to believers. He applied Israel's traditional epithets to believers, but called them to holiness, not halakah."[140] While it is certainly the case that Peter did not call his addressees to some form Pharisaic *halakhah* that helped them know how to apply the Torah to their circumstances, he did nevertheless provide them with a governing framework for how to practice the will of the God of Israel as gentiles. In this sense, Peter extends a form of Jewish identity to his addressees that is analogous to the pattern found in Exodus 19-23 and Leviticus: they are declared to be the God of Israel's people and then called to be holy. For gentiles, however, holiness is discerned and practiced, not by walking in keeping with Torah but instead by following in the footsteps of Israel's Messiah.[141] As they wait in the wilderness of fiery trials, their fidelity to the God of Israel will be measured in accordance with the example that Jesus left to follow. But Peter is also quick to remind his addressees that this same Jesus is also at the right hand of the Father, where he performs covenant maintenance as they await their inheritance.

In some regards these conclusions about the limits and boundaries of gentile identity are somewhat disappointing or anticlimactic. Frustratingly, Peter does not tell us all we might want to know about what distinguishes Jewish and gentile identity in Christ. But it seems to be the case that for Peter, what he has written is sufficient for the situation he seeks to address, which is itself illuminating. As we have said before, it appears that Peter is not so much concerned with what distinguishes Jewish and

---

140. Marcar, *Divine Regeneration and Ethnic Identity*, 17 (emphasis mine).

141. With this statement I am not suggesting that Torah and fidelity to Christ are in opposition in any way, or that Christ nullifies the Torah.

gentile allegiance to Jesus as he is focused on helping gentiles find ways in which they are united to the people of the God of Israel.

## Conclusions

The ethnic reasoning displayed in 1 Peter is not intended to suggest that "the church" replaces Israel as the new people of God. Neither is it merely a technique or a rhetorical strategy. Instead, it is the very substance of the identity of these addressees. By attuning carefully to the argumentation of 1 Peter and the ways that it shows evidence of engagement with the text-plots of several key Jewish eschatological traditions, we see that Peter's ethnic reasoning has more texture and depth than earlier studies have captured. First, we see that the ethnic reasoning language is intricately connected to the larger story of the God of Israel's commitment to restore the covenant with Israel. This insight flips a common orientation to 1 Peter on its head. That is, often, Primopetrine scholars wonder why Peter does not explain how Israel in the flesh fits into the letter. But our examination shows that the pressure runs the other direction. That is, one way to understand this apparent silence is to deduce that God's ongoing fidelity to Israel is *assumed* and therefore unquestioned. What *is* in question, however, is whether and how gentiles fit into what the God of Israel is doing through Israel's Messiah. This is the rhetorical exigence of the letter. Second, rather than draw on ethnic categories as a means to generate a new (generic) ethnic identity, more accurately, Peter extends a form of *Jewish* ethnic identity to his gentile addressees: they also belong to the people of the God of Israel, and this reality is so profound that it requires that they subordinate their inherited gentile identity to Israelhood. The profundity of this new identity entails learning a new way of life, but one that does not demand Torah adherence as would a Jewish proselyte. Instead, Peter presents this new way of life as a kind of pneumatological-christological *halakhah* for gentile members of the οἶκος πνευματικός.

Additionally, one further implication of this study is that we should give more consideration to the way in which οἶκος in 1 Pet 2:5 works to characterize the addressees as a household or dynasty. What is more, it also suggests that it is perhaps unnecessary to determine which image—either the temple/building or the community/household—is in the fore of 1 Pet 2:5.[142] It seems that to mark out one connotation as more

---

142. *Pace* Elliott; Williams and Horrell, who, while noting that "The mixture of

prominent than the other seems to minimize the semantic flexibility and thus the rhetorical effect of choosing οἶκος to describe the addressees.

---

metaphors and images the author weaves together—from newborn infants, to stones and buildings, then to priests offering sacrifices—means that the connections between them cannot be neatly sewn," nevertheless conclude that "it would seem that the image of a building is to the fore" (1 Peter, 616).

# *Conclusion*

## Summary and Implications

### A Summary of the Argument

IN CHAPTER 1, I called attention to a potential problem with the identity-formation strategy of 1 Peter: it seems to be dependent upon the premise that Israel has been replaced by a newer and truer people of God. Or, said in another way, Peter is purported to take the promises and privileges given to Israel (by God) and hand them over to a new entity, whom he refers to as Christians. It has not been until recently that 1 Peter scholars have characterized this move as problematic. One way to resolve this issue, some have suggested, is to recognize that the letter is silent regarding whether God's original covenant with Israel continues to be in effect. In other words, 1 Peter seems to be ambivalent and unclear about the relationship between the addressees and the Israel from whom they derive their new identity. This silence, they propose, creates hermeneutical space to go outside the text to resolve the problematic identity-formation strategy of the letter. But I showed that going outside the text can also be problematic because the standard canonical narrative exerts hermeneutical pressure to fill "the silence of 1 Peter" with supersessionist assumptions. Instead of going outside of the letter to resolve the ambiguity, I demonstrated briefly how attending more carefully to the reference "god" along with the implicit narrative in the letter as well as the way in which gentiles are exhorted to embrace a non-gentile, Israel-centric way of understanding what God is up to in the world and their place in it press against the purported supersessionist posture of 1 Peter. As a result, I contended that fresh research on the identity-formation strategy of 1 Peter was in order.

But the supposed problematic identity-formation strategy of 1 Peter is dependent upon a foundational assumption that, if proven otherwise, would radically change our perception of the kind of shaping that is happening in the letter. That consensus assumption among scholars is that the letter is written to a predominantly or exclusively gentile audience. In chapter 2, I suggested that there are some compelling reasons to question this established modern consensus. In fact, in reexamining this commonly held view, I showed that most of the proof texts (1 Pet 1:14, 18, 21; 2:9–10) used to support a predominant or exclusive gentile audience can also be leveraged to argue for an exclusively Jewish audience. Importantly, in the course of exploring the ethnic identity of the addressees, as we examined how Peter's critique of the futile ways of the fathers (1 Pet 1:18) coheres with similar examples of intra-Jewish debate, we learned that Peter presumes that God's covenant restoration promises are applicable to his recipients. What is more, we saw in brief that the imagery used to convey covenant restoration in 1 Peter was dependent on a particular tradition of Jewish restoration eschatology that characterizes the first stages of restoration as a new exodus/wilderness journey in which fidelity will be tested with fiery trials on the way to an inheritance (e.g., Isa 40; 42–43; Hos 2 recapitulating Exod 19:4–6). I showed how this new exodus/wilderness imagery is both implicitly as well as explicitly drawn from the Hebrew Bible and that it serves to incorporate the addressees into God's ongoing commitment to Israel. Given some of the erroneous foundational assumptions of the modern consensus as well as a renewed awareness of how Jewish restoration eschatology is interwoven throughout 1 Pet 1:1—2:10, I argued that it is necessary to examine further the ethnic makeup of the recipients. Since it turns out that Jews do in fact talk to other Jews like Peter does in this letter, and given that the letter seems to suggest that God's covenant with Israel has been restored through Jesus, and because these addressees are seamlessly included in this restoration, perhaps it is the case that 1 Peter is written exclusively to Jews.

So, in chapter 3 I analyzed the best extant proposal for a Jewish audience but determined that it did not accurately reflect what we know about the audience from the text and from the socio-historical context of the letter. Rather than fixate on the proof texts that are often used in order to debate about the ethnic makeup of the addressees of 1 Peter, I instead considered how exploring the theme of suffering might be a better way of discerning the ethnic identity of the recipients. In the end, I concluded that the kind of suffering described in 1 Peter would have been unique to gentile followers of Jesus, and that the ideal or imagined audience was made up of gentiles who suffered because faithful allegiance to Jesus entailed a new way of life that was seen as shameful, offensive, and even hostile to their gentile family, friends, and neighbors. In the midst of ascertaining this, I called attention to the profound disorientation these gentile addressees faced as they were cut off from their traditional networks of support and belonging. I also underscored that the primary concern that Peter addresses is what we might call intragentile conflict—that is, gentiles telling other gentiles that they do not belong because they do not live honorable lives. What is more, I explored the development and meaning of the term Χριστιανός, and this shed further light on the tenuous and ambiguous status of gentile followers of Jesus. The term was coined by outsiders in a context in which gentiles were welcomed into the people of the God of Israel through their belonging to this distinct expression of Jewish identity. But as time went on, gentile followers of Jesus within this mixed group increased, while the population of Jewish followers of Jesus did not keep pace. Concomitant with this demographic change was the development of the term Χριστιανός as an indicator of criminal status. Within this scenario, I suggested that these gentile followers of Jesus were not only facing the threat of criminal punishment, not only were they being ostracized by their own people, but they may also have been experiencing an erosion of their sense of belonging within their new host family, the people of the God of Israel. In other words, the development of the meaning of "Christian" may point to the fact that the addressees' new roots in Jewish identity were also being questioned at the time of the composition of 1 Peter—either by the addressees themselves, by other gentiles, or perhaps even by Jews.

I sought to confirm this hypothesis by considering the genre and the rhetorical exigence of 1 Peter. I concluded that as a diaspora letter, 1 Peter is presented as quasi-authoritative correspondence from a Jewish apostle of Jesus who is remembered for his mission to the gentiles. I also explored the rhetorical exigence of 1 Peter by comparing it with the letter from the Jerusalem Assembly (Acts 15). The comparison brought further depth and clarity to our understanding of the genre discussion. In short, 1 Peter is best regarded as an authoritative letter written to provide apostolic affirmation to gentile followers of Jesus regarding their full legitimacy and inclusion within the people of the God of Israel. Thus, considerations about the genre and the rhetorical exigence of 1 Peter confirmed my hypothesis regarding the intended or imagined addressees being gentiles who needed to know that (and how) they belonged to the people of the God of Israel *as gentiles*.

As I sought to discern the ethnic makeup of the addressees of 1 Peter, we became more attuned to the way in which the Roman Empire, or more particularly Roman imperial ideology, had a significant impact in generating negative responses from gentiles to gentiles who reoriented their way of life around Jesus. So, in chapter 4, I analyzed how Peter responded to the challenges of Roman imperial ideology—and in particular its claims of realized eschatology—by once again pointing to Jewish restoration eschatology or, we might say, a uniquely Jewish way of understanding what God is up to in the world. To be more specific, I demonstrated that Peter appeals to the inaugurated but deferred hope of the eschatological Davidic shepherd king. What is important to underscore, especially for the purposes of this study, is that Peter's solution to the problem of empire and the way in which it has alienated these newly formed gentile followers of Jesus is to welcome them into the people of the God of Israel by including them as beneficiaries of what the God of Israel is doing in and through the Davidic king, Jesus. In other words, in the end, Peter's solution to a uniquely gentile problem is "Israelhood," that is, for gentile followers of Jesus to inhabit, even participate in, a uniquely Jewish way of being in the world by following in the footsteps of the radical and transforming pattern of enemy-love embodied by the eschatological Davidic king Jesus, who it should be noted also confronts and reshapes Jewish self-understanding.

In chapter 5, I began to explore two central themes of the most problematic passage in the letter, 1 Pet 2:4–10. That is, I showed how temple and priesthood imagery is integral to the identity-formation strategy of 1 Peter, that this imagery has often been interpreted as a polemic against the Jerusalem temple (and by extension Judaism), and that such judgments often intensify into claims that constitute the church or Christians as the "new" and/or "true" Israel. I demonstrated, however, that there are no grounds for such a reading of this imagery in 1 Peter. In contrast to repudiating and replacing Israel with the church, I suggested that when we pay attention to where Jesus is and what he is doing (from the perspective of the letter), we see more clearly that Peter constructs the identity of the gentile addressees *in continuity with and even under the pressure of the logic of covenant and sacrifice*. That is, through the unjust suffering and death of Jesus, which Peter characterizes in relation to the Passover lamb, the suffering servant, and the eschatological Davidic shepherd, God's covenant with Israel has been restored—and 1 Peter makes the apostolic claim that gentiles *qua* gentiles have been included in this restoration. But this account of the death of Jesus should not be confused or conflated with the ongoing covenant maintenance that Jesus presently supplies at the right hand of God in the heavenly temple, where he sprinkles his blood as an offering of atonement. It is this ongoing ministry of purification, consecration, and expiation, coordinated with the sanctifying work of the Spirit, that enables Peter to confidently claim that the Spirit of glory and of God rests upon his imagined recipients; that they are a "spiritual house" that offers up "acceptable spiritual sacrifices"; and that the addressees will faithfully persevere in the wilderness of testing. In the course of developing how the logic of covenant and sacrifice works in 1 Peter, I also underscored the importance of acknowledging that the claims of 1 Pet 2:5 ("you are a spiritual house") and 1 Pet 4:14 ("the Spirit of glory and of God rests upon you") are only possible *by means* of the activities of both the Spirit and Jesus Christ. That is, the impetus for the claim that these gentile followers of Jesus are holy space in which God is found is not derived from polemical concerns with the Jerusalem temple and Judaism more generally. Instead, these claims are pneumatologically and christologically generated in keeping with covenantal logic. Finally, I concluded chapter 5 by noting that if there is any sort of polemic going on with temple and priesthood imagery in 1 Peter, it is more likely directed toward Rome and its realized eschatology (*pax Romana*), which is said to be maintained through faithful allegiance to the Roman emperor, who bears the title *pontificus maximus* for his priestly role in keeping the *pax deorum*. Here we see once again how Peter points his gentile addressees to an Israel-centric solution to their problem, this time by calling attention to the logic of covenant and sacrifice, interpreted through the life, death, resurrection, and ongoing priestly ministry of Jesus, in order to help them understand how their daily acts of fidelity testify to their belonging to the God of Israel and the people of God.

In chapter 6 I considered the concentration of terms in 1 Pet 2:9–10 which seem to suggest that Israel has been replaced by a new people called Christians. I discussed the helpful insights and limitations of recent scholarship that has highlighted the "ethnic reasoning" found in 1 Peter, ultimately concluding however that they do not go far enough— for the ethnic reasoning of 1 Peter is more than a rhetorical technique; it is more precisely *Jewish* ethnic reasoning. I followed the assessment of recent attempts to make sense of the "race, nation, and people" imagery with a reconsideration of the term *oikos*. I explored the way that *oikos* is developed in 1 Peter by comparing it with the unique Jewish restoration program of Zechariah 9–14. Attentiveness to the text-plot of the eschatological David shepherd program of Zechariah 9–14 not only helped make sense of several puzzling features of 1 Peter, it also provided a compelling explanation for why Peter chose to refer to the addressees as the οἶκος τοῦ θεοῦ and the οἶκος πνευματικός, instead of the ἐκκλησία—namely to declare that they belong to the restored people of the God of Israel and the slain and vindicated Davidic shepherd, but also that, in keeping with that well-known eschatological program, they must pass through fiery trials as they wait for their inheritance.

I concluded chapter 6 by highlighting yet another display of Pentateuchal logic that informs the identity-formation strategy developed in 1 Peter. An elect and redeemed people are gathered and told who they are in light of God's saving actions (1 Pet 1:1—2:10)[1] and are then given instructions about how to live in light of this reality (2:11—4:11). But I also called attention to the fact that instead of requiring these gentile followers of Jesus to become Torah-observant proselytes, Peter anchors their new way of life to the faithful obedience of Israel's Messiah, the Davidic king, showing how his pattern of life is to be instantiated in a variety of contexts—from the household to life under the Roman Empire. While it is certainly the case that Peter did not call his addressees to some form Pharisaic *halakhah*, he did nevertheless provide them with a governing framework for how to practice the will of the God of Israel as gentiles. In this sense, Peter extends a form of Jewish identity to his addressees that is analogous to the pattern found in Exodus 19–23 and Leviticus: they are declared to be the God of Israel's people, and then called to be holy. For gentiles, however, holiness is discerned and practiced, not by walking in keeping with Torah but instead by following in the footsteps of Israel's Messiah.

In short, 1 Peter is *not* silent concerning the relationship between the addressees and Israel in the flesh. We do not need to go outside the text to solve its purported ambiguity. And the letter does not promote a supersessionist posture towards Israel in the flesh. Peter may not say all that we want to know, but there is nothing in the letter that presses us to assume discontinuity between what God promised to Israel in the

1. See chapter 2 for all the ways 1 Pet 1:1—2:10 draws upon exodus and new exodus imagery.

past and what Peter is claiming is true for these gentile addressees (as he draws from Israel's privileges, promises, and prerogatives). Too often it is the case that supersessionist assumptions cloud and confuse our perceptions about how Peter is constructing identity in the letter. It is not the case that he is taking privileges and promises that were originally given to someone else and is now handing them over to these gentiles. I have shown that the grain runs the other direction. Instead, what we have in 1 Peter is a Jewish apostle of the Jewish Messiah extending the benefits of God's covenant restoration of Israel to these beleaguered gentile followers of Jesus by providing apostolic affirmation regarding their full legitimacy within the people of the God of Israel—Israelhood. I have sought to demonstrate that this is the intended punchline of the letter: that "the prophets prophesied of the grace intended for *you* [gentiles]" (1 Pet 1:10); that Christ "was revealed at the end of the ages for *your sake* [gentiles]" (1 Pet 1:20); and that "*you* [gentiles] have been returned to the shepherd and overseer of your souls" (1 Pet 2:25).

## Some Implications

This study has important, though to some extent limited, implications for the overarching aim of NTAS series, which is to provide an exegetical basis for post-supersessionist theology.[2] First, it affirms the God of Israel's ongoing, irrevocable covenant with the Jewish people as a central and coherent part of ecclesial teaching. I have demonstrated that 1 Peter rejects understandings of the new covenant that entail the abrogation or obsolescence of God's covenant with the Jewish people. However, given the nature of the situation that Peter was addressing, it does not offer instruction on whether Torah observance continues to be a demarcator of Jewish communal identity, though neither does it deny it. What it does affirm, however, is that gentile followers of Jesus are not obligated to practice Torah in order to know and do the will of the God of Israel.

Messianic Jewish biblical scholars have highlighted the relationship of interdependence and mutual blessing between Jews and gentiles in Messiah Jesus. First Peter does not offer much in terms of what gentiles offer to Jews. Rather, Peter seems to stress the blessings of salvation, hope, fellowship with God, and belonging that are rooted in being incorporated into the people of the God of Israel.

---

2. See the series preface statement at the front of the book.

This raises a further uncomfortable implication of our study, one that might be due to limits of the situation being addressed in the letter. First Peter seems to project a fairly negative view of gentile heritage prior to conversion. That is, the ethnic heritage of the addressees prior to their new birth is presented in exclusively negative terms in order to shape this new identity in which belonging to Jesus means belonging to the people of the God of Israel. So, while in this study we have focused on the problem of supersessionism in 1 Peter, our examination raises another potential problem that merits further consideration: is the kind of identity formation that is done in 1 Peter problematic in the other direction? That is, in calling for an "Israelhood" identity that supersedes all other ethnic identities, does this generate new concerns for the identity-formation strategy of the letter? And, if so, do we need to go outside the text to find solutions, or might the letter itself provide the clarification?

And yet, if Jesus points us to the God who has revealed his identity to the world through his interaction with the particular people of Israel, what are we to make of this God's fidelity and reliability if we embrace supersessionism? In other words, if the God of Israel is indifferent to a people that he once promised an inheritance, then how seriously can we take promises he is said to make to other peoples at other times? Or, if the God of Israel is capable of raising up a people only to abandon them for another, how sure can we be that he will not do the same to his new chosen people?

Which god is the Father of our Lord, Jesus Christ (1 Pet 1:3)? Ultimately, this is what is at stake as we seek to discern whether the identity-formation strategy of 1 Peter promotes a supersessionist posture towards Israel.

# Bibliography

Achtemeier, Paul J. *1 Peter*. Hermeneia. Minneapolis: Fortress, 1996.
Anderson, Bernhard W. "Exodus Typology in Second Isaiah." In *Israel's Prophetic Heritage: Essays in Honor of James Muilenburg*, edited by Bernhard W. Anderson and Walter Harrelson, 177–95. London: Harper and Brothers, 1962.
Ando, Clifford. *Imperial Ideology and Provincial Loyalty in the Roman Empire*. Berkeley: University of California Press, 2000.
Aune, David E. *Revelation 1–5*. Word Biblical Commentary 52A. Dallas: Word, 1997.
Balch, D. L. *Let Wives Be Submissive: The Domestic Code in 1 Peter*. SBLDS 26. Chico, CA: Scholars, 1981.
Barclay, John M. G. *Pauline Churches and Diaspora Jews*. WUNT 275. Tübingen: Mohr Siebeck, 2011.
Bauckham. "James, 1 and 2 Peter, Jude." In *It Is Written: Scripture Citing Scripture: Essays in Honour of Barnabas Lindars*, edited by D. A. Carson and H. G. M. Williamson, 303–17. Cambridge: Cambridge University Press, 1988.
Bauman-Martin, Betsy. "Speaking Jewish: Postcolonial Aliens and Strangers in First Peter." In *Reading First Peter with New Eyes: Methodological Reassessments of the Letter of First Peter*, edited by Robert L. Webb and Betsy Bauman-Martin, 144–77. LNTS 364. London: T&T Clark, 2007.
Beale, Gregory K. *The Temple and the Church's Mission: A Biblical Theology of the Dwelling Place of God*. Downers Grove, IL: InterVarsity, 2014.
Bechtler, S. R. *Following in His Steps: Suffering, Community, and Christology in 1 Peter*. SBLDS 162. Atlanta: Scholars, 1998.
Bhabha, Homi. *The Location of Culture*. London: Routledge, 1994.
Bird, Michael, et al., eds. *Paul Within Judaism: Perspectives on Paul and Jewish Identity*. WUNT 507. Tubingen: Mohr Siebeck, 2023.
Black, M. C. "The Christological Use of the Old Testament in the New Testament." *New Testament Studies* 18 (1971) 1–14.
———. "The Rejected and Slain Messiah Who Is Coming with His Angels: The Messianic Exegesis of Zechariah 9–14 in the Passion Narratives." PhD diss., Emory University, 1990.
Bockmuehl, Markus. *Jewish Law in Gentile Churches: Halakhah and the Beginning of Christian Public Ethics*. London: Bloomsbury, 2022.
———. *Simon Peter in Scripture and Memory: The New Testament Apostle in the Early Church*. Grand Rapids: Baker Academic, 2012.
Boring, M. Eugene. *1 Peter*. Abingdon New Testament Commentaries. Nashville: Abingdon, 1999.

———. "Narrative Dynamics in First Peter: The Function of Narrative World." In *Reading First Peter with New Eyes: Methodological Reassessments of the Letter of First Peter*, edited by Robert L. Webb and Betsy Bauman-Martin, 7–40. LNTS 364. London: T&T Clark, 2007.

Bosetti, Elena. *Il Pastore: Cristo E La Chiesa Nella Prima Lettera Di Pietro*. Supplementi alla Rivista Biblica 21. Bologna: Edizioni Dehonian, 1990.

Botner, Max. "The Essence of a Spiritual House: Misunderstanding Metaphor and the Question of Supersessionism in 1 Peter." *Journal of Biblical Literature* 139.2 (2020) 409–25.

Boyarin, Daniel. *Border Lines: The Partition of Judaeo-Christianity*. Philadelphia: University of Pennsylvania Press, 2004.

Brox, Norbert. *Der Erste Petrusbrief*. 2nd ed. EKKNT 21. Zurich: Benzinger, 1986.

Burnhope, Stephen. *Atonement and the New Perspective: The God of Israel, Covenant, and the Cross*. Eugene, OR: Pickwick, 2018.

Campbell. Barth. *Honor, Shame, and the Rhetoric of 1 Peter*. SBLDS 160. Atlanta: Scholars, 1998.

Carter, Warren. "Going All the Way? Honoring the Emperor and Sacrificing Wives and Slaves in 1 Peter 2.13—3.6." In *A Feminist Companion to the Catholic Epistles* edited by Amy-Jill Levine and Maria Mayo Robbins, 14–33. London: T&T Clark, 2004.

Cervantes Gabarrón, José. *La Pasión de Jesucristo en La Primera Carta de Pedro: Centro Literario Y Teológico De La Carta*. Institución San Jerónimo 22. Estella (Navarra): Verbo Divino, 1991.

Chae, Y. S. *Jesus as the Eschatological Davidic Shepherd*. WUNT 2.216. Tübingen: Mohr Siebeck, 2006.

Chester, Tim, and Steve Timmis. *Everyday Church: Gospel Communities on Mission*. Wheaton, IL: Crossway, 2012.

Christensen, Sean M. "The Balch/Elliott Debate and the Hermeneutics of the Household Code." *Trinity Journal* 2 (2016) 173–93.

Coggins, R. J. *Haggai, Zechariah, Malachi*. Old Testament Guides. Sheffield, UK: Sheffield Academic Press, 1987.

Conzelmann, Hanz. *1 Corinthians*. Hermeneia. Philadelphia: Fortress, 1975.

Crossan, John Dominic, and Jonathan L. Reed. *In Search of Paul: How Jesus's Apostle Opposed Rome's Empire with God's kingdom: A New Vision of Paul's Words & World*. San Francisco: HarperSanFrancisco, 2004.

Davids, Peter H. *The First Epistle of Peter*. NICNT 21. Grand Rapids: Eerdmans, 1990.

deSilva, David. "1 Peter: Strategies for Counseling Individuals on the Way to a New Heritage." *Ashland Theological Journal* 32 (2000) 33–52.

Deterding, Paul E. "Exodus Motifs in First Peter." *Concordia Journal* 7.2 (1981) 58–65.

Dodd, C. H. *According to the Scriptures: The Sub-Structure of New Testament Theology*. London: Nisbet, 1952.

Doering, Lutz. *Ancient Jewish Letters and the Beginnings of Christian Epistolography*. WUNT 2.298. Tübingen: Mohr Siebeck, 2012.

———. "First Peter as Early Christian Diaspora Letter." In *The Catholic Epistles and Apostolic Tradition*, edited by Karl-Wilhelm Niebuhr and Robert W. Wall, 215–36. Waco, TX: Baylor University Press, 2009.

———. "'You Are a Chosen Stock . . .': The Use of Israel Epithets for the Addressees in First Peter." In *Jewish and Christian Communal Identities in the Roman World*, edited by Yair Furstenberg, 243–76. Leiden: Brill, 2016.

Donaldson, Terence L. "Supersessionism and Early Christian Self-Definition." *Journal of the Jesus Movement in Its Jewish Setting* 3 (2016) 1–32.

Dryden, J. W. *Theology and Ethics in 1 Peter: Paraenetic Strategies for Christian Character Formation*. WUNT 209. Tübingen: Mohr Siebeck, 2006.

Dubis, Mark. *1 Peter: Handbook on the Greek Text*. Waco, TX: Baylor University Press, 2010.

———. *Messianic Woes in 1 Peter: Suffering and Eschatology in 1 Peter 4:12–19*. Studies in Biblical Literature 33. New York: Lang, 2002.

———. "Research on 1 Peter: A Survey of Scholarly Literature Since 1985." *Currents in Biblical Research* 4.2 (2006) 199–239.

Duguid, Iain. "Messianic Themes in Zechariah 9–14." In *The Lord's Annointed: Interpretation of Old Testament Messianic Texts*, edited by P. E. Satterhwaite et al., 265–80. Grand Rapids: Baker, 1995.

Dunn, James D. G. *Beginning from Jerusalem*. Vol. 2. of *Christianity in the Making*. Grand Rapids, Eerdmans, 2009.

Eberhart, Christian A. *The Sacrifice of Jesus: Understanding Atonement Biblically*. Reprint, Eugene, OR: Wipf and Stock, 2018.

Egan, Patrick T. *Ecclesiology and the Scriptural Narrative of 1 Peter*. Eugene, OR: Pickwick, 2016.

Eisenbaum, Pamela. *Paul Was Not a Christian: The Original Message of a Misunderstood Apostle*. New York: HarperCollins, 2009.

Elliott, John H. *The Elect and the Holy: An Exegetical Examination of 1 Peter 2:4–10 and the Phrase "Basileion Hieratenma."* Leiden: Brill, 1966.

———. *1 Peter: A New Translation with Introduction and Commentary*. Anchor Yale Bible 37B. New York: Doubleday, 2000.

———. *A Home for the Homeless: A Sociological Exegesis of 1 Peter, Its Situation and Strategy*. Philadelphia: Fortress, 1981.

Esler, Philip F. "Paul's Contestation of Israel's (Ethnic) Memory of Abraham in Galatians 3." *Biblical Theology Bulletin* 36.1 (2006) 23–34.

———. "Religion, Race, Whiteness in Constructions of Jewish and Christian Identities." *Expository Times* 133.7 (2022) 284–89.

Fagbemi, Stephen A. A. *Who Are the Elect in 1 Peter? A Study in Biblical Exegesis and Its Application to the Anglican Church of Nigeria*. Studies in Biblical Literature 104. Oxford: Lang, 2007.

Fee, Gordon D. *The First Epistle to the Corinthians*. NICNT. Grand Rapids: Eerdmans, 1987.

Feldmeier, Reinhard. *The First Letter of Peter: A Commentary on the Greek Text*. Waco, TX: Baylor University Press, 2008.

Fishbane, Michael. *Biblical Interpretation in Ancient Israel*. Oxford: Oxford University Press, 1985.

Galinsky, Karl. *Augustan Culture*. Princeton, NJ: Princeton University Press, 1996.

———, ed. *The Cambridge Companion to the Age of Augustus*. Cambridge: Cambridge University Press, 2005.

Gane, Roy E. *Cult and Character: Purification Offerings, Day of Atonement, and Theodicy*. Winona Lake, IN: Eisenbrauns, 2005.

Gärtner, Bertil E. *The Temple and the Community in Qumran and the New Testament: A Comparative Study in the Temple Symbolism of the Qumran Texts and the New Testament*. SNTS. Cambridge: Cambridge University Press, 1965.

Goppelt, Leonhard. *A Commentary on 1 Peter*. Grand Rapids: Eerdmans, 1993.

———. *Typos: The Typological Interpretation of the Old Testament in the New*. Grand Rapids: Eerdmans, 1982.

Green, Joel. *1 Peter*. Two Horizons New Testament Commentary. Grand Rapids: Eerdmans, 2007.

Gregerman, Adam. "The Challenges of Post-Supersessionism in Contemporary Christianity." Paper presented at *The Identity of Israel: Jews, Christians, and the Bible*, Wycliffe Centre for Scripture and Theology, Toronto, Canada, May 19, 2019. Video. https://www.youtube.com/watch?v=qMA9OOxA3Ss&t=1372s.

Gupta, Nijay K. "A Spiritual House of Royal Priests, Chosen and Honored: The Presence and Function of Cultic Imagery in 1 Peter." *Perspectives in Religious Studies* 36.1 (2009) 61–76.

Harink, Douglas. *1 & 2 Peter*. Brazos Theological Commentary on the Bible. Grand Rapids: Brazos, 2009.

Harland, Phillip. *Associations, Synagogues, and Congregations: Claiming a Place in Ancient Mediterranean Society*. Minneapolis: Fortress, 2003.

Hengel, Martin. *Saint Peter: The Underestimated Apostle*. Grand Rapids: Eerdmans, 2010.

Hillyer, C. N. "'Rock-Stone' Imagery in 1 Peter." *Tyndale Bulletin* 22.1 (1971) 58–81.

———. "Spiritual Milk . . . Spiritual House." *Tyndale Bulletin* 20 (1969) 126–27.

Himmelfarb, Martha. *Ascent to Heaven in Jewish and Christian Apocalypses*. Oxford: Oxford University Press, 1993.

Hockey, Katherine M. *The Role of Emotion in 1 Peter*. SNTS 173. Cambridge: Cambridge University Press, 2019.

Holloway, Paul A. *Coping with Prejudice: 1 Peter in Social-Psychological Perspective*. WUNT 244. Tubingen: Mohr Siebeck, 2009.

Horrell, David G. "Aliens and Strangers? The Socioeconomic Location of the Addressees of 1 Peter." In *Engaging Economics: New Testament Scenarios and Early Christian Reception*, edited by Bruce Longenecker and Kelly Liebengood, 176–202. Grand Rapids: Eerdmans, 2009.

———. *Becoming Christian: Essays on 1 Peter and the Making of Christian Identity*. LNTS 394. London: T&T Clark, 2015.

———. "Between Conformity and Resistance: Beyond the Balch-Elliott Debate Towards a Postcolonial Reading of 1 Peter." In *Reading 1 Peter with New Eyes: Methodological Reassessments of the Letter of First Peter*, edited by Robert L. Webb and Betsy J. Bauman-Martin, 111–43 London: T&T Clark, 2007.

———. "'Das im Unglauben verharrende Judenvolk': 1 Pet 2:4–10, Its History of Interpretation in Germany (1855–1978), and the Important Contribution of Leonhard Goppelt". In *Bedrängnis und Identität: Studien zu Situation, Kommunikation und Theologie des 1. Petrusbriefes*, edited by David du Toit, 327–52. Berlin: de Gruyter, 2013.

———. "Ethnicisation, Marriage and Early Christian Identity: Critical Reflections on 1 Corinthians 7, 1 Peter 3 and Modern New Testament Scholarship." *New Testament Studies* 62 (2016) 439–60.

———. *Ethnicity and Inclusion: Religion, Race, and Whiteness in Constructions of Jewish and Christian Identities*. Grand Rapids: Eerdmans, 2020.
———. *1 Peter*. New Testament Guides. London: T&T Clark, 2008.
———. "Judaean Ethnicity and Christ-Following Voluntarism? A Reply to Steve Mason and Philip Esler." *New Testament Studies* 65.1 (2019) 1–20.
———. "The Label Χριστιανός: 1 Peter 4:16 and the Formation of Christian Identity." *Journal of Biblical Literature* 126.2 (2007) 361–81.
———. "'Race', 'Nation', 'People': Ethnic Identity-Construction in 1 Peter 2.9." *New Testament Studies* 58 (2011) 123–43.
———. "Whose Faith(fulness) Is in 1 Peter 1:5?" *Journal of Theological Studies* 48.1 (1997) 110–15.
Horsley, Richard A., ed. *Paul and the Roman Imperial Order*. London: Bloomsbury, 2004.
Hunzinger, Claus-Hunno. "Babylon als Deckname für Rom und die Datierung des 1. Petrusbriefes." In *Gottes Wort und Gottesland*, edited by Hans-Wilhelm Hertzberg, 67–77. Göttingen: Vanderhoeck and Ruprecht, 1965.
Janowski, Bernd. "He Bore Our Sins: Isaiah 53 and the Drama of Taking Another's Place." In *The Suffering Servant: Isaiah 53 in Jewish and Christian Sources*, edited by Bernd Janowski and Peter Stuhlmacher, 48–74. Grand Rapids: Eerdmans, 2004.
Jauhiainen, Marko. *The Use of Zechariah in Revelation*. WUNT 2.199. Tübingen: Mohr Siebeck, 2005.
Jennings, Willie J. *The Christian Imagination: Theology and the Origins of Race*. New Haven, CT: Yale University Press, 2012.
Jobes, Karen. *1 Peter*. Baker Exegetical Commentary on the New Testament. 1st ed. Grand Rapids: Baker, 2005.
———. *1 Peter*. Baker Exegetical Commentary on the New Testament. 2nd ed. Grand Rapids: Baker, 2022.
———. "The Septuagint Textual Tradition in 1 Peter." In *Septuagint Research: Issues and Challenges in the Study of the Greek Jewish Scriptures*, edited by W. Krause and R. G. Wooden, 311–33. Leiden: Brill, 2006.
Johnson, Dennis. "Fire in God's House: Imagery from Malachi 3 in Peter's Theology of Suffering (1 Pet 4:12–19)." *Journal of the Evangelical Theological Society* 29.3 (1986) 285–94.
Johnson Hodge, Caroline E. *If Sons, Then Heirs: A Study of Kingship and Ethnicity in the Letters of Paul*. Oxford: Oxford University Press, 2007.
Joseph, Abson P. *A Narratological Reading of 1 Peter*. LNTS 440. London: T&T Clark, 2012.
Keener, Craig S. *1 Peter: A Commentary*. Grand Rapids: Baker Academic, 2021.
Kim, Seyoon. "Jesus—the Son of God, the Stone, the Son of Man, and the Servant: The Role of Zechariah in the Self-Identification of Jesus." In *Tradition and Interpretation in the New Testament: Essays in Honor of E. Earle Ellis for His Sixtieth Birthday*, edited by Otto Betz and Gerald F. Hawthorne, 134–48. Grand Rapids: Eerdmans, 1987.
Kinzer, Mark S. *Jerusalem Crucified, Jerusalem Risen: The Resurrected Messiah, the Jewish People, and the Promised Land*. Eugene, OR: Cascade, 2018.
———. *Post-Missionary Messianic Judaism: Redefining Christian Engagement with the Jewish People*. Grand Rapids: Brazos, 2005.

Klawans, Jonathan. *Purity, Sacrifice, and the Temple: Symbolism and Supersessionism in the Study of Ancient Judaism.* Oxford: Oxford University Press, 2006.

Korner, Ralph. *The Origin and Meaning of Ekklēsia in the Early Jesus Movement.* Ancient Judaism and Early Christianity 98. Leiden: Brill, 2017.

———. *Reading Revelation After Supersessionism: An Apocalyptic Journey of Socially Identifying John's Multi-Ethnic Ekklēsiai with the Ekklēsia of Israel.* New Testament After Supersessionism. Eugene, OR: Cascade, 2020.

Kraus, Hans-Joachim. *Psalms 60–150: A Continental Commentary.* Minneapolis: Fortress, 1993.

Laniak, T. S. *Shepherds After My Own Heart.* Studies in Biblical Theology 20. Downers Grove, IL: InterVarsity, 2006.

Larkin, K. J. A. *The Eschatology of Second Zechariah: A Study of the Formation of a Mantological Wisdom Anthology.* Kampen, Netherlands: Pharos, 1994.

Leithart, Peter J. *Deep Exegesis: The Mystery of Reading Scripture.* Waco, TX: Baylor University Press, 2020.

Levenson, Jon D. *Resurrection and the Restoration of Israel: The Ultimate Victory of the God of Life.* New Haven, CT: Yale University Press, 2006.

Levering, Matthew. *Jewish-Christian Dialogue and the Life of Wisdom: Engagements with the Theology of David Novak.* New York: Continuum, 2010.

Levine Amy-Jill. "Supersessionism: Admit and Address Rather Than Debate or Deny." *Religions* 13.2 (2022) 1–12.

Liebengood, Kelly D. *The Eschatology of 1 Peter: Considering the Influence of Zechariah 9–14.* SNTS 157. Cambridge: Cambridge University Press, 2014.

———. "Participating in the Life of God: Exploring the Trinitarian Foundation of 1 Peter's Missional Identity." *Midwestern Journal of Theology* 15.2 (2016) 74–91.

———. "The Problem(s) of Reading 1 Peter after Supersessionism." *Religions* 14.2 (2023) 206. doi.org/10.3390/rel14020206.

Lindbeck, George. "What of the Future? A Christian Response." In *Christianity in Jewish Terms*, edited by Tikva Frymer-Kensky et al., 357–73. Boulder, CO: Westview, 2000.

Lockett, Darian. Review of *A Narratological Reading of 1 Peter* by Abson P. Joseph. *Journal of the Evangelical Theological Society* 56.2 (2013) 443–45.

Marcar, Katie. "Building a Holy House." In *Muted Voices of the New Testament: Readings in the Catholic Epistles and Hebrews*, edited by Katherine Hockey et al., 41–54. LNTS. London: T&T Clark, 2017.

———. *Divine Regeneration and Ethnic Identity in 1 Peter: Mapping Metaphors of Family, Race, and Nation.* SNTS 180. Cambridge: Cambridge University Press, 2022.

Marshall, I. Howard. *New Testament Theology: Many Witnesses, One Gospel.* Downers Grove, IL: InterVaristy, 2004.

Martin, Troy W. *Metaphor and Composition in 1 Peter.* SBLDS. Atlanta: Scholars, 1992.

———. "Peter and the Expansion of Early Christianity in the Letters of Acts (15:23–29) and First Peter." In *Delightful Acts: New Essays on Canonical and Non-Canonical Acts*, edited by Harold W. Attidge et al., 87–99. WUNT 391. Tübingen: Mohr Siebeck, 2017.

Mason, Rex. *The Use of Earlier Biblical Material in Zechariah IX–XIV.* London: University of London Press, 1973.

Mason, Steve, and Philip Esler. "Judaean and Christ-Follower Identities: Grounds for a Distinction." *New Testament Studies* 63.4 (2017) 493–515.

Mbuvi, Andrew M. *Temple, Exile, and Identity in 1 Peter*. LNTS 345. London: T&T Clark, 2007.
Meyers, C. L., and E. M. Meyers. *Zechariah 9–14*. Anchor Bible 25C. New York: Doubleday, 1993.
Michaels, J. Ramsey. *1 Peter*. Word Biblical Commentary 49. Nashville, TN: Thomas Nelson, 1988.
Milgrom, Jacob. *Leviticus: A Book of Ritual and Ethics: A Continental Commentary*. Minneapolis: Fortress, 2004.
Millar, Fergus. "Ovid and the Domus Augusta: Rome Seen from Tomoi." *Journal of Roman Studies* 83 (1993) 1–17.
Mitchell, David C. *The Message of the Psalter: An Eschatological Programme in the Book of Psalms*. JSOTSup 252. Sheffield, UK: Sheffield Academic, 1997.
Moffitt, David M. *Rethinking the Atonement: New Perspectives on Jesus's Death, Resurrection, and Ascension*. Grand Rapids: Baker Academic, 2022.
Moo, Douglas J. *The Old Testament in the Gospel Passion Narratives*. Sheffield, UK: Almond, 1983.
Nanos, Mark D., and Magnus Zetterholm, eds. *Paul Within Judaism: Restoring the First-Century Context to the Apostle*. Philadelphia, Fortress, 2015.
Ok, Janette H. *Constructing Ethnic Identity in 1 Peter: Who You Are No Longer*. LNTS 645. London: T&T Clark, 2021.
Page, Sydney. "Obedience and Blood-Sprinkling in 1 Peter 1:2." *Westminster Theological Journal* 72.2 (2010) 291–98.
Paget, James. "Jewish Christianity." In *The Cambridge History of Judaism III*, edited by William Horbury et al., 731–77. Cambridge: Cambridge University Press, 1999.
Paul VI. "Nostra Aetate." Declaration delivered October 28, 1965. https://www.vatican.va/archive/hist_councils/ii_vatican_council/documents/vat-ii_decl_19651028_nostra-aetate_en.html
Petersen, David L. *Zechariah 9–14 and Malachi: A Commentary*. Louisville, KY: Westminster John Knox, 1995.
Presbyterian Church, USA (PC[USA]). "A Theological Understanding of the Relationship Between Christians and Jews." Texted adopted by the 199th General Assembly of the PC(USA), June 1987. https://www.presbyterianmission.org/wp-content/uploads/christiansjews1.pdf.
Price, S. R. F. *Ritual and Power: The Roman Imperial Cult in Asia Minor*. Cambridge: Cambridge University Press, 1984.
Ramage, Edwin S. *The Nature and Purpose of Augustus' 'Res Gestae'*. Stuttgart: Steiner, 1987.
Redditt, Paul L. *Introduction to the Prophets*. Grand Rapids: Eerdmans, 2008.
Regev, Eyal. "Community as Temple: Revisiting Cultic Metaphors in Qumran and the New Testament." *Bulletin for Biblical Research* 28.4 (2018) 604–31.
Reicke, Bo. *The Epistles of James, Peter and Jude*. Anchor Bible 37. Garden City, NY: Doubleday, 1964.
Rillera, Andrew R. *Lamb of the Free: Recovering the Varied Sacrificial Understandings of Jesus's Death*. Eugene, OR: Wipf and Stock, 2024.
Rudolph, David J. "Describing the Church in Relation to Israel." In *Covenant and the People of God: Essays in Honor of Mark S. Kinzer*, edited by Jonathan Kaplan et al., 219–32. Eugene, OR: Pickwick, 2023.

———. *A Jew to the Jews: Jewish Contours of Pauline Flexibility in 1 Corinthians 9:19-23.* WUNT 2.304. 2nd ed. Eugene, OR: Cascade, 2016.

———. "Messianic Judaism in Antiquity and the Modern Era." In *Introduction to Messianic Judaism: Its Ecclesial Context and Biblical Foundations,* edited by David Rudolph and Joel Willitts, 21–36. Grand Rapids: Zondervan, 2013.

Runesson, Anders. "What Does It Mean to Read New Testament Texts 'Within Judaism'?" *New Testament Studies* 69.3 (2023) 299–312.

Sargent, Benjamin. *Written to Serve: The Use of Scripture in 1 Peter.* LNTS 547. London: T&T Clark, 2015.

Schultz Montalbetti, María José. *La estrategia misionera de la Primera carta de Pedro: edificar una casa espiritual por medio de la buena conducta.* Estella-Navarra, Spain: Editorial Verbo Divino, 2022.

Schutter, William L. *Hermeneutic and Composition in 1 Peter.* WUNT 2.30. Tübingen: Mohr Siebeck, 1989.

Scott, James C. *Domination and the Art of Resistance: Hidden Transcripts.* New Haven, CT: Yale University Press, 1990.

Segal, Alan F. "Jewish Christianity." In *Eusebius, Christianity, and Judaism,* edited by Harold Attridge and Gohei Hata, 326–48. Leiden: Brill, 1992.

———. *Paul the Convert: The Apostolate and Apostasy of Saul the Pharisee.* New Haven, CT: Yale University Press, 1990.

Selwyn, Edwin. G. *The First Epistle of St. Peter.* 2nd ed. London: Macmillan, 1958.

Severy, Beth. *Augustus and the Family at the Birth of the Roman Empire.* London: Routledge, 2003.

Skarsaune, Oskar, and Reider Hvalvik, eds. *Jewish Believers in Jesus: The Early Centuries.* Grand Rapids: Baker Academic, 2007.

Smith, Shively T. J. *Strangers to Family: Diaspora and 1 Peter's Invention of God's Household.* Waco, TX: Baylor University Press, 2016.

Soulen, R. Kendall. *The God of Israel and Christian Theology.* Minneapolis; Fortress, 1996.

———. "The Standard Canonical Narrative and the Problem of Supersessionism." In *Introduction to Messianic Judaism: Its Ecclesial Context and Biblical Foundations,* edited by David Rudolph and Joel Willitts, 282–91. Grand Rapids: Zondervan, 2013.

———. "Supersessionism." In *Encyclopedia of Jewish-Christian Relations Online,* edited by Walter Homolka et al. Berlin: De Gruyter, 2019. https://www.degruyter.com/database/EJCRO/entry/ejcro.9724136/html.

Spicq, C. *Les Épitres de Saint Pierre.* Paris: Librairie Lecoffre, 1966.

Starling, David I. *Not My People: Gentiles as Exiles in Pauline Hermeneutics.* BZNW 184. Berlin: de Gruyter, 2011.

———. "'She Who Is in Babylon': 1 Peter and the Hermeneutics of Empire." In *Reactions to Empire: Sacred Texts in Their Socio-Political Contexts,* edited by John Anthony Dunne and Dan Batovici, 111–28. WUNT 2.372. Tübingen: Mohr Siebeck, 2014.

Sun, Joyce Wai-Lan. *This Is True Grace: The Shaping of Social Behavioural Instructions by Theology in 1 Peter.* Carlisle, UK: Langham Monographs, 2016.

Sweeney, Marvin A. *The Twelve Prophets: Micah, Nahum, Habakkuk, Zephaniah, Haggai, Zechariah, Malachi.* Berit Olam 2. Collegeville, MN: Liturgical, 2000.

Thiessen, Matthew. *Jesus and the Forces of Death: The Gospels' Portrayal of Ritual Impurity Within First-Century Judaism.* Grand Rapids: Baker Academic, 2020.

———. *A Jewish Paul: The Messiah's Herald to the Gentiles*. Grand Rapids: Baker Academic, 2023.

Thompson, Michael. *Clothed with Christ: The Example and Teaching of Jesus in Romans 12.1—15.13*. JSNTSup 59. Sheffield, UK: JSOT, 1991.

Tigchelaar, E. J. C. *Prophets of Old and the Day of the End: Zechariah, the Book of Watchers and Apocalyptic*. Leiden: Brill, 1996.

Tite, P. L. *Compositional Transitions in 1 Peter: An Analysis of the Letter-Opening*. San Francisco: International Scholars, 1997.

Trebilco, Paul. *Outsider Designations and Boundary Construction in the New Testament: Early Christian Communities and the Formation of Group Identity*. Cambridge: Cambridge University Press, 2017.

———. *Self-Designations and Group Identity in the New Testament*. Cambridge: Cambridge University Press, 2012.

Tucker, J. Brian. *Reading Romans After Supersessionism: The Continuation of Jewish Covenantal Identity*. New Testament After Supersessionism. Eugene, OR: Cascade, 2018.

Tucker, J. Brian, and Wally Cirafesi. "Paul's Segmentary Grammar of Identity: Ex-Pagan Gentiles within Synagogues and the Importance of the Eschatological Pilgrimage Tradition." In *Paul Within Judaism: Perspectives on Paul and Jewish Identity*, edited by Michael Bird et al., 119–45. WUNT 507. Tübingen: Mohr Siebeck, 2023.

Van Maaren, John. "How Can the New Testament Writings Be Within Judaism? Distinguishing Ways of Asking and Answering the Question." *Zeitschrift für die neutestamentliche Wissenschaft* 114.2 (2023) 264–303.

Volf, Miroslav. "Soft Difference: Theological Reflections on the Relation Between Church and Culture in 1 Peter." *Ex Auditu* 10 (1994) 15–30.

Wan, Wei Hsien. *The Contest for Time and Space in the Roman Imperial Cults and 1 Peter: Reconfiguring the Universe*. LNTS 611. London: Bloomsbury, 2020.

Wilken, Robert L. *The Land Called Holy: Palestine in Christian History and Thought*. New Haven, CT: Yale University Press, 1992.

Williams, Travis B. *Good Works in 1 Peter*. WUNT 337. Tübingen: Mohr Siebeck, 2014.

———. *Persecution in 1 Peter: Differentiating and Contextualizing Early Christian Suffering*. Novum Testamentum Supplements 145. Leiden: Brill, 2012.

Williams, Travis, and David G. Horrell. *1 Peter: A Critical and Exegetical Commentary*. 2 vols. London: T&T Clark, 2023.

Willitts, Joel. *Matthew's Messianic Shepherd-King: In Search of "The Lost Sheep of the House of Israel."* BZNW 147. Berlin: de Gruyter, 2007.

Windsor, Lionel J. *Reading Ephesians and Colossians After Supersessionism: Christ's Mission Through Israel to the Nations*. New Testament After Supersessionism. Eugene, OR: Cascade, 2017.

Witherington, Ben. *A Socio-Rhetorical Commentary on 1-2 Peter*. Vol. 2 of *Letters and Homilies for Hellenized Christians*. Downers Grove, IL: IVP Academic, 2007.

Yoder, John Howard. *The Jewish-Christian Schism Revisited*. Edited by Michael Cartwright and Peter Ochs. Grand Rapids: Eerdmans, 2003.

Zanker, Paul. *The Power of Images in the Age of Augustus*. Ann Arbor, MI: University of Michigan Press, 1988.

Zoccali, Christopher. *Reading Philippians After Supersessionism: Jews, Gentiles, and Covenant Identity*. New Testament After Supersessionism. Eugene, OR: Cascade, 2017.

# Author Index

Achtemeier, Paul J., 6n14, 6n16,
    11n1, 12n5, 14n11, 16n20,
    32n4, 44n29, 80n105,
    83n115, 113n85, 116nn102–
    3, 137n57, 138, 139n66,
    140n66, 154n129, 161n154,
    186n60, 186n66, 187n67,
    187n69, 188n73, 189n78,
    199n107, 207n130, 208n133
Anderson, Bernhard W., 46n32
Ando, Clifford, 95n30, 96, 96n35
Aune, David E., 33n6

Balch, D. L., 88, 89, 89n5, 91
Barclay, John M. G., 90n11
Bauckham, Richard, 115, 115n97,
    117, 118n108, 183,
    183nn50–51, 184, 202
Bauman-Martin, Betsy, 4–5, 5nn11–
    12, 13n8, 14n9, 15, 15nn15–
    18, 17n28, 21, 21n40, 29, 90,
    90n13, 179–80
Beale, Gregory K., 127n14
Bechtler, Steven R., 35, 35n16,
    75n86, 102, 102nn51–53,
    103, 104n59, 185n59,
    187n68, 189n77, 189n79
Beza, Theodore, 34
Bird, Michael, 9n26, 57n31, 90–91,
    90n13
Black, M. C., 111n77, 111n79
Bockmuehl, Markus, 8n25, 206n125
Boring, M. Eugene, 103, 104nn58–
    59, 127n14

Bosetti, Elena, 12n3, 113, 113n88,
    114nn90–91, 115n93, 201,
    202n116
Botner, Max, 12n3, 13n7, 127n15,
    131–32, 132nn33–37, 135,
    135n50, 147n96, 150n106,
    176n32
Boyarin, Daniel, 9n28
Brox, Norbert, 112n82
Burnhope, Stephen, 9n29

Calvin, John, 34
Campbell, Barth, 44n30, 45n30,
    187n68, 189n77, 207n130
Carter, Warren, 90, 90n13
Cervantes Gabarrón, José, 113n84,
    116n100
Chae, Y. S., 110n72
Chester, Tim, 12n4
Christensen, Sean M., 205n119
Cirafesi, Wally, 108n68
Coggins, R. J., 114n93
Conzelmann, Hanz, 115n98,
    116n104
Crossan, John Dominic, 98n40

Davids, Peter H., 35n17
deSilva, David, 12n4
Deterding, Paul E., 48n37
Dodd, C. H., 111n77, 111n79
Doering, Lutz, 7, 7nn17–18, 12n3,
    16–17, 16nn21–23, 17n24,
    17n28, 20, 21n40, 27, 29,
    33, 33nn8–9, 48n39, 77–79,
    77nn89–91, 78nn92–94,

233

Doering, Lutz (*continued*)
  79nn95–100, 80, 100,
  100n47, 181
Donaldson, Terence L., 1n1
Dryden, J. W., 102–3, 103nn54–55,
  103nn56–57, 104, 104n59
Dubis, Mark, 12n5, 43n27, 44n28,
  113, 113nn88–89, 114,
  114nn90–92, 186n60,
  190n80, 190n82, 190n84,
  191n86
Duguid, Iain, 115n93, 201n111
Dunn, James D. G., 33, 33n11,
  43n26

Eberhart, Christian A., 151,
  152n117, 152n123, 153n125,
  160, 160nn144–48, 162n155,
  163, 163n166
Egan, Patrick T., 12n3, 32n4, 43n27,
  105n65
Eisenbaum, Pamela, 9n26, 57n31
Elliott, John H., 6nn14–15, 8, 8n23,
  12n5, 26, 26n51, 32n4,
  34n14, 47n36, 52, 52n7,
  52n9, 89, 89n6, 113, 113n85,
  113nn87–89, 114n90,
  116n101, 117, 118n108, 122,
  122nn116–17, 123, 125,
  125nn2–3, 136, 136n53,
  137, 137nn59–60, 138,
  138n61, 139n65, 155n130,
  157n138, 159n143, 174, 183,
  183nn48–49, 183nn51–52,
  184, 184n53, 185, 185n59,
  186n60, 186n65, 187n69,
  188n72, 190, 190n81,
  190n83, 191n86, 191n89,
  197–98, 197nn98–100, 202,
  207, 207nn129–30, 212n142
Esler, Philip F., 170n2

Fagbemi, Stephen A. A., 12n4
Fee, Gordon D., 115n98, 116n104
Feldmeier, Richard, 127n14, 186n60
Fishbane, Michael, 46n32

Galinsky, Karl, 95n30, 96–97,
  97n36, 98n41
Gane, Roy E., 151
Gärtner, Bertil E., 127, 127n15
Gil, Carlos, 148n97
Glenny, Edward, 11n2
Goppelt, Leonhard, 45n31, 116n102,
  127n14, 131, 131n31,
  155n129, 186n61, 186nn63–
  64, 187n66
Green, Joel, 26, 26n49, 33n8, 35–36,
  36n18, 43n27, 44n28, 126,
  126n5, 156n131, 157n136,
  190, 190n81, 190n83, 199,
  199n107, 206n124, 207n130
Gregerman, Adam, 3, 3n4
Gupta, Nijay K., 150n106

Harink, Douglas, 13n7, 154n128
Harland, Phillip, 63n47, 88,
  88nn2–3
Hengel, Martin, 57, 58nn33–35
Hillyer, C. N., 109n70, 191n88
Himmelfarb, Martha, 153n124
Hockey, Katherine M., 12n3
Holloway, Paul A., 75n84
Horrell, David G., 6nn14–15, 7n19,
  8n23, 8n25, 11n2, 12n3,
  12n5, 14n13, 15–16, 16n19,
  17, 17nn25–28, 20, 21n40,
  29, 33, 33nn8–10, 52n5,
  67n59, 69n66, 71, 88n4, 89,
  89nn6–8, 90n13, 91, 99–
  100, 99nn44–45, 100n47,
  100n48, 122nn118–19, 125,
  126, 126n4, 126n6, 128n19,
  129–31, 129n23, 130nn24–
  29, 131n30, 131n32, 136n52,
  136n54, 137, 137n58, 138,
  138nn62–63, 140n66, 148,
  148nn98–99, 148n102, 149,
  149n100, 150, 150nn103–6,
  157n137, 158nn141–42, 161,
  161n150, 162, 162nn156–
  159, 163n160, 164, 165n169,
  170–72, 170nn1–2, 171nn3–
  9, 176–77, 177n35, 177n39,
  178, 178n40, 179–80, 181,

183n48, 184, 184nn54–57,
    197, 197n101, 198nn102–3,
    205, 205n119, 205nn120–23,
    206, 206n126, 208n132,
    208n134, 209n136, 212n142
Horsley, Richard A., 90n9, 95n31
Hunzinger, Claus-Hunno, 6, 7
Hvalvik, Reider, 9n26

Janowski, Bernd, 164, 164n167
Jauhiainen, Marko, 112n81
Jennings, Willie J., 28, 28n58
Jobes, Karen, 3n3, 26, 26n52, 50n1,
    51n2, 52n5, 112n83, 113,
    113n88, 115n94, 116n102,
    126, 126n8, 127n14, 137n56,
    174, 189n79, 190, 190n83,
    207n130
Johnson, Dennis, 185n58
Johnson Hodge, Caroline E., 9n26,
    57n31
Joseph, Abson P., 102n50, 104,
    104nn60–62, 105nn63–64

Keener, Craig S., 205n119
Kim, Seyoon, 109n69
Kinzer, Mark S., 1n1, 8, 8n20, 8n22,
    57n32, 139n64, 141–47,
    141nn71–72, 142nn73–76,
    143nn77–79, 144nn83–84,
    145nn85–87, 146nn88–92,
    147n93, 153n124, 161
Klawans, Jonathan, 132–35,
    133nn39–42, 134nn43–45,
    134nn47–48, 135n49,
    144n80, 144n82, 168,
    176n32
Korner, Ralph, 11n2, 26, 27n54, 59,
    59n37, 60nn39–41
Kraus, Hans-Joachim, 39n21, 40,
    40nn22–23

Laniak, T. S., 47n37, 109n72,
    115n93, 200n110
Larkin, K. J. A., 115n93
Leithart, Peter J., 123n121
Levenson, Jon D., 22n43
Levering, Matthew, 14n10

Levine, Amy-Jill, 4, 4nn7–10, 5
Liebengood, Kelly D., 12n3, 22n42,
    22n44, 28n59, 32n4, 42n24,
    43n27, 47n34, 48n39,
    109n70, 110nn75–76,
    115n95, 118nn110–12,
    147n95, 155n129, 157n138,
    161n154, 164n168, 186n62,
    189n76, 191n87, 193n92,
    194nn94–95, 195n96,
    208n135
Lindbeck, George, 9, 10n30, 10n31
Lockett, Darian, 105n64
Louw, Johannes P., 136n51, 158n140

Marcar, Katie, 12n3, 14n13, 43n27,
    139nn64–65, 140, 140nn67–
    68, 140n70, 174–76, 174n24,
    175nn25–31, 176nn32–34,
    177, 178, 178n41, 179–80,
    181, 182, 211, 211n140
Marshall, I. Howard, 14n14, 51,
    51n3
Martin, Troy W., 44n30, 45n30,
    80–84, 80nn101–104,
    81nn106–8, 82nn110–11,
    82n113, 83n114, 83n116,
    123, 125n3, 187n67, 200,
    200nn108–9
Mason, Rex, 201n112
Mbuvi, Andrew M., 12n3, 43n27,
    125n1, 126, 126n7, 126n9,
    127–28, 127nn10–13,
    127n16, 128nn17–18,
    156n133, 163nn163–65,
    165n170
Meyers, C. L., 115n93, 201nn111–12
Meyers, E. M., 115n93, 201nn111–
    12
Michaels, J. Ramsey, 6n14, 8n24,
    12n5, 14n12, 26, 26n50,
    31n2, 32, 32n3, 33, 33nn6–8,
    34n12, 35, 35n17, 113n85,
    115n96, 155n129, 185n59,
    186n60, 186n63, 187n66,
    188n69, 188n72, 189n78,
    190n84, 199, 199nn104–6,
    202n115, 207n130

Milgrom, Jacob, 151, 151n107
Millar Fergus, 98n40
Mitchell, David C., 111n79
Moffitt, David M., 148n97, 151, 152nn117–22, 157nn110–16, 161nn151–53, 162n155, 163nn161–62, 164, 164n167
Moo, Douglas J., 111n78

Nanos, Mark D., 9n26, 57n31
Nida, Eugene, 136n51, 158n140

Ok, Janette H., 5n13, 12n3, 26n52, 74n83, 172–74, 172nn10–11, 173nn12–16, 173n18, 174nn19–24, 176, 177, 177n36, 177n38, 179–80, 179nn42–43, 181, 182, 203, 203n117, 207n128, 210, 210nn138–39

Page, Sydney, 157n139
Paget, James, 9n27, 180n46
Paul VI, 3n5
Petersen, David L., 42n25
Pierce, Chad T., 43n27
Price, S. R. F., 89n8, 95n29

Ramage, Edwin S., 97, 204n118
Redditt, Paul L., 201, 201nn113–14
Reed, Jonathan L., 98n40
Regev, Eyal, 132n38, 134n46, 139n64, 144n81, 160, 161n149, 176n32
Reicke, Bo, 128n19
Rillera, Andrew R., 151n109
Rudolph, David J., 2n2, 9n26, 10n31, 57n31
Runesson, Anders, 57n31

Sargent, Benjamin, 32n4, 43n27, 105n65
Schrenk, 47n36, 155n130
Schultz Montalbetti, María José, 12n3
Schutter, William L., 12n3, 32n4, 115n96, 117, 117n107, 185n59, 190n84

Scott, James C., 90, 90n10, 90nn11–12, 95
Segel, Alan F., 9n27, 180n46
Selwyn, Edwin G., 34n13, 35, 35n15, 51, 51n4, 127, 127nn14–15, 137, 186n60, 188n69, 188n73
Severy, Beth, 95n30, 98n40, 204n118
Skarsaune, Oskar, 9n26
Smith, Shively T. J., 174
Soulen, R. Kendall, 1n1, 17–20, 17n29, 18nn30–34, 19nn35–37, 20nn38–39
Spicq, Ceslas, 118, 118n109, 127n14
Starling, David I., 87n1, 90–92, 90nn13–15, 91nn16–21, 92nn22–23
Stendahls, Krister, 33n6
Sun, Joyce Wai-Lan, 12n4
Sweeny, Marvin, 200n110

Thiessen, Matthew, 9n26, 57n31, 151n108
Thompson, Michael, 112n80
Tigchelaar, E. J. C., 115n93
Timmis, Steve, 12n4
Tite, P. L., 155n129
Trebilco, Paul, 26n53, 27n55, 70n73, 71, 71nn74–77, 72n78, 73nn81–82
Tucker, J. Brian, 9n26, 57n31, 108n68

Van Maaren, John, 57n31
Volf, Miroslav, 12n4

Wan, Wei Hsien, 63n49, 93–94, 93n24, 94n25, 94nn27–28, 96n32, 96n34, 97n37, 98, 98n39, 98n42, 99n43
Wesley, John, 34
Wilken, Robert L., 8, 8n21
Williams, Travis B., 6nn14–15, 7n19, 8n23, 8n25, 12n5, 55–59, 56nn26–29, 61–75, 61n42, 62nn43–45, 64n52, 65nn53–55, 66nn56–57,

67n58, 67nn60–61, 68nn62–63, 69nn66–70, 70nn71–72, 72n79, 72n80, 75n85, 85, 88n2, 100n47, 122nn118–19, 125, 126, 126n4, 126n6, 129–31, 129n23, 130nn24–29, 131n30, 131n32, 136n52, 136n54, 137, 137n58, 138, 138nn62–63, 140n66, 148, 148nn98–99, 148n102, 149, 149n100, 150, 150nn103–6, 157n137, 158nn141–42, 161, 161n150, 162, 162nn156–59, 163n160, 164, 184, 184nn54–57, 197n101, 205, 205nn120–23, 206, 206n126, 208n132, 208n134, 209n136, 212n142

Willitts, Joel, 110n72
Windsor, Lionel J., 9n26, 57n31, 206n127
Witherington, Ben, 44n30, 45n30, 52–57, 52n6, 52n8, 52n10, 53nn11–17, 54nn18–20, 55nn21–23, 58nn35–36, 59, 62n46, 186n60
Wycliffe, John, 34, 34n13

Yoder, John Howard, 9n28

Zanker, Paul, 95n30, 96, 96n33, 97, 97n38
Zetterholm, Magnus, 9n26, 57n31
Zoccali, Christopher, 9n26, 57n31

# *Scripture Index*

## OLD TESTAMENT

### Genesis

| | |
|---|---|
| 1:1—2:3 | 142 |
| 48:15 | 109n71 |
| 49:24 | 109n71 |

### Exodus

| | |
|---|---|
| | 162 |
| 1:17 | 45 |
| 1:19 | 45 |
| 12:11 | 45 |
| 19 | 191 |
| 19:1–6 | 46 |
| 19:5 | 46 |
| 19:5–6 | 22, 23, 46, 107, 129 |
| 19:6 | 13, 45, 46, 162, 178 |
| 19–23 | 211 |
| 24 | 162 |
| 24:3 | 162 |
| 24:3–9 | 162 |
| 24:7 | 162 |
| 25:8 | 142 |
| 25:9 | 142 |
| 25:40 | 142, 161n152 |
| 29:38–42 | 145n86 |
| 32:9 | 38, 39n21 |
| 34:7 | 40 |

### Leviticus

| | |
|---|---|
| | 152, 160, 211 |
| 2:1 | 160 |
| 2:1–16 | 160 |
| 2:2 | 160 |
| 2:4 | 160 |
| 2:7 | 160 |
| 2:12 | 160 |
| 3:7 LXX | 149n101 |
| 3:12 LXX | 149n101 |
| 4:1—5:13 | 153n125 |
| 4:3 LXX | 149n101 |
| 4:14 LXX | 149n101 |
| 11:44 | 13, 23, 45, 156 |
| 11:45 | 45 |
| 16:1–34 | 153n125 |
| 17:1–9 | 156 |
| 17:3 | 152 |
| 17:11 | 162 |
| 18:1–5 | 156 |
| 19:1–8 | 156 |
| 19:2 | 13, 45, 156n134 |
| 20:7 | 13, 45, 156n134 |
| 20:26 | 13, 156n134 |
| 21:8 | 156n134 |

### Numbers

| | |
|---|---|
| 28:1–8 | 145n86 |
| 34:2 | 45n31 |
| 36:2 | 45n31 |

## Deuteronomy

| | |
|---|---|
| 7:9 | 40 |
| 10:16 | 38 |
| 12:9 | 45n31 |
| 30:3 | 47n35 |
| 30:3–5 LXX | 117n105 |
| 32:5 | 39n21 |

## Joshua

| | |
|---|---|
| 1:15 | 45n31 |
| 13:1 | 45n31 |

## Judges

| | |
|---|---|
| 2:6 | 45n31 |
| 18:1 | 45n31 |
| 21:23 | 45n31 |

## 2 Samuel

| | |
|---|---|
| 7 | 109 |
| 7:8 | 109n71 |
| 7:11–16 | 193 |

## 2 Kings

| | |
|---|---|
| 17:14 | 39n21 |

## 2 Chronicles

| | |
|---|---|
| 6:27 | 45n31 |
| 31:1 | 45n31 |

## Ezra

| | |
|---|---|
| 9:9 | 47n35 |

## Nehemiah

| | |
|---|---|
| 9:16 | 41 |
| 9:17 | 41 |
| 9:19 | 41 |
| 9:26 | 41 |
| 9:28 | 41 |
| 9:29 | 41 |
| 9:30–33 | 41 |
| 9:34–35 | 41 |
| 9:36 | 40 |

## Psalms

| | |
|---|---|
| | 38, 39n20, 112 |
| 2:8 | 45n31 |
| 18:50 | 193 |
| 23 | 23, 109n71 |
| 28:9 | 109n71 |
| 33 LXX | 46, 107 |
| 33:4 LXX | 46 |
| 34 | 46, 92 |
| 34 MT | 46 |
| 34:8 | 46 |
| 34:9 | 92 |
| 59:4 LXX | 117n105 |
| 65:10 LXX | 186n64 |
| 67:10 | 45n31 |
| 74:1 | 109n71 |
| 76:9 LXX | 47n35 |
| 77:20 | 109n71 |
| 78 | 39 |
| 78:1–8 | 39 |
| 78:3–4 | 39 |
| 78:7 | 40 |
| 78:7–8 | 39 |
| 78:8 | 39n21 |
| 78:9–72 | 39 |
| 78:22 | 39 |
| 78:41 | 39 |
| 78:52–55 | 109n71 |
| 78:56 | 39 |
| 78:70–71 | 109n71 |
| 79:13 | 109n71 |
| 80:1 | 109n71 |
| 84:8 | 47n35 |
| 84:11 | 47n35 |
| 89:4 | 193 |
| 89:29–37 | 193 |
| 95:7 | 109n71 |
| 97:3 | 47n35 |
| 102:3 LXX | 117n105 |
| 105:45 | 47n35 |
| 106 | 39, 40, 41 |
| 106:20 LXX | 117n105 |
| 106:24–27 | 40 |
| 106:27 | 40n22 |
| 106:47 | 40, 40n22 |
| 110:6 | 45n31 |
| 114:1–2 | 143 |

| | | | |
|---|---|---|---|
| 117:22 LXX | 128 | 49:8 | 45n31 |
| 118 | 37, 166, 177 | 49:9–13 | 110n73 |
| 118:22 | 22, 23, 49, 109, 128, 194 | 49:10 | 47n35 |
| | | 49:13 | 47n35 |
| 129:7 | 47n35 | 52:7–8 | 143 |
| 132 | 109 | 52:11–12 | 143 |
| 132:11–12 | 193 | 53 | 22, 113, 114, 114n92, 116, 117, 123, 164, 177, 209 |
| 134:12 | 45n31 | | |
| 135:21 | 45n31 | | |
| 135:22 | 45n31 | 53:5 LXX | 117n105 |
| 135:23 | 47n35 | 53:5–6 LXX | 115 |
| 146:3 LXX | 117n105 | 54:7–8 | 47n35 |
| | | 54:10 | 47n35 |
| | | 55:7 | 47n35 |
| | | 56:1 | 47n35 |
| | | 57:18–19 LXX | 117n105 |
| | | 60:10 | 47n35 |
| | | 61:1 LXX | 117n105 |
| | | 63:7 | 47n35 |
| | | 63:15 | 47n35 |

## Isaiah

| | |
|---|---|
| | 39n20, 143n77 |
| 1:2 | 48 |
| 2:20 | 35 |
| 6:1–5 | 142 |
| 8:14 | 22, 23, 49, 109 |
| 9:7 | 193 |
| 11 | 196n97 |
| 11:1 | 188, 189, 193 |
| 11:2 | 118, 187, 188, 188n71, 189, 195, 196 |
| 12:1–6 | 47n35 |
| 14:1–3 | 47n35 |
| 28:16 | 22, 23, 49, 109, 194 |
| 29:13 | 37 |
| 30:18–19 | 47n35 |
| 30:26 LXX | 117n105 |
| 33:2 | 47n35 |
| 40 | 22, 92, 107, 177 |
| 40:1–11 | 110n74 |
| 40:6–8 | 45 |
| 40:10–11 | 110n73 |
| 40–55 | 46, 119n113, 143 |
| 40–66 | 112 |
| 42:12 | 13, 46 |
| 43 | 46, 107, 191 |
| 43:20 | 13, 22, 46 |
| 43:20–21 | 23, 46, 47, 129, 178 |
| 43:21 | 45, 46 |
| 44:22–23 | 47n35 |
| 45:8 | 47n35 |

## Jeremiah

| | |
|---|---|
| | 195 |
| 2 | 42 |
| 2:5 | 42 |
| 2:5 LXX | 35, 42 |
| 2:7 | 45n31 |
| 2:11 | 42 |
| 3:19 | 45n31 |
| 10:25 | 35 |
| 11:8 | 42n25 |
| 12:15 | 47n35 |
| 12:25 | 45n31 |
| 16:18 | 45n31 |
| 23 | 23, 110, 110n74, 115n93, 194, 200 |
| 23:2 | 110n73 |
| 23:5 | 193 |
| 25:5 | 42n25 |
| 29:4–23 | 33 |
| 30:18 | 47n35 |
| 31:10 | 110n73 |
| 33:6 LXX | 117n105 |
| 33:15 | 193 |
| 35:15 | 42n25 |
| 50:19 | 110n73 |

## Lamentations

| | |
|---|---|
| 3:32 | 47n35 |

## Ezekiel

| | |
|---|---|
| | 119n113, 143n77, 144, 195, 201 |
| 1:1–28 | 143 |
| 8:3–5 | 143 |
| 8:4 | 143 |
| 8:6 | 143 |
| 8–11 | 143, 190 |
| 9:3 | 143 |
| 9:6 | 23, 191, 191n86, 191n87 |
| 9:6 LXX | 190 |
| 10:1–22 | 143 |
| 10:19 | 143 |
| 10:20 | 143 |
| 11:15 | 45n31 |
| 11:16 | 143 |
| 11:23 | 143 |
| 20 | 41 |
| 20:4–17 | 41 |
| 20:18 | 41 |
| 20:24 | 41 |
| 20:30 | 41 |
| 20:36 | 41 |
| 25:4 | 45n31 |
| 25:10 | 45n31 |
| 33:11 | 42n25 |
| 34 | 22, 23, 110, 110n74, 113, 114, 114n92, 115n93, 117, 164, 177, 194, 200, 201 |
| 34:3–4 | 200 |
| 34:4 | 114n92 |
| 34:4–11 | 114n92 |
| 34:5 | 114n92 |
| 34:6 | 114n92 |
| 34:8 | 114n92 |
| 34:10 | 114n92, 200 |
| 34:11 | 114n92 |
| 34:16 | 114n92 |
| 34:23 | 114n92, 201 |
| 34:23–24 | 193 |
| 34:31 | 110n73 |
| 36 | 196n97 |
| 36:20–30 | 194 |
| 36:25–27 | 201 |
| 37:23 | 195 |
| 37:24 | 193 |
| 37:24–25 | 201 |
| 39:25 | 47n35 |
| 40–48 | 142 |
| 43:2 | 143 |
| 45:1 | 45n31 |

## Daniel

| | |
|---|---|
| | 112 |
| 9:9 | 47n35 |
| 9:18 | 47n35 |

## Hosea

| | |
|---|---|
| | 47 |
| 1:6 | 22, 29, 47, 129 |
| 1:9 | 22, 47 |
| 1:9–10 | 22, 29, 53, 129 |
| 1:10 | 22 |
| 2 | 47, 107, 177, 191, 194 |
| 2:15 | 47 |
| 2:23 | 22, 29, 45, 119, 129, 178, 195 |
| 2:25 | 47 |
| 5:11 | 35 |
| 12:13 | 109n71 |

## Joel

| | |
|---|---|
| 2 | 196n97 |

## Proverbs

| | |
|---|---|
| | 39n20 |
| 3:34 LXX | 92 |
| 27:21 | 186n64 |

## Amos

| | |
|---|---|
| 5:15 | 47n35 |

## Micah

| | |
|---|---|
| 2:12–13 | 110n73 |
| 4:6–8 | 110n73 |

| | |
|---|---|
| 4:14—5:5 | 110n74 |
| 7:14–15 | 110n73 |
| 7:18–20 | 47n35 |

## Zechariah

| | |
|---|---|
| | 119, 193, 195, 196 |
| 1:4 | 42, 42n25 |
| 1:12–17 | 47n35 |
| 3:8 | 118, 193, 196 |
| 6:12 | 118, 193, 196 |
| 9:1–17 | 193 |
| 9:8 | 193, 198 |
| 9:9 | 111, 111n78 |
| 9:9–10 | 111, 118n111, 193 |
| 9–10 | 194 |
| 9:11–13 | 201 |
| 9–14 | 42n24, 48n39, 108, 108n68, 110, 110n76, 111, 111n77, 112, 112n81, 114, 114n93, 115n93, 116, 117, 118, 118n110, 118n111, 119, 119n113, 120, 123, 164, 177, 182, 185, 189, 192, 193, 195, 196, 196n97, 201n114, 209 |
| 9:14–15 | 193 |
| 9:16 | 110n73, 119, 194 |
| 10 | 123 |
| 10:1–5 | 200 |
| 10:1—14:21 | 193 |
| 10:2 LXX | 115, 117, 209 |
| 10:2 MT | 200 |
| 10:3 | 118, 196, 200 |
| 10:4 | 194 |
| 10:4–12 | 119 |
| 10:5 | 201 |
| 10:6 | 195 |
| 10:6–12 | 119, 194, 195 |
| 10:8–10 | 110n73 |
| 10:8–12 | 119 |
| 10–13 | 200, 201 |
| 11:4–14 | 110 |
| 11:4–17 | 194, 209 |
| 11:7–9 | 110 |
| 11:8–14 | 195 |
| 11:12–13 | 111 |
| 12:7—13:1 | 201 |
| 12:8 | 118, 194, 196, 201 |
| 12:8–12 | 198 |
| 12:8—13:2 | 209 |
| 12:8–14 | 194 |
| 12:9–10 | 109 |
| 12:10 | 111, 111n78, 119, 194, 195, 209 |
| 12:10—13:1 | 201 |
| 12:10–14 | 194 |
| 12:11–14 | 111 |
| 13:1 | 111, 194 |
| 13:1–2 | 194, 196 |
| 13:1–6 | 194 |
| 13:2 | 194 |
| 13:7 | 23, 110, 111, 111n78, 118, 118n111, 193, 195, 196, 209 |
| 13:7–9 | 111, 119, 195, 200 |
| 13:8 | 195 |
| 13:8–9 | 110, 195 |
| 13:9 | 190n85, 195, 200 |
| 14 | 119, 142 |
| 14:3–20 | 110 |
| 14:3–21 | 195, 201 |
| 14:4 | 195 |
| 14:4–15 | 195 |
| 14:8 | 111 |
| 14:16 | 49 |
| 14:20–21 | 198 |
| 14:21 | 195, 196 |
| 36:26–27 | 194 |

## Malachi

201n114

# DEUTEROCANONICAL BOOKS

## 2 Maccabees

| | |
|---|---|
| 1:1–10a | 33 |
| 1:10b—2:18 | 33 |

| | |
|---|---|
| Baruch | 33, 38 |
| 3:8 | 42 |
| | |
| Epistle of Jeremiah | 33 |
| | |
| Jubilees | |
| 23:29 | 117n105 |
| | |
| Wisdom of Solomon | |
| 14:22 | 35 |

## PSEUDEPIGRAPHA (OLD TESTAMENT)

| | |
|---|---|
| 2 Baruch | |
| 73:2 | 117n105 |
| 78:1—87:1 | 33 |
| | |
| 4 Ezra | |
| 13:50 | 117n105 |
| | |
| Psalms of Solomon | |
| 17–18 | 193 |
| 17:32 | 188n71 |
| 17:37 | 188n71 |
| | |
| Testament of the Twelve Patriarchs | |
| Testament of Zebulun | |
| 9:8 | 117n105 |

## DEAD SEA SCROLLS

| | |
|---|---|
| 4Q521 | 117n105 |
| QpIsa | |
| 8–10 iii, 11–25 | 188n71 |
| Temple Scroll | 135 |

## ANCIENT JEWISH WRITERS

| | |
|---|---|
| Josephus | 71n75 |
| Philo | 71n75 |

## RABBINIC WORKS

| | |
|---|---|
| Midrash | |
| Genesis Rabbah | 188n71 |
| | |
| Targums | |
| Isaiah | 188n71 |
| Zechariah | 111n78, 194n93 |

## NEW TESTAMENT

| | |
|---|---|
| Matthew | |
| | 111n77 |
| 5:11–12 | 188n69 |
| 10:16–23 | 37n19 |
| 11:7–19 | 37n19 |
| 11:20–24 | 37n19 |
| 15:1–19 | 37 |
| 21:5 | 111 |
| 21:12–13 | 111 |
| 21:33–46 | 37n19, 128n21, 129 |
| 21:42 | 49n40 |
| 23:13–36 | 37 |
| 23:31 | 37 |
| 23:32 | 37 |
| 23:37–39 | 37 |
| 26:15 | 111 |
| 26:31–32 | 111 |

## SCRIPTURE INDEX 245

| | |
|---|---|
| 27:9–10 | 111 |

### Mark

| | |
|---|---|
| | 111n77 |
| 6:1–6 | 37n19 |
| 7:1–13 | 37 |
| 9:41 | 187n66 |
| 11:1–11 | 111 |
| 11:15–17 | 111 |
| 12:1–12 | 37n19, 128n21 |
| 12:38–40 | 37n19 |
| 13:3–13 | 67 |
| 14:27–28 | 111 |
| 24:3–14 | 67 |

### Luke

| | |
|---|---|
| | 111n77, 145 |
| 4:16–30 | 37n19 |
| 6:26 | 37 |
| 11:39–52 | 37 |
| 13:31–35 | 37n19 |
| 19:29–40 | 111 |
| 20:9–19 | 128n21, 129 |
| 21:7–19 | 67 |
| 22:15 | 116n100 |
| 23:27 | 111 |
| 24:26 | 116n100 |
| 24:46 | 116n100 |

### John

| | |
|---|---|
| | 111n77, 146 |
| 1:13 | 159 |
| 1:32 | 188n71 |
| 2:16 | 111 |
| 3:1–8 | 159 |
| 8:22–44 | 130 |
| 10:11 | 111 |
| 10:16–17 | 123n120 |
| 12:15 | 111 |
| 15:17 | 111 |
| 16:32–33 | 111 |
| 19:34 | 111 |
| 19:34–37 | 111 |
| 21:18–19 | 79 |

### Acts

| | |
|---|---|
| | 37, 38, 76, 136, 145 |
| 1:3 | 116n100 |
| 2 | 145 |
| 2:40 | 38 |
| 3:1 | 145 |
| 3:17 | 38 |
| 3:18 | 116n100 |
| 3:19–21 | 38 |
| 3:26 | 38 |
| 3:27 | 38 |
| 4:8–11 | 128, 129 |
| 4:11 | 49n40, 128 |
| 7 | 38, 136 |
| 7:10 | 136 |
| 7:20 | 136 |
| 7:42 | 136 |
| 7:46 | 136 |
| 7:47 | 136 |
| 7:51–53 | 38 |
| 7:53 | 158n140 |
| 10 | 57n32, 145 |
| 10:1—11:18 | 79 |
| 10:3 | 145 |
| 10:44–45 | 83 |
| 11:26 | 26 |
| 12:17 | 79 |
| 13:3—14:20 | 76n88 |
| 13:13—14:20 | 57n30 |
| 13:50 | 76n88 |
| 14:2 | 76n88 |
| 14:15 | 35 |
| 15 | 58, 58n35, 82 |
| 15:2 | 83 |
| 15:7–11 | 83 |
| 15:23 | 82 |
| 15:23–29 | 79, 80 |
| 15:24 | 81 |
| 15:27 | 80 |
| 16:16–40 | 68 |
| 17:1–9 | 68 |
| 17:1–15 | 57n30, 76n88 |
| 17:3 | 116n100 |
| 17:5 | 76n88 |
| 17:7 | 76n88 |
| 17:30 | 35 |

## Acts (*continued*)

| | |
|---|---|
| 18:1–17 | 57n30, 76n88 |
| 18:12–13 | 76n88 |
| 18:12–17 | 68 |
| 23:24–26 | 68 |
| 23:25–30 | 68 |
| 26:28 | 26 |
| 27:5 | 82 |

## Romans

| | |
|---|---|
| 3:8 | 190 |
| 3:9–18 | 38 |
| 5:6 | 115n98 |
| 5:8 | 115n98 |
| 9–11 | 130 |
| 9:31–33 | 49n40 |
| 15:12 | 188n71 |

## 1 Corinthians

| | |
|---|---|
| 1:12 | 79, 187n67 |
| 5:1 | 56 |
| 8–10 | 54 |
| 9:1–3 | 83 |
| 9:5 | 79 |
| 10:18 | 130n28 |
| 12:2 | 56 |
| 15:3 | 115, 115n98, 116, 116n99 |

## 2 Corinthians

| | |
|---|---|
| 5:14 | 115n98 |

## Galatians

| | |
|---|---|
| 2 | 58n35 |
| 3:28 | 179 |
| 4:21–31 | 130n28 |
| 5:10 | 190 |
| 6:16 | 16 |

## Ephesians

| | |
|---|---|
| 2:3 | 38 |
| 4:18 | 35 |

## 1 Thessalonians

| | |
|---|---|
| 2:14–16 | 130 |
| 4:5 | 35 |

## 2 Thessalonians

| | |
|---|---|
| 2:8 | 188n71 |

## Titus

| | |
|---|---|
| 3:5 | 159 |

## Hebrews

| | |
|---|---|
| | 146, 153 |
| 1:3–4 | 153, 153n126 |
| 3:6 | 192n90 |
| 7:18–19 | 130n28 |
| 8:1–2 | 153 |
| 8:6–13 | 130n28 |
| 9:11–15 | 130n28 |
| 9:13–14 | 153 |
| 9:24–28 | 153 |
| 9:26 | 116n100 |
| 10:12–13 | 153 |
| 13:12 | 116n100 |

## James

| | |
|---|---|
| | 79 |
| 1:1 | 33, 48n38 |
| 1:2–4 | 102n49 |

## 1 Peter

| | |
|---|---|
| 1:1 | 8, 9, 13, 33, 48n38, 61, 79, 83, 99, 107, 119, 154 |
| 1:1–2 | 154–65 |
| 1:1—2:3 | 175 |
| 1:1—2:10 | 47, 211 |
| 1:1—4:11 | 185 |
| 1:1b–2 | 155 |
| 1:2 | 3, 125, 139n65, 156, 157, 157n139, 158, 159, 162, 164, 165, 167, 173n14, 204 |
| 1:2–3 | 3 |

# SCRIPTURE INDEX

| | |
|---|---|
| 1:3 | 24, 28, 45, 120, 125, 148, 154, 204, 210 |
| 1:3—2:10 | 48n39, 119, 174 |
| 1:3—2:19 | 147 |
| 1:3-4 | 46 |
| 1:3-5 | 101 |
| 1:3-7 | 52n5 |
| 1:3-9 | 101, 147, 185 |
| 1:3-12 | 44, 186 |
| 1:4 | 45, 122, 165, 175 |
| 1:5 | 101, 165, 165n169, 185, 189 |
| 1:5—2:10 | 29 |
| 1:5-7 | 45, 119, 147, 155, 185, 186, 189, 192 |
| 1:5-9 | 147, 186, 186n65, 190 |
| 1:6 | 61, 75, 101, 120, 190, 198-99 |
| 1:6-7 | 101, 185 |
| 1:6-8 | 185, 186, 186n60 |
| 1:7 | 101, 102n49, 147, 165, 185, 186, 200 |
| 1:8-9 | 101 |
| 1:9 | 147, 185 |
| 1:10-12 | 13, 22, 24, 45, 92, 94, 105n65, 106, 122, 155, 156 |
| 1:11 | 189 |
| 1:12 | 3 |
| 1:13 | 23, 24, 28, 65, 66, 101, 106 |
| 1:13—2:10 | 44, 45, 45n30 |
| 1:13-16 | 44n30 |
| 1:14 | 34, 35, 36, 38, 43, 43n26, 44, 48, 50, 51, 53, 54n18, 65, 83, 107, 139n65, 210 |
| 1:14—2:10 | 44n30 |
| 1:14-15 | 156 |
| 1:14-16 | 79 |
| 1:14-18 | 156 |
| 1:15 | 27, 45, 65, 107, 159, 205n123, 210 |
| 1:15-16 | 13, 23, 156 |
| 1:16 | 45 |
| 1:17 | 27, 52n5, 65, 91, 204, 205n123 |
| 1:17—2:10 | 44n30 |
| 1:18 | 12, 23, 27, 28, 34, 35, 36, 42, 43, 43n26, 44, 48, 49, 50, 51, 53, 54n18, 77, 84, 107, 205n123, 210 |
| 1:18-19 | 147 |
| 1:19 | 3, 22, 107, 114, 163, 173n14 |
| 1:20 | 22 |
| 1:20-21 | 122 |
| 1:21 | 12, 23, 34, 35, 36, 38, 42, 43, 44, 48, 50, 51, 83, 84, 101, 106, 107 |
| 1:22 | 65, 79, 159, 204 |
| 1:23 | 28, 45, 139n65, 159, 175 |
| 1:24-25 | 22, 92 |
| 2:1 | 65 |
| 2:1-3 | 139n65 |
| 2:2 | 28, 175 |
| 2:3 | 46, 92 |
| 2:4 | 28, 118, 129, 130, 154, 167, 183 |
| 2:4-5 | 110, 115, 183, 184 |
| 2:4-8 | 120, 129, 129n22, 167, 176n32, 183, 191 |
| 2:4-10 | 23, 28, 29, 46, 86, 108, 115, 117, 119, 125, 126, 128, 129, 131, 165, 171, 176, 183, 184, 191, 204, 205 |
| 2:5 | 3, 7, 13, 109, 118n112, 119, 122, 125, 126, 128, 132, 133, 135, 136n52, 137, 137n56, 139, 139n65, 147, 154, 160, 161, 167, 175, 182, 183, 184, 185, 191, 192, 196, 197, 198, 202, 207, 210, 212 |

## 1 Peter (continued)

| | | | |
|---|---|---|---|
| 2:6 | 194 | 2:19 | 61, 208 |
| 2:6–8 | 23, 37, 49, 118, 196 | 2:19–20 | 65 |
| | | 2:20 | 61, 62, 64, 64n51, 75, 206, 208, 208n133 |
| 2:6–10 | 115, 183, 184 | | |
| 2:7 | 26, 128, 130 | 2:21 | 61, 113, 115, 116, 158, 159, 179, 206, 208 |
| 2:7–8 | 130 | | |
| 2:8 | 194 | | |
| 2:9 | 13, 23, 46, 83, 122n119, 125, 154, 159, 162, 170, 171, 172, 173, 179 | 2:21–23 | 27 |
| | | 2:21–25 | 66, 112, 114, 115, 116, 117, 206, 207, 208, 209, 210 |
| 2:9–10 | 3, 12, 24, 26n52, 43n26, 44, 79, 84, 107, 110, 122, 123, 129, 129n22, 130, 147, 164, 170, 177, 178, 182, 183, 184, 185, 192, 202, 203 | 2:22 | 149, 208 |
| | | 2:22–23 | 113, 116 |
| | | 2:22–24 | 116n101 |
| | | 2:22–25 | 22 |
| | | 2:23 | 121, 154, 158, 208 |
| | | 2:23–24 | 119 |
| | | 2:23–25 | 47, 196 |
| | | 2:23–35 | 118 |
| 2:10 | 22, 29, 34, 35, 43, 45, 47, 50, 51, 53, 54n18, 83, 107, 114, 119, 176, 178, 200 | 2:24 | 65, 113, 116, 117, 164, 209 |
| | | 2:24–25 | 3, 47n34, 114, 119, 121, 123, 209 |
| | | 2:25 | 23, 28, 108, 109, 112, 113, 114, 114n92, 164, 193, 200, 208, 209 |
| 2:11 | 65, 101 | | |
| 2:11—3:12 | 44n30, 88, 182 | | |
| 2:11—4:11 | 45n30, 92, 126, 205, 211 | | |
| 2:11–12 | 26n52, 52n5, 120, 155, 205 | 3:1 | 26, 27, 65, 205n123, 209 |
| 2:11–17 | 75 | 3:1–6 | 75 |
| 2:12 | 23, 25, 26n52, 27, 32, 47, 49, 53, 55, 64n51, 65, 75, 88, 154, 205, 206 | 3:1–7 | 206 |
| | | 3:2 | 27, 91, 205n123 |
| | | 3:2–4 | 65 |
| | | 3:3 | 65 |
| 2:13 | 208 | 3:5 | 22 |
| 2:13—3:12 | 205, 205n119, 207, 210 | 3:6 | 64n51, 65, 206 |
| | | 3:7 | 65, 210 |
| 2:13–14 | 65 | 3:8 | 65, 79, 204, 210 |
| 2:13–17 | 206 | 3:8–12 | 66, 206, 207 |
| 2:14 | 64n51, 206 | 3:9 | 65, 75, 121, 158, 159 |
| 2:15 | 64n51, 206 | | |
| 2:16 | 207, 207n131 | 3:9–11 | 65 |
| 2:17 | 65, 88, 91, 210 | 3:9–12 | 27 |
| 2:18 | 65, 88, 91, 207 | 3:9–17 | 154 |
| 2:18—3:7 | 204, 205n120 | 3:10–12 | 46, 209 |
| 2:18–20 | 206 | 3:11 | 64n51, 206 |
| 2:18–25 | 207, 210 | 3:12 | 65 |

| | | | |
|---|---|---|---|
| 3:12—5:11 | 44n30 | | 185n59, 187, |
| 3:13—4:11 | 44n30 | | 187n67, 191, 199, |
| 3:14 | 61, 62, 64n51, 65, | | 199n107, 201, 202 |
| | 206 | 4:13 | 61, 185, 186, 187, |
| 3:14–16 | 75 | | 188, 188n72, 191 |
| 3:15 | 24, 101, 106 | 4:14 | 3, 75, 118, 119, |
| 3:16 | 32n5, 62, 64n51, | | 141, 147, 165, 167, |
| | 65, 205n123, 206 | | 186, 187, 188, |
| 3:16–17 | 206 | | 188n72, 191, 192, |
| 3:17 | 61, 64n51, 154 | | 195, 196, 201, 202 |
| 3:18 | 3, 61, 148, 148n99, | 4:14–17 | 109, 110 |
| | 149, 150, 154, 167 | 4:14–19 | 196 |
| 3:18–22 | 148, 150, | 4:15 | 61, 65 |
| | 150n106, 151, 153 | 4:15–16 | 66 |
| 3:20–21 | 32n5 | 4:16 | 3, 26, 67, 187, |
| 3:21 | 148 | | 188n72, 191 |
| 3:22 | 148n99, 149, 150, | 4:17 | 67, 118, 185, 189, |
| | 153, 154, 167 | | 190, 190n80, 191, |
| 4 | 210 | | 191n86, 191n87, |
| 4:1 | 61, 154 | | 192, 196, 197, 201, |
| 4:1–2 | 158 | | 207, 210 |
| 4:1–3 | 65 | 4:17–19 | 185, 186 |
| 4:1–6 | 199n107 | 4:18 | 23, 65 |
| 4:2–3 | 43n26 | 4:19 | 22, 61, 64n51, |
| 4:2–4 | 35 | | 121, 158, 165, 185, |
| 4:3 | 26, 58, 63 | | 206 |
| 4:3–4 | 12, 25, 26n52, 27, | 5 | 202 |
| | 34, 50–51, 52–55, | 5:1 | 199 |
| | 56, 62, 73, 84, 85 | 5:1–4 | 200, 201 |
| 4:4 | 75 | 5:1–5 | 44n30, 192, 199, |
| 4–5 | 199n107 | | 199n107, 200 |
| 4:7 | 65 | 5:2 | 65, 192, 200 |
| 4:7–11 | 199n107 | 5:4 | 23, 190, 192–93, |
| 4:8 | 65, 79 | | 201 |
| 4:9 | 65 | 5:5 | 65, 92 |
| 4:10 | 210 | 5:5–6 | 210 |
| 4:10–11 | 65 | 5:5–7 | 65 |
| 4:11 | 210 | 5:6 | 189 |
| 4:11d | 188n72 | 5:6–9 | 44n30 |
| 4:12 | 61, 185, 186, 190, | 5:8 | 65 |
| | 199, 200 | 5:8–9 | 121 |
| 4:12—5:11 | 45n30 | 5:8–10 | 147 |
| 4:12—5:14 | 44n30 | 5:9 | 59, 61, 74, 75, 79 |
| 4:12–13 | 186n60 | 5:9–10 | 147 |
| 4:12–15 | 201 | 5:10 | 61, 101, 119, 154, |
| 4:12–17 | 101, 155 | | 159, 165 |
| 4:12–19 | 44n30, 75, 119, | 5:10–11 | 44n30 |
| | 147, 154, 185, | | |

## 1 Peter (continued)

| | |
|---|---|
| 5:12 | 6, 80, 83 |
| 5:13 | 6, 7, 33, 52, 100 |
| 9:6 | 191n86 |
| 9:7 | 191n86 |
| 9:9 | 191n86 |
| 417b–18 | 190n81 |

## 2 Peter

| | |
|---|---|
| 2:3 | 190 |

## 1 John

| | |
|---|---|
| 2:29 | 159 |
| 3:9 | 159 |
| 4:7 | 159 |
| 5:1 | 159 |
| 5:9–10 | 159 |
| 5:18 | 159 |

## Jude

| | |
|---|---|
| 1:4 | 190 |

## Revelation

| | |
|---|---|
| | 90, 100n46, 112n81, 146 |
| 17 | 190 |

---

# APOCRYPHA (NEW TESTAMENT)

## 1 Clement

| | |
|---|---|
| 5:3–4 | 79 |

## Ascension of Isaiah

| | |
|---|---|
| 4:2–3 | 79 |

## Epistle of Barnabus

| | |
|---|---|
| 16:5–8 | 130n28 |

---

# EARLY CHRISTIAN WRITINGS

| | |
|---|---|
| Augustine | 34n13 |
| Didymus | 34 |
| Epiphanus | 34 |
| Eusebius | 34n13 |
| *Ecclesiastical History* | |
| 3.1.2 | 34 |
| 3.4.2 | 34 |

Ignatius of Antioch
*Epistle to the Romans*

| | |
|---|---|
| 4:3 | 79 |
| Jerome | 34, 34n13 |
| Melito of Sardis | 18 |
| Origen | 34, 34n13 |

---

# GREEK AND ROMAN LITERATURE

| | |
|---|---|
| Pliny | 76 |
| *Letter to Trajan* | 68, 69 |
| Tacitus | 76 |

www.ingramcontent.com/pod-product-compliance
Lightning Source LLC
Chambersburg PA
CBHW030823230426
43667CB00008B/1348